HOLLYWOOD'S UNOFFICIAL FILM CORPS

Wisconsin Film Studies

PATRICK MCGILLIGAN, series editor

HOLLYWOOD'S UNOFFICIAL FILM CORPS

*American Jewish Moviemakers
and the War Effort*

Michael Berkowitz

THE UNIVERSITY OF WISCONSIN PRESS

The University of Wisconsin Press
728 State Street, Suite 443
Madison, Wisconsin 53706
uwpress.wisc.edu

Copyright © 2025
The Board of Regents of the University of Wisconsin System
All rights reserved. Except in the case of brief quotations embedded in critical articles and reviews, no part of this publication may be reproduced, stored in a retrieval system, transmitted in any format or by any means—digital, electronic, mechanical, photocopying, recording, or otherwise—or conveyed via the Internet or a website without written permission of the University of Wisconsin Press. Rights inquiries should be directed to rights@uwpress.wisc.edu.

Printed in the United States of America
This book may be available in a digital edition.

Library of Congress Cataloging-in-Publication Data

Names: Berkowitz, Michael, author.
Title: Hollywood's unofficial film corps : American Jewish moviemakers and the war effort / Michael Berkowitz.
Other titles: Wisconsin film studies.
Description: Madison, Wisconsin : University of Wisconsin Press, [2025] | Series: Wisconsin film studies | Includes bibliographical references and index.
Identifiers: LCCN 2024016396 | ISBN 9780299349509 (hardcover)
Subjects: LCSH: Rosten, Leo, 1908-1997. | Jews in the motion picture industry—United States. | World War, 1939-1945—Motion pictures and the war.
Classification: LCC D743.23 .B47 2025 | DDC 940.53089/924—dc23/eng/20241009
LC record available at https://lccn.loc.gov/2024016396

for
Faith and Jim Gray
&
Carol and Eric Haun
&
Cynthia and Mike McHale
&
Ernie and Isabel Oliveri

I don't know whether what we do is an art or a business. Joe Mankiewicz gets angry every time I say "the film industry." He contends that it isn't an industry. It is an art. I don't think semantics has a damn thing to do with it. Films are an influence, a tremendous influence.
    —Walter Wanger, oral history interview in *The Real Tinsel* (1970)

I'm such an admirer of Mrs. Roosevelt that I agree with everything she says or does, or has ever said and done.
    —Leonard Spigelgass, in *The Scuttle Under the Bonnet* (1962)

I think that even those [in Hollywood] who opposed and hated Roosevelt nevertheless had a feeling that what he was trying to do was, in human terms, valid and good.
    —Leo Rosten, *Oral History Interview* (June 1959)

Mrs. Miniver was more powerful in the war effort than the combined work of six military divisions.
    Mrs. Miniver has done more for the Allied cause than a flotilla of battleships.
    Mrs. Miniver was propaganda worth 100 battleships.
    —Attributed to Winston Churchill, concerning the American feature film *Mrs. Miniver* (dir. William Wyler, 1942)

Contents

Preface and Acknowledgments   ix

Introduction   3

1   Launching Countercurrents   27

2   Artful Dodges   55

3   Credit(s) Where Credit Is Due?   90

4   Fathers and Sons, Home and Away   112

5   Hard-Boiled Hollywood Justice   139

6   Reckonings—or Not   176

Epilogue   196

Notes   205

Bibliography   255

Index   269

Preface and Acknowledgments

The idea for this book was sparked by a comment that I read while perusing the papers of refugee photographer John Gutmann at the Center for Creative Photography (University of Arizona, Tucson, 2014). I was then engaged in research on Jews and photography. I didn't think much of the comment at the time. Gutmann wrote: "I entered WWII as a still and motion picture cameraman for the OWI [the Office of War Information]."[1] I couldn't find any record of Gutmann's motion-picture work under government auspices. Later, when I was investigating Jews from the United States who were photographers during the Second World War, mainly with the US Army Signal Corps, I spotted similar remarks by several photographers, along the lines that they had "also shot motion picture film." This happened during my research stints at Yad Vashem (Jerusalem, 2016) and the United States Holocaust Memorial Museum (USHMM, Washington, DC, 2017). Again, I looked and found nothing. This struck me as odd, because some of these photographers were well-known when they entered the military, and some achieved fame afterward.

While in Washington I sought information about these expert cameramen who seemed to have been unnoticed. I began reading about the OWI and American filmmaking during World War II. I was mildly intrigued by a reference to Leo Rosten in *The Propaganda Warriors: America's Crusade Against Nazi Germany* (1996) by Clayton D. Laurie, who noted usually convivial relations between officials from vastly different backgrounds, even before the United States' entry into the war.[2] Rosten was familiar to me mainly as a lighthearted humorist, the author of *The Joys of Yiddish* (1968).[3] I also started looking at film in the USHMM collection that contained any reference to the US Army Signal Corps. There was a lot—hundreds of segments. I proceeded to write down as much information as recorded—often not a lot—and started tracking down the references in the United States National Archives and

Records Administration (NARA) in College Park, Maryland, and the Library of Congress. I stumbled on Leonard Spigelgass, leading to his writing partner and friend, Leo Rosten—then Garson Kanin, Anatole Litvak, Stanley Kramer, George Cukor, Jesse Lasky, and Jesse Lasky Jr. The papers at NARA revealed that Rosten had been a major player in US moviemaking during World War II, and his handiwork extended to areas such as book publishing and radio. I continued to research the activities of Rosten, Spigelgass, and their cohort during World War II at the Motion Picture Archives and the Herrick Library in Los Angeles, and later at the Wisconsin Historical Society at the University of Wisconsin–Madison. While in Los Angeles I came to appreciate the role played by Budd Schulberg in the use of film at the Nuremberg trial and found that historical scrutiny of his service in this sphere was sparse. I saw that rarely used papers of Schulberg were held at Dartmouth College, his alma mater.

At various points in my research, I greatly benefited from conversations (real and virtual, from lengthy to very brief) with film scholars David Shneer (z"l), Noah Isenberg, Toby Haggith, Eylce Rae Helford, Lary May, and Patrick McGilligan. Steven Carr, the leading scholar of Rosten's academic career and Hollywood's complicated relations with Jews and things Jewish, deserves special mention for his deep insight and advice. Steven Ross shared a wonderful story with me about a personal encounter with Rosten, which remains his to tell (or not). Chris Yogerst offered wisdom and support at a few critical junctures. All my work in this field is influenced by my friendship with Judith E. Doneson (z"l), a pioneering scholar of Holocaust film,[4] and later conversations with Laurie Baron and Nathan Abrams. I continue to be mindful of the example set by, and extraordinary scholarship of, my colleague Miriam Hansen (z"l).[5] Heartfelt gratitude is due to Andy Bachman for just about everything. Colleagues and friends Bob Abzug, Leslie Adelson, Laura Almagor, Rachel Altstein, Brain Amkraut, Len Arzt, Ofer Ashkenazi, Liz Astaire, Mark Astaire, Fred Astren, Leora Auslander, Oksana Baigent, Joel Berkowitz, Azriel Bermant, Sam Bloom, John Boyer, David Brenner, Michael Brenner, Suzanne Brown-Fleming, Alex Busansky, Justin Cammy, Nina Caputo, Bridget Cogley, Gary Cohen, Judy Cohen, Caroline Sturdy Colls, David Conway, Deborah Dash-Moore, David De Vries, Leonard Dinnerstein (z"l), Skye Doney, Jacob Dorfman, Daniella Doron, Leo Doulton, Arie Dubnov, John Efron, Bob Ericksen, Laura Hobson Faure, Rachel Feldhay Brenner (z"l), Katie Fleming, Diego Flores-Jaime, David Franklin, Richard Freund (z"l), Bernie Friedman, Peter Fritzsche, Charles Gallagher, Ali Garbarini, Jay Geller (Case Western), Jay Geller (Vanderbilt), Michael Geyer, Sharon Gillerman (z"l), Sander Gilman, Ann Goldberg, Monica Gonzalez, Adam Gower, Danny Greene, Felicity Griffiths, Atina Grossmann, Malachai Hacohen, Mitch Hart, Stephen M.

Hart, Patricia Heberer-Rice, John Hoberman (Texas), Janine Holc, Nick Howe (z"l), Maryam Nabeelah Ismail, Jack Jacobs, Kala Jerzy, Marion Kaplan, Dennis Klein, Bob Koehl (z"l), Dennis Koepke (z"l), Ken Koltun-Fromm, Steve Kale, Haydn Kirnon, Susanne Kord, Yvonne Kozlovsky Golan, Gary Krueger, Konrad Kwiet, Ulrich Lehmann (z"l), Paul Lerner, Gail Levin, Amy-Jill Levine, Mitch Levine, Abby Lewis, Jonathan Lewis, Dan Magilow, Ruth Mandel, Jann Matlock, Jürgen Matthäus, Julie Mell, Dan Michman, David Myers, Kitty Millet, Leslie Morris, George Mosse (z"l), Stephen Naron, Joanna Newman, Marta Niccolai, Peter Novick (z"l), Tudor Parfitt, Andrew Patner (z"l), Avinoam Patt, Samantha Paul, Derek Penslar, William Pimlott, Alexandra Przyrembel, Mark Quigley, Andy Rabinbach, Linda Raphael, Marc Raphael, Wojtek Rappak, James Renton, Clemente Renton-Gonzalez, Jim Rice, Moses Rischin (z"l), Ruth Rischin, Bernard Rosenberg (z"l), Dan Rosenberg, Eric Rosenthal, Howard Sachar (z"l), Steven Samols, Alex Samson, Robert Sandler, Jay Satterfield, Anne Schenderlein, Robert Segal, Eli Shai, Clive Sheldon, Marci Shore, Lisa Siverman, Richard Sonn, David Sorkin, Scott Spector, Alan Steinweis, Lynda Stevenson, Marshall Stevenson, Dan Sussman, Kevin R. Thomas, John Tortorice, Barry Trachtenberg, Larry Trachtman, Joel Truman, Katie Trumpener, Jeff Veidlinger, Arlo Velmet, Marc Volovici, Jane Wells, Richard Wetzell, Larry Wolff, Louise Wolitz, Seth Wolitz, and Lindsay Zarwell have contributed, in important ways, to this book. Former student and colleague Frank Dabba Smith deserves his own sentence for service well beyond the call of duty. Thanks to Sara Halpern in Columbus and Sam Astaire in London for assistance with research. Besides tracking down dates and directors, Sam's breadth and depth of film knowledge helped tremendously. Sam Sheldon managed to provide me with a complete version of Leo Rosten's 1959 interviews at Columbia University, which filled critical gaps and illuminated several facets of this story. I also greatly benefited from two unpublished papers: those of Chris Simmons, who produced a superb essay on Hollywood and Jewishness (University of Chicago, MA seminar, 1998), and David Kimberly, author of a fine study of Jewish themes in the films of Alexander Korda (University College London, finalist essay, 2016).

I am grateful for a Josef Breitenbach Fellowship from the University of Arizona Center for Creative Photography (summer 2014); a research fellowship from Yad Vashem (spring–summer 2016); the William J. Lowenberg Memorial Fellowship on America, American Jews, and the Holocaust, at the Mandel Center for Advanced Holocaust Studies, United States Holocaust Memorial Museum, Washington, DC (fall 2016); and a Remarque Institute Fellowship at New York University (January–May 2017). The Remarque Institute Fellowship gave me time to read in the New York Public Library and the opportunity to meet Joan Juliet Buck, who generously shared memories and material from her father, Jules Buck, an important subject in this book. While at New York University, I was able to begin presenting my findings about film to university and general audiences, and I learned a lot from colleagues and attendees. Settings for discussion were graciously afforded by Haverford College, the University of Chicago, Cleveland's Jewish Community Forum and Case Western Reserve University, Mt. Zion Synagogue in St. Paul (MN), Yale University, the University of Florida, Florida International University's Jewish Museum, Monash University (Melbourne), the Sussex branch of the Jewish Historical Society of England, Aberdeen University, and the Institute of Jewish Studies and seminars of the Department of Hebrew & Jewish Studies, University College London. The thoughtfulness of Professor Susannah Heschel facilitated my visit to Hanover in 2017 for research in the papers of Budd Schulberg, and I wish to thank her for her graciousness and generosity.

In addition to fellowships, I have incurred more than the usual measure of academic debts. For an earlier phase of this book's journey, I wish to thank Jerry Singerman. For its materialization with the University of Wisconsin Press, I am extraordinarily grateful to Dennis Lloyd and his assistant, Jackie Krass, for their interest in this book and perseverance in seeing it through to publication. I am especially thankful to them for having found committed readers who gave me exceptionally sound advice. I also wish to thank project editor Jessica Smith and copy editor Mary Magray for their dedication, good sense, and expertise.

I offer profound thanks to my colleagues in the Department of Hebrew & Jewish Studies at University College London: Chimen Abramsky (z"l), Seth Anziska, Helen Beer, Sima Beeri, Sara Benisaac, Alinda Damsma, Mark Geller, Shirli Gilbert, Sonia Gollance, Gillian Greenberg (z"l), Francois Guesnet, Emma Harris, Casey Johnson, Lily Kahn, Lia Kann-Zajtmann, John Klier (z"l), Lior Libman, Neill Lochery, Raphael Loewe (z"l), Tali Loewenthal, Carlos Yebra López, Simo Muir, Tsila Ratner, Ada Rapoport-Albert (z"l), Vanessa Richards, Belinda Samari, Shoshana Sharpe, Willem Smelik, Sacha Stern, Michael Weitzman (z"l), and Leon Yudkin (z"l). It is impossible to imagine a better next-door office mate than Professor Guesnet.

It is typical for academic books to be overdue. This one has been stewing for years and taken off the burner completely on a few occasions. When I returned to London in May 2017 from my sabbatical, I was about to launch into writing. I almost immediately headed back to the United States, however, due the failing health of my mother, Gloria Berkowitz (1929–2017), who died mid-June, and my sister, Edie Needleman (1958–2018), who died several months later. They are much in my thoughts, as is my father, William Berkowitz (1917–1995). I cannot possibly specify how my sense of World War II, which ended fourteen years before my birth, has been enhanced by my father's service as a GI in the Pacific. Alas, when one figures the pandemic into the mix, I suspect that I have left many loose threads, personally and professionally. I would not be surprised to learn that I have short-changed several people for whom gratitude is due.

As ever, I wish to thank my daughter Rachel, my son Stephen, and my wife Debby, with love, for putting up with me. Even as adults the kids are just too much fun.

HOLLYWOOD'S UNOFFICIAL FILM CORPS

Introduction

In late October 1942, President Franklin Delano Roosevelt's (nearly) private screening of *Prelude to War*, the first of the *Why We Fight* series, was momentous in the history of American filmmaking and spectatorship during World War II.[1] By the time FDR saw *Prelude to War*, supervised by the esteemed director Frank Capra, millions of US servicemen had already watched it. Although a media blitz along the lines of *Why We Fight* was conceived for general audiences,[2] Capra's remit originally was for "shorts" restricted to armed forces personnel.[3] But the top brass, notably Generals George C. Marshall and Frederick H. Osborn, thought that *Prelude to War* should be offered to the home front.[4] On seeing it, FDR, too, was adamant that *Prelude to War* be dispatched to US movie houses as swiftly as possible.[5]

Well, why not? Commonly held views about federally funded film at the time prompted immediate pushback from the US Bureau of Motion Pictures and other quarters. Putting these movies in theaters, for the general public, was supposedly forbidden. Long-standing convention held that US tax dollars could not be used to create film for general consumption, since this would promote a particular viewpoint and thereby violate the First Amendment of the Constitution. Hence *Why We Fight* and many of the films to be considered here, such as the "Private Snafu" cartoons, were, at least initially, unavailable to the public. The government could make and distribute movies for specific purposes, such as for military training and advice for essential occupational groups, like farmers and munitions factory workers—and that was that. Or was it?[6] Early in FDR's presidency, the moguls were "alarmed" at the prospect of administration "involvement in the business of making motion pictures."[7]

We shall see that other policies generated by US advisers on wartime film contradicted, circumvented, or else complicated this prohibition. Movies with dedicated objectives, it was proposed, also might be shown to public audiences at schools and community centers, and theaters were not precluded. Objectives could be quite broad, such as "morale." The target audience might even encompass the entire population of the United States. That strategy arose mainly from little-known Donald Slesinger, then director of the American Film Center, and from the slightly better known Leo Calvin Rosten, PhD, chief of the motion picture division of the US government's short-lived Office of Facts and Figures founded in 1940.[8] Both held vague but high-level advisory positions throughout the war. Slesinger's inspiration derived, in large part, from knowledge of the governmental "film program" dubbed "The Celluloid Circus" as executed in the United Kingdom, with similar efforts across the British empire, since 1940.[9] The efforts of Rosten and Slesinger were abetted, as well, by a growing "collaboration between the motion picture industry and the US government during Franklin D. Roosevelt's presidency," as the moguls sought to avoid judicial penalties for antitrust violations.[10] Hollywood also was painfully aware, by 1938, that Hitler's increasing control of Europe was bad for business.[11]

In 1939 Britain, Canada, and the United States "began to need films and film people, for a variety of causes," Leo Rosten said in a 1959 interview. The Canadians and the British started "to make a great many pictures for training purposes. The US Government needed film people to start making films," likewise, "in the armed forces, because, remember, we began to arm desperately once it looked as if the war might spread. Also, the government was interested in heightening the awareness of Americans about what was going on in the world."[12] Since 1940 Rosten had himself advocated and worked knee-deep in the creation of an immense range of movies of all genres, whether expressly governmental or from established Hollywood studios, to blanket the United States, as long as they conveyed clear, consistent messages and were well-produced. He prompted and administered both quantity and quality.[13]

At this crucial screening of *Prelude to War*, the president was not alone.[14] FDR went with Harry Hopkins, one of his closest advisers, particularly on matters pertaining to the war. Hopkins spearheaded the Lend-Lease program of US support for Great Britain. He also was a key administration player in safeguarding the film industry from antitrust prosecution, which allowed studios to keep theaters under their ownership and generally evade challenges to their "oligopoly."[15] The president and Hopkins were joined by the flamboyant Alexander Woollcott, a writer for newspapers and *The New Yorker*, who was a foremost arbiter of taste in the nation. Often bypassed by historians, "for nearly twenty years" Woollcott "was the most conspicuous persuader in America."[16] FDR, Hopkins, and Woollcott were accompanied, as well, by Harpo Marx.[17]

Harpo was the hyperkinetic member of the Marx Brothers troupe who wore a blonde, curly wig, chased women across stage and screen, and honked a horn instead of speaking. Pianist and composer Oscar Levant, Harpo's frequent houseguest who stayed for months on end, accords Harpo the status of Hollywood's most sought-after personality in the late 1930s, along with Charlie Chaplin.[18] One could expect bankers, academics, all kinds of musicians, and even a cabinet member to turn up at Harpo's pool or dinner table in Beverly Hills.[19]

Harpo's presence may be attributed to the fact that Alex Woollcott was one of his dearest friends.[20] But Woollcott, the ringleader of the Algonquin Round Table conversation club, had many beloved associates, who, on the surface, might have made more appropriate company. Either FDR asked for Harpo or else he was thrilled when Woollcott suggested him. Harpo's brother Groucho, the family intellectual, was (and remains) more renowned for his support of Roosevelt.[21]

We have no record of the conversation between the president, Hopkins, Woollcott, and Harpo. From FDR's response it seems that his guests encouraged the movie's public dissemination. Harpo, therefore, may have had more to do with the fate of *Why We Fight* than the director of the Bureau of Motion Pictures, Lowell Mellett, or the bureau's Hollywood branch director, Nelson Poynter.[22] Harpo knew a lot more about movies than these earnest administrators, who mainly had newspaper experience behind them.[23]

Harpo's autobiography, *Harpo Speaks!*, mentions neither this occasion nor the fact that he had any relationship with FDR. (In 1939, Oscar Levant wrote that Harpo's inscribed photo of the president was among his "most treasured possessions.")[24] Harpo was not shy about revealing his role in another clandestine operation. He writes effusively about serving as a courier/spy for the US government in the wake of a trip to the Soviet Union in the early 1930s. To be sure, Harpo is self-deprecating, as a man who "never finished the second grade." He does, however, boast that

> I've played piano in a whorehouse. I've smuggled secret papers out of Russia. I've spent an evening on the divan with Peggy Hopkins Joyce. I've taught a gangster mob how to play Pinchie Winchie. I've played croquet with Herbert Bayard Swope while he kept Governor Al Smith waiting on the phone. I've gambled with Nick the Greek, sat on the floor with Greta Garbo, sparred with Benny Leonard, horsed around with the Prince of Wales, played ping-pong with George Gershwin. George Bernard Shaw has asked me for advice. Oscar Levant has played private concerts for me for a buck a throw. I have golfed with Ben Hogan and Sam Snead. I've based on the Riviera with Somerset Maugham and Elsa

Maxwell. I've been thrown out of the casino at Monte Carlo. . . . I've been a member of the two most famous Round Tables since the days of King Arthur—sitting with the finest creative minds of the 1920s at the Algonquin in New York, and with Hollywood's sharpest professional wits at the Hillcrest.[25]

So why would Harpo, in a (nearly) tell-all tale, not say that he had been with the president and his closest adviser, and his pal Woollcott, at this decisive screening? Had the likes of American antisemitic radio priest Father Charles Coughlin and "isolationist anti-Semite" Senator Gerald Nye (R-ND)[26]—not to mention Joseph Goebbels and other Nazis who claimed that Roosevelt was a closet Jew—gotten wind of FDR and Harry Hopkins privately conferring with Harpo Marx, their heads would have exploded. They also would have been beside themselves had they known that Leo Rosten, a Jew born in Lodz, Poland, was on close enough terms with General Osborn, General Marshall, and Harry Hopkins to allow him to pick up the phone and ask, personally, for favors.[27]

General George C. Marshall is lionized as "one of the nation's most distinguished leaders in war and peace."[28] Frederick Henry Osborn, in contrast, "who ran the Army's Information and Education Division as a Major General during World War II," often misidentified as "Osborne," largely has been ignored.[29] In 1940 Osborn was appointed by FDR "to head the Civilian Committee on Selective Service. A year later, he was named chairman of the Army Committee on Welfare and Recreation, and, at the outbreak of war, was made a general, leading the Army's Morale Branch, which he shaped into the Information and Education Division."[30]

On film matters, Osborn listened attentively to Leonard Spigelgass, a screenwriter. Spigelgass was one of the first Hollywood people to make Leo Rosten's acquaintance in 1937, when Rosten and his wife were stranded in Los Angeles.[31] Spigelgass wrote the screenplay for *All Through the Night* (dir. Vincent Sherman, 1942), a comic caper about Nazi spies in New York for which Leo Rosten penned the "story" under the pseudonym Leonard Q. Ross. With many writing credits since the early 1930s, Spigelgass was famed for the screenplay of *Gypsy* (dir. Mervyn LeRoy, 1962) and was nominated in 1950 for an Academy Award for "best writing, motion picture story" for *Mystery Street* (dir. John Sturgess). By early 1942 Spigelgass had already served with Frank Capra making US Army Orientation Films before his military induction. After the stint with Capra, Rosten "got him a job with the Office of Facts and Figures." Spigelgass was soon returned to Capra's unit, and within weeks was commissioned a US Army captain.[32] He emerged in 1945 as a lieutenant colonel, proving that the army reckoned his collaboration with Capra, Garson Kanin, Anatole Litvak, Julian Blaustein, Daniel Taradash, Hebert Baker, Stanley Kramer, Arthur Lewis, and David Miller as highly valuable to the war effort.

On learning of the imminent public release of *Prelude to War* and viewing it in the US Senate chamber, isolationist Senators Rufus C. Holman (R-OR) and John A. Danaher (R-CT) groused that "government motion pictures and magazines, ostensibly produced to further the war effort, were being used to promote a fourth term for President Roosevelt." The "real purpose" of the film, they charged, was "personal, political propaganda."[33] Indeed, America's relationship to Europe and the wider world, as presented in *Prelude to War*, was not their cup of tea. In addition to imagery and narration, which they took to be a paean to FDR, its very film techniques might have rankled them. Had the senators from Oregon and Connecticut been aware that Russian-born Anatole Litvak, commissioned a US Army lieutenant colonel, was one of Capra's underlings, whose vision was vital in *Why We Fight*, their ire would have been at a white heat.[34]

Jesse Lasky, like Harpo, was reticent to acknowledge his encounters with FDR. His firm was front and center in the government antitrust suit against the industry.[35] Lasky was a founding Hollywood mogul who helped foster the Marx Brothers' movie career, and he was unabashed about tooting his own horn. In a book of 2017, Pat Silver-Lasky, a daughter-in-law of Lasky, writes that in 1939 her husband's dad "was granted a private audience with Franklin D. Roosevelt." Lasky was then working at RKO studios, after falling out with his partners at Paramount. "The president discussed Hitler's progress through Europe and made a pointed suggestion to him to produce a film that would sway the hearts of isolationist America into entering the war on the side of Great Britain."[36] In Lasky's 1957 autobiography, although he writes extensively about producing *Sergeant York* (dir. Howard Hawks, 1941), which brilliantly satisfied FDR's request, he is silent about being personally instructed by the president. Lasky's lone mention of the president is an anecdote about seeing him *after* the gala premiere of *Sergeant York*.[37]

In addition to Jesse Lasky, Harry Warner (of Warner Bros.) and independent producer Walter Wanger enjoyed warm relations and frequent access to FDR.[38] The Warner brothers and Wanger were fierce New Dealers, anti-isolationists, and ardent supporters of the president. A Wanger-produced movie, *Gabriel Over the White House* (dir. Gregory La Cava, 1933),[39] which was widely perceived as shilling for the 1932 candidacy of FDR and urging his forceful control of the administration, had a special place in the president's heart. "Roosevelt always used to joke with me about it," Wanger recalled in the 1960s. "I went to the White House a great deal in those days."[40] But Wanger did not often talk about this in public at the time.[41]

The Hollywood figure who spurred the initial research for this study is the aforementioned Leo Calvin Rosten. This is the same Leo Rosten who would later gain fame as a Jewish humorist. In an article for a political science journal in 1947, Rosten described himself, along with being a screenwriter and magazine author, as having "served as the deputy director of the Office of War Information, special consultant to the Secretary of War's Office, chief of the Motion Picture Division of the Office of Facts and Figures, and chief of the Motion Picture Bureau of the National Defense Advisory Commission."[42] The latter commission, about which there is limited scholarly discussion, was under the auspices of the Office for Emergency Management.[43] Rosten suggests that his government duties commenced in the spring of 1940, when he "was called in by Lowell Mellett, who was then one of Roosevelt's six anonymous assistants, and had been appointed government film coordinator." But Rosten reveals that he had already been advising the administration for over a year prior to that. While the precise timing is unclear, he was notably summoned "to meet with them on the whole problem of movies and the defense effort." According to Rosten, the president set up the National Defense Advisory Commission (NDAC), "under [William S.] Knudson and [Sidney] Hillman, just after the fall of France."[44] Knudson is best remembered for leading the General Motors corporation. Some nine months afterward, a profile of Knudson in *The New Yorker* reported that "the vague character of Knudson's job and the whole NDAC reflected Roosevelt's state of mind as he felt his way over difficult ground." Officially, Knudson was the chief of the Office of Production Management, "the supreme defense council supplementing the Advisory Commission to the Council on National Defense," which included labor leader Sidney Hillman as its associate director general.[45] Rosten explained that "once France fell and the Germans were all over the Continent, the whole world picture changed."[46]

Leo Rosten, therefore, "in terms of the defense effort," became engaged in the open-ended enterprise of "our commitments to the British and the French," with the task of steering clear of "some of the mistakes of the First World War, when Wilson had set up the Committee of Public Information under George Creel, and when, in the years after World War I, there was a strong revulsion against 'propaganda.'" In 1959 Rosten made a point to remind his audience of the "propaganda posters and movies, all of them hostile to Germany, favorable to Britain, in the First World War." While Hitler looked to be in firm control of Europe, "there was an awareness that we had to think out some policy and some programs. The movie people," he said, "were very much concerned that the government would try to move in on film, and would try to use the feature film as a propaganda instrument. My position was something like this: that no matter what happened, the public wanted and was entitled to movies which would entertain them; that the shorts were the form which legitimately permitted the communication of facts, of information; *that we should never get into the business of propaganda, but that you couldn't seal off the movie-house from the currents of life.*"[47] Without being explicit about when his official Washington role began, Rosten continued that "on the basis of many discussions in Washington, and then in Hollywood with the heads of the studios, we organized a kind of loose liaison between the movie industry and Washington, *and I worked in Hollywood for several years as a kind of two-way channel.*" After the Japanese attack on Pearl Harbor, Rosten says that he "was called back to Washington, and then we opened an office in Hollywood under Nelson Poynter, while I remained in Washington, and in this way we began to systematize the flow of information both ways, and I think we began to get pretty good shorts about various aspects of the war effort, about the war in Europe, about training, and all the rest of it."[48]

One of the most extraordinary disclosures in the course of this oral history is Rosten admitting his centrality in the small Washington cohort that "organized all sorts of programs which brought into government service and into the armed forces some of the most gifted people in Hollywood," including Frank Capra. Capra was commissioned a major and was directed to set up "the army film unit."[49] Historians' discussions of the bold government move to bring Capra and other movie people into both government service and high ranks in the US armed forces, formally, have never counted Rosten as a designer and instigator of this policy. Capra was, indisputably, one of America's and the world's greatest movie directors. Although left unspoken, it also helped that Capra was a Gentile. He was a master at appealing to the Christian American masses. "Some of the Frank Capra pictures," Rosten said, "were deceptively simple, and yet actually dealt with the story of the Crucifixion. See, Capra did three films in a row which were a story of a good man maligned, persecuted, and crucified by the Philistines of this world. That's a funny way to talk about it, but in fact that's what *Mr. Deeds* and *Mr. Smith* and several other of his stories were about—stories that echo some of the most ancient themes in human drama."[50] Likewise, Rosten extolled director John Ford, also a Gentile, as a Christian storyteller. "John Ford's *The Informer* was a very great movie in which you saw a group of people caught up in the political crisis of the Irish Revolution. It was a story of betrayal, the story of Judas."[51] Compared with giants like Ford and Capra, Rosten was Hollywood small fry. He had, however, already forged an unusual role for himself as an expert about the movie industry, as detailed by historian Steven Carr.[52] But because of the pressures of the moment, Rosten helped to install the biggest directors expressly into the US armed forces.

Rosten had great esteem, as well, for Garson Kanin, "a superb movie director." He especially venerated Kanin for how he worked his way up and carefully studied the craft of moviemaking. Arriving in Hollywood after Rosten was tied to a studio in 1937, Kanin "was working for [Sam] Goldwyn as a sort of assistant, not as a director at all." Committing himself to becoming a director, Kanin would "sit in a projection room and have run for him, over and over, day after day, hour after hour, one or two movies that he greatly admired. He learned the method by which the movie had been put together, in terms of scenes, cuts, camera angles and all the rest of it."[53] Kanin had enlisted in the army on his own volition and was taken into its film branch, directing and codirecting a number of important productions. Kanin, as a Jew, like his friend George Cukor, would occupy the strata below that of Capra, Ford, George Stevens, and John Huston, and was uncredited for his biggest wartime film, *The True Glory* (1945). William Wyler, whom Rosten regarded as in the same league as Capra, George Stevens, and Orson Welles,[54] was the exception to the rule of reserving top billing for non-Jewish directors.

In that interview Rosten explained that it would have been naive to believe that the American film industry, by the late 1930s, could be immune from politics. Although many studio heads and producers were conservative, numerous actors, writers, directors, and technicians became politically sophisticated and progressive. This was certain to influence the character of movies—although there were Hollywood people on the right, as well, who were against intervention in Europe and the New Deal. Democratic party activist actors such as Humphrey Bogart and Melvyn Douglas were recognized as potentially huge vote getters. Studio heads and producers leaned "isolationist," but this was more in the sense of their business practices. Actors, directors, writers, and technicians, however, realized that dealing with dictatorships was a short-sighted strategy, even from a profit-margin perspective. These regimes, including Japan, Spain, the Soviet Union, and Italy—as well as Nazi Germany—both "censored and barred" selected Hollywood films. Much of the American film industry stood to be shut out from what had once been an enormous, open market.[55] After war with the Axis powers was engaged in 1941, however, this controversy over doing business with dictatorships was largely moot. Concern over the nexus between the movies, politics, and governmental control, however, would not disappear.

Rosten's tenure throughout the war, in which he was in and out of uniform, was marked by a steadfast conviction: that it was absurd to think there could be an absolute division "between something called 'entertainment' and something called 'propaganda.' This muddy distinction implied that what is entertaining cannot be significant, and that what is significant (dealing with group, rather than individual problems) cannot be entertaining." Rosten scolded unnamed studio heads and movie producers for having fed this fiction when it suited them.[56]

The principals in this story concurred wholeheartedly with Rosten concerning the absurdity of trying to separate "entertainment from propaganda." They were motivated to make movies that would matter, along with sincerely having answered the call of duty. (The term "propaganda," though, became impolitic.) Rosten was a driver behind the notion that movies could serve US war aims in specific as well as general ways and also be compelling—even enjoyable. It was in the government's interest, therefore, to produce and facilitate the making of movies that were unmatched in power and speed to influence opinion and to have the best industry people serving in the US military.[57] "I had been very much interested in public opinion," Rosten said, "how it is formed, and in those things that influence people. I had done a lot of graduate work in propaganda, public opinion analysis, and so on."[58] Efforts to make movies, in studios and with independent producers and directors, to fulfill war-related objectives both at home and abroad continued full throttle under Rosten and company. Why are discussions of Rosten's ideas and activities during wartime, many of which were consequential, so elusive?[59]

Interestingly, one of the early films produced by the Office for Emergency Management, titled *Fellow Americans* (1942), was an appeal for American social solidarity after Pearl Harbor. It was narrated by actor Jimmy Stewart, directed by Garson Kanin, with music by Oscar Levant. A certain "Wallace Russell" was the (credited) screenwriter.[60] Wallace Russell, who also is listed as writing another Office for Emergency Management film, *Ring of Steel*, narrated by Spencer Tracy (dir. Garson Kanin, 1942), does not seem to have existed. The latter film solemnly begins: "I am the American soldier." The final scene of *Ring of Steel* has Tracy intone: "I, the American solider, am the shield." The soldier depicted is not silhouetted by the sea or amber waves of grain—but the skyline of New York City.[61] Homage to Manhattan would be even more spectacular, set to a booming rendition of George Gershwin's *Rhapsody in Blue*, in the "War Comes to America" segment of *Why We Fight*. Anatole Litvak, correctly, gets directing credit for "War Comes to America," which was "Orientation Film No. 7" (reel 2) for US soldiers and, later, was shown to the broad US public.[62] In 2017 several people in Cleveland attested that they had seen it as kids, in different parts of the United States, during the Second World War. Consistent with Slesinger and Rosten's ideas, *Why We Fight* and related films were, in fact, shown to Americans far and wide.

This book addresses a taboo that, in the third decade of the twenty-first century, is difficult to fathom as a touchy subject: the engagement of Jews with motion picture making—from policy to screenwriting, editing, camera work—in and for the United States during the Second World War.[63] Charges that any government role in filmmaking, even during wartime, was "obviously a non-essential expenditure" and "a waste of public funds" were usually tainted with anti-Hollywood, antisemitic prejudice.[64] Recognition of connections between Hollywood, Roosevelt, and Jews, then, were often subdued, and a great many who were involved stayed quiet about it for their entire lives, others, for decades. But broad conceptual contours and nitty-gritty details of how the United States used film during the war were shaped, in no small part, under Leo Rosten, an intimate of FDR and key members of the press corps,[65] and carried through by scores of Hollywood types, including Budd Schulberg, Garson Kanin, George Cukor, and Stanley Kramer.

Leonard Spigelgass and Anatole Litvak put their own stamp on film work, including *Why We Fight*, that mainly is subsumed under the directorship of Frank Capra. Jules Buck was more of a collaborator, not just a cameraman, for John Huston. Buck's quasi-governmental film work, supporting Britain and intervention, began before Pearl Harbor, which also is true for Garson Kanin.[66] The modest photographer Philip Drell happily worked under director George Stevens. But the direction he received was sometimes minimal. Drell found that as a still and movie cameraman, at critical moments, he was in front of the action—which made its way on screen, as he caught it. Jesse Lasky Jr. was an intrepid soldier in the Philippine jungle (with a rifle and cameras) and, overall, creator of film that came out of US training camps, the film center in Astoria, Queens, battles with the Japanese, and the European theater toward war's end. Lasky Jr. had been engaged in anti-isolationist moviemaking before 1942. His films did not, until decades later, indicate their creators. At the close of the conflict, Budd Schulberg, who had made and substantially improved wartime films,[67] and distinguished himself in conventional military engagements, was critical in determining how movies would be used to convey the recent history of the Nazi menace and to portray how National Socialism used film to realize its grotesque designs.[68] Schulberg was the most proactive Hollywood and Washington interlocutor preventing Hitler's favorite director, Leni Riefenstahl, from resuming her film career after the Nazi defeat.[69] Budd Schulberg was delighted to shower praise on those who helped him and said little about his wartime service for most of his life. To the extent that credit for his efforts were offered, it was extended to directors George Stevens and John Ford.

But because Hollywood had been accused of "warmongering" and the movies had a disproportionate number of Jews among its moguls and staff, and because isolationists (including unabashed antisemites) alleged that going to war in Europe was ignited by, and in the chief interest of, Jews—FDR's administration and the Hollywood establishment were not keen to publicize the extent to which they had worked, in harmony, with those who happened to be Jews. When FDR proposed putting *Prelude to War* into theaters, he was accused by his conservative opponents of using it to boost his own prospects for reelection in 1944. The public showing of *Prelude of War* and all of *Why We Fight*, including a number of off-shoots, went full steam ahead, mainly to loud acclaim.[70] But consistent with their respective approach to the problematic Jewishness of Hollywood, both Washington and Hollywood were wary of casting a spotlight on the part of Jews in making film an effective instrument in waging war, galvanizing the home front, and forging the peace at war's end.

This book tells a story of those who are relatively obscure in the history of World War II filmmaking in the United States. It argues that the creation of American movies during the Second World War looks different when one considers the factor of ethnicity, not just antisemitism, anti-Black racism, or anti-Asian sentiment as it was perceived at the time. One dimension of this book will startle nobody: Jews played a large role in wartime filmmaking. During the Second World War, experience in Hollywood studios—typically combined with a liberal-arts education[71]—constituted a highly valuable sort of cultural capital, in the terms of Pierre Bourdieu. I intend to show—counterintuitively, by Hollywood logic—that individual Jews had a pronounced impact because they voluntarily stepped aside if and when credit was assigned. We also learn the extent to which key Jewish personnel, even many who achieved fame later on, have been slow to be accorded honor in America's "Good War," to steal a phrase of Studs Terkel.

What was the state of the American motion picture industry, in particular its "studio system," when Rosten assumed the leadership of the film division of the Office of Facts and Figures? A large chunk of the answer may be gleaned from Rosten's study, *Hollywood: The Movie Colony, The Movie Makers* (1941). Seen from the 2020s, many aspects of moviemaking, under the vague rubric of Hollywood, seem to have changed little for nearly a century. Beginning in the 1990s, a great deal of attention, both scholarly and popular, has been paid to the impact of the Motion Picture Producers and Distributors of America, which was formed in 1922. This formidable body claimed to be "morally" driven but also had clear, conservative biases. "Will Hays, chairman of the Republican National Committee and Postmaster General in the Harding administration," Rosten wrote, "was made president of this organization, which became known as the 'Hays office,' under a contract which placed his salary at $100,000 a year and was later revised to give him $150,000 a year. The movie colony and moving pictures became the objects of an organized, long-range clean-up."[72] Hays hired Joseph L. Breen to lead the Production Code

Administration, a strong censorship instrument. Breen managed to tamp down his earlier anti-Jewish rants.[73] Besides being shaped by this type of control, at the close of the 1930s, Hollywood's studio system was in a state of flux in many other respects. A cornerstone of moviemaking, however, present from its outset and ongoing, is that "the work" conducted there "is a form of play, and the people love their work."[74]

Beginning in the 1910s, the "classical" film business, according to Thomas Schatz, comprised a "period when various social, industrial, technological, economic, and aesthetic forces struck a delicate balance" that fostered "a consistent system of production and consumption."[75] Indeed, "despite the perennial crises in the motion picture industry (labor strife, wholesale lay-offs, shrinking box-office receipts) Hollywood possesses," Rosten wrote in 1941, "a sense of insulation" from economic turbulence.[76] Building on increasing sophistication and depth of stories in the silent film era, what Chris Simmons calls "performed narrative,"[77] major advances in 1920s film technology included sound, such as featured intermittently—yet strikingly—in *The Jazz Singer* (dir. Alan Crosland, 1927, Warner Bros.) starring Al Jolson, widely considered the first "talkie." Soon afterward, it was expected that all films would have consistent, spoken dialogue. This development obviously enhanced storytelling. "That Hollywood attaches great importance to the Story," Rosten wrote, "is no news, although few producers seem to be as cognizant of its decisive importance as Mr. Goldwyn."[78] While black-and-white filmmaking continued to predominate, the late 1930s witnessed a vast improvement in Technicolor, culminating in the spectacular musical, *The Wizard of Oz* (dir. Victor Fleming, 1939, MGM) starring Judy Garland in her sparkling, ruby-red slippers. Immediately before the United States entry into World War II, Rosten remarked that "The American press is read only where English is read; the American radio is heard only where English is comprehended; but the American movie is an international carrier which triumphs over differences in age or language, nationality or custom.... Through the movies ... the United States has effected a 'cultural colonization' of the world. And trade follows the films as well as the flag."[79]

Hollywood, in the narrow sense, was and remains a part of the sprawling, seemingly uncentered city of Los Angeles, California. Currently, the sections to its "West" and "North" supposedly denote distinct areas. In 1941 Rosten specified that "there are two Hollywoods: the Hollywood where people live and work, and the Hollywood which lives in the mind of the public like a fabulous legend."[80] It "is a place which has been so ballyhooed that it has become preposterous, and so lampooned that the ridicule ceases to carry credence."[81] Yet viewed from a distance, it was not so different from other specialized industries in the United States.

Perhaps, though, more than any occupational sector, it is impossible to talk about Hollywood and ignore money—that which flows in and is paid out. The movie business, famously, offered big salaries to studio executives, stars, producers, and directors. "The motion picture industry," around 1941, had "a capital investment in the United States alone of approximately two billion dollars—in movie production, theaters, and distribution."[82]

Hollywood, "the industry," signifies, as well, its major studios, the larger of which were tied to theater chains and vast distribution networks. In roughly descending order of their size, measured by profits and holdings, these comprised eight "majors," which accounted for "approximately eighty percent of the total production value of all the feature pictures made in the United States": "Paramount Pictures, Inc.; Twentieth Century-Fox Film Corporation; Warner Bros. Pictures, Incorporated; Loewe's, Inc. (of which Metro-Goldwyn-Mayer was the production subsidiary); RKO (Radio-Keith-Orpheum) Corporation; Universal Corporation; Columbia Pictures Corporation; and United Artists Corporation."[83] United Artists, at that time, distributed films made by "leading independent producers: Charles Chaplin, Samuel Goldwyn, David O. Selznick, Walter Wanger, Alexander Korda, Hal Roach, James Roosevelt, Edward Small, and others."[84] Together, the big eight "produced 376 pictures in 1939. In the same year only 1,133 new books of fiction were published in the United States."[85] The studio of Walt Disney was up and coming, along with many smaller players. Actors and actresses, producers, directors, and writers were often committed to one studio, while others were "independents."

Although Hollywood was amorphous, geography mattered—more so as Los Angeles became crisscrossed by freeways and automobiles were seen as extensions of personalities. Around 1940 RKO, Paramount, Columbia, and the United Artists group were "in Hollywood or Los Angeles proper," and "the independent 'quickie' producers clustered around what was known as 'Poverty Row.'" The massive Warner Bros. facility, along with Universal Pictures and Disney Productions, were some five miles north of Hollywood; Twentieth Century-Fox was in West Los Angeles; MGM in Culver City, "several miles south of West Los Angeles, along with Hal Roach and Selznick Pictures."[86] Ruminating on the initials MGM, Budd Schulberg recalled L. B. Mayer, likely repeating stories told by his parents:

> On young Louie's wedding day [June 1904] some sense of the grandiose impelled him to add a middle initial to his signature on the marriage license. So he became, with a flourish of the pen, Louis B. Mayer, a precursor of the godlike figure he would eventually become when the second M in the enormous MGM sign over the great studio in Culver City stood for him. He would rule with a

draconian hand not only his own studio but in effect The Industry, all of Hollywood as we knew it in the Twenties, Thirties, and the Forties.[87]

Louis B. Mayer also faced a giant-sized payout upon his divorce from Margaret Shenberg in 1947, to the tune of a $3,250,000 "cash settlement."[88]

A Hollywood myth that Rosten reinforced, rather than punctured, concerned the whopping salaries doled out to studio executives, directors, and star performers. Its essential "workers," though, had more earthly wages. In total, not counting the staffing of theaters in the United States and worldwide, the movie industry had a reported workforce of nearly a quarter million in 1939.[89] Although there were numerous exceptions, studios became known for certain strengths and genres. Each was thought to have "a personality":[90] Warner Bros., "melodrama and drama," often with gritty crime; Paramount, comedy; Universal, horror; and Disney, animation.[91] The studios had little choice but to embrace "the Star System," in which groups of films and trends clustered around highly prized popular actors and directors.[92]

From the 1930s to nearly 1942, in addition to the constant push for bigger audiences and profits amid fierce competition between the entrenched studios and several upstarts, another pressure, both foreign and domestic, was mounting. The largest studios were most threatened by looming, US antitrust legislation. All of them had already been deflated from the effect of Nazi control in Europe.[93] "The war on Hollywood," Rosten wrote in 1941, "antedated the firing of cannon. The political advertency of Hollywood preceded the political awakening of America."[94] While ideas popped up to develop markets in South America and elsewhere, the loss from Europe took quite a bite.[95] It is now recognized that "antitrust action against the major motion picture studios during the 1930s *led to unprecedented collaboration* between the Roosevelt administration and the industry during World War II."[96] This complemented the impulse of many Hollywood insiders toward US intervention in Europe, especially after the start of the war in 1939. A federal criminal lawsuit began against Warner Bros. in 1935, which also included Paramount and RKO, for interfering with interstate commerce. In 1938 United States v. Paramount was launched, in which "eight major studios, twenty-five affiliates and subsidiaries, and one-hundred-thirty-two industry executives were named in the suit, making it one of the largest antitrust cases filed by the US government against an industry in history."[97] Yet remarkably, the case is rarely mentioned in the correspondence dealing with moviemaking itself, and censorship through Motion Picture Code regulation only occasionally surfaces. "The remarkable point," perhaps only slightly exaggerated by Rosten, "is that Hollywood's elite has no respect for itself." Therefore it "is singularly deferential to the prestige of others [so] it is almost craven before politicians, professors, or playwrights."[98]

The studios were acting with some integrity when they "pledged their full support to the Roosevelt administration on June 5, 1940," hoping that "the president himself would instruct the Department of Justice to cease its antitrust inquiries into the industry."[99] In contrast to its obliviousness to politics in the early 1930s, Rosten argued that

> during the world crisis in September, 1939, four movie producers had teletype machines installed in their offices to clatter out the minute-by-minute pulse beat of Europe; Hollywood parties rang with fevered talk and were gripped by dark apprehension; committees sprang up to aid Poland, France, Britain, China; and through every nerve of a community reputed to be somnambulistic, there raced the throbbing pains of the world's agony. Those who knew Hollywood twenty years ago, or fifteen, or ten, would have been dumbfounded by the tension which electrified the men and women of the movie colony. "Hollywood," someone cried, "has put on political long pants."[100]

The fact that these otherwise competing entities, coming together in concert in such a manner—led by Leo Rosten—were coordinated from the outset as a governmental accomplice was barely noticed. What began as the Motion Picture Committee Cooperating for National Defense was renamed after Pearl Harbor and the official American entry into the war as the more sharply focused War Activities Committee (WAC). "The coordinated efforts of the WAC's seven divisions—the Theatres Division, the Distributors Division, the Hollywood Division, the Newsreel Division, the Trade Press Division, the Foreign Managers (overseas) Division, and the Public Relations Division—exemplifies," in the analysis of Mary Gelsey Samuelson, "Hollywood's strategic 'voluntary' cooperation with the US government during World War II."[101] All of this, though, ran considerably through the efforts of Rosten, beginning with his role as head of the motion picture division of the Office of Facts and Figures. The distinctions between units, while a matter of policy and administration, hardly ever figured into the working out of picture making. The five newsreel corporations—20th Century-Fox Movietone News, Metrotone News (later, News of the Day, distributed by MGM), Paramount News, Universal News, and Pathé News, which served local theaters, also were in the loose remit of Rosten. The 1930s, furthermore, saw the rise of several independent documentary filmmakers, some of whom had their own companies. Many of these, who often began as still photographers, were from the activist left.[102] The next chapter will show how Rosten selectively appropriated these as well.

Why, one may ask, is this book largely concerned with Hollywood's Jews, who are so often portrayed as seeking to abandon any trace of Jewish distinctiveness? In *Prequel: An American Fight Against Fascism* (2023), Rachel Maddow argues that Louis B. Mayer concocted a lavish, expensive event, on April 27, 1939, to keep his "megastars"—William Powell, Myrna Loy, Mickey Rooney, Jean Harlow, Norma Shearer, Rosalind Russell, Robert Montgomery, Hedy Lamarr, Jimmy Stewart, Joan Crawford, and Clark Gable—away from the premiere of *Confessions of a Nazi Spy*, an openly anti-Nazi, Warner Bros. picture directed by Anatole Litvak.[103] Warner Bros. has been noted as "the first to personally offer to screen films for the Roosevelt family for free in the White House. Harry and Jack Warner first met Roosevelt in 1932 during his bid for the presidency. Although many associate the men and their studio with the Democratic party, the brothers were longtime Republicans" prior to 1932.[104]

Yet many of those under L. B. Mayer at MGM, and every other big studio, had consulted with Rosten or Spigelgass about adjusting their films, since May 1940, to an anti-Nazi, war-preparedness footing. With Hollywood Jews at the forefront, numerous projects that were backing Britain's war effort, including feature films and shorts, were polished off or underway. Calling out Jews as the vanguard of anti-fascism, however, was not a matter to be treated lightly, if at all. The same argument that Vincent Brook musters to undergird his study of Jewish émigré directors and film noir applies here: "The significance of these individual's Jewishness, and the impact of their ethno-religious identification on their work, has remained almost wholly unexplored."[105] In this instance, expertise in filmmaking enhanced the power of challenges to the Nazis. Rosten's comprehensive study, *Hollywood: The Movie Colony, the Movie Makers*, appearing as a single volume in 1941—as we will see, almost at the moment when Pearl Harbor was bombed—began with the crucial, and still relevant, assertion that "the name 'Hollywood' provokes either amusement or indignation in those whose conception of Hollywood has been formed by publicity and gossip."[106] Although Rosten claimed to have examined the film industry "under the microscope of social science,"[107] he chose to shy away, or remained highly selective, concerning the perceptions of Hollywood that derived from the Jewishness of its constituents.[108] "In few areas of American life," Rosten wrote, "is there such a miasma of myths and misconceptions as that which surround Hollywood."[109] No doubt the "lurid reputation" of Hollywood was enmeshed with antisemitism.[110] "Hollywood also served," Rosten wrote, "as the scapegoat for traditional and familiar hostilities," such as "the rural for the cosmopolitan,"[111] which would later be seen as bound up with Jew hatred.[112] Rosten was not shy, however, to praise the film industry for being cosmopolitan.[113] Hollywood in the 1930s to 1940s was immeasurably enhanced by the movie people who escaped from Hitler's Europe. Noah Isenberg argues that the extremely significant wartime film, *Casablanca* (dir. Michael Curtiz, 1943, Warner Bros.), would have been inconceivable without the numerous refugees in critical parts both in front of and behind the camera.[114] Rosten never specified how many of the foreign-born Hollywood directors, who comprised 28.7 percent of the total, happened to be Jews.[115]

A further rationale for focusing on Jews, and those who otherwise remained under the radar, was that "the desire for circumspection [was] particularly marked in Hollywood . . . because of the pitiless publicization to which the movie colony is exposed."[116] Rosten, with more generosity than deserved, wrote in 1941 that "the farce of 'Communist Hollywood' was conceived in the days when political innocents assumed that any and all opposition to Fascism was Communist in origin or purpose."[117] This charge was raised to a fever pitch due to the scorn, often laced with antisemitism, heaped on FDR that was spearheaded by Congressman Martin A. Dies (R-TX), which veered into fascism, accusing Hollywood of Communist sympathies.[118] Dies's House [of Representatives] Committee on Un-American Activities, formed in 1938, was known by its shorthand, "the Dies Committee."[119] "*It will be to Hollywood's credit* that its anti-Fascist activities predated the swing in American public opinion and diplomacy. *It will be to Hollywood's credit* that it fought the Silver Shirts, the German-American Bund, and the revived Ku Klux Klan at a time when few realized their ultimate menace."[120] In film history, such credit would only be forcefully articulated in the work of Chris Yogerst, *Hollywood Hates Hitler!* (2020).[121] And we are now aware that this effort of Hollywood's men and women was abetted by the courage and fortitude of attorney Leon Lewis and government official Leon Tourou.[122]

Hollywood also was discreet on more expressly economic grounds "because of the precarious health of an industry whose heart's blood can be choked off overnight by sudden shifts in public taste, by organized pressure groups, or by international politics; because of the salaries which flaunt Hollywood's fortune while the rest of the land is constricted with crisis; because of the conduct which parades indiscretion before the eyes of a public *wracked by social fevers*" that now could be termed "moral panic."[123] The press is scoured, Rosten continued, "to find whipping boys for its rage; because actors and showmen have always been easy targets for demagogues and crackpots; [and] because those movie leaders who are Jewish are easy prey for the manipulators of anti-Semitism, those who are Catholic are easy targets for the purveyors of anti-Catholicism, and those who are Protestant are alarmed by the mounting demands of anti-movieism. . . . The movies are exposed on a dozen more fronts than most enterprises in America today."[124] In public discourse, however, the hostility to Hollywood was most loudly tied to antisemitism.

Certainly there were non-Jews who were critical players in the relationship between the Roosevelt administration and Hollywood, such as the president's press secretary, Stephen T. Early, who had been in the movie business himself,[125] and FDR's son-in-law, John Boettiger.[126] The president's son, James, had briefly worked for Sam Goldwyn.[127] Rosten noted him as an "Independent Producer" under United Artists.[128] Historians have referred to documentarian Pare Lorentz as "the president's filmmaker."[129] This masks the much larger and effective phalanx, however underground, coordinating FDR interventionism (and, later, war) and Hollywood. The role of Rosten and the cohort explored here far outpaces and the entire output the United States Film Service, although here, too, Rosten had a heavy hand.[130] While not a puppet master, Rosten had helped put newspaper men Lowell Mellett and Nelson Poynter, with whom he was very close, into leading wartime film administration positions.

I will argue that Rosten, from a vague but lofty perch, and the second and third tier of moviemakers helped to usher in an improvisational style, informed by practical and real-world concerns including strained and nonexistent budgets, that would come to be recognized as characteristic of pathbreaking American movies in the 1960s.[131] Echoing Rosten, those actually making films showed that it was possible for movies to be "significant" as well as "entertaining." It has been recalled that some who were famous before and others who went on to illustrious Hollywood careers, such as Stanley Kramer, George Cukor, Irwin Shaw, and Garson Kanin, had meaningful apprenticeships during World War II. I would hesitate to say that they became "*auteurs*" in wartime, or even proto-*auteurs*, in the sense of Andrew Sarris's famous and now somewhat disparaged terminology. (George Stevens, a major subject of Mark Harris's *Five Came Back* [2014], regularly acknowledged how much his World War II experience changed the kind of films he did afterward.)[132] I believe, though, that these men under Stevens, Capra, Ford, and Huston were inspired by similar intellectual sensibilities and a desire to shake things up that characterized the later (mainly) French "new wave" cinema. Inherent in their film work, whether it be studio or explicitly governmental, was a tempered moral outrage at Japanese imperialism, but more so at the Nazi demolition of democracy and any semblance of human rights. They mixed an ecumenical ("do unto others") creed with bits of irreverence toward authority. National chauvinism was not as sharp as it might have been, and war, in itself, was not glorified. A sing-along cartoon, "When G.I. Johnny Comes Home Again" (dir. Seymour Kneitel, 1945), to the tune of "When Johnny Comes Marching Home Again" promised that

> When Johnny comes march-in' home again
> Hur-ray, hur-ray
>
> We're gonna sing hal-le-luh-jah on
> That hap-py day
>
> We will take the hel-met that Johnny got
> And turn it into a flow-er pot
> And we'll be so gay
> When Johnny comes march-in' home
> . . .
> When Johnny comes march-in' home
> Upon this shore
> Again
> We'll pray that he never
> Has to go to war
> Again . . .[133]

Their superiors (largely) let them get on with it, even if they were young or at lower military rank than those to whom they issued orders.

Richard Maibaum, who was on the Inter-Services Film Committee and was inundated with footage gathered from US Army, Navy, Marines, and Coast Guard film units to make documentaries, recalled that "wonderful work was done there, and I think the American documentary came of age during the war." He was "the youngest officer in grade in [his] outfit." Among the films in which Maibaum had a strong, but anonymous, hand were *Appointment in Tokyo*, *The Liberation of Rome*, and *Twenty-Seven Soldiers*.[134] In the latter, the national, racial, linguistic, and religious diversity of the Allied forces facing fascist Italy was exalted, where "the only thing that was universal was the jeep." I believe that these films influenced not just documentaries, but the evolving, liberal, freewheeling, tersely written character of movies overall. "The master race," it was proclaimed wryly in *Twenty-Seven Soldiers*, "surrendered to a dozen lesser breeds."[135]

While much of the effort of film and policymakers who happened to be Jews was by the seat-of-the-pants and rather extemporaneous (even exuberantly so), there was a more or less fixed dimension of their approach: excessive concern with the picture, that is, with the quality of photography in their domain. Cinematography, to them, was moving photographs. This obsession with photography is true even of those on the screenwriting side, such as Rosten and Spigelgass. Jesse Lasky Jr., mainly known as a screenwriter, was central to a photography (including motion picture) training center in the Pacific that enabled the military and the home front to engage, realistically and with empathy, to this far-flung and unromantic theater of war.[136] Anatole Litvak may have been more influenced than he cared to admit by the revolutionary Soviet film, *Man with a Movie Camera* (dir. Dziga Vertov, 1929), with its exaggerated still-photographic sensibilities. In the same way that directors such as Stanley Kubrick and Ernst Lubitsch are better appreciated through understanding their earlier careers as (still) photographers, each of those considered here markedly improved the photography that came out of the war, which could not be separated from their acumen at storytelling. George Cukor has been seen as moving toward a more documentary style from his Army service,[137] and conversely, the documentary filmmaker Henwar Rodakiewicz adopted a lighter, more story-friendly touch. Budd Schulberg truly knew what he was doing in barring Leni Riefenstahl from peering behind movie camera lenses after 1945.

As a group, however, the (mainly) men of Jewish origin on whom I focus were not preoccupied with matters that inform much of the historical reflection about wartime film: censorship and maintaining the separation, or even the appearance of a strict division, between the film produced by Hollywood studios and the efforts for express military purposes. There is little evidence that these burning issues troubled them as they went about their business. Rosten professed to understand, and even to sympathize, with Joe Breen, the head of the Hays Office, which was the movies' "internal policing system" that Rosten thought "worked pretty well."[138] He described Breen as "remarkable"—"a wonderful, straight, direct, outgoing Irish extrovert, and we got along fine." Will Hays, too, was forthcoming with Rosten when he was conducting his film industry research. Breen even shared his files with Rosten.[139] Beyond Rosten, however, the Hollywood-Washington group was aloof from the Office of War Information (OWI), the Motion Picture Bureau, and the War Activities Committee.[140] Dealing with these competing authorities and vexing problems was left, in large measure, to the non-Hollywood and non-Jewish men who were the nominal heads of the Hollywood-Washington nexus: Lowell Mellett and Nelson Poynter. The fact that Rosten had infiltrated and become part of "an elite boys' club" of newsmen, in which Jews were typically excluded, seems to have flown under the radar of FDR's enemies.[141] Mellett and Poynter faced a different series of challenges than Maibaum, Richard Brooks, Anthony

Veiller,[142] Bernie Feins, Spigelgass, Jules Buck, Lasky Jr., Budd Schulberg, and Daniel Taradash, who were up to their eyeballs in making pictures.

It was no secret that the Nazis hated Jews above all and that National Socialism had real-life masters and slaves. Rosten frequently reminded his correspondents that the Nazi institutionalization of forced labor and outright slavery were bizarre and reprehensible aspects of their regime. By anyone else's standard, the Nazis were criminals. What we see in wartime American filmmaking, under the level of the "big five" directors (Frank Capra, John Huston, George Stevens, John Ford, and William Wyler), is not only tolerance for those of different backgrounds and religions but also beaming pride in the inherent goodness of US racial and ethnic diversity beginning with Kanin's *Fellow Americans* (1942). They emphasized teamwork between men and nations, and that human foibles are unavoidable. Powers that be are not simply exalted. At times they must be criticized, even laughed at, for not upholding their own rules or not doing the right thing. Several characters in this book shared a similar joke: that they had to salute before giving orders—because of their junior status. While during World War II, few of these men dealt directly with what would later be termed the Holocaust, they frequently problematized issues of race, inequality, sexism, and the legacy of slavery with greater consistency, and forcefulness, than had previously been articulated in film. Their own ethnicity may be seen as inflecting, yet not overdetermining, "the content, form, and style" of their pictures.[143]

But the fact that they did not directly deal with the catastrophe of the European Jews as it was unfolding may have contributed to their silence about their wartime endeavors. It is highly significant that their efforts were sandwiched between well-publicized spectacles that sought to vilify Hollywood and had expressly antisemitic dimensions, as Chris Yogerst has shown: the US congressional hearing immediately before the country's entry into World War II about "warmongering" and agitating against national interests, and the post–Second World War "Red Scare" orchestrated by Senator Joseph McCarthy (R-WI).[144] McCarthyism has come to signify the blacklisting of "the Hollywood Ten" and knee-jerk discrimination against hundreds of others who had committed no crime, many of whom had substantially assisted the United States in war. Victor Navasky, in his classic book on the Red Scare, correctly discerns it as both antisemitic and "at some level" an internecine Jewish battle.[145] Budd Schulberg, in particular, did not emerge well from the McCarthyite wreckage, regarded as an all-too-obliging witness. Rosten, called "a centrist" amid "the inquisition in Hollywood" who evaded being party to the Red Scare,[146] rose as famous for something quite distinct from his wartime hats: a conflation of old-country and American Jewish humor.

This book's first chapter, while not comprising full-scale biographies, begins to situate Rosten and Schulberg in their American Jewish, intellectual, international, and Hollywood settings, including reflections on how they have been viewed.

Chapter 2 sets out how Rosten and his closest collaborators, such as Leonard Spigelgass and Donald Slesinger, applied themselves to the tasks at hand: the strategies they developed that came to fruition in diverse government filmmaking enterprises, including making newsreels fit for their purposes and studio films in which they had had a heavy hand in editing and publicizing. They were not the movies' producers or directors, but they facilitated and influenced film in crucial ways. Rosten, meticulous in every regard, was acutely sensitive to the photographic aspects of anything that would appear in a visual form. Rosten and company also promoted films made outside the United States to further the war effort, such as *The 49th Parallel* (dir. Michael Powell, 1941), released in the United States as *The Invaders*.

Chapter 3 explores the crafting of film treatments of the conduct of the war as it was being waged, concomitant with presentations of the rationale for the United States entering and pursuing the war, in large part through the efforts of Anatole Litvak. A great deal of thought and energy was devoted to seemingly mundane topics that the Washington-Hollywood crew attempted to make compelling for the military and the home front. Credits were simply not to be found in most wartime films. Who made the movies, and how?

The fourth chapter recounts the efforts of Jesse Lasky, a force behind the movie *Sergeant York*, which was released around the time of the bombing of Pearl Harbor. Rosten often cited *Sergeant York* as an example of how to incorporate essential war-related aims into popular film.[147] One of Lasky's leading studio writers, Robert Presnell, was a key figure in film work in the Pacific theater, as was Lasky's son, Jesse Lasky Jr., whom Presnell apparently handpicked for the job. Lasky Jr. devised ways to film troop activity with integrity, in extraordinarily challenging conditions. He rarely spoke or wrote publicly about what he did, although his father could not resist talking about his son's daring. Robert Presnell's son, Robert Presnell Jr., wrote the screenplay for an underappreciated film on the Holocaust, *Conspiracy of Hearts* (dir. Ralph Thomas, 1960), and both father and son were progressive idealists in the post-1945 film world. This also was part of Rosten's and Spigelgass's vision, in which the Allies were transformed into the United Nations. Blending into the immediate postwar period, the Washington-Hollywood Jews, with Schulberg prominent among them, sought to render, in film, commitment to the idea of a liberal, quasi-unified Europe that would be enmeshed with the well-being of the United States and permanently congenial to world Jewry. The preeminence of the United Nations was not, however, reserved for the endgame. It had been part of the struggle since 1942.

Chapter 5 focuses on the exploits of Budd Schulberg, Hollywood's earlier *enfant terrible* as author of *What Makes Sammy Run?* (1939), around the close of the war. Schulberg, with the assistance of his brother Stuart and others, was a leading operative for the Office of Strategic Services (OSS, forerunner to the CIA) in capturing what remained of German movies. He also was animated by a burning desire to locate explicit atrocity footage, which eluded him. Budd Schulberg was instrumental in the use of film as a major part of the Nuremberg prosecution of Nazi war criminals and, not coincidentally, in the apprehension of famed German director Leni Riefenstahl.[148] The story of her confrontation with Schulberg underscores Riefenstahl's uneasy relationship with Hollywood, a Jewish counterhistory of wartime film.

The sixth chapter explores Budd Schulberg's efforts to hold the National Socialist film industry to account, which was not, however, taken up by US military authorities. It addresses the extent to which Rosten's cohort engaged the catastrophe of European Jewry in their efforts. It poses the difficult dilemma of the Washington-Hollywood nexus in facing what we now recognize as the Holocaust. For quite understandable reasons, Jews themselves were involved in the Jewish story being swallowed in the dramatic whole of universalizing myths of "The Good War."[149] Germany's and Europe's besieged Jews were not excluded from *Prelude to War*, but there was no dwelling on their plight. We also shall see, however, greater engagement, through film, with Jewish issues during and after the war than have typically been discerned. Many members of the "tribe" of filmmakers who did exceptional work with Leo Rosten, Frank Capra, and for the US war effort overall suffered from Senator Joseph McCarthy's charges of Communist infiltration, which had a precedent in the Senate hearings into motion pictures in 1941. In this regard, Spigelgass and Rosten, and especially Schulberg, come off as less than admirable in the postwar period.[150]

While the (yet unnamed) Holocaust might have been subdued, the wartime films of America to some extent succeeded in showing how anti-Jewish prejudice was unacceptable in the evolving ethos of the Allies. Included in the US Army Signal Corps offerings were instructional films that expressly dealt with antisemitism and possibly hundreds of other movies that tackled Jewish questions in understated and coded ways, such as the treatments of African Americans, Mexicans, and American Indians.[151] The Washington-Hollywood cohort helped make it possible to claim that Jews were (and are) like everybody else and simultaneously maintain that Jews are different, special, and that the Jews within the Nazi *Weltanschauung* and hyperaggression were remarkably singled out as victims. Despite antisemitism within the US armed forces, and lingering suspicions about ties between Jews and the film industry, Hollywood's Jews were enthusiastic to exploit their filmmaking talents for the war. Richard Koszarski, in his studies of moviemaking at the former Kaufman studio in Astoria, Queens (famous for the Marx Brothers movies), discusses the antisemitism faced by the Jewish soldier/filmmakers.[152] One may note, however, that this did not seem important to (most of) the Jews themselves. It was crucial for them to contribute and be a part of the team, even if they were occasionally disparaged. The suspicion that Hollywood's Jews were up to no good never totally vanished from Congress, especially the doggedly conservative US Senate. In significant measure, Hollywood's unofficial film corps managed to work its magic on behalf of the perseverance and overall well-being of the United States, congenial to the ideals of FDR. It is important to recall, though, that "even those" in Hollywood "who opposed and hated Roosevelt nevertheless had a feeling that what he was trying to do was, in human terms, valid and good."[153] Jews behind the creation of movies helped to teach Americans how to be Americans and, eventually, Europeans how to be Europeans, by seeing themselves over and against the Nazis—before, during, and after the onslaught of the Axis—mainly at the behest of the US Army. This was a good thing for them to do, from the perspectives of liberal humanitarianism and the ever-annoying question of "what's good for the Jews." It is hoped that this study will deepen our understanding of American filmmaking surrounding World War II and enhance historical perspectives on untidy Jewish identities as experienced in the modern world.

I

Launching Countercurrents

Vietnam, it is claimed, was the first television war. Attitudes toward the conflict in Southeast Asia were increasingly affected by what was televised, especially for the American public.[1] World War II, in no small part, was the first motion picture war. Although the extent of film's influence is contested, the production and deployment of movies was, indisputably, highly consequential in the Second World War. Nazi Germany is regarded as strikingly successful, even cutting edge, in harnessing film to its cause. Leni Riefensthal, who shot to fame through her movies of the 1934 Nazi party-day rally in *Triumph of the Will* and the 1936 Berlin Olympics, was particularly acknowledged as the world's preeminent film propagandist.[2] The Nazis pursued moviemaking with a less diverse body of professionals than had been the norm in Weimar Germany. Film producers, under Joseph Goebbels, threw Jews out of the industry after the National Socialist takeover of power in 1933 amid the denunciation of Jewry as the antithesis of Germany's "Aryan" stock.[3] Although the bulk of National Socialist movies were comedies and melodramas and "not overtly political," among the purposes of Nazi film was to serve the Third Reich's war aims, including the ruthless destruction of Poland and the stigmatization, persecution, and, eventually, systematic murder of Europe's Jews.[4]

Despite the widely publicized films of Leni Riefenstahl, and scores of renowned movie people fleeing Central Europe, there was little awareness in Hollywood, or almost anywhere outside of Germany, about the character of movies pumped out in the Third Reich—except for film, in total, being in the tight grip of Goebbels. Budd Schulberg, as we shall see, was one of the American-born Hollywood denizens who was closely attuned to European-wide cinema in the 1930s, and he would have a formidable hand in US film work in the Second World War and its aftermath—which went largely unrecognized.[5] Adolf Hitler's vehemently antisemitic worldview and his immediate assault on Germany's Jews, however, were unmistakable. Almost from the moment the Nazis seized power in 1933, the Hollywood community—if such a term is appropriate—made no secret of its hatred for Hitler. Historians Chris Yogerst and Steven Carr have detailed how this sentiment, until late 1941, played a large part in "the US Senate investigation into warmongering in motion pictures."[6] The inquisition and public scold of Hollywood, on the eve of America's entry into the war, is less remembered than the "witch hunt" under Senator Joseph McCarthy in the 1950s, but it is crucial in reflecting on the story told here. Yogerst and Carr's interpretations, along with the recent work of Steven Ross and Laura Rosenzweig,[7] stand in stark contrast to the deeply flawed thesis that the US film industry "colluded" with Nazi Germany.[8] Building on the analyses of Yogerst and Carr, in addition to those of Kathryn Cramer Brownell, James Myers, Thomas Doherty, Michael Birdwell, and Allan Winkler, on attempts to control and censor film, the focus here, instead, is on the conception, production, and dissemination of movies for both armed service personnel and the general public.[9]

The assertion of the Office of War Information that "motion pictures designed to educate servicemen were relatively easy to make" was blithely accepted by almost everyone beyond Hollywood and certain confines of Washington. "The Army or the Navy provided the equipment and men," the Office of War Information guidebook proclaimed, "while the studios lent technical services involving cameramen, sound experts, narrators, directors, and if necessary, star actors or actresses. In many cases the stars and high-paid directors provided their time without compensation to make these movies."[10] Such a summary would have been regarded as between sardonic and hilarious to the Hollywood people who made wartime movies. Jesse Lasky Jr. admitted that, when faced with creating films about barrage balloons, "the work is very difficult."[11] A month later, he was still reporting that "many phases of my work have been tremendously difficult."[12] He found that he needed the skills of "a mathematician, a chemist, an astronomer, a mechanic, and an electrical engineer!!"[13] Movies were expected to be expertly made with "mini-budgets."[14] Bernie Feins, a Hollywood literary agent and story editor for Paramount, later a European vice president for Panavision, was tasked to make a film about the capabilities of the M-10 tank and became embroiled in conflicts over its usefulness. He was pressed to deal with the fact that the tank didn't function as the film was supposed to demonstrate. "Strictly entre-nous," he wrote to Daniel Taradash, "the Tank Destroyer, M-10, is not a very good instrument. General Bruce wants no part of it. It seems the goddam things cannot turn their turrets to fire unless the ground is as level as pavement or at least a billiard table."[15] Feins needed "good writers" to make this film as well as others experienced with problematic artillery to help the soldiers who would be using the equipment.[16] More than a half century later, these films on barrage balloons and tanks are watchable, informative, literate movies. I will show that, beginning in 1942, the lines between so-called instructional, recruitment, morale-building, and studio film became increasingly and intentionally blurred, as did the lines between documentary, combat, and event-based feature film.[17] Lasky Jr. was indeed correct when he described his job as "without boundaries."[18] The work required tremendous energy and creativity on the part of those who made the movies for America's wartime purposes. A large portion of those engaged in such enterprises, which mostly was due to the historical ethnic composition of Hollywood itself, happened to be Jews—but the US government was loathe to shine a spotlight, or even strike a solitary match, on this reality.

The Office of War Information was the generic tent under which Rosten and others operated, overlapped, and took cover and was one of the more important, if unwieldly, newly created government divisions. The War Activities Committee of the Motion Picture Industry, as discussed by historian Thomas Doherty, also was fresh on the horizon, engaging the government-Hollywood landscape. Headed by Francis Harmon, it was the official representative of leading studios and other components of the movie business, which openly made and promoted films. It served as the more public face of Hollywood than the bureau headed by Lowell Mellett, and its Victory shorts were well received.[19] Noah Isenberg, illuminating the wrangling of these bodies over scenes in *Casablanca* (dir. Michael Curtiz, 1942), observes the Production Code Administration, which Harmon had previously represented, and the Office of War Information as "dueling" in imposing "moral" strictures.[20] Similar to the august-sounding Bureau of Motion Pictures, the War Activities Committee was fronted by a distinguished Gentile, Harmon, who had been the general secretary of the Young Men's Christian Association (YMCA) from 1932 to 1936. In 1937 he joined the Motion Picture Producers and Distributors as the executive assistant to Will H. Hays, in charge of the Eastern Division of the Production Code Administration, which was reluctantly accepted by Hollywood.[21] After some fifteen years in and around the movie industry, Harmon led the Federal Council of Churches, which merged into the National Council of Churches in 1950, one of the more significant religious organizations in the nation. Under his leadership, the War Activities Committee was "acclaimed for its services to the Government and the armed forces."[22] While these organizations, contributing a fraction of wartime moviemaking, were not quite window dressing, they were, perhaps, necessary for the government to make the case that the film industry was behaving itself and under watchful eyes.

Because of the character of animus directed against President Roosevelt, not the least of which was his supposed catering to Jewish interests, both Hollywood and Washington tried to preserve the edifice of absolute separation between the movie business and the government.[23] But after America was pressed into war, there was broad agreement that Hollywood should be mobilized for the cause.[24] Despite the dramatic attack by Japan on Pearl Harbor, US citizens' cohesion and enthusiasm for the war effort was more fragile than is often assumed.[25] Even during the war, Roosevelt's opponents in Congress charged that government films, as a rule, had become pro-FDR propaganda. Jews, as Americans serving their country, became central to (truly important) film work, both officially and unofficially, for the US government. In a number of capacities, they made movies an extraordinarily effective and significant tool in helping the military work better and binding the disparate community of Americans together. The Jews behind American moviemaking in World War II furthermore assisted their countrymen's commitment and willingness to sacrifice as prescribed by the government. In so doing they helped change the character of filmmaking. In certain respects the work of these key Jewish Hollywood men may be seen as a bridge to "the new Hollywood" that would emerge in the 1960s (as brilliantly explored by Mark Harris): creating films "without stultifying overpreparation," often evincing "a European texture," that were short on "the Old Sentimentality" and that served as "beacons of tolerance and cross-cultural understanding" and were "relevant" in diverse ways.[26] Their métier was "message cinema" that proved to be compelling and entertaining.[27]

The disproportionate presence of Jews in the motion picture industry is legendary. The historical trajectory of European Jewry as a migratory, marginal people seeking fresh opportunities in the early twentieth century and picture shows as a nascent form of entertainment and commercial enterprise coalesced in a way that prompted Jews to the forefront of moviemaking.[28] The history of film as a popular medium is inseparable from the secularized Jewish origins of its founders and, later, many of its leading figures. This is especially true in the first generation of Hollywood's studio moguls, who in the (somewhat exaggerated) words of historian and critic Neal Gabler, created "an empire of their own."[29] In Europe, too, Jews played outsized and pioneering roles in film in Russia and the Soviet Union, Poland, Germany, Austria, France, and Britain, which also impacted American movies, however indirectly. But there remain little-studied dimensions of the activity of Jews in film as relate to the United States in World War II.[30]

While Jews in the mix of wartime movie history have not been ignored,[31] a quantitatively large and qualitatively important piece of filmmaking during World War II—centering on Jews—has thus far received limited attention.[32]

The inception of a deliberate effort to apply Hollywood to the war was originally entrusted, in large part, to Leo Rosten—who rarely has been investigated, or even noticed, for this role.[33] In 1959 Rosten revealed that upon the fall of France, FDR forcefully initiated a "loose liaison between the movie industry and Washington" in which Rosten himself was "a kind of two-way channel."[34] This lacuna has recently been partially addressed by Chris Yogerst, who is one of few to recognize that Rosten was given the significant task, in 1940, of advising Hollywood's "national defense films" through the Division of Information of the National Defense Commission. Rosten's research into the film industry provided ammunition for all sides of its defense. Most crucial, though, was that he helped protect Hollywood leading up to the Senate Propaganda Hearings of 1941. The very threat of those hearings had been the elephant in the room in 1940. As detailed by historian Steven Carr, many saw Rosten's unmatched research into the motion picture industry as exonerating Hollywood of the accusations that films were engaging in propaganda.[35] Nevertheless, along with Major General Charles S. Richardson in 1941, Rosten—identified as a liaison "between Hollywood and the US government"—was accused by Senator Gerald Nye of stoking "war hysteria," which was un-American, anti-American, and was meant to line the pockets of "European immigrants."[36] The making of government movies from 1942 to 1946, while brilliantly undertaken by famed directors supervised by, and including, Frank Capra, were the handiwork of many, but especially Leonard Spigelgass and Anatole Litvak,[37] who are far less lionized than Capra and the marquis directors John Huston, John Ford, George Stevens, and William Wyler.

Litvak, however, had a known critical reputation before his work in the *Why We Fight* series. The *New York Times* lavishly praised his direction for *Mayerling* (1936),[38] and Litvak went on to make a number of important A-list Hollywood films after 1940, including two big hits in 1948, *The Snake Pit* and *Sorry, Wrong Number*, as well as the Ingrid Bergman vehicle *Anastasia* (1956).[39] While it was primarily nervousness over federally funded film that kept names besides Frank Capra from the list of wartime credits as *Why We Fight* penetrated US movie theaters, there was added incentive for not spotlighting personalities such as Litvak and Spigelgass—which would have raised the specter of Roosevelt, Hollywood, and Jews. Although not quite front-page news, many were sure to have remembered that Litvak was summoned before the Senate subcommittee "investigating alleged dissemination of war propaganda in film" for directing *Confessions of a Nazi Spy* and, alongside Charlie Chaplin, writer, director, and star of *The Great Dictator*.[40]

Capra and his fellow headliners, while military grade, were also working with the (Gentile) civilian heads of wartime movies Lowell Mellett and Nelson

Poynter—neither of whom had previous filmmaking experience. As an aide to FDR serving as a "media liaison," Mellett began dealing explicitly with the movie industry only in 1941,[41] but he somehow was considered an "old friend" of Hollywood.[42] Most Hollywood insiders were "perplexed by the president's choice" of Mellett, and Poynter was "not an avid filmgoer and did not follow the industry with any regularity."[43] Mellett and Poynter were talented newsmen, skilled administrators, and certainly not puppets. Yet both were apparently cherry-picked for their position—with Rosten having a hand.[44] To no small extent, they were the Gentiles forced to deal with censorship issues foisted on them by self-declared guardians of public morality and oversight of supposed federally funded politicking.[45]

Toward the end of the war, while Rosten was serving in a broad advisory capacity between Washington and London, US authorities asserted that Nazi film ought to be prominent in the prosecution for war crimes. Budd Schulberg emerged as central in this endeavor. Schulberg was a Hollywood brat who wrote one of its scathing exposés, *What Makes Sammy Run* (1941),[46] and had threatened the studio system as a youthful Communist.[47] He also was among the Hollywood crowd who objected to the 1939 visit of Leni Riefenstahl, seeing her glorification of Hitler and the Nazis as obscuring antisemitism and other brutal aspects of the regime.[48]

Schulberg has garnered more attention for his service at the close of the war than has Rosten for his meaningful role at the beginning. Yet neither are well-known for their activity, which went substantially beyond the call of duty. Jesse Lasky Jr., too, was something of a Hollywood stepchild, attached to a dethroned mogul (his father, Jesse Lasky). Lasky Jr. was crucial, though, in making movies that would serve US interests from the Pacific theater. Spigelgass, Litvak, Lasky, and others who were so critical in wartime film conceived and executed films and series for which the paper trails are barely salvageable from history's dustbin. A share of the US wartime movies vanished, such as one written by S. J. Perelman (of Marx Brothers' comedies fame) and at least two directed by George Cukor.[49]

A tie between this core group is that many were first-generation college educated in their families, landing in Hollywood by way of the Ivy League and otherwise elite universities.[50] They might be regarded as an invisible moviemaking "brain trust" beneath the more illustrious "brain trust" assembled by FDR. The most concrete connection was Rosten's tutelage under Louis Brownlow, who he knew as a student at the University of Chicago. Leonard Spigelgass quipped that while at the Office of Facts and Figures in Washington, it resembled a University of Chicago seminar, where "I've never known clearer or more incisive brains."[51] Critically, the young film crowd was enabled by FDR, family members including his wife Eleanor and son James (in Hollywood, working for Samuel Goldwyn beginning November 1938), and the president's eclectic entourage. They were ranked mainly under Frank Capra and John Ford, not typically "directors" in name (with the exception of Kanin and Cukor), but were vital, "conscious artists" who made a difference.[52]

The reasons for the absence of the Jewish movie men from much of the public record, and acclaim, however, are integral to this story. First, it is important to recall that there were many pieces of the war effort that were kept confidential, including those concerned with "propaganda," both inside and outside of the United States. To be sure, governmental filmmaking enterprises, as of late 1942, were being conducted largely in the open.[53] But before Pearl Harbor, the Roosevelt administration took pains to show that it had nothing to do with movies that might be seen as warmongering or preemptively setting the country on a war footing.[54] As mentioned previously, in 1939 FDR implored Jesse Lasky Sr., who happened to be the brother-in-law of his eldest son's employer, Sam Goldwyn, to make an anti-isolationist picture.[55] Given FDR's access through back and side channels, and the extent to which he prided himself on being a Hollywood crony, there is no reason to doubt this account. But had it gone public, there would have been firestorms of protest. The meeting between Lasky and FDR was probably at the forefront of Lasky's mind when he "dared" Senator Gerald Nye, who was itching to implicate Hollywood as "warmongering" on behalf of Jews, to investigate the origins of his production of the movie *Sergeant York*, which was seen as priming public acceptance of a European war.[56] Interestingly, Jesse Lasky Sr. chose to leave this scintillating tidbit out of his autobiography.

Yet before *Sergeant York* appeared, in 1939 the Warner Bros. studio "had had the audacity to produce Anatole Litvak's *Confessions of a Nazi Spy* and other major studios tried to halt production, claiming that it would put a damper in the export of Hollywood films to an increasingly Nazified Europe."[57] The movie *Blockade* (dir. William Dieterle, 1938), about the Spanish Civil War, also conveyed a strident anti-Nazi theme. "Motivated by the closing Continental market and sincere anti-Nazism," Thomas Doherty writes, "the industry ventured boldly into oppositional action not only in the docu-dramatic *Confessions of a Nazi Spy* (1939) but also in romantic melodramas such as *The Mortal Storm* (1940) and *The Man That I Married* (1940)."[58] Shortly after the Nazi defeat, Rosten wrote that in response to *Blockade* and *Confessions of a Nazi Spy*, in particular, "the leaders of public opinion began to realize the political potential of movies—as a catalyst of political attitudes and as a lever on Congress and American foreign policy. The controversy about these first 'political' films was significant not simply because of the position which those films took: what alarmed the politicos was the fact that movies dared to say anything about matters which were believed to be outside of Hollywood's jurisdiction."[59] Rosten and Leonard Spigelgass were largely responsible for *All Through the Night* (dir. Vincent Sherman, 1942), an American-set comedic take on *Confessions of a Nazi Spy* starring Humphrey Bogart in one of his more forgettable roles.

Of course, this was moot—or should have been—after December 7, 1941, under the imperative of comprehensive mobilization. Military audiences (in the United States and abroad) and diverse communities on the home front saw the fruits of government filmmaking endeavors (that is, they watched movies) in countless assemblies (both compulsory and voluntary) and as the ticket-buying public. But the genesis, planning, and means devised of carrying out the film program, and supporting filmmaking generally, also was conducted behind the scenes or completely under wraps, even though many of the men involved were not pledged to secrecy. It was, after all, a different age. For those born in the first two decades of the twentieth century, theirs was not a confessional, tell-all generation.

Participants in the ideal Good War of the United States tended to stress teamwork.[60] Men and women were not in it for themselves, chasing individual glory, but selflessly working toward victory for their country and all freedom-loving peoples. This would not have been dismissed as a cliché. It was typical for a soldier's stint in the US Army Signal Corps, in which he might have been instrumental in the film effort, to be omitted totally in a biography or obituary, or dismissed in only a line or phrase, as "service during wartime." Upon the death of Julian Blaustein, the *New York Times* did not mention his wartime experience, while *Variety* reported that he was "involved in the production" of over 250 movies, "including training, information, and docu films."[61] Scores, if not hundreds, of Jews in Hollywood, including some of its prominent producers, directors, writers, and cinematographers as well as non-Hollywood photographers—no matter their age or physical condition—desperately wanted to contribute to the war effort. But they were wary that their Jewishness would hamper the reception of their work—a concern appreciated by the Roosevelt administration. The story that unfolds in this book is how this conundrum was worked out. It has less to do with antisemitism per se than with both the government and Hollywood trying to avoid a perception of filmmaking that might be construed as being in a Jewish interest.

Many of these men, once in service, tended to the jobs to which they were assigned without trying to influence their placement. Depending on age, family circumstances, and draft status, some had volunteered, and a number of them made concerted efforts to apply their movie skills to government work.

A few Hollywood Jews, such as writer Irwin Shaw, sought to be regular GIs, but the government insisted that their special talents be put to use. One extremely weighty element of filmmaking, however, in which Jews were distinctly involved, might have led to controversy had it been noticed. Along with moviemaking in the more conventional sense, Spigelgass, Harold Jacobs, Herb Miller, and Leo Rosten, dramatic personae of this story, were involved in shaping newsreel shorts that appeared along with feature films in American theaters. This was a systematic and intensive endeavor that applied Hollywood know-how to shaping public opinion in the entirety of the United States.

Especially toward the end of the war, the news was also influenced by close cooperation between Washington and London, mainly through Sidney Bernstein (1899–1993), a towering figure in British cinema.[62] Bernstein himself meticulously prescribed the movements of American and British forces, as the war was winding down, with an eye to supplying the most usable material for film. His "American Deputy" for unspecific projects was director Garson Kanin.[63] For Bernstein's film *German Concentration Camps Factual Survey* (1945), one of the key cameramen in Austria and Germany was Sergeant Philip Drell, whose work is prominent in archives of "liberation" photos.[64] Bernstein's "survey" was not released in its full form until its restoration by the Imperial War Museum of London in 2016.[65] But both the British Broadcasting Company [BBC] and Public Broadcasting Service [PBS, US] aired unfinished versions of *German Concentration Camps* several times throughout the 1980s and 1990s, so many were aware of this film's existence before the 2016 restoration.

Although Bernstein himself was frustrated by its failure to appear promptly on (big) British and international screens, the work had an impact on still photography that emerged from the liberation as well as scenes that appeared in other films, as evinced by photos now credited to Drell, Harold Bloom, Henry Gerzen, and others. Some of the soldiers who believed they encountered concentration camps by accident likely had been put on the trail by Bernstein and others seeking to ensure that Nazi atrocities would be caught by Allied cameras. But such planning was not discussed publicly in order to preserve the myth of the objectivity of the press (including newsreels).[66] Scholars take for granted the idea that all news is to some extent mediated and never a simple reflection of events. Had there been suspicions that the wartime newsreels were affected by Hollywood (and London) Jews along with top military brass and coordinated from Washington, a loud outcry would no doubt have ensued.

The overt, intentional shaping of the newsreels, to be discussed in detail below, is an exceptional case, however. The nonconspiratorial camouflage of further aspects of wartime filmmaking to be illuminated here also derives from the dissemination (or not) of information from the government itself, which ultimately decides to make its wartime historical records accessible to the public. The armed forces of the United States are, in fact, concerned with, and highly skilled at writing, their history. It is unlikely that this book would have been imagined without the official histories of the US Army Signal Corps photographic division as the basis for my own understanding.[67] Military and other historians have been keen to seek access to what they need in order to write professional accounts. On the other hand, the government withholds documents if they are thought to involve continuing matters of national security or otherwise sensitive ones. And perhaps some of the material related to filmmaking was not regarded as important enough to be saved in the first place. The policy and operations concerning filmmaking fell into the murky realm of "national emergency" questions. This means that data concerning wartime film were released in different stages, and documents used here were unavailable to many of those who have written previously on the subject.

From the period of the war itself through the immediate postwar period, the story of American Jews involved in filmmaking has been largely obscure for historically specific reasons. The United States government wanted to avoid giving any credence to Nazi antisemitism or even to stir the embers of Jew hatred in America. In "news" that penetrated the United States through diverse channels, the Nazis frequently and vehemently charged that there was selfish influence of Jews in the United States—especially in newspapers and movies in league with the government. According to the Nazis, Jews coming from Europe most recently were those behind the stage, the puppeteers pulling the strings of supposedly autonomous non-Jewish leaders. Prior to the United States' entry in the war—before being attacked by Japan, and Germany's declaration of war on the United States—Hitler and Goebbels railed that it was mainly America's Jews who were meddling in Germany's affairs from abroad and encouraging confrontation.

This was echoed, albeit in subtler tones, by men such as US Representative John E. Rankin (D-MS), "an open supporter of the Ku Klux Klan, [who] accused 'a group of our international Jewish brethren' of pushing the United States into war."[68] After the United States was engaged as an enemy of the Third Reich, the Nazis continued to allege that Jews were in control of decision-making and media in the United States. To a much greater extent than historians (until recently) have tended to observe, the enemies of the Nazis—the very nations of Britain, the United States, and the Soviet Union (after June 1941)—were imagined and portrayed for the Germans and their accomplices as synonymous with "the Jewish enemy."[69] This was part of the

Nazi policy to paint all Jews, and any entity that allowed Jews in its midst, as "criminal."[70]

Such claims were vacuous, outrageous distortions or else utter garbage. But the United States was left in something of a quandary. Movies were indeed important. Jews were all over and inextricable from every facet of the American movie business. Jews should be active in filmmaking and not squandered as a vital, distinctive wartime resource. But the movies, as the most supremely visible of the arts and entertainment, had to be treated gingerly, with kid gloves. The conglomeration of the movies and government was not to be associated with Jews. The government, especially, did not want to publicize the vague, unarticulated relationships at all. While only a few attempts at being intentionally duplicitous (such as in changing or not mentioning Jewish-sounding names) are present in the record,[71] the United States government, with full cooperation of Hollywood, made a concerted effort to assure that those at the public apex of filmmaking during wartime were non-Jews: Darryl Zanuck, Lowell Mellett, Nelson Poynter, Francis Harmon, Archibald MacLeish, and Frank Capra. Capra did emerge as the greatest force in US filmmaking from 1942 to 1945. In his superb study of wartime filmmaking, *Five Who Came Back* (2014), Mark Harris identifies the most critical American directors as Frank Capra, George Stevens, John Ford, John Huston, and William Wyler. Only one of these, William Wyler, is Jewish.[72] Yet there was a great deal going on—above and below the strata of the "five"—that also deserves scrutiny. Jews who ranged from world-famous to virtually unknown helped facilitate the spectacular work of Capra and the other (rightfully) esteemed—mainly Gentile—directors and administrators.

It is important to recognize that hundreds of thousands and, more likely, millions of Americans and Europeans had their perspectives informed from so-called propaganda film by not only Frank Capra and Darryl Zanuck but also a host of American Jews and émigrés whose names are much less familiar and celebrated (in this context), including Anatole Litvak, Leonard Spigelgass, Jesse Lasky Jr., Walter Wanger, Garson Kanin, Stanley Kramer, Robert Riskin, David Miller, Harold Jacobs, Donald Slesinger, Leon Schlesinger, Jules Buck, Julian Blaustein, Ernst Lubitsch, George Cukor, Arthur Laurents, Irwin Shaw, Herbert Baker, Carl Foreman, Paddy Chayefsky, Stanley Cortez, Jerome Chodorov, Harold Tannanbaum, Daniel Taradash, Julius Epstein, Arthur Lewis, Shepard Traube, Gottfried Reinhardt, Emmanuel Cohen, Irving Jacoby, Henwar Rodakiewicz, Ralph Steiner, Richard Maibaum, Friz Freleng, Mel Blanc, Dmitri Tiomkin, Henry Brant, Kurt Weill, and others. Some of the critical areas in which Jews were invaluable included music, editing, scriptwriting, and cinematography—in all varieties of film. Although Walt Disney and his studio are lauded for their inestimable contribution to wartime movies, there are few animated films from 1939 to 1945 that did not count Jews as writer, producer, or director or as among the animators.[73] The first cartoon appealing to Americans to buy war bonds starred a strutting Bugs Bunny, joined by Porky Pig and Sylvester. "Scrape up the most you can—Here comes the freedom man—Askin' you to buy your share of freedom—today!" His clever routine in "Any Bonds Today?" (1941) included an impersonation of Al Jolson in blackface from *The Jazz Singer* (dir. Alan Crosland, 1927), which decades later would be considered racially insensitive.[74] Despite Disney's reputation for unfriendliness to Jews, and having employed crude antisemitic images in some early cartoons, the defense of the studio after 1942—for employing Jews as artists and executives—is more formidable than the taint of prejudice.[75] Leo Rosten explicitly takes credit for getting "Disney to begin making pictures for the aircraft industry" and "different branches of the government" well before 1943.[76]

One of the most important American wartime film projects emerged as *Why We Fight*, the series commonly attributed to Frank Capra. The Sicilian-born Capra, best known for *It Happened One Night* (1934), *Mr. Smith Goes to Washington* (1939), and *Meet John Doe* (1941), oversaw the grand effort, but the sea of diverse film work over which he presided was too vast for him to have firm control over any but a fraction of it. A large share of the power of *Why We Fight* derives from the genius of émigré director Anatole Litvak ("Tola") in particular, for whom Russian and German film techniques were second nature.[77] Although there were occasions when Capra was generous in sharing credit, Litvak has not received the full, subsequent attention he deserves—despite being a frequent subject of press attention in his lifetime. This is partly due to Capra being allotted star billing and also because Litvak was embroiled in a sex scandal in 1940, with lingering effects that damaged his reputation. Certainly, Tola was appreciated by his colleagues and his luster has persisted with more observant film scholars. But he never became a household name in America like other big directors. *Why We Fight* also was marked by the inclination of the Hollywood Jews to consider all film as a potential *Gesamtwerk* (as a production that would enjoin as many of the senses as possible) and an opportunity for telling a story. How else can one explain why a documentary film about military procurement, *Substitution and Conversion* (1943), would demand a leading scriptwriter with literary pretensions, such as David Miller, or why an "instructional" film, *A Salute to France* (1944), would require the music of avant-garde composer Kurt Weill?

As mentioned previously, *Why We Fight* was eventually released to the general public after having been officially produced for the military. It was, however, conceived as an offering to the general American public.[78] It took the direct intervention of President Roosevelt, as we have seen, in the company of Harpo Marx, to speed its release into theaters at home.[79] Along with Hollywood, the Algonquin Roundtable and the Hillcrest Country Club set also relished informal communication with FDR.

There were smaller scale film vehicles produced simultaneously that proved highly effective, such as the *Army-Navy Screen Magazine* and *Staff Film Report*, which were in large part the province of Leonard Spigelgass and Stanley Kramer, supervised by Frank Capra. Like the jump of *Prelude to War* (and *Why We Fight*) from soldiers-only to the general public, many segments of these projects found their way into mass-distribution documentaries, studio films, and newsreels—and edited into *Why We Fight*. Both of these film journals boasted of providing up-to-the-moment and largely unfiltered accounts of the war, inside reports from allied and occupied nations, insight from the United States top brass and home fronts, and entertaining interludes—including cartoons. The cartoons also served important purposes, such as the "Private Snafu" misadventures that called for better attitudes and behavior on the part of GIs. These authoritative but edgy productions helped create a relatively liberal, progressive consensus among American servicemen. The main complaint heard of such films was that there should be more of them.

Along with *Why We Fight* and other movies expressly commissioned by the government to boost morale, there are a number of feature films whose genealogies stem, to a significant extent, from the Washington-Hollywood-Jewish nexus. Film scholar R. Barton Palmer argues that George Cukor's *Winged Victory* (1944), based on a play by Moss Hart, possessed "a truthfulness that the stage version could never provide" through Cukor's expertly managed "location shooting at several USAAF bases in California," making for "an important document of Hollywood's extensive contribution to the war effort," and was "a Cukor film that deserves better than it has hitherto received from the director's critics."[80] The classic of William Wyler, *The Best Years of Our Lives* (1946), for instance, would have been far less compelling had it not drawn on the "training film" by Julian Blaustein, *Diary of a Sergeant*. Although it is no secret that Wyler discovered the amputee Harold Russell from his part in *Diary of a Sergeant* and took the bold step of featuring the nonprofessional actor in *The Best Years of Our Lives*, far more was borrowed from Blaustein's work than is usually discussed.[81] Wyler's masterpiece also shares many features with the late World War II film *Welcome Home* (1945) by one of Blaustein's close friends, Daniel Taradash.[82] The body of wartime (and immediate postwar period) film, including animation, typically attributed to Capra, John Huston, Disney, and others, bears a profound imprint of Jews—who were not necessarily "non-Jewish Jews"—as creative forces.[83] In the transition to peacetime, Garson Kanin directed *The True Glory* (1945) about Eisenhower and the Allied invasion of Europe, which was as much an offspring of Washington as it was of Hollywood.

There is a prehistory of Mark Harris's wartime (deservedly lauded) "five" that also merits more attention. Jews in American filmmaking during the period from the Nazi takeover of power (January 1933) up until the outbreak of the war (September 1939) and the United States' entry into the war (December 1941) also calls for further analysis. For instance, Jules Buck's battlefield work is well-remembered, but his government film service did not begin with his assignment to John Huston's crew in 1943. He had worked with Jack Warner in the year prior to Pearl Harbor, assisting in movies to lend sympathy for Blitz-ravaged Britain.[84] Anatole Litvak's *Confessions of a Nazi Spy* (1939), which was initially a box office flop, was the most ardently anti-Nazi American film prior to Pearl Harbor, and parts of it were recycled for the final segment of *Why We Fight* (*War Comes to America*). It served as fodder for antisemitic abuse and charges of a "Jewish monopoly" over motion pictures.[85] Matt Bernstein shows that Walter Wanger's work took on a decided edge after Hitler's ascension to power. Like Litvak, in 1951 Wanger's legacy was undermined by scandal, which was worse than that of Litvak. Wanger served time in prison for shooting a Hollywood agent he accused of sleeping with his wife.[86]

In addition to his unequivocal anti-Nazi stance after 1933, Wanger was more expressly supportive of intervention on behalf of Britain than most of his cohort in the Hollywood colony. This was especially important after the start of the war, when it was interpreted by many as nefarious Jewish "warmongering" in the movies.[87] One may, however, perceive sympathy for the British and anti-Nazi allies, as exemplified by Wanger and others who felt wholeheartedly American, and believed themselves to be acting in the United States' best interests, as a kind of Jewish response to the threat faced by Europe. Even after the United States' entry into the war, Jews played a distinctive role in coordinating the film programs of America and Britain, and more generally, in attempting to smooth over tension, which sometimes grew quite testy, over how each was portraying the other in their movies and newsreels during World War II.[88]

Another characteristic is shared by Wanger and many of the American Jewish men (and fellow travelers) who greatly influenced wartime film. Wanger was a college boy, a graduate of Dartmouth. This background certainly factored into Wanger's urge to remain autonomous, to be his own man in the studio world—which in some ways was feudal, dependent on personal services rendered and perceptions of loyalty. Budd Schulberg also was a Dartmouth grad, who, like Wanger, would remain dedicated to his alma mater. With the exception of Budd Schulberg and Jesse Lasky Jr., it seems no mere coincidence that many of those who played key roles were distinct, as was Wanger, from the founding studio moguls and had backgrounds in higher education—several from the most prestigious American universities. Leo Rosten, Robert Presnell, and Stuart Schulberg were all products, to some degree, of the University of Chicago. Bernie Feins and Julian Blaustein were together at Harvard; Samuel Spewack went to Columbia; Daniel Taradash was a graduate of both Harvard College and Law School. Herbert Baker was a Yale man, as was Arthur Lewis; Sidney Kingsley went to Cornell; Arthur Laurents, Cornell; Irving Reis, Columbia; Carl Foreman, the University of Illinois and Northwestern; Don Ettlinger, Stanford and the University of Chicago; Stanley Kramer and Leonard Spigelgass, New York University; Richard Maibaum, Universisty of Iowa; Irwin Shaw, Brooklyn College. These pedigrees likely contributed to intellectualized approaches to film, even in lighthearted or seemingly mundane offerings produced during the war. Almost everything was clever. Brown University–educated (but not quite graduated) humorist S. J. Perelman, often recalled for his collaborations with the Marx Brothers, wrote a script for an instructional film on how Americans should prepare, especially in cold climates, for the coming winter. Officials of the Office of War Information expressed their pleasant surprise with how engaging the film was despite so tedious a subject.[89] Perelman, who turned anything into an article, never publicly discussed either his government film work or efforts for the Council on Books in Wartime.[90]

This book especially illuminates two figures who are far from unknown—but rarely recognized for their wartime endeavors—Leo Rosten and Budd Schulberg. Rosten was a humorist for the *New Yorker*, *Look* magazine, and other middle- to high-brow popular journals. He is most famous as the author of *The Joys of Yiddish* (originally 1968), a witty introduction to Americanized Yiddish in the form of a lexicon, and a warm and humorous novel about an immigrant trying to improve himself and become a real American: *The Education of H*y*m*a*n K*a*p*l*a*n* (first published in 1937 under the pseudonym Leonard Q. Ross), both of which were bestsellers and ran several editions.[91] *The Joys of Yiddish* is not highly regarded by most Yiddish specialists. Rosten himself decided not to use some of the material he solicited from experts, perhaps because he felt it did not fit the light-hearted tone of the book.[92]

Rosten was a vital force in American filmmaking from 1941 to 1947, which is nowhere stated explicitly. Above all, Rosten was empowered by Washington to assist in channeling the collective American filmmaking know-how and energy into the war effort. In a matter of months, he played a part in putting

Lowell Mellett and Nelson Poynter in place, advancing the impression of a firm barrier between Washington and Hollywood, and in assuring that all film content was adhering to evolving censorship practices and otherwise serving war aims. In sum, it meant that widespread and rather disparate film work could go ahead, largely unimpeded. Although there is no reason to believe that Rosten was not satisfied and fairly rewarded for his service to the United States, the government never publicly acknowledged that Rosten was as essential as he was in moviemaking in the United States nor that he was a key interlocutor between Hollywood and the Roosevelt administration. There is no evidence that Rosten himself ever sought to bring attention to what he did during the war—except for reporting a few escapades that occupy a tiny portion of his literary output, including one in particular that will be illuminated below.[93] His wartime service was exactly that: service to his country. His activity was rarely in the public eye, and he respected the secrecy of his work.

After the United States entered World War II, Budd Schulberg's first impulse was to join the US Marines. The Marines had long held a reputation as the toughest of the American armed forces, the most demanding of physical exertion and, possibly, sacrifice. Schulberg was encouraged, though, to put himself forward for a movie-related posting. His record was impressive, even patrician. He had been editor in chief of the student newspaper at Los Angeles High School, perhaps the best-known public secondary school on the West Coast. He then went to Deerfield Academy, a prestigious East Coast boarding school, where he was associate editor of their newspaper and school magazine and played football and tennis. It was the kind of institution that served as a feeder for the Ivy League schools. Schulberg went on to Dartmouth College, graduating in 1936 with a bachelor of arts degree, cum laude, with honors in sociology and a named fellowship in English. At Dartmouth he was editor in chief of the student daily newspaper and associate editor of the college's humor and literary magazines, also winning a prize in the intercollegiate short story competition. After Dartmouth he mainly styled himself as a writer, publishing short stories in magazines including *The Saturday Evening Post, Colliers, Liberty, Esquire, Story,* and *The New Yorker*, several of which were selected for "best of" lists and special editions. In his curriculum vitae, Schulberg laconically states that in 1941 he wrote the novel *What Makes Sammy Run?* published with Random House, "which became a national best-seller and has been translated into various languages."[94]

With the rising specter of fascism, Budd Schulberg imagined himself saving humankind as a fighting marine, bayonet in his teeth. He wound up happily ensconced in the US Naval Reserve as an Office of Strategic Services (OSS) man. In "frontline intelligence" he faced enemy fire toward the war's end and helped to save lives and secure Allied victory. After Germany's unconditional surrender, he continued his military service and applied his Hollywood expertise and *yichus* (proud ancestral heritage) to bringing Nazi war criminals to justice. He did not just step in and do the job. Budd Schulberg helped to shape the very terms of engagement between the Nuremberg International Tribunal and Nazi film, bringing ferocious intensity and depth of commitment to the challenge. In the end, although the Nuremberg prosecutors were keen to project movies in the courtroom and to use Nazi film as evidence, they were less enthusiastic to pursue meaningful charges against the Germans who had made the films that served Hitler and his henchmen so well. Leni Riefenstahl's status as a pariah to the postwar film industry, outlasting the Third Reich by fifty-plus years in her long life, was the exception to the rule. She had ventured into associated realms, particularly photography, and up to Hitler's demise was frequently feted for her National Socialist film work. But after 1945 she never again garnered an invitation to direct a major film, and eventually she learned that a certain Hollywood prince, Budd Schulberg, was critical in her undoing.

Schulberg's renown would grow with the publication of *The Disenchanted* (1950), a novel based on his exasperating attempt to work with a broken-down F. Scott Fitzgerald, and his 1954 Academy Award–winning screenplay for *On the Waterfront* (dir. Elia Kazan). Schulberg became notorious for testifying before the House Un-American Activities Committee about his "Communist affliliation" and identifying at least fifteen of those who were in the party and later subjected to "blacklisting."[95] Despite being snubbed by many in Hollywood and beyond, he enjoyed an illustrious career mainly as a screen writer and writer and editor on boxing.[96]

Because these revelations about the importance of Rosten, even more so than Schulberg, may seem surprising, it is helpful to revisit how Leo Rosten came to occupy such a role. For someone who wrote a great deal, and quite a bit about himself as a central figure, Rosten has left little grist for a conventional biography. His personal story, given that he was a longtime best-selling author, remains obscure. Rosten and his research loomed large, though, in the rancorous "warmongering" hearings, and his "type"—as a foreign-born Jew— was explicitly lambasted by the film industry's detractors.

In many respects Leo Rosten does not fit the classic immigrant story. He was two years old when his family made their way from Lodz, Poland, to the west side of Chicago in 1910. Leo rarely spoke or wrote about what his family did for a living. He made it clear, however, that while they were neither poor nor rich, they were comfortable by the standards of the time. Although he had to work to help pay for his undergraduate education at the University of Chicago, he was never pressured to contribute toward his family's sustenance.

Most pertinent to the immediate background of this story is that at the moment of the United States' entry into World War II, Rosten was an aspiring but seemingly well-grounded Hollywood screenwriter. Even more important is the fact that he was author of two highly respected works sponsored by the leading think tanks and foundations in the United States, the Carnegie Corporation and the Rockefeller Foundation, about the origins and operations of the movie industry and the relationship of the movies to public opinion: *Hollywood: The Movie Colony* (1939), which was incorporated into a second volume, *The Movie Makers* (1941).[97] These books were written in an accessible way, buttressed by rigorous research.[98] One of the reasons why Rosten is widely remembered for *Joys of Yiddish* and *Hyman Kaplan*, and known (almost) exclusively to specialists for his movie book, is because of—in some respects—highly unfortunate timing: "My opus on Hollywood retains one indisputable and historic distinction. It was reviewed, with hosannas of praise, on the front page of the Sunday *New York Times* book section, in a long and laudatory review in the Sunday *New York Herald Tribune*, and in the Sunday book sections up and down the republic—on December 7, 1941."[99]

Rosten, smug, "had received advance copies of some of these "encomiums." So, truly enjoying his breakfast

> that lovely Sunday morning, preening with pride and telling myself that the years of drudgery were really worthwhile: the gruelling gobs of statistical analysis, the inescapable disappointments and frustrations, even the rumors with which my name had been blackened. (The Communists in Hollywood regarded my politics and my project with special venom, and spread canards that I was a secret agent of the producers; that I was really being financed by the Chase National Bank to undermine the guilds—I was a member of the Screen Writers Guild; that my "naïve liberalism," evidenced in government service for the Roosevelt administration, was a snare designed to deceive the proletariat and reduce their militancy.)

Moving from cereal to grapefruit, gently dabbing his mouth, Rosten "thought of all this charitably now, reflecting that all over America people were reading the tributes to my brain-child, and tomorrow they would hasten to bookstores" and buy *Hollywood: The Movie Makers, the Movie Colony*. But the glaring ring of a "telephone interrupted my blissful reverie, and a friend's voice, oddly thick, asked: 'Have you been listening to the radio? I just caught the goddamnedest news bulletin. The announcer says the Japs have bombed Pearl Harbor.' Yes, it was Sunday morning, December 7, 1941."

Situating himself, half tongue-in-cheek, as a world historical figure, Rosten predicted that "when historians in the future reconstruct that terrible day, they may say that what America was reading at Armaggedon was—of all things!—a sociological tome on Hollywood. But they will be wrong."[100]

He was forced to admit that "Pearl Harbor, Hitler's declaration of war, our entry into war with Japan—during such days, who cared about the gaudy night life of the stars? The next morning, I received a phone call from Lowell Mellett, one of President Roosevelt's six assistants with 'a passion for anonymity.' (The phrase was Louis Brownlow's and it is still a dandy.)"[101]

Now comes the muddled partial truth: "I had been serving as a consultant to the National Defense Advisory Committee, working on the ways to use films for training purposes in the armed forces and what later became known as the I.E.&O. (Information, Education, Orientation) program. I flew to Washington, was enlisted by Archibald MacLeish for his Office of Facts and Figures, and subsequently became Deputy Director of the Office of War Information. But all that, as they say, is another story—another time, another universe."[102]

Overall, this in an accurate summary. But it's a teeny bit *Ferkokte*—as Rosten might have said in *Joys of Yiddish*—screwed up, misinformed, and, well, wrong. It contains an immense, deliberate falsification. He was already in place, as the head of motion pictures, for the Office of Facts and Figures on that fateful December 7. Over twenty years after the events, he wished to preserve the fiction that FDR's government had not been interfering in the movie business before the actual outbreak of war, an uncomfortable role he helped to foist on Lowell Mellett.[103]

At least as early as 1939, the American government was interested in what he had to say, as it wished to use movies to inform and shape public opinion, as obviously had been done to great effect in Germany. Nobody knew more about the subject than Leo Rosten. In the 1930s there were two universities that had recognized "public opinion" as a major subject and approximating its own discipline: Columbia University and the University of Chicago. Although he had set out no grand plan leading to the pinnacle of government-administered filmmaking, the stages of Rosten's career made him the ideal choice.

After having embarked on an academic track, but not attaining a college teaching or research position, Rosten's experience led to his becoming an insider in both Washington and Hollywood. His PhD dissertation, published as his first book, was a survey and analysis of the Washington press corps, with an emphasis on the relationships of the correspondents to their social surroundings, elected officials, bureaucrats, editors, and fellow journalists and their impact on newspapers' readership.[104] This helps to explain his exceptionally cozy relationship with FDR's press secretary, Stephen Early.[105] Rosten's methodology comprised written surveys, face-to-face interviews, and perhaps most important, schmoozing with reporters, informally and formally, in diverse settings. During his first extended period in Washington, DC, when he was pursuing his dissertation research, Rosten was employed by one of his former professors from the University of Chicago, Louis Brownlow (1879–1963). "When I came to Washington" in the mid-1930s, "I was hired by Louis Brownlow, that bucolic, rumpled, immensely knowledgeable adviser to four presidents—and the John the Baptist of professional public administration in America. 'Brownie' retained me, with White House funds, to make a study of the growth of the powers of the presidency" beginning with the Continental Congress.[106] Brownlow had been recruited for President Roosevelt's "brain trust." Considered one of the most astute experts in public administration, Brownlow was charged with the daunting task of making the government more efficient. Interestingly, Brownlow himself had an unusual background and was something of an outsider. He was a former newspaperman from a poor family—distinct from the vast majority of his peers on the faculty of the University of Chicago and in the Roosevelt administration. Brownlow was the main link between Rosten and FDR.[107] The FDR connection also might have been enhanced by Beulah Roth, the sister of his close friend and collaborator Leonard Spigelgass, who is said to have worked as a speechwriter for Roosevelt. It was, then, Rosten's immersion in the press milieu—not only the movies—that helped land him in his commanding position. It is no accident that some of those appointed to leading wartime motion picture positions, such as Nelson Poynter and Lowell Mellett, also hailed from newspapers—as Rosten most likely helped select them.[108]

Rosten's second major project after the Washington correspondents' study, *The Hollywood Colony*, was the more immediate springboard for his appointment as the first chief of the motion picture division of the Office of Facts and Figures established by Roosevelt in October 1941.[109] Before this, along with General Charles Richardson (who was soon reassigned), he was the Hollywood-Washington liaison to the body of movie executives FDR called to order in the summer of 1940 in a larger gathering of industrialists. The movie producers' committee was hamstrung immediately, however, because the government did not want to be seen as taking any initiative in Hollywood—with Rosten himself on record as verifying their supposed neutrality, if not idleness. Despite being disparaged by historians as ineffective, it seems that some divisions of the Office of Facts and Figures were more effective than others and that significant initiatives were launched from Rosten's domain. It was a large and cumbersome unit, so it is understandable that scholars investigating the Office of Facts and Figures, and its later incarnations such as the Office of War Information, did not acquaint themselves with the entire range of its activities. Interestingly, James Rogers recalled how much he enjoyed his time at the

Office of War Information with the "reformer-intellectuals" of the New Deal, which featured "a barrel full of Jews."[110]

In the big picture Rosten contributed magnificently to the US war effort. Ideas developed by Rosten for radio, newspapers, and public events, originating from a wide array of correspondents and colleagues, were adapted for film. He helped concoct a superadhesive that held the nation together. Along with his part in moviemaking and propagandizing to the United States and occupied Europe, there was at least one instance when Rosten had a role in the actual military conduct of the war. Budd Schulberg, along with media and movie-related roles, also influenced some key events on the ground during wartime. Later in life he discussed these in detail. Rosten, it seems, never talked about his exploits before a camera. But despite his reticence, Rosten couldn't resist writing about it. He was the father of one of the more spectacular bombing raids against Nazi Germany. He seems to have only told the tale once, in one of the many anthologies of his writing, *Passions and Prejudices: Or, Some of My Best Friends Are People* (1978).[111] It is likely that he could have placed it in a prestige and widely read venue such as *LOOK* or the *New Yorker*—but he did not.

The story told by Rosten is as follows. In the weeks leading up to the tenth anniversary of Hitler's seizure of power, January 30, 1943, the Allies were aware that the Nazis intended to generate a great amount of publicity for their celebrations on that date. Among other festivities, the Nazis planned to mark the occasion with an address by Hitler from Berlin to Germany and all Nazi-occupied Europe. They wished to time it precisely for 11 a.m., when (according to their reckoning) the Nazis were installed. In the winter of 1942, Rosten was in London serving on a secret, high-level advisory committee to the Allies, in which each member from the United States was "twinned" with a British counterpart. Rosten's partner could barely have been more different from himself: David Bowes-Lyon, the brother of England's wartime queen, Elizabeth ("queen mother" of Queen Elizabeth II, b. 1926). "He was very handsome," Rosten recalled, "charming, impeccably tailored. He conducted himself with that air of confidence and amusement that is the special style of the English aristocrat. When he offered an idea, it was with an apologetic air—and a twinkle of the eye that belied it."[112]

In a planning meeting, Rosten made a bold suggestion: that the Allies should attempt to bomb the location of the broadcast set for January 30 in order to severely disrupt it. This was an unusually audacious proposal, because at that time the bombing of Berlin was being conducted by the British, and only at night. Daylight bombing was considered extremely risky. Rosten had added incentive in making the request: January 30 also happened to be the birthday of President Roosevelt. What better gift might the Allies bestow than causing havoc and destruction in Berlin at the very moment the Nazis wanted to proclaim to the world their eternal invincibility?[113]

We may assume that it was with the greatest respect that Rosten beseeched his colleague, David Bowes-Lyon, to have the Royal Air Force depart from its established policy and conduct the bombing during the day. Lyon's initial response was to emit a sort of distinctly English, aristocratic noise that signified he had heard the question but could not possibly give any sort of answer. Rosten was caught by surprise some days later when Lyon came into his office and said: "Our chaps will do it." "Do what?" "Bomb Berlin. Eleven A.M. January thirtieth."[114]

The raid occurred on the dot: bombs started falling just moments after the start of the Nazi transmission. The only disappointment was that Hitler, as the featured speaker, had been replaced by Field Marshal Hermann Goering. Although, officially, Hitler chose to be "with his soldiers" on the occasion,[115] the American and British were aware that the Führer had a sore throat.[116] Rosten recalled that British bombers returned to base with no losses, but the *New York Times* page 1 story, jubilant over the raid, reported that one Mosquito plane was lost. "Displaying an audacity unsurpassed in the war," James MacDonald wrote,

> Royal Air Force bombers struck at Berlin twice today in the first British daylight attacks on the strongly defended enemy capital. The raids were made by the R.A.F.'s new twin-motored Mosquito planes, said to be the fastest bombers in the world and capable of carrying four 500-pound bombs each. The first raid hit Berlin at 11 A.M. at the precise moment that Reich Marshal Herman Goering was to begin a broadcast speech in connection with the tenth anniversary observance of Adolf Hitler's regime. The second struck the Nazi capital just before 4 P.M. when Propaganda Minister Joseph Goebbels was to address a big gathering in Berlin's Sportpalast.[117]

The Germans now had even more to fear: bombs might rain down during the day as well as at night. Hitler, the world's greatest purveyor of lies and double standards, complained that the Allies were not fighting fair by having bombed Berlin during the day. There were even reports that the (variously scorned) Jew Roosevelt, or else the Jews behind Roosevelt, had perpetrated the dastardly deed as a perverse birthday present for FDR.

Rosten's published version of the story concludes with a reminiscence of a meeting in France shortly after V-E (Victory over Europe) day with one André, a partisan from the French underground who had been imprisoned, tortured, escaped, recaptured, and tortured again. How was it, Rosten asked, that André had the wherewithal to keep on fighting and not give up? The answer shocked him. "'Oh, sometimes a thing would happen: a sign of hope. *Par exemple*, I was working in the Renault plant, where they made tanks. I was making sabotage, spoiling parts. Came one day—eleven o'clock, January 30. All work stopped. We must stand by our machines and listen to a speech. From Berlin. From Hermann Pig Goering himself. For the tenth anniversary of Nazism! . . . *Alors!* First we hear the drums and trumpets. Then Goering starts.' Andre's eyes glinted. 'Then—mon Dieu! Bombs, Bombs! Falling on Berlin! Yes! In the daytime! Yes! . . . We heard the bombs.'" "'The Nazis are running around their radio station frantic, shouting orders, and again—boom, boom, *boom*! . . . And poof! Off goes the sound. Silence . . . We realize what has happened! A tremendous cheer—again and again—in the factory. We know a turning point has arrived. The *Boche* [French slang for German soldiers] are not invincible! Berlin itself is bombed! The plant guards run around and strike blows on us with sticks, and the machines begin again, we must resume work. . . . But it was never as before. We knew now the Allies could win.'"[118]

Rosten could see how grateful he was for that show of solidarity. He knew that it was a first-page story in the French resistance press,[119] along with the *New York Times*. Having some inkling of the kind of role Rosten had played in the war, his French friend asked: did your people have anything to do with it? Rosten demurred that he had never heard about it. It is hard to imagine that Rosten did not consider this as a great idea for a movie.

If Jews were integral to wartime film in the United States, we are left with a potentially disturbing question: what about the Holocaust? Why wasn't a greater effort made to bring attention to the distinctive fate of Europe's Jews, which certainly must have been known to those in the government film world? Rosten himself was born in Lodz and must have had family that remained in the country. How might one possibly account for the fact that the fate of the Jews only became notable in American films around the time of liberation, and even then, great pains were exerted to show that they were part of a broad tapestry of Nazi victims? In great part, this was first challenged by Budd Schulberg at Nuremberg. Similar to the argument of David Shneer in his excellent study of Soviet Jewish photojournalists, American Jews themselves—as filmmakers during the Second World War—mainly sought to universalize Jews within the broader wartime landscape and humanitarian story.[120] When pressure was exerted by the American Jewish Committee on Lowell Mellett in February 1943 to dramatize the fate of European Jewry, his response did not seem to make sense.[121] That is, unless one reads it as a way to make it seem as if Hollywood, and anyone officially involved in film, was as disinterested in the Jews as possible.

Lowell Mellett wrote to the American Jewish Congress in early February 1943, "advising that the Hollywood office of the bureau had taken soundings among the various studio heads and found that the reaction was that 'it might be unwise from the standpoint of the Jews themselves to have a picture dealing solely with Hitler's treatment of their people, but interest has been indicated in the possibility of a picture covering various groups that have been subject to the Nazi treatment. This of course would take in the Jews.' The reaction to this advice was one of disbelief as it was expressed in a letter" on behalf of the American Jewish Congress "of 13 February to Mellett." Historian K. R. M. Short, one of the few to address this question, writes that "Hiter's persecution of the Jews of Europe posed a profound problem for Allied propagandists, whether they represented the official opinion of the governments of the United States and Great Britain or private efforts of individuals (not always Jewish) of how to bring the appalling enormity of virulent anti-Semitism into focus for the citizens of the Western democracies." Short mentions that a reason for this reluctance was the spotlight it might cast on antisemitism, which was certainly alive in America and Britain.[122] But more important was the anxiety that it might cause the war itself to be seen as a Jewish war.

The fate of Jewish refugees was not, however, anywhere near the top of administration priorities. Historians Richard Breitman and Allan J. Lichtman have recently argued that despite staunch opposition, "FDR's second-term policies likely helped save the lives of well over 100,000 Jews."[123] From a slightly different angle, Peter Hayes asserts that "America performed terribly in the face of the crisis of European Jewry, except in comparison to every other country."[124] The recent work of Tracy Campbell reminds us of the fragility of the US consensus, even in the wake of Pearl Harbor.[125]

In the few instances when Rosten himself articulated messages about Jews as Nazi victims, he responded with courtesy but not alacrity, repeating, almost verbatim, Mellett's response.[126] In retrospect, perhaps it was the increasing attention paid to the Holocaust and the emergence of the issue of "rescue" that made the Hollywood-Washington Jews in this study reluctant to be effusive about their wartime activity. The Holocaust is what brought Schulberg to the surface. All of them, up to the war's end, had, in fact, a wonderful answer to the proverbial question, "What did you do in the war, Daddy?" (or Grampa)? They did quite a bit, thank you, and some of them were under fire. But this could not have been echoed as a response to "What did you do about the Holocaust"?

One of the few wartime projects to which Leo Rosten affixed his name was an exhibition he designed at New York's Rockefeller Center, which premiered in late May 1943, "The Nature of the Enemy."[127] This comprised a number of outdoor "photo murals": "It dramatically depicts what would be America's fate if the Allies did not win the war." According to its coverage in *The New York Times*, there was apparently no particular focus on the fate of Germany's or Europe's Jews.[128] Interestingly, the exact same term, "The Nature of the Enemy," was used some three months later in an unattributed piece in the *New York Times*. It announced the publication of two separate reports, one of which, from the Institute of Jewish Affairs, said that 1.6 million Polish Jews had been killed since 1939. The other, from the Inter-Allied Information Committee, claimed that the Polish Jewish death toll was 1 million.[129] "The Jews come first in this awful tabulation. They were the first to be attacked when the Nazis began their civil war in Germany. They are always among the first to be attacked when a reactionary drive starts," the article proclaimed. "But sympathy for those who are being so hideously persecuted is not enough." Providing a rationale remarkably consistent with that of Rosten when he did address the Jewish plight specifically, the article concluded:

> If we realize the deeper meaning of Americanism, and of its counterparts in other democratic countries, we do not segregate the Jews, the Catholic, the Protestant as such. It is enough to know that there are just two kinds of people in this world at present: those who support the Axis regimes and philosophies and those who do not.
>
> We hope that our government will do anything it can to rescue innocent and persecuted people in Europe. If it does this it will come to the aid of the martyred Jews. But we hope that this will be done with a realization that it is not any man's religion or any man's race that matters, but rather the fact that he is suffering for freedom's sake. Our enemy's enemies, whoever they are, are our next of kin. If he shuts them up to starve in a ghetto all free men are in that ghetto with them. If he kills them, freedom is wounded with them. All barriers among free people go down if this danger is fully realized. The sufferings of Czech and Yugoslav, of Frenchman and Netherlander, of Jew, Catholic, and Protestant, the devotion of millions of soldiers of a score of races and all religions, bring the free together in a new brotherhood.
>
> Such is the nature of freedom, made manifest by the nature of freedom's enemy.[130]

Part of the reasoning behind the lack of coverage of Europe's Jews is parallel to the motive behind not wishing to bring attention to the Jews running the movies in the United States. At bottom there was a desire not to make Jews into a separate wartime subject. It was more important that they were part of a whole. To the extent that antisemitism was addressed—and it was—this occurred mainly in the context of depictions of prejudice in the United States. The case also may be made that the Washington-Hollywood Jews, while having a mixed record in advancing integration and equal treatment for African Americans in the United States generally, and in its armed forces particularly, regarded antisemitism and anti-Black racism as kindred and intertwined.[131] But the American versus European compartmentalization of Jewry, and universalizing of the Jews in wartime, does not mean that the Hollywood-Washington cohort was categorically insensitive to alleviating the plight of their brethren.

Although they would not have put it in such terms, I believe that Rosten and his colleagues firmly and sensibly believed that the best way to help Europe's Jews was to work toward the most expedient end of the war—that it had to be won as quickly as possible. To the extent that they were able to express personal opinions, it seems that they were fierce interventionists before Pearl Harbor and proponents of the opening of a second front of the war far earlier that it happened (June 1944). In the best of worlds, D-Day should have happened some two years earlier, in the spring of 1942. They also put stock in the notion that the occupied peoples under the Nazis could be inspired to rise up, en masse, against their oppressors. The Germans had succeeded, in part, through a cynical strategy of "divide and conquer," which could be overcome through the triumph of a spirit of unity to throw off the Nazi yoke and relieve the plight of the imprisoned and distressed.[132] Rosten and company also pushed for greater cooperation between American forces and their (Free) French, British, and Soviet allies with greater enthusiasm than those who were entrusted with military planning and decisions per se. The importance of Soviet assistance in Schulberg's story could help to explain why he was quiet about this work for many years. Of course, an earlier D-Day would have been too late for over a million Jews, but there is no doubt that it would have saved many and radically altered the course of the war.

The "Riegner Telegram" of August 1942, sent from the Geneva headquarters of the World Jewish Congress to Washington and London, warning of the planned, mass slaughter of European Jewry by the Nazis, is now a firm part of the historical record. It commonly serves as the basis for charging the Allies and neutrals with some degree of complacency. But the mission of Polish emissary Jan Karski and that of the Jewish escapee from the Warsaw ghetto Shmuel Zygielbojm, compellingly warns that exposure to the truth of the destruction of European Jewry was rarely a spur to action. Numbness or paralysis was the typical reaction.[133] Rosten's reaction to the Holocaust also may be seen as consistent with his intellectual contortions in avoiding the Jewishness of Hollywood in his film industry studies.[134]

In addition to having a view of European Jewry that was not unusually prescient, any valorization of Rosten and, more so, Schulberg is also clouded by their responses to the postwar anti-Communist hysteria, which was frequently accompanied and driven by antisemitism.[135] Rosten studiously avoided appearing political, with the exception of being pro-American and pro-Roosevelt. He did, however, make a concerted effort to bring selected leftist filmmakers into the government fold during the war. But he also was cozy with none other J. Edgar Hoover, founding and longtime head of the FBI (Federal Bureau of Investigation). Rosten even wrote the original screenplay for *Walk East on Beacon* (1952), about the FBI's pursuit of Ethel and Julius Rosenberg.

Rosten did, however, help to steer Hoover and the FBI, in the midst of the war, to focus on the Nazi threat. Rosten made detailed "suggestions" for J. Edgar Hoover's speech to commemorate the tenth anniversary of the Nazi regime for January 30, 1943, arranged by himself, which stressed the need to recognize the entire National Socialist enterprise as "criminal":

1. The Nazi leaders started a plot against the people of the world on the day they took power: the record from 1933 to 1943 reveals the step by step by step development of the Nazi plot for world conquest and domination.
2. These men use terrorism, violence, torture, starvation, lies, betrayals, brutality as deliberate tools of political conquest and control. Nazi atrocities are *intended*; they are cold-blooded measures for the achievement of consciously chosen goals.
3. The Nazi leaders are world criminals: like criminals they have broken laws, looted, robbed, ravaged.
4. Adolf Hitler, on August 1, 1923 (twenty years ago), while he was in jail for having led an armed mob through the streets of Munich, said "There are two things which can unite men: common ideals, and common criminality." The world of democracy, of decency, strives to unite men on the basis of common ideals. The Fascist leaders have chosen to unite their political regimes through "common criminality."
5. We in America have the phrase: "Public enemies." The free peoples of the United Nations must smash the greatest gang of "world enemies"—not simply public enemies—in the history of mankind.
6. This is a war between law and crime, between order and criminality. The world must prevent crimes against peaceful people and countries of the world.[136]

This set an important precedent for how Nazism was to be treated in American public discourse, which would largely be respected in official circles until the second decade of the twenty-first century.[137]

As much as their heartfelt aim was attaining complete victory over the Nazis as swiftly as possible, the Hollywood-Washington Jews, in agreement with the administration of the United States under FDR and Truman, also were looking to the emergence of a postwar order that would be more hospitable to Jews and other minorities than any previously known. In addition to work in film, they would help achieve such an end through radio, print media, and even public pageantry such as parades. The main point was to permanently institutionalize the cooperative effort of the Allies into the future United Nations. In fact, these terms—Allies and United Nations—were nearly interchangeable. Like so many others, the Jewish film men did not seem to grasp, until it was too late, that the vast majority of Jews from Eastern Europe had been murdered—three million from Poland and some three million others, leaving the Baltics, southeastern Europe, and part of the Soviet Union with few survivors; western European countries lost between one-third and three-quarters of their prewar Jewish populations. While ever cognizant of the Holocaust, this study reveals that the American Jews in film saw their country's mission as the leader of the fight against Nazism and champion of the free world as their most urgent concern.

2

Artful Dodges

To a much greater degree than reflected in retrospective accounts, as far as American motion pictures during the first year of the Second World War were concerned, Leo Calvin Rosten helped run the show.[1] Along with matters of the moment, he charted the course for moviemaking in wartime overall and well into the post-1945 period. (He also kept up the front of being a "regular" scriptwriter, playwright, and humorist, which he was.)[2] Consistent with his earlier scholarly work, he would make no "outright reference to anti-Semitic attacks on the [movie] industry."[3] In the projects in which he was involved, many with highly specific instructions, his word was nearly uncontested.[4] In wartime, Rosten rarely, if ever, described in detail what he did, but his advice and working methods are abundantly recorded. Perhaps the closest he came to describing his function was to say in early 1942 that his division of the Office of Facts and Figures "will have to carry out the burden of supplying a continuous stream of material and information to Hollywood people—through Nelson Poynter, who will be [Lowell] Mellett's representative [in Los Angeles] and with whom I shall work in very close liaison. Poynter will be a two-way funnel feeding requests to me, and getting materials from us."[5]

I have detected no paper trail showing, definitively, how Rosten came to occupy his initial government position as director of the Motion Picture Division of the Office of Facts and Figures, to which he was appointed before the United States' entry into the Second World War. While Rosten's activity is one of the red threads in this story, what follows is by no means a comprehensive treatment of his role. He took meetings that were not minuted, and he liked to talk on the phone. And given the scope of wartime filmmaking, which mixed the work of cameramen in the field of battle, stock footage editing, movies shot at military bases, the ongoing work of established Hollywood and New York film studios, and at least three film operations on the East and West

Coasts expressly for government film purposes, he never could have exercised tight control over the entirety of the enterprise. But Rosten nevertheless put a strong stamp on it, and the emphasis here will be on the important "creatives" who were in his orbit, for whom recognition, in this respect, is in inverse proportion to their impact.

Although Rosten had worked in Washington previously, his official entrée to his wartime role occurred in the summer of 1940 when he served as the "Hollywood representative of the advisory commission of the Council for National Defense," part of "the Motion Picture Committee for Cooperation for National Defense," which was among a group of "industrialists" gathered by President Roosevelt. General Richardson, his armed forces counterpart, was reassigned in July 1941.[6] For the first three months of its existence, however, the Motion Picture Committee "remained quiescent" because it did not want its activities to "be regarded as political or as bearing on the recently settled Federal anti-trust suit" against Hollywood. Even though that case was closed, and an important election was behind FDR, it was said that "the government remains leary of the word 'propaganda.' The term 'controlled' screen is anathema to all concerned."[7] That smacked of Goebbels. Hence the agencies stressed their "advisory" role with respect to "cooperative bodies." The point was driven home that any initiative in Hollywood that might possibly be interpreted as warmongering did not originate "from the government."[8]

In December 1940 Rosten told Thomas Brady, a *New York Times* reporter, that his role was "to provide information to producers who wish to make defense subjects of a non-military nature." That he did. Another "member of the production committee" Brady approached "indicated that he expected Rosten to suggest ideas for such pictures, but Rosten said that he had no such intention. Rosten said he will compile information which will be available to studios asking for it, but that he will avoid any appearance of instituting propaganda." That would remain his watchword: throughout the war, Rosten attempted "to avoid any appearance of instituting propaganda" himself.[9] What he did, though, was to incessantly "suggest ideas" for pictures that would materialize as government and Hollywood studio films for the next four or five years. He was walking a tightrope, yet out of public view, because of the remaining tension over public funding for movies as well as the competing and overlapping authority of official bodies such as the Motion Picture Bureau, the War Activities Committee, and the branches of the US armed forces.

Rosten did, however, give some taste of what he was up to in that 1940 interview. MGM ("Metro"), he told Brady, "has in view an over-all treatment of the non-military aspects of national defense in a documentary short, which may be followed by other, more detailed films; and Warners will probably issue some similar shorts on their next year's program."[10] Rosten was crucial in turning this trickle into a flood. Despite having relinquished his Facts and Figures job in late 1942 for vague yet formidable advisory roles to FDR (later Harry Truman), Rosten nevertheless continued to exert influence. In 1964, in one of many capsule biographies supplied for his books, Rosten wrote that in addition to heading the motion picture section of the Office of Facts and Figures, he also served as a "special consultant to the Secretaries of War and Air, chief of the Motion Pictures Division of the National Defense Advisory Committee [which might have overlapped with the Facts and Figures role], deputy director of the Office of War Information, and consultant to the Commission on National Goals."[11] Although he spent time in Los Angeles, he mainly worked out of an annex of the Library of Congress in Washington.

Rosten's appointment as chief of Motion Pictures for the Office of Facts and Figures most likely materialized through face-to-face conversations or over the telephone at the behest of the previously mentioned presidential adviser Louis Brownlow and poet Archibald MacLeish (1892–1982), who became Librarian of Congress in 1939.[12] MacLeish was the founding head of the Office of Facts and Figures, precursor to the Office of War Information. Both MacLeish and Rosten had been writers for Henry Luce's *Fortune* magazine, which MacLeish served as an editor. They probably collaborated on a special *Fortune* project, *The Jews of America*, that appeared in the magazine as well as a separate, small hardcover book in 1936.[13] Although neither MacLeish's name—nor that of any other individual—appears in the book form of the publication, MacLeish is (now) credited with its authorship, which was claimed to be the work of "the editors of *Fortune*." The series clearly meant to push back against a growing wave of antisemitism in the United States at that time, which emphasized alleged Jewish control over various industries, including the media. That the series appeared at such a time was indeed significant. It mainly, however, was something of a debunking exercise, intended to undermine myths about Jewish control of the American economy, media, and government and to immunize the United States against the spread of Nazi-type antisemitism. The two appendices of the book are titled "A. Principal Anti-Semitic Organizations" and "B. Ownership and Control of Moving-Picture Companies." The latter argued that outside of the clothing industry,[14] the only realm where individual Jews possessed economic clout well out of proportion to their numbers was the movies—and that motion pictures were "the chief point of anti-Semitic reference." It explained that while Jews did own or have a majority stake in some of the studios, it was not nearly the Jewish "monopoly" that many thought. They were a diverse, highly competitive lot who made no effort to coordinate themselves as Jews.[15] Rosten most likely supplied the data.

MacLeish and Rosten ran in many of the same circles—despite MacLeish being far more accomplished and a blue blood and Rosten, a comparative greenhorn and an upstart (to use a favorite phrase of Groucho). Both were politically progressive, anti-Communist, fiercely anti-isolationist, and devoted to FDR and had vast experience in the press. Although MacLeish was a deservedly renowned poet and committed public intellectual, he was not known for work in the movies and was skeptical that they were up to the wartime task.[16] For administrative decisions that involved motion pictures, he conceded it as Rosten's bailiwick. Interestingly, Rosten and Leonard Spigelgass did succeed in getting MacLeish into the movies—to deliver the prologue to a Warner Bros. short, *This Is Your Enemy* (1942), for which he is credited as director.[17]

MacLeish was, in fact, comfortable with the likes of Rosten and Spigelgass. He was keenly interested in public engagement in many forms, and he understood that pictures and words complemented each other. He also shared with Rosten a sense that photography was critical in shaping public opinion. Shortly before the war, MacLeish was involved in an unusual publication that appeared as *The Land of the Free* (1938), in which one of his long poems accompanied the work of photographers under the auspices of the Resettlement Administration (later the Farm Security Administration), a signature program of the New Deal. Among those who provided photos for this work, now considered a classic, were Margaret Bourke-White, Walker Evans, the previously mentioned John Gutmann, Dorothea Lange, Arthur Rothstein, and Ben Shahn. In a poignant expression of modesty, MacLeish said that it was "the opposite of a book of poems illustrated by photographs. It is a book of photographs illustrated by a poem." He labeled his poem "The Sound Track," and the layout of the book by Robert Josephy had a filmlike feel. "The original purpose," MacLeish wrote, "had been to write some sort of text to which these photographs might serve as a commentary. But so great was the power and the stubborn inward livingness of these vivid American documents that the result was a reversal of that plan."[18] MacLeish, who some historians maintain was not very effective as the head of the Office of Facts and Figures, probably should be given more credit for recognizing the potential power of photography and film and for delegating control of the movies to Rosten.[19]

Reflecting on his life as a writer, Rosten said that photography had always been one of his passions, and his film work evinces a sharp concern for cinematography and the more photographic aspects of movies, along with meticulous attention to scripts, treatments, editing, and straightforward matters of content. As a young man Rosten aspired to write a "dazzling masterpiece" on photography—which never materialized.[20] His advice for shaping newsreels (institutionalized as the "Newsreel Box Score"), in consultation with Leonard

Spigelgass and Harold D. Jacobs, often hinged on their photographic dimension. In the confidential "Newsreel Critique" of December 19, 1942, Jacobs wrote of the offerings by Fox, MGM, Pathé, and Universal: "The most interesting story" of the week "was the Lend-Lease report featuring Ed Stettinius." Lend-Lease, "an Act to Promote the Defense of the United States" (March 11, 1941) was the official means by which the United States supplied oil, food, ships, airplanes, and other war-related materiel to the United Kingdom, Free France, and other Allied nations including the Republic of China and the Soviet Union. It was an incremental but decisive step toward engaging in the European and Pacific war. Stettinius, a former executive of US Steel and General Motors, was important as a public face of Lend-Lease. Jacobs wrote that "each newsreel editor used his own ideas in presenting this story," allowing for some autonomy. "The excellent photography and selection of subjects used by our New York Production Unit afforded considerable opportunity for selection." Apparently, the Army Signal Corps film unit in Astoria had supplied much of this news footage. "In the introductory shot of Stettinius presenting his report to the President, *Lt. Spencer's Navy camera crew got one unusual close-up which was a real work of art. Probably the best job was done by Fox, which used Stettinius' voice for the commentary throughout practically the whole story.*"[21]

Jacobs was scathing, though, about "two personality shots carried by most of the reels that presented rather doubtful value. The worst example was the picture of Donald Nelson summarizing the accomplishments of WPB [War Production Board] throughout the last year." Jacobs lamented that the "photography was poor, Nelson was not at his best and the message he carried was pretty dull. The other picture was that of Secretary Morgenthau telling what had been accomplished in the sale of bonds during the last year."[22] This was not as dismal as the Nelson piece "but still turned out pretty dull." Fox came through admirably with an "exclusive Christmas feature" in the form of "a message by Monsignor [Fulton J.] Sheen. This was a little too long but Sheen's personality, the importance of the message, and the fact that he is unusually photogenic, made the feature above the average."[23] Rosten and his charges were not just "keeping score." They used the information to try to intensify the cumulative effectiveness of the newsreels. Bishop Sheen did have that chiseled, matinee-idol quality, which contributed to his gracing the cover of *Time* (1954) and becoming a leading upstate New York TV personality in the 1960s and 1970s.

One of the few instances in which Rosten reflected contemporaneously on his wartime film assignment was when he appealed to an executive at Disney Studios, Robert Spencer Carr, to leave Disney to work for him. He clarified that "the following is strictly off the record and represents a personal rather than an official communication." On February 13, 1942, Rosten wrote that "I am now working as the Special Assistant to the Film Coordinator of the United States, Mr. Lowell Mellett, as well as Chief of the Motion Picture Division of the Office of Facts and Figures, directed by Archibald MacLeish."[24] It is true that Mellett, a distinguished and intrepid journalist from a modest midwestern background, was "the senior federal liaison between the film industry and Washington during the early years of the war." He was "President Roosevelt's point man for the Hollywood studios, working to promote productions that supported FDR's internationalist orientation and the nation's war goals."[25] But his junior colleague, Rosten, was more deeply enmeshed in both the Hollywood studios and media generally, and Rosten had far greater creative input in the broad sweep of filmmaking during the war. Mellet's métier was, nevertheless, extremely important—smoothing over how the press handled Washington's relationship with Hollywood and trying to regulate the tricky balance between the government and studios—but he engaged little with moviemaking in and of itself.

"*All I need to tell you,*" Rosten explained to Carr, "*is that my present duties are, by all odds, the most satisfying, intelligent and pointed I could wish for. They represent access to the heart of policy making on the broadest possible lines of public information.*" Rosten was not one to blow his own horn, but he wanted to let Carr know that as *his* assistant, Carr would have tremendous opportunities. As much as Rosten held the utmost respect for Mellett, it is doubtful that he would have characterized his position in such a way to Carr if he had been in a traditional role as an undersecretary or assistant. Although Rosten was wary of "taking a valuable member" away from the Disney operation, which was important for wartime films, he made it clear to Carr that their domain would extend far beyond the remit of a single studio and that his work would be interwoven into diverse filmmaking realms.[26] Rosten was, in fact, in the Executive Office of the President of the United States, Office for Emergency Management—which did not seem to have fixed boundaries. It became a source of humor and consternation that it was hard to figure out exactly where Rosten and his closest colleague, Spigelgass, were located in the administration. Allen Rivkin, an MGM colleague, wrote Rosten that the address he was given didn't seem to be right. "It doesn't make any sense. OFF [the Office of Facts and Figures] isn't OEM [Office of Emergency Management] and neither is it the Executive Office of the President, is it?"[27]

Rosten repeated, and perhaps an organizational chart somewhere confirmed, that he was indeed subordinate to Mellett, the "film coordinator." But the character of their interactions indicate that Rosten was at least coequal and not in an inferior position. Although Rosten received many queries and requests from Mellett and others, a huge share of the directions, in all of moviemaking, emanated from Rosten. Had he actually been an assistant, it is doubtful that the degree of satisfaction and autonomy in which Rosten was basking, as revealed in the missive to Carr, would have been possible. While accepting tasks in the form of questions and assignments, it did not seem that Rosten was answerable to a superior exercising control. This is not to say that Rosten simply did whatever he wished. He often expressed his frustration, owing to numerous structures to which he was beholden. But his ability to influence how movies were made, which movies were made, and the general character of the enterprises was extraordinary.

Robert Carr did not become Rosten's assistant. But Rosten's interactions with Carr reveal his long-standing effort to integrate animation into wartime film, which was already in place when Frank Capra came on board. One of the many kudos lavished on Capra was that he had pioneered the integration of Disney-style animation into his *Why We Fight* series and other wartime films. Although Disney would garner the greatest praise for the animations in Capra's *Why We Fight* and other government films, there were competitors of Disney, noted and nurtured by Rosten, such as the firm of Philip Ragan, which already had been commissioned by the Canadian Film Board. Ragan's "wartime short-shorts" featuring an everyman character named "Plugger," such as *He Plants for Victory* and *Empty Rooms Means Idle Machines*, are clever and captivating. "You will remember my mentioning Philip Ragan and Associates to you," Rosten wrote to Capra. They

> do the maps for *Fortune*. I have held several discussions with him: he is extremely able and conscientious. He is anxious to do what he can in the war effort and is at present producing a series of films for the Canadian government on their war economy. Ragan is equally adept in the production of animated maps, pictorial statistics, charts, diagrams, etc. He showed me samples of his work, both black and white and in color: it is simply first rate. In discussing another kind of project with him, which involved a visualizer, writer, sound man, researcher, photographer, animator, map maker, colorist, graphic designer, head draftsman, four assistant draftsmen and a secretary, he quoted a maximum price of $500 per minute of screen time. He is also willing to work on a cost plus basis. He has an organization and technique which can turn stuff out very rapidly.[28]

Capra was thankful for the reminder and assured Rosten that he would be in touch with Ragan immediately.[29] Even if Capra preferred working with Disney, Rosten's introduction to Ragan was critical. Capra was, therefore, well equipped for dealing with Disney and other such outfits. Ragan also was called on after the end of war to create a "short" warning of the dangers of nuclear warfare, *One World or None* (1946), complementing the admonition that all nations must work together to avoid global catastrophe. In addition to Ragan, animator Max Fleischer, who had made some of "the very first training films" in the First World War, also was brought back into the government fold with the Jam Handy Organization.[30]

Since there was no precedent in the United States for what Rosten was trying to do, much of his work was improvisational, a result of trial and error. The core idea and many features associated with the *Why We Fight* series, officially under Frank Capra, emerged from outside of the movies. In addition to what he gleaned from film, Rosten sometimes learned from radio what might be done with motion pictures. He simultaneously wanted to make all forms of media more gripping. Rosten approached H. L. McClinton of the National Association of Broadcasters with the ostensible purpose of praising a radio program he had heard. But Rosten also offered stern advice, which shaped his idea of the signature offering of the film program. "In regard to *This Is War*," a radio show, "I heard the program on February 14 [1942]. I won't comment on the many virtues of the program, but here are several comments which might interest you."[31] Although Rosten was cordial, and not quite giving an administrative or military order, it was expected that McClinton would act on Rosten's resolve.

The most pressing matter was the title: "*This Is War* struck me as too objective a title. A title with a 'we' value seems much preferable." *Why We Fight*, the title taken for Capra's grand project, was either Rosten's doing or an extraordinarily happy coincidence. Continuing his commentary on the radio show, Rosten said that "there seems to be far too much direct narration. . . . Some of the points made by the narrator could have been more effective if they had been acted out in [the] story." This is classic Hollywood advice: don't tell the story—act it out. McClinton also was implored to consider who was behind the voice: "If you use a movie actor people are inclined to think that what he is saying simply represents his interpretation. Note the technique of *March of Time*, where an impersonal, strong, decisive voice presents the news in such a way that the public feels that they are actually witnessing history and taking part in it—rather than being 'told' about it."[32]

There was probably even more in the wisdom Rosten imparted to McClinton, Capra, and others that was borrowed from the *March of Time* radio and "shorts" series than was admitted, as it combined both documentary and dramatization with a liberal sprinkling of reenactments. The bias of the twenty- to thirty-minute *March of Time* films, stridently anti-fascist and mainstream liberal, was also to Rosten's liking, and they were a hit with movie audiences. It seems that Rosten had a strong hand in the making of their two-feel film, *Main Street on the March* (1941), which was accorded the "best short subject" Oscar.[33] Predictably, Senator Nye's "warmongering committee in 1941 denounced the *March of Time* series as objectionable because of pro-war or interventionist themes."[34] In the wake of the wave of anti-Jewish violence in Germany, later known as *Kristallnacht*, of November 9–10, 1938, *March of Time* broadcast a show called *The Refugee* that dealt specifically with the plight of Jews as well as those considered "racial" Jews by the Nazis. The creative heads of the series were the brothers Louis and Richard de Rochemont, who traced their ancestry to French Hugenots fleeing to New Hampshire in the early nineteenth century. *March of Time*, perhaps because of its well-established patterns, was not consistently included in the newsreel "scorecards" and improvement exercises overseen by Rosten—but he and Spigelgass did "offer certain suggestions" about the shows *India in Crisis* and *India at War*, which aired in April and May 1942. These "were accepted by the *March of Time* people, and the film [was] reedited before release."[35] The de Rochemonts were also feature film producers, who in 1951 bought a screenplay by Leo Rosten, *Walk East on Beacon* (dir. Alfred L. Werker, 1952), derived from "J. Edgar Hoover's account of the national-wide F.B.I. offensive against Communist espionage in the United States," from *Reader's Digest* that featured the case leading to the conviction and execution of Ethel and Julius Rosenberg.[36] Richard de Rochemont, "although not officially credited in any of Stanley Kubrick's films," is said to have "played an important role as a mentor early on in Kubrick's career."[37]

Rosten cultivated a relationship with Albert E. Sidlinger, who was then head of marketing and promotions for *March of Time*, in order to establish a routine for his office's review of their scripts. Sidlinger is remembered as a founder of the polling industry with George Gallup. "I was much impressed by your last two releases: *The New United States Army* and *India in Crisis*," Rosten wrote Sidlinger. He found a way to diplomatically give himself and Spigelgass a share of the credit for the success of the India film. "I thought the latter profited enormously by the cutting and changes in the script which the final version had." Rosten's explanation of his work was not quite full disclosure, but not far off: "The Office of Facts and Figures, among its other activities, is conducting a scientific analysis of the content of motion pictures, shorts, and newsreels. It would help us tremendously if we could have copies of the narration of each *March of Time* issue: as it is now, we employ a stenotypist to take the narration from the screen." The subtext was that his office was anxious to see the scripts before editing and to continue to "offer suggestions."[38]

The same point raised with McClinton about the freighted significance of titles arose in communication with William B. Lewis concerning "the upcoming radio shows."[39] Lewis was not much older than Rosten but he already was a powerhouse in American radio. After being named commercial program director for CBS (Columbia Broadcasting System) in 1935, Lewis "became head of all CBS programs and the network's youngest vice-president" the next year. Among his brilliant moves was assigning Edmund R. Murrow to London shortly before the outbreak of the Second World War. Lewis began his own wartime service as chief of the radio division of the Office of Facts and Figures.[40] "I think," Rosten advised, "'Our Navy,' 'Our Army,' 'Our Air Force,' are more effective that 'Your Army,' 'Your Navy,' 'Your Air Force.'" "'We' symbols" were preferable, as was "avoiding impersonal and objective titles."[41] He did not spare his criticism:

> The titles for Programs Nos. 8, 9 and 11 ('No Danger: Men at Work,' 'Curbstone Colonel' and 'A Day in the Life of a Defense Bond'), respectively, are ineffective. It seems to me there is not sufficient firmness in determining what effect should be created; hence the present titles might represent almost any kind of radio show. 'Curbstone Colonel' could certainly be a corny serial; 'A Day in the Life of a Defense Bond' does not carry any sense of urgency. If we want to keep the public constantly aware of the war, our language should convey a sense of militancy and urgency.[42]

If one were looking for the kind of transformation undergone by Capra's wartime work, this is precisely the tone that was adopted: "a sense of militancy and urgency" characterized nearly every film presentation, especially *Why We Fight*.

Early in the war, as it was becoming clear that Americans would have to make sacrifices that many would find uncomfortable, if not damaging to their normal routines, Rosten articulated a strategy for dealing with such problems in media generally and especially in newsreels. His "Statement on Rubber" turned out to be a model for how films dealing with supply and demand would proceed. Rosten contended that "Any statement on the rubber situation should, I believe, make the following points." First, that it "is very critical. This must be an authoritative statement" to counteract "false optimism" and confusion that had arisen from contradictory messages of government officials. The most fundamental question had to be tackled immediately:

> *Why* do we lack rubber?" Because we got our rubber from Malaya and the Dutch East Indies—and the enemy has taken these areas. Your rubber is cut off because the Japanese have driven the British out of Malaya and Singapore, and are driving the Dutch out of strategic points in the Dutch East Indies. (This offers a

simple lesson in global warfare; it emphasizes to the public that the war is a war of the United Nations, that it *is* taking place on a world front, that it is a total war, economic war, and that we are smack in the middle of it.)[43]

While trying to stave off unrealistic hopes, he also specified that the public needed to be told that "several plans" were being undertaken by the government "to make our rubber go as far as possible. (This will help deflate the dangerous public feeling that Washington is unprepared, or feels helpless, etc.)" There was to be no question that "military needs will come first; everything else must be secondary." There must be "several methods" illustrated "of handling the civilian rubber problem" in the form of "suggestions." But the bottom line was that "'no matter what is decided upon by the experts, *you* will find it extremely difficult or impossible to get rubber.' (This should be said flatly.)" Even more emphatically, Rosten continued: "You won't get rubber *because*: (1) tires will go first to the army, the navy, and the air force; (2) tires available for civilian use must go to those who are most important in the war effort: officials engaged in civilian defense, hospital agencies, doctors, etc.; (3) after these needs are fulfilled the men who work at the defense factories—airplane plants, shipyards, ordinance plants—must get tires so that they can get to work."

He stressed that "'The production of war materials cannot be hindered in any way; it must be kept at maximum output.' This points out to the civilian that his deprivation has a purpose; that the individual is sacrificing for something important; that his sacrifice is a *positive* contribution, as well as a deprivation, which *helps* the war effort. We thus underline two things: the citizen's sense of participation; the citizen's sense of sacrifice *for an intelligible purpose* which is all part of the war effort."[44]

The final two points resurface in almost every government film presentation during the war: that American citizens, in total, must participate in the war effort, and that personal sacrifice was for a purpose that could be justified and comprehended through reason. This cannot be overemphasized. In the case of rubber, as with many other subjects, Rosten's advice concluded with practical instructions: "You can do your part in this war by conserving the rubber you now possess. Watch it; keep it in repair; make it go a long way; cooperate with your neighbors and pool your tire resources, etc. This is how *you* can help. Keep rubber consumption down to an absolute minimum."[45] These were no platitudes. Rosten was deadly serious: Americans had to cooperate with the authorities and their neighbors. This was the way to prevent resentment and divisions, a theme he would revisit repeatedly.

A project to which Rosten devoted substantial effort was called "The Boys Write Home," which was first conceived as either a single film or a series.[46]

This was initially pitched to MGM studios, where Rosten had himself worked, and was particularly impressed with its operation.[47] No such title seems to have been produced.[48] But many of its ideas, and letters exchanged between family members, were central to an instructional film, *Fighting Men: Keep It Clean*, of 1943, which was mainly devoted to rules concerning keeping one's rifle prepared for immediate use. The underlying theme was that apparently excessive or nitpicky regulations could mean the difference between life and death in the field of battle.

Rosten spelled out how his prescriptions were to be carried out on screen through the "Newsreel Presentation of the Statement on the Rubber Situation." Rosten knew the nuts and bolts of "newsreel companies" operations. Government spokesmen had to be aware that the newsreel editors routinely "cut speeches to 150 words or less." Rosten furthermore warned that "speeches in which a public official looks into the cameras and reads off a dry statement" tend to be chopped up or thrown out. "To make the points graphic and more memorable in newsreels," he asserted, "several devices ought to be used." First, the presenter "should have a large map of the world to which he could point to drive home his geographical comments. He might also have a graph with "pictorial statistics" technique—which will show the rubber situation in terms of symbols: our stockpiles, our military demand, and the little amount available for civilian use." Again demonstrating his familiarity with the process, he advised that "when the newsreel companies photograph" the speaker—"photograph" is this sense referring to motion pictures—"they will also photograph the map and other visual materials. It will also be possible for them to take close-up shots of the graphic materials and, perhaps" permit the speaker's voice, when he was off-screen, "to remain on the sound trace as narrator."[49]

As Hollywood professionals increasingly came to direct and shoot government films, even straightforward speeches were transformed. Although George Cukor, reputedly "MGM's highest-paid director," tended to disparage his work for the Signal Corps, among his notable achievements was an assignment in Washington to film a speech by the secretary of war, Robert Patterson. Cukor's initial projects for the Signal Corps had included "an instructional film about the building and placement of latrines" (which has vanished) and a short about the Merchant Seamen Canteen (also lost). For the address of the secretary of war,

> when they went into his office to set up the equipment, Cukor instructed Patterson as to the proper line reading, although Patterson didn't have the slightest idea who Cukor was. The director treated him as he would any actor. After Patterson tried his speech, Cukor told him, 'That's fine, but look, we don't want

acting, we want you. Your personality. When you say your lines, I want you to believe every word.' Cukor even tilted Patterson's chin for the best camera angle. Everyone else in the room seemed terrified. An aide pulled Cukor aside and asked him, 'How can you speak to Secretary Patterson that way?' Cukor said, 'How else would I talk to him?' When finally Patterson discovered that Cukor was a prominent motion-picture director, they all began asking him for autographs.[50]

This was exactly Rosten's intention: to harness the talent of Hollywood, as directly as possible, to create the most effective films. Cukor also was asked to direct a film about women in the armed forces, the Women's Army Auxiliary Corps (WAACS),[51] which is not surprising considering his reputation as a "director of women."[52]

Despite the imperative to hire seasoned professionals, Rosten preferred to leave little to chance. "We may have to provide the newsreel companies with maps and 'pictorial statistic' graphs which they can photograph quite independently" of the speech, Rosten advised. They also might want to use "their own narrators to drive home the essential point-concepts outlined. We should, obviously, check their commentary before it is recorded; we should, therefore *supply the newsreel people with the basic ideas* which it is imperative to get across to the public." Rosten was polite but the message was firm: he was the one giving the orders: "We should suggest to Arch Mercey, Deputy Film Coordinator for Lowell Mellett, that the newsreel companies might use 'stock shots' which will give the public concrete evidence of the use to which rubber is being put (shots of airplane wheels, army trucks, the rubber used in battleships, tanks, etc.)."[53] In this context, to "suggest" was nothing short of an order.

This was to be continued throughout the war and even into the postwar period. Rosten's insider knowledge left nothing vague, with the absolute procedure to be followed clearly stated. "We shall have to work with the newsreel companies through Mr. Mellett's office. The newsreel companies are organized in a committee headed by Claude Collins," a former daredevil cameraman, therefore, "our information can be channelled to all the newsreel companies simultaneously."[54] It is possible that Rosten himself had a part in the composition of the War Activities Committee for which Collins was appointed "Newsreel Coordinator."[55] Interestingly, the War Activities Committee has been given retrospective credit for "organizing and coordinating" "all activities of the US film industry."[56] Rosten wanted to be sure that the lessons applied to rubber were not lost in the greater motion picture effort. One of the many films in which these ideas were presented was the 20th Century Fox short, narrated by Henry Fonda, *It's Everybody's War* (1942). Although Rosten receives no screen credit, much of the content is nearly identical with his prescriptions—similar to *Keep It Clean* (1943) and *Fellow Americans* (1942).

Rosten expressed very strong opinions about how shows were titled and how disruptions in the daily lives of Americans should be handled. He was aware, nevertheless, that he could not possibly exert absolute control over all the films whose production he shaped and facilitated. On the one hand, he tried assiduously to ensure that wartime movies were of the highest quality and on message. Rosten also believed in the principle "the more the better"—the greater the number of movies produced covering certain topics, the better the chance that governmental war aims would be widely and effectively disseminated. This was not a scattershot approach but, rather, his realization that different types of media, and varieties of presentation, could work better for different audiences. For instance, in addition to George Cukor's movie about how to position latrines in the field, a cartoon by Hugh Harman was commissioned on the same subject for the Navy: *Commandments for Health: Use Your Head* (1945). "Head" here refers to thinking—as well as to the slang for the toilet, "the head." To this end Rosten seized the opportunity to encourage the participation of socially and aesthetically minded documentarians to become integrated and benefit from the US government's film activity.

This was always going to be a tricky proposition because it was no secret that many photographers and documentary filmmakers were from the political left. Rosten's recruitment of Henwar Rodakiewicz underscores his attempt to promote a genre that was not primarily associated with the Hollywood studios—and occasionally perceived as their antithesis. Given the tendency to omit credits for most government films during the war, it is difficult to identify precisely the films for which Rodakiewicz was responsible. It is likewise frustrating, if not impossible, to reconstruct the government work of Rodakiewicz's sometime collaborators, Ralph Steiner and Leo Hurwitz. Hurwitz was blacklisted in the McCarthy red scare. Hurwitz had made films for "the Office of War Information, the British Information Service, and other government agencies," after having been "a cameraman and co-writer of Pare Lorentz's landmark documentary on the dust bowl, *The Plow That Broke the Plains* (1936)."[57] It is not easily discernible which government films are Hurwitz's handiwork.

Henwar Rodakiewicz was a photographer turned documentary filmmaker who had begun as a disciple of Alfred Stieglitz. When he was in the midst of this shift, Rodakiewicz was anxious that Stieglitz should recognize his work as having the same integrity and seriousness of purpose as (still) photography—which Stieglitz was happy to grant.[58] Rodakiewicz had assisted one of the most illustrious photographers who had turned to film, Paul Strand, with the direction of his film *Redes* (1936, released as *The Wave* in the United States). This movie about skilled and athletic fisherman had begun as a documentary, commissioned by the Mexican government, but was transformed into a drama and mainly lauded for its exceptional cinematography.

Rodakiewicz approached George Barnes, then in the Office of War Information, with word that he intended to direct a film about scarcity during wartime and its social implications. Prior to the war Barnes was a newspaperman who later moved to the US Department of Agriculture as director of information in the Soil Conservation Service.[59] In a letter to Rodakiewicz (April 24, 1942), Rosten said that the message to Barnes was passed to him, and he confirmed reports already beginning to spread that "the motion picture producers are planning to produce 26 to 30 shorts, using material and information which they have requested from the government." Rosten did not, however, indicate that he was a prime source from which the program emanated. Rodakiewicz wrote that his company was "anxious" to pursue a dramatization to illustrate the catastrophe that could result if the enemy's strategy of "Divide and Conquer" gained traction in the United States. One of the early mass-circulated pamphlets that Rosten had produced for "public education" dealt with this.[60] For Rosten and his colleagues, it was one of the most important subjects to be engaged—applied to both Europe and the United States. The segments of *Why We Fight* would repeatedly emphasize that the success of the Nazis was in great part due to this tactic, of Hitler turning the citizens of European nations, formerly cohesive populations, against each other. For the United States it was a matter of preventing the exacerbation of social, economic, and political divisions due to the hardships and stress of the war.

"Could you give me any further information on the project you are contemplating?" Rosten asked. "Would the film be done for theatrical distribution or are you intending to reach the non-theatrical audience?" He wanted to know if it was being shot in 35mm, for theaters, and/or 16mm, which was typically for schools, community groups, and smaller audiences. "What arrangements do you have for distribution and release? If I had more detailed information I could help you in this undertaking."[61] Rosten's response to Rodakiewicz was constructive compared with a typical answer he gave to those inquiring about government support for film projects—that his bureau simply did not produce films.

Rodakiewicz seemed surprised that Rosten's reply was positive and was happy that Rosten—with whom he was somewhat familiar—had pursued the enquiry. "I'm so sorry we never came closer to meeting than a few telephone conversations in Hollywood," Rodakiewicz wrote. Now Rosten wished to pave the way for Rodakiewicz to be included in the government film program—but

Rodakiewicz did not apparently understand Rosten's critical role in the process. "Our plans for the production and distribution of civilian defense films," Rodakiewicz continued, "have been thrown into some confusion by the announcement that the industry," the Hollywood studios, "was to make about thirty of these." He wished to know "what subjects they would cover but as yet have been unable to do so." He was puzzled because he had received "a letter from Arch Mercey the other day" informing him "that when these will be announced, he will let us know"—which Rodakiewicz understood as "don't call us, we'll call you."[62]

Mercey was a heavyweight in his own right. "A former tutor, ditch digger, librarian, truck driver, reporter, radio columnist, coal miner and college teacher," he "came to Washington in 1935 as an information specialist with the Agriculture Department's Resettlement Administration. He subsequently served as assistant director of information," taking part in the making of *The Plow That Broke the Plains* and *The River*, "which set an all-time record for documentary films when they were shown in 4,400 theaters" in the United States "and later distributed throughout the world." Beginning in 1938 Mercey "was assistant director of the US Film Service, an arm of the National Emergency Council created as a clearing house for all federal film projects." After Pearl Harbor he "served as a motion picture consultant to the president" and "to the Office of War Mobilization and Reconversion," and later, "chief information officer for the World Health Organization."[63] Despite Mercey's tepid response, Rodakiewicz was beginning to realize that Rosten was the key to decision-making: "Therefore, *your advice* that a *dramatization* of 'Divide and Conquer' will be one of them is of great interest to us."[64]

Rodakiewicz proceeded to explain to Rosten where things stood—which touched on a number of points that piqued Rosten's interest. Although Rodakiewicz was not as esteemed as Pare Lorentz, the director of *The Plow That Broke the Plains* and *The River*, Rosten was familiar with his work and wanted him on board. His own patch was decidedly Hollywood, but Rosten knew that segments of the public were more attuned to the emerging genre of documentary film—which was, with a few exceptions (such as Strand, Steiner, Hurwitz, and Rodakiewicz), not notably a Jewish domain with which he had extensive contacts. The documentary filmmakers also tended to be more politicized than Rosten, who had mainly plied his trade for academia, the mass market of Hollywood, respectable journalism (such as *Fortune* magazine), and eventually a more elevated public through his work with middle-of-the-road think tanks. It seems that Rosten's taking over the handling of Rodakiewicz was a means of taming the thorny issue of leftist politics and harnessing the talents of its filmmakers.

Rodakiewicz told Rosten that, initially, he and his colleagues' "plan had been to produce a series of civilian defense pictures to be released on 16mm through the usual channels of such distribution." This meant they would be mainly shown at schools—not theaters. Rodakiewicz found himself confronting "innumerable delays, restrictions and bottlenecks," which was especially frustrating, if not tragic, because he sensed an urgent need for exactly this kind of film. "If we can find some way of defraying the cost of production through 35mm distribution," Rodakiewicz wrote, "you can be sure that we will jump at it. We've been working at this problem and have found one interested sponsor who is very willing to withhold his name from the credits, and we're in touch with a major distributor who is willing to accept the picture and release it through his organization. Such an arrangement seems a step forward to us and we hope that we can put it through. The subject of this film is not 'Divide and Conquer' but another equally important one which happened to appeal particularly to the sponsor. . . . As yet we have not found anyone who is willing to finance this production. We have this idea as well as several others on file in Kenneth MacGowan's office [at MGM]." Rodakiewicz was miffed that he had not received the go-ahead for production. "We understand that within a month or so the situation may clear up, but our past experience with that office does not augur well for quick action on their part." Rodakiewicz's main fear was that a project already underway on the subject would preclude his company from making such a film: "If 'Divide and Conquer' is definitely set for the studios to do, then we shall have to drop it from our list, but if there is any way in which this subject could be diverted from Hollywood production, could you let us know?"[65]

Rosten had likely seen Rodakiewicz's film, *Hidden Hunger* (1942), which apparently was in production prior to Pearl Harbor. Although classified as a documentary, it featured a seasoned actor, Walter Brennan. Made under the auspices of the Federal Security Agency, *Hidden Hunger* was praised for its "lively, amusing plot" concerning a farmer (Brennan) who tries to persuade his friends to "use food wisely and thereby stop extravagant waste of our abundant foodstuffs and at the same time 'get themselves an equal chance for health, the way they've got themselves an equal chance to vote.'"[66] Rodakiewicz's codirector and writer for that film, Joseph Krumgold (1908–80)—who gained fame as a Hollywood screenwriter, documentarian, and children's author—was certainly part of Rosten's crowd. It was the sort of combination of the intelligent, entertaining, and useful that Rosten prized. Rodakiewicz's hand may be detected in *The Autobiography of a Jeep* (1943), a clever short that Krumgold is credited with writing.

Rosten informed Rodakiewicz that he passed his letter on to Lowell Mellett "with my own comments urging that we integrate the *informational activities* of the Hollywood and *non-Hollywood* producers. You may be interested to know that Mellett and Donald Slesinger," to be discussed below, "had a long talk on just this point several days before your letter was written." This was meant as a signal to Rodakiewicz that the kind of politicized and socially conscious filmmaking he practiced would have a place in the government program. Rosten, it seems, was the moving force behind such a meeting between Mellett and Slesinger. "I suggest," he instructed Rodakiewicz, "that you talk to Mr. Mellett if you can get down to Washington." Rosten was adamant, however, that he did not believe Rodakiewicz's plan for a film on the "Divide and Conquer" theme should be scrubbed. "It is our feeling that more than one film can be made on the subject, and as a matter of general information policy there ought to be several approaches to one problem, and more than one film on any one problem. The war information needs are so great that a certain amount of 'over-lapping' may be necessary. There is no reason why you should not continue" with this "or any other theme which studios in Hollywood put into their shorts."[67]

The precedent was established, therefore, to take as many different angles on important subjects as possible—including the more intellectual. Later, on being notified that Rodakiewicz and his colleagues wished to make a film about the black market, Rosten reiterated that multiple treatments of the same subject actually is desirable. He was not, however, issuing Rodakiewicz carte blanche: "We would want to know who the sponsor is and whether any private interest is being served by the sponsorship of the subject matter. If there is no commercial angle, and if the film meets with [a] favorable reaction from a Government agency, it might be that the Coordinator of Films would recommend the picture to the War Activities Committee of the Motion Picture Industry." Rosten wanted Rodakiewicz to be aware that there would be a large potential audience and that there was good chance for subvention.

> Films accepted by the War Activities Committee are distributed to 12,000 theaters. In order to get wide distribution, it would be best to have the film produced by or for some agency of the Government. . . . What obviously is needed now is a much more detailed indication of the nature of the film you are proposing—and a more specific outline of the arrangements for production. Any picture which tackles the problem of inflation or any of its ramifications (price-fixing, rationing, hoarding, etc.), can be of immense service at this time. Any film, therefore, proposed with reference to this field is certain *to attract the greatest interest from this office and from Mr. Mellett's office.*[68]

Here Rosten reveals that his remit was distinct from that of Mellett, to whom he was supposedly subservient.

Above all, Rosten wished to assure Rodakiewicz that he need not fret "about the possibility of 'overlapping'"—either with contemplated Hollywood or expressly government productions. "It is possible that a film on inflation, or one of its sub-divisions, will be made by a studio in Hollywood. It is also true that the office for Emergency Management's Film Division is contemplating a short, to go into the works soon, on the problem of inflation. But this does not exclude further contributions to the field—the problem of inflation is so great and critical that a campaign of far more than any one picture is required. Mr. Mellett tells me that any short film which you do, that handles the subject of inflation with accuracy and intelligence, would be of great interest to his office—and that you can expect his cooperation." While Rosten was being honest, and there seemed no difference of opinion between Mellett and himself, the policy derived, in the first instance, from Rosten. "The problem of censorship, as I mentioned before, prevents any further commitment until the nature of the sponsor and the nature of the script are made clear." Perhaps Rosten was trying to steer Rodakiewicz away from murky associations that might have raised political red flags. "But any film which helps the war effort at this time, whether intended for theatrical or non-theatrical distribution, would gain our interest."[69]

Although Rodakiewicz did not seem to be terribly hopeful when he first approached Rosten, his proposal was bold. He knew enough about Rosten, though, to speak his mind. He had originally pitched "two separate projects" and distinct "deals" that seemed, possibly, "a great waste." He sought a promise that would enable him to produce "a series" of films. "While we can see," Rodakiewicz wrote, "that there are some advantages to the government in having the industry make a group of them and distribute them, one can't help feeling at the same time that there is a considerable amount of talent outside of the industry which is eager and willing to go into production. I've had a talk with Donald Slesinger about this and he feels, as you know, very much the same way. Have you any suggestion as to how this might be accomplished?"[70] There are few names Rodakiewicz might have dropped that would have had greater resonance with Rosten than that of Slesinger.[71]

Rosten was inclined to give him a green light in any case. Rodakiewicz went on to make a number of films with the US government even into the postwar period. The project that sparked the discussion with Rosten appeared as *It's Up to You!* (1943), sponsored by the Department of Agriculture—explaining that rationing was necessary in order for American farmers to feed both the soldiers in the field and those on the home front, and it also served as an admonition about indulging in the black market. The film features a rousing tune at the close and stars Margaret Hamilton, whose performance resembles her classic portrayal as the Wicked Witch of the West in *The Wizard of Oz* (dir. Victor Fleming, George Cukor [uncredited], and Mervyn LeRoy [uncredited],1939). The cinematography of *It's Up to You!*, utterly brilliant and inventive in its incorporation of everyday scenes and wartime posters, was the work of Paul Strand. Another surviving government work of Rodakiewicz, *The International Ice Patrol* (1949), is a well-crafted short edited by Alexander Hammid, an émigré avant-garde filmmaker, which continued the cooperativist, internationalist agenda of wartime. Rosten helped assure that there was significant continuity between the finest documentary and government filmmaking that had appeared before the war and what was sponsored during wartime.

The previously noted Donald Slesinger (1897–1977) was the head of the American Film Center yet played a largely unheralded role in US wartime film. Slesinger was a psychologist who had been associate dean of the Division of Social Sciences at the University of Chicago, which is probably where he made Rosten's acquaintance. Later he became a professor and dean of the University of Chicago Law School. Slesinger was one of the originators of the use of "psychological insights to determine the reliability of witness testimony," which came to the attention of Robert Maynard Hutchins, then at Yale, who became his mentor. Slesinger followed Hutchins to the University of Chicago when he assumed its presidency in 1930. "In 1938, [Slesinger] began a nine-year stint as director of the American Film Center, a Rockefeller Foundation project to help to upgrade the production of health, education, and medical films. In World War II he served as a consultant to the military and other Government training programs."[72] But what did he know about the movies? In no small part, it was a family affair. His brother Stephen (1901–53), is regarded as an American media pioneer, "the father of the licensing industry" dealing with literary creations, such as Winnie the Pooh, and comic book characters, such as Dick Tracy, Blondie, and Tarzan.[73] Slesinger's sister, Tess (1905–45) was one of the most successful women Hollywood screenwriters of her time, having written the adaption of Pearl S. Buck's *The Good Earth* (1937) and with her (second) husband Frank David, *A Tree Grows in Brooklyn*, for which they were nominated for the Academy Award for Best Screenplay (1946). Tess David did not live, though, to personally collect it, struck down by cancer before age forty.[74]

Donald Slesinger, perhaps unsurprisingly, was involved in moviemaking and distribution in myriad ways, and he was already well established, however vaguely, in the US government and military well before Pearl Harbor. He was instrumental in conceiving films, generally, in deploying film as widely as possible (through theaters as well as venues such as schools and libraries equipped for 16mm) and in developing and distributing feature films, shorts, instructional movies, and filmstrips. In all these phases, Slesinger was especially significant in providing Rosten with information about how the British had handled wartime filmmaking and distribution and what they had learned through their film program's evolution. Slesinger's brainstorming with Rosten reveals most clearly the origins of the US film program that came to fruition primarily under Frank Capra. An important fact, which did not need to be spelled out between Rosten and Slesinger, was that in Britain, before Hitler's launch of the war, "there seemed to float in the air a general acceptance" that the country "was being drawn into the European war on behalf of the Jews."[75]

In March 1942, Slesinger sent Rosten a detailed letter (which he called "a brief sketch") on pursuing an investigation of how "the British Ministry of Information has handled its film problem. For six months or a year they apparently had gone through the same sort of chaos that we are experiencing now." At the time of his writing, it was three months and two weeks since the United States was officially at war. "Then when the German planes darkened the skies" in the Battle of Britain, "it seemed necessary to do something, and a coordinated plan was worked out [in the UK] in very short order." Despite Rosten's best efforts, this had not yet happened in the United States. The UK (nearly) immediately instituted "a 10 minute MOI [Ministry of Information] film on every theatrical program, and series of 90 short subjects that went on 16mm film to the non-theatrical projectors." Slesinger knew that the effort, no matter how successful, could not simply be duplicated. "Two things in England made it easier to handle a coordinated set-up. In the first place, there was only one strictly government producing unit and that was in the post office. In the second place, England has no Hollywood."[76] The latter contention is not as simple as it may seem. Rosten knew Britain fairly well, having studied at London School of Economics and maintained a stream of contacts. What Slesinger probably meant by "England has no Hollywood" is that the studios comprising the UK film industry were not nearly the powerhouses that the established Hollywood outfits were. Both Slesinger and Rosten were enamored of British film, including the work of Jewish émigrés, but the quantity and consistent quality of output could not match that of Hollywood.

"There was some concern in the beginning," Slesinger continued, "about the possibility of the MOI films driving people from the theaters, but the reverse turned out to be the case. In fact, managers all over England now report that many patrons ask if the new MOI film is going to be shown before going into a theater." This was exactly the kind of fillip and information Rosten sought. He would be able to confirm that a government film program would complement and not detract from overt Hollywood fare, and this would sweeten the deal for the studios—which were already largely on board, along with the distribution networks. "Of course the theatrical films are not just hit-or-miss bright ideas. They are carefully thought through and are coordinated with the government's general information policies." This confirmed that Rosten and Spigelgass were on the right path, with the time and energy they were devoting to feature films, to be discussed below. "They report on the state of the nation and explain the complexity of global warfare, the reasons for rationing, and the methods than can be employed to combat the growing rodent menace." Such an approach already had materialized in Rosten's detailed prescriptions concerning rubber. "Proposals come from the various government departments and they are acted upon at once by the ministry, which either turns the project down, produces the film itself with the cooperation of the ministry suggesting it, or contract it to an outside producer."[77] This was already happening, but the evidence provided by Slesinger helped Rosten to turn it into policy to be executed by others.

Both Slesinger and Rosten were favorably impressed by the British government–sponsored *Target for Tonight* (1941), which was classified as a documentary ("an authentic story") while featuring numerous reenactments. Beginning with a British photo-reconnaissance officer detecting a new, "colossal" military installation in Germany, his aide responds: "Certainly is a peach of a target, isn't it Sir?" It details how a bombing raid originated and was carried out. Slesinger learned that the film was "conceived as a two-reeler but grew into a feature."[78] It was directed by Harry Watt (1906–87), who was a director for the *March of Time* series in Britain and had previously produced two highly acclaimed documentaries in a similar mold to the work of Rodakiewicz: *England's Tithe War* and *Night Mail* (both 1936). Not surprisingly, *Target for Tonight* was eventually distributed to American audiences through Warner Bros. The US Army Air Force film, *Target for Today* (1944), for which there are no screen credits, obviously derives from its British predecessors and is yet another textbook example of the application of Rosten's ideas.

Slesinger carefully detailed the methodology of the Ministry of Information. It

> announces that it wants to make a film on the bomber command. It then draws lots to see who is to handle the production. The company that is selected proceeds to make the film under government subsidy and, of course, it can have complete government cooperation. The company that makes the film also releases it commercially to the theaters and divides the proceeds in the usual manner: 70 percent to the government, 30 percent to the distributing corporation. In England, as in this country, the money that is paid to the government goes

into the treasury and is not placed to the credit of the MOI or any other government department.

Another important part of the template was delineated: "Of the ninety non-theatrical films, about half are suggested by the various ministries and the other half are planned directly by the Ministry of Information. Tom Baird, who is in charge of the distribution, has eight or ten (I forget the exact number) regional offices, each one with projector, personnel and some storage space for films." As anyone who has shown a film to a group knows, sometimes things go wrong. The British already had debugged the process. "The projectionists are carefully trained, and with the mobile units reach an audience of some five million. And through other non-theatrical film another five million is reached. The 16mm films are extremely important in their general program and they often include prints of the MOI theatrical releases."[79] While this might seem technical, it was extremely important to have a sense of how to obtain the widest possible release for films.

Slesinger continued with his largely sanguine picture of how it was done in Britain: "Cooperation has been very satisfactory, but the government has an ace-in-the-hole for the recalcitrant. Since everything is rationed in England, it is almost impossible to get celluloid and plyboard unless a film is approved. It should be clear that the Ministry of Information has no control over the activities of the Ministry of Supply and occasionally strong government departments have been able to surpass the priority wishes of the MOI. By and large, however, all the ministries work together and a well-rounded program results." Slesinger saw this as nothing short of a blueprint for Rosten. In something of an understatement, he asserted "If that experience is worth anything as a lesson to us I think it is clear that we must be willing to exert pressure, and that it is only fair to exert that pressure *in terms of a genuine program.*"[80] This is the clearest genealogy of what was to become the US government film program as enacted under Frank Capra and the other (mostly Gentile) esteemed directors: John Ford, John Huston, George Stevens, and William Wyler—the latter, the odd man out as a Jew.

"Since I have returned to New York," Slesinger continued, "I have been trying to get some inside information concerning the philosophy of the War Activities Committee." This high-level group did not count either Slesinger or Rosten as an official member. In the next two months, however, Spigelgass would confer with them.

> I think it is accurate to say that committee considers itself on the defensive against the government rather than [as] an instrument to facilitate the carrying

out of government policies. Its tremendous fear is that government production will be so good and so much in demand as to cut into the return of the industry's. It might help to change that attitude if we adopted some such policy as the one described above in connection with *Target for Tonight*. But I am also convinced that it will be necessary for the coordinator of films, or who ever has the final authority, to be willing from time to time to issue orders and *to use the whip-hand which he will possess through the government control of celluloid.*[81]

Although it has a rather unromantic sound, in the same way that print was beholden to paper supply, movies could not be made without motion picture film. Even if designs for the control of the industry in this manner were far from complete when bestowed on Capra, he had been given no small part of the means to fulfill his mandate through the designs of Slesinger and Rosten.

Slesinger was keenly aware that making the deepest impact on public consciousness meant utilizing, to the best of the government's abilities, 16mm film as well as 35mm outlets. "On the 16mm side," he wrote, "the problem is much simpler because it does not involve a fight" with studios and distributors, and other possible conflicts between stakeholders in the film industry, "but merely a putting together of existing personnel and coordinating them in terms of a general plan. The key to the success of the 16mm program is the tight and comprehensive organization of the distribution. The War Production Board recently reported that 36,000 16mm sound projectors were manufactured in 1939, 1940, and 1941" in the United States. "If that is only half true, it means that there will be more 16mm projectors in this country than there are theaters. If the available projectors were gathered together in a distribution system centrally controlled and regionally administered, the government film program would be as important as it really deserves."[82]

Slesinger had firm ideas about how this could be done: "We can accomplish that coordination within the Federal Security Agency and the Department of Agriculture both with a regional set up and extensive systems of distribution. They could be asked to organize the film distribution under a single responsible head. This distribution chief could work directly under the Coordinator or under one of the other departments. The other possibility is to have the whole job of organization, supervision and administration taken over by the American Film Center," Slesinger's own organization, "or set up a similar non-profit corporation. The only advantage of the second type of setup would be that it would be possible to present to the exhibitors films produced by government and non-government sources."[83]

The final but critical piece of wisdom imparted by Slesinger was a perfect fit with Rosten's developing role in the administration. "In addition to the general planning that we hope will go on in this country," Slesinger concluded, "I believe it is essential to do some international planning because part of our future problem is going to be to keep friendly [relations] with our present friends and to keep them understanding us." The film program needed to think, expansively, of how its work could be applied to the Allied nations.

> I know that there is fairly strong feeling in some camps in this country against the British soldiers that are brought over here for training. I know, also, that in England there is at least a seed of resentment against this country for always coming in at the end. There is also, so far as this country and England are concerned, the future possibility of economic friction in South America partly, at least, due to the fact that the British have sold most of their industries there in order to acquire exchange for the purchase of raw materials. While I don't have any figures before me, I am reasonably certain that American capital has moved in on many places where British capital has moved out. For those reasons, and others, it is essential that we provide for some coordination, at least in the British and American film programs, both in the theatrical and non-theatrical field.[84]

In this regard Rosten was keen to promote British films in the United States that could further this purpose, as well as devising new methods to coordinate the activity and further goodwill between the Allies. Rosten found that two movies set in Canada during the war, *The Forty-Ninth Parallel* (dir. Michael Powell, 1941) and *Captains of the Clouds* (dir. Michael Curtiz, 1942) were unusually effective in fostering improved relations between the United States and the UK.

As part of a strenuous effort to translate Slesinger's report into policy, Rosten requested a meeting, in person, with the film officer of the British Press Service, a Mr. G. S. G. Walker, and specifically asked for information about the government's "Mass-Observation reports." The "Mass Observation" initiative, begun in 1937, was similar to the kind of academic work in which Rosten had been involved that focused on trends in daily life. Rosten carefully read and marked up detailed lists of British films. Although there is no mention of this in the historiography, what emerged as the film program of the US Army Signal Corps and other armed forces was in large measure modeled on what the British called "The 'Celluloid Circus.'" Rosten knew enough about Britain to not be thrown off—on the one hand, this referred to the American understanding of a circus, a big show under tents with clowns, acrobats, and wild animals. But the term "circus" here also meant something like a traffic "circus," a circle or roundabout: that is, how one designs the movement of a large number of vehicles—and how to get them to their "non-theatrical" destinations in the most efficient way, touted as "twelve months' achievement by the Ministry of Information." "Out from the Ministry of Information a year ago went a fleet of mobile film units. Since then they have travelled thousands of miles, setting up their equipment each night to show their films in the village halls of Britain. It is a business of 'one night stands,'" a term that did not (then) have a sexual connotation in Britain. They would proceed "on to the next village the next day." Rather than adopting a rigid schedule, the timing was adjusted to wartime demands. "Sometimes it will be 'a midnight matinee' between shifts at an armaments factory; sometimes it will be a 'fit up' in a barn for a group of the new agricultural workers. There are now 70 units on the road. In the afternoons the mobile units keep engagements with Women's Institutes and Townswomen's Guilds to show films about food and wartime housewifery; and in the mornings shows are given to children in school, who see special films about the Empire, our Allies and the life of Britain."[85]

Rosten could not help but be impressed and to imagine the possibilities for the United States with its varied social landscape. Slesinger continued:

> But the shows are not all in villages. Town social clubs, adult educational groups and church societies all have their visits from M.O.I's unit, see the films about the war, discuss the problems raised and learn how they can adjust themselves to wartime life. The M.O.I.'s "Celluloid Circus," as it is affectionately known in the Ministry's Film Division, is creating again the market place discussion; the public forum is returning to village and town alike with a new orator—film—to lead a lively and well-informed discussion of the country's wartime problems. Shows have been given in many outlying places where the population does not otherwise have an opportunity of seeing films. . . . *20,000 shows have been given in this first year of operation and over 3 million people have attended them.* It has not always been easy to carry out the schedule of shows. The units were hardly on the road when the blitz struck London. They had to carry on.[86]

Consistent with the kind of advice Rosten had been giving to his studio colleagues, the stated objective of the British "non-theatrical films" was to

> help people to think about the general trends of the war and to gain a conspectus on subjects on which they are constantly receiving direct instruction. They are designed to help people see their own activities in the general picture of the nation at war. . . . The non-theatrical film can cater for the specialised audience and for the people who are already gathered together in a group with a special interest. The non-theatrical work is in a deeper sense public education. In the hundreds of adult education groups these films are now appearing as authoritative

and vivid reports of the life of the nation at war. They become the case studies and the raw material of free discussion. The general policy of the Films Division is to produce Five-Minute films for campaigns, especially those campaigns which have a short term, and to produce for non-theatrical distribution films which deal more with the continuing themes of Britain's social life. The general rule is, therefore, to exclude from the non-theatrical scheme those campaigns whose success depends upon a wide and immediate coverage and to include those themes which are best treated in general terms and on the deeper educational basis.[87]

The principle was that "the non-theatrical scheme is not an alternative to the theatrical scheme. It is a supplement to the theatrical scheme." This also was part and parcel of Rosten's agenda. He was at home with the expressed "*aim behind all this work,*" which was "*to put people in possession of the facts of the war; to give them the information they need to be useful citizens in wartime Britain; and to remind them of the ideals which continue to permeate the life of this country.*"[88]

Although it is impossible to prove conclusively, a memorable part of the *Army-Navy Screen Magazine* of Leonard Spigelgass and Stanley Kramer—the frequent animated character of Private Snafu (voiced by Mel Blanc)—might have derived from the characters of "Goofer" and "Mr. Proudfoot" of British shorts that were noted by Rosten. In *Goofer Trouble*, an eight-minute film, "Goofer" is a guy

> who emerges from his shelter during an air raid to judge the performance of fighter pilots. "Why do you suppose he let that one get away?" he asks as he watches a Canadian fighter give up attack on a low flying Heinkel. The answer is that Mr. Goofer would have been killed by the shrapnel in machine gunning, and his unnecessary presence cost an enemy plane. As the fighter pilots report in after the raid without having made their record because of "the one that got away," the squadron leader explains the phenomenon of the goofer to a young pilot, and tells how he hampers a pilot's work. At the close he turns to beg the audience to stay safely under cover during raids, and leave the fighting to the air force.[89]

In *Mr. Proudfoot Shows a Light*, likewise a one-reeler of under ten minutes, the character is also, in American terms, a "screwup":

> Mr. Proudfoot is very casual about air raids—he's been through many, they don't frighten him. The blackout is, of course, a good idea, necessary and all that, but one must let some fresh air into the house. No one would want to bomb his

town anyway. Of course, there's an aircraft factory in B—— a few miles away, but that's not here. So Mr. Proudfoot's glaring window fixes the course for an enemy airman, and as he passes over to demolish a factory he leaves a "calling card" to thank Mr. Proudfoot for his help. In this film the problem of enforcing the blackout is presented in a short comedy, played by professional actors.[90]

Although one could ascribe the similarities to the American products to the generic character of filmmaking, these lighthearted treatments to correct serious problems of discipline were applied to films for American servicemen. Rosten carefully studied these not only with the intention of determining what to show to American audiences but also to help set a course for what the film program might borrow and integrate into their own productions.

In addition to the British, the work of the Canadians and Australians could also be emulated. "The other day," Rosten wrote to C. M. Vandenburg, MacLeish, and others, "I had the opportunity to preview a new industrial film prepared for distribution by the Army and produced by outstanding Hollywood technical talent," *The Arm Behind the Army*, which showed large-scale armament production. "It so happened," Rosten continued, "that this film was followed by an Australian short dealing with the identical subject." Although he knew there were vast differences between the countries' filmmaking, Rosten was nevertheless surprised by "the astonishing difference in technique. From a technical standpoint, there could be no question that the Hollywood film was superior. Its musical score was outstanding and the entire production was as hard and polished as a blue diamond. It moved swiftly—almost mechanically, and was interlaced with photo-montage inserts that were impressive, but more than a little confusing. It was a production in symbols and in no place did it have that human touch that distinguished the Australian film," which was not nearly as expertly produced. "My first reaction to the Australian film," Rosten admitted,

> was a desire to slide down in my seat and relax. Most of it was done in soft focus, while the narration was quiet, direct, and full of purpose. Worker comment was frequent throughout the film and the remarks seemed sincere and spontaneous. Outstanding was the performance of a grey-haired intelligent-looking Australian minister who works in a steel factory six days and preaches on the seventh. He turned away from the furnace he was tending to deliver a straight from the shoulder sermon on the workingman's view of the war. It was a good documentary film and I can't help but feel that we could learn something from this technique.[91]

There are any number of films on similar themes stemming from the American film program that built on this unnamed Australian movie. From this point there would be a more determined effort to bear in mind the kind of human touch that so impressed Rosten. Was there anyone better at implementing this than Frank Capra?

Rosten received credit for one wartime film himself, *All Through the Night* (dir. Vincent Sherman, 1942), for which he penned the story. Yet he had a huge influence over the totality that appeared on the screen. The Warner Bros. movie, *Air Force*, directed by Howard Hawks, began with a treatment Jerry Wald sent to Rosten for comment in February 1942 titled *The Young and the Brave*. (Wald, thought to be the model for Budd Schulberg's Sammy Glick, could cynically be seen as having matured considerably.) Rosten's main objective was to turn it into an effective recruiting tool for the US Air Force as well as to impart consciousness of the government's war aims. The suggestions to Wald would be repeated in several discussions with producers and directors. Rosten's advice also is apparent in *Pride of the Marines* (dir. Delmer Daves,1945), produced by Wald and starring John Garfield, which was a box office smash.

While on the one hand the subject itself—the men of the Air Force—had great potential, the treatment Wald shared with Rosten of *The Young and the Brave* was unimpressive. The plot was dull and weak, and "the sub-plotting seems to be forced; the rivalry between the pilots, and the love story, seem dragged in by the heels. I am sure that the story will go through many script stages, and that you and your writers will add devices, plot points, and general intricacies and plotting." But Rosten was more concerned that "there doesn't seem to me to be any place in the treatment in which any one of the characters is directly concerned with issues greater than his individual reaction or desire. No one seems to articulate the *meaning* of the war; no one seems to be aware of the significance of the conflict; no one seems to be *concerned*, as a matter of fact, with the contribution which either characters or the Air Force are making to the total war effort." Rosten's next line was damning: "The story, as it now stands, might just as well have been written two years ago—except for the sequences which come after the Pearl Harbor incident; and since these are nothing but battle scenes, without reference to the present war and the present enemy, they merely serve as spring boards for exciting scenes of planes in action."[92]

His instructions to Wald, while for this particular project, also were forceful statements about how Warner Bros. should go about its business during wartime: "*It seems to me that you and your writers have to do the next job now—of breathing life into the story and putting political flesh onto the structure.*" Rosten was sending Wald back to the drawing board.

> It isn't enough to have a boy want to join the Air Force just because his father was a flyer; that places the story in the old stereotype, and removes it from the

contemporary and the political. Men join the air force for more profound reasons, of political thought and moral conviction, than simply because their fathers were flyers. *In other words, motivations and purpose, the thinking and 'political awareness' of the characters needs a great deal of thought.* None of the characters in your story joins the Air Force for a really relevant reason. Americans who enlist, enlist for a great many other reasons—not the least of which is a firm conception that we *are* threatened by destruction, that we have been attacked and invaded, that this world is burning around us and that no one can measure and insure the overwhelming threat to his own safety and future.[93]

Wald had approached Rosten with the idea that the movie was in no small part rather traditional propaganda, "to show that the 'American Air Force' is better equipped, better manned and better trained than any Air Force in the world; and second, to give the parents of the young boys confidence in the Air Force, so that they will be cooperative in granting permission to their sons to enlist." With that as the objective, Rosten saw the execution as terribly flawed.

If this is the basic idea, then the sections which show how the Air Corps is trained becomes all-important—and that will have to be emphasized, of course, in the film itself. I do not think that the present story line will particularly impress parents. You must certainly sharpen the importance of the air force, the importance of the flyers; you must, that is, build a story with a logical connection between mere fighting-in-planes and men who understand the great and fateful conflict in the world.[94]

Rosten then drew the most Hollywood of cards: he referred to another movie. "The thing that made *Sergeant York* such a remarkable film was just this: it was not a traditional story about a soldier; it was, as well, as serious analysis of the moral problems of a soldier, and the resolution of doubt in heroic action which had a *point*. Sergeant York knew why he was fighting; he knew why he and his country had to fight. I would like to see your characters have a similar clarity and maturity of consciousness." Rosten would frequently cite *Sergeant York* as the kind of movie to be matched. "I am aware of all the problems that are involved," he assured Wald, "and I don't mean to imply that all the problems can be solved in a first treatment of the kind you sent me. Let me know how I can help. You know, of course, that the script and the picture will require considerable cooperation from the Army and the Air Force—and that they will probably have to pass upon the script."[95] In his tome on the film industry, Rosten had explicitly "approved the courageous stand Warner Bros. and independent producer Walter Wanger took."[96] This helps to foreground

Rosten's forceful intervention in the work of other studios after his appointment by FDR.

Rather than a defensive reaction, Wald had nothing but praise for Rosten's criticism, which he deemed "excellent" and was now in good hands under the direction of Howard Hawks, sure that he would "turn out a hell of a picture." Wald also wanted to go full steam ahead and asked Rosten for specific suggestions. "As you know, Leo," he wrote,

> Warner's are always anxious to keep ahead of the times and, if possible, try to do front page stories. *Is there anything we can do out here towards making the type of pictures that you think are needed at the present time? I'm well aware that you have your fingers on the pulse of the type of pictures that are required at the present time, and if you could see your way clear to suggest to me what we could do out here,* I'd be most appreciative.
>
> For some time, I've been considering the possibility of doing a picture about G-2 [information gleaned from intelligence], and weaving the story through the training of men for espionage and counter-espionage work. Into this setup I had planned to inject as much subtle propaganda as possible.... *The important thing that I want to stress in this note, Leo, is that Warner's are very anxious to make good propaganda pictures, not obvious ones but anything along the lines of* All Through the Night, *which, as you know, managed to get a couple of good kicks in at the Axis and to do quite a little good.* I've received copies of several editorials written in papers throughout the country which stressed how much they liked *All Through the Night* and the way it handled the propaganda.[97]

Rosten did not comment on the latter part of the message—because he was one of the screenwriters, under the pseudonym of Leonard Q. Ross, for *All Through the Night*, along with Leonard Spigelgass and Edwin Gilbert. Gilbert, too, made government and Hollywood films during the war. There is a fair chance that the editorials about *All Through the Night* were indebted to Rosten's press connections. While Wald continued along these lines with Warner Bros. during the war, he also launched into a movie on the Merchant Marine, in which he attempted to directly apply Rosten's advice for the Air Force film. Rosten also worked with Warner Bros. in attempting to blur the lines between "commercial pictures" and government films, such as for *This Is Your Enemy* (dir. Archibald Macleish, 1942).[98]

Like his work with Wald on *The Young and the Brave*, Rosten offered extensive comments to Collier (Collie) Young of MGM for *Swing Shift*, which is best known for its 1984 incarnation directed by Jonathan Demme, starring Goldie Hawn and Kurt Russell. Young wrote Rosten that "personally, I feel that there is a theme and message here, which should be brought forward right now. I have met a lot of these kids around the factories, and aside from their paychecks, somehow or another I would like to see them get an orchid pinned on them in a picture of this kind."[99] Rosten's main concern, to which Spigelgass chimed in, was that the circumstances surrounding the reason for the male lead being in the factory, and not drafted, had to be as realistic as possible. "There are certain points," Rosten advised Young, "which I think you should reconsider: 1. I am reasonably certain that the draft board cannot prevent a man from enlisting in the Air Corps because he is engaged in a vital defense industry. Once he enlists and is ready to entrain, it becomes all the more unlikely. (I checked with General Hershey's office, and the answer was 'It's damned improbable.') 2. Even if it *were* possible, I should like to suggest that it would be unfortunate to tell Americans that they have no free choice in the services." Repeating what he had told Wald and others, Rosten urged Young to demonstrate the importance of the factory work though the story, as opposed to speeches. His advice here would even be apparent in what contributed to the popularity and critical acclaim for the 1984 version of the film. "The characters seem to be living in a vacuum," Rosten asserted. "They have little relation to the outside world. Both dramatically and realistically, would it not be wise to show how this work requires them to deviate from the normal? Night turned into day, for instance. The problems of the workers are not exclusively in the factory; what happens to the rest of their lives?" Certainly, this would strike a chord with the hundreds of thousands doing such round-the-clock work. Overall, though, Rosten felt it was a great basis for a movie. *Swing Shift* presented "an excellent way of combining entertainment with the new problems caused by the war, and solved by the war. My chief criticism is that, in the present script, only a limited number of these are covered. The subject matter obviously offers a far greater opportunity than has been realized, and an extension into the private lives, attitudes, and adjustments of its characters would contribute both to its drama and effectiveness. If you feel it may be helpful, I shall be happy to read any further versions of the script."[100] Young was happy to receive such a thorough response and was truly grateful to Rosten.

    No small part of Rosten's effort was devoted to locating films produced elsewhere that served US war aims and to making them available—and stoke their popularity—in America. The prime source was obviously going to be England. One such example is the film by the team of director Michael Powell and writer Emeric Pressburger, *49th Parallel*, which was released in the United States as *The Invaders* (1942). The film dramatized a Nazi attempt to disrupt shipping from Canada in an early stage of World War II. Something similar actually did occur a few months after the movie's release. In *49th Parallel*, the Nazi band escapes and tries to make its way through Canada, revealing their treachery and inhumanity. The movie's climax is set at the [Indigenous] "Indian Days" celebration at Banff National Park. While the Nazis are interspersed in a crowd, a "Mountie" reads descriptions of the men, and they are discerned by Indians. The function of Indians here may also recall the myth of Indians in the Americas in popular culture as the "Lost Tribes" of ancient Israel.

49th Parallel epitomized precisely what the isolationist American congressmen and antisemites feared: it was a vehicle imagined as a way to draw the United States into the war or, at the very least, to galvanize support for the Nazis' opponents. But by the time it made it to American screens, the United States already had been attacked. The main contact of Rosten's who was distributing *49th Parallel* in the United States was Robert Taplinger of Columbia Pictures. In addition to seeking Rosten's help with that movie, Taplinger was in touch because he was keen to enlist and serve the armed forces in a filmmaking capacity—but the path to such a placement was not clear. He pleaded with Rosten: "If you uncover any opportunity regarding that personal matter about which I spoke to you, please let me know as I can do a bang-up job in the right spot—Army, Navy, or Civic."[101]

Along with the appeal for himself personally, Taplinger's message to Rosten was an overwhelming confirmation of the impact of the movie, in the United States, spilling over into different realms in which the men were concerned. The first measure of its success was the box office. "Thought you would be gratified to know" Taplinger wrote,

> that *The Invaders* looks as though it will set the pace as a big money-maker, not only for this Company—but for others, as well. It is now in its third week at the Capital, and during its first week's engagement, did $12,000 more business than *Johnny Eager* with Robert Taylor and Lana Turner. Seattle, the second opening date, was a tremendous success and out-grossed any picture played there since *Lost Horizon*—including Capra's biggies. Just had a wire that in the four key openings today, business is even beyond expectations. Therefore, I want to thank you for your faith, encouragement and help on behalf of *The Invaders*. We can exchange "I told you so's" on this one. *I am particularly pleased it is a big smash because I know it is the type of picture which is so important now and one which you fellows are widely interested in seeing produced.* If there is any special setup you have in mind for Washington, just call Nate Spingold at Columbia in New York.[102]

Spingold, then an executive at Columbia, was exactly the kind of guy who Rosten would call. He had studied law and began as a journalist for Chicago's

Examiner, Record Herald, and *Tribune* before beginning his Hollywood career as an agent for William Morris. Spingold also gained fame as an art collector and philanthropist and has been described as "one of the most influential men in bridge administration between 1937 to 1943," whose name is still associated with Contact Bridge.[103]

While he certainly was enormously pleased, Rosten was careful not to comment to Taplinger on the financial side of the deal. "It is especially gratifying to me," he wrote, "to see the coverage that the picture got in *LIFE* and *Look*." Apparently Rosten had given him precise instructions about how to get such publicity. Rosten himself, however, had personally contacted Allen Grover, vice president of Time-Life, considered the right-hand man of Henry Luce, with the most effusive praise for the movie. "Last night," he wrote, "I saw a private preview of a film which will be ready for release in a month. It is called *The Invaders*. It will be distributed by Columbia Pictures. The cast includes Laurence Olivier, Leslie Howard and Raymond Massey. The picture was directed by Carol Reed (*Night Train [to Munich]*)." Rosten was incorrect about the director, but Reed's *Night Train to Munich* was certainly in the same vein—attempting to alert the world to the Nazi menace. "I do not hesitate to say," Rosten audaciously stated,

> that the United States could not make a better film if we tried. The movie is right on the head and makes any number of basic points about 'the strategy of the truth,' 'the enemy; who he is, what he stands for,' with remarkable skill and precision. The picture is, besides, one of the most exciting melodramas in many a year. The whole movie is so directly in line with what we have been discussing in the Office of Facts and Figures, that I urge that we do everything we can to encourage the widest possible audience for this film. I can arrange a special showing for our Board, or for the Operations people who might be helpful in an unofficial campaign to widen public knowledge of the picture.[104]

With the movie continuing to fare well, Rosten followed up with another note to Grover expressing his gratitude for Grover's assistance. "I think we can all take a little bow on the current success of the Columbia picture *The Invaders*." Columbia was the distributor, certainly not the producer of the film, but Rosten was proud of its American appropriation. "I am informed that this film will be one of the top grossers of the year for Columbia. Its box office business today is about 230% above average. Columbia expects to get two million dollars gross out of the United States and Canada. The publicity coverage in *LIFE, Look*, and *Time* have unquestionably played a large part in calling this film to the attention of the public—especially since the picture has no 'love story,' no outstanding female star, and few of the other supposed factors for natural box office success."[105] Rosten was certainly correct to shower praise on Grover and himself for their efforts to promote *The Invaders*. At the time, however, he was oblivious to the fact that the quality of the film owed a great deal to the team of Powell and Pressburger, who were only beginning to be recognized as a power in British film.

Rosten also supplied Taplinger with advice about how to get himself into service. Similar to Rosten's methodical advice to Rodakiewicz on how to turn his idea into a government film, he was as specific as possible in telling Taplinger how he could best realize his objective. It is possible that at that time he was helping to support family members.

> With reference to your personal problem: there can be no doubt that selective service will become increasingly more inclusive. General Hershey has indicated dependency will no longer grant deferment. You should remember that if you are called up, then there is no chance of getting a commission. If you are called, you must take the basic training in the army, and then apply for special training in the officers training corps. In other words, if you want a commission, you had better apply at once and not wait. It is getting harder to get commissions all the time. It is difficult to advise you on a decision of such importance, but it would be my feeling that sooner or later your dependency will not count and that your number will be called.
>
> You can see General Osborn, I believe, just by getting in touch with him. You can mention my name. If you are interested, you might also sound out the army and navy people. Jock Lawrence, of course, has a Major's commission under Lt. Col. E. Mason Wright here in Washington in the Film Division of the Public Relations Department of the Army.[106]

Rosten was, indeed, the best source for such information, which paid off for Taplinger. He became a lieutenant in the Navy and "helped organize the combat photographic division."[107] As is evident in the films *Target for Today* and *Memphis Belle* (to be discussed below) and through the varieties of advice that Rosten dispensed for movies and movie people, Washington's Hollywood Jews would make a striking difference in how movies served US interests during the war.

3

Credit(s) Where Credit Is Due?

Wartime producers, directors, writers, composers, editors, and cameramen were engaged with the cloistered yet well-connected Leo Rosten and the esteemed American director Frank Capra. Capra was one of the half dozen Hollywood people who befriended Rosten when he arrived in 1937, and their relationship was enhanced by Rosten's friendship with Jo (Joseph) Swerling, who was famed for writing "numerous quality screenplays for Capra, [Frank] Borzage, [John] Ford, [Rouben] Mamoulian, Hitchcock, Wyler, and other distinguished Hollywood directors."[1] Swerling, like Rosten, came to America from the old country with his parents. Capra was, and remains, the preeminent public face of the US film program of the Second World War. The lesser known figures, even those who were famous before or after the war, have largely escaped notice, in part because wartime film work was collaborative to an extraordinary degree. The making of Capra's *Why We Fight* series, for instance, was intertwined with the barely remembered *Army-Navy Screen Magazine*. The Roosevelt administration and its Hollywood army did not wish to publicize the multitude and centrality of Jews in its sprawling filmmaking enterprises. Along with the Jews there are several non-Jews whose wartime work in movies also deserves revisiting, including writers William Saroyan, an Armenian American, Robert Presnell Sr., Robert Benchley, Anthony Veiller, and John Cheever.[2]

All these men accomplished highly significant work in a collective effort, conscious that they were part of a coherent, interwoven whole—what the photographer and cinematographer Jules Buck referred to as "one tribe."[3] Their social relationships, often originating before the war, were integral to the film work to which they contributed immensely. Even the more illustrious among them, such as Carl Foreman, Garson Kanin, Stanley Kramer, Irwin Shaw, Paddy Chayefsky, and George Cukor, are not widely recognized for what they achieved during the war and the indebtedness of postwar movies to their Signal Corps or wartime studio experience. Ideas and scenes from pre-1945 governmental films sometimes resurfaced in later Hollywood features, and their products were frequently recycled, such as *Swing Shift* (originally 1942) and *Memphis Belle* (originally 1944). Wartime relationships often held over into postwar partnerships. And compared with Capra, Stevens, Ford, Huston, and Wyler, the film work of this second and third tier overall has frequently been ignored or even disparaged. One of the exceptions is the continued attention lavished on *Casablanca* (1942).

Cinematography itself, the explicitly photographic dimension of movies as opposed to the subject matter and supposed ideological tinge of the stories, is of signal importance in understanding the influence of these uncredited or lesser regarded individuals. Some of the camera work, such as by Jules Buck, Philip Drell, and Stanley Cortez, was unconventional for the time and occasionally executed under harrowing conditions. Cameramen were calling and framing shots, and writer-directors, or else director-writers, worked with sketchy scripts, highly improvised scripts, or no script at all to devise what often turned out to be quality products. Rarely did the artists and technicians behind these movies have the sort of well-defined, discrete function that is typically revealed in film credits. Interestingly, among the five most esteemed directors, William Wyler (the lone Jew among them) was notable for occasionally serving as a cameraman for his own movies—particularly his renowned short film, *Memphis Belle*, in which his own life was endangered and his hearing was permanently impaired.[4] As a matter of policy, cameramen were intentionally put in positions where they were behind photographic lenses as opposed to gun sights, because what they were ordered to capture was of inestimable value to the war effort. In one of the movies exploring the US armed forces filmmaking, *The United States Army Air Forces Presents the First Motion Picture Unit* (1944), cameramen were portrayed as expecting to "fight the war as well as to film it."

Whether or not they were aware of it, these men were entrusted with realizing the agenda set forth by Leo Rosten, Leonard Spigelgass, and Donald Slesinger—along with that of Frank Capra. Their basic assignments and means of completing the tasks at hand had largely been determined when Rosten was at the helm of the motion picture division of the Office of Facts and Figures, which was assumed to be of little consequence, and its remnants, moribund. An example of the perseverance of Rosten's approach is that stories of the wartime Allied interconnectedness, through movies such as *I Was a Male War Bride* (screenplay initially by Spigelgass and Don Ettlinger, 1949) and *The Bridge Over the River Kwai* (dir. David Lean, 1957), for which Carl

Foreman supplied the first adaption, may be seen as a continuation of admonishments toward international understanding advanced by Rosten. "United Nations" was not just a term for a postwar institution but also an idea of how the Allies were supposed to conceive of themselves and behave. The constituents of the Allied nations, individually and as members of their respective countries and armed forces, Rosten urged, must demonstrate that they are accountable to each other and unified through core values despite cultural differences and the inevitable pressures and tensions of wartime.[5]

Perhaps most important: few of these men surrounding the "five (who) came back" wrote a dedicated memoir or left a substantial record of what they did during the war. There is, however, ample evidence of continuity between the liberal-humanitarian, social documentary, utilitarian, and didactic imperatives from 1938 to 1941,[6] wartime, and immediate postwar periods.[7] This is part of what makes *Five Came Back* such a great book and documentary: the work of these filmmakers, Mark Harris realized, was taken for granted. Only a select few besides "the five" were sought by journalists, other filmmakers, or volunteers soliciting testimony about their wartime work. Therefore, we are left with a sharp contrast between typically effusive Hollywood types versus the paucity of accounts. Like the obscured wartime history of Rosten, there is no central address to learn what they attempted and accomplished, outside of the operation centered in Astoria, as richly illuminated by Richard Koszarski.[8]

Although Rosten himself left snippets of his activities, most of the creative material that followed his lead is scarcely credited. At the time, no parties involved believed it was necessary to provide credits, in principle, for governmental and especially armed forces films. The added incentive was to ignore the Hollywood Jews (and occasional Gentiles) despite their part in the war effort beyond the field of battle itself. In the few instances in which the story behind the filmmaking is told, greatest credit during the war—and even in retrospect by the principles—is given to the specifically military figures who were the commanding officers. Whenever possible, the preferred name was that of a Gentile. Budd Schulberg, with no hint of irony, always gave credit to John Ford for his unit's work on film for the Nuremberg trial—from which Ford was thousands of miles removed.[9] Occasionally, though, government citations for merit provide precise information about an individual's activity.

Leonard Spigelgass was a close friend and writing partner of Leo Rosten whose contributions are difficult to disentangle from those of Rosten. He was born in Brooklyn in 1908 and graduated from New York University. His undergraduate years included "a side trip to the conservatory of the League of Nations in Geneva," most likely for music. A brief autobiography states that he "first entered the motion picture industry in the New York office of Metro and Fox."[10] From there he was transferred to Hollywood by Al Lewis of Fox and wrote or cowrote several movies, including a few starring Nancy Davis and Ronald Reagan. Before the war his projects included *The Boys from Syracuse* (dir. A. Edward Sutherland, 1940), in which he shared writing credits with several others including Shakespeare, *Tight Shoes* (dir. Albert S. Rogell, 1941) and *Big Street* (dir. Irving Reiss, 1942), both based on a Damon Ruyon story; and his movie with Leo Rosten, *All Through the Night* (dir. Vincent Sherman, 1942), which was in production when America went to war.

In 1985 Rosten recalled that *All Through the Night* was "the first flatly political movie made in Hollywood," conceived and produced "during a 'controversial' time" when it was rare for studio pictures to be "explicitly anti-Nazi."[11] In 1939, though, *Beasts of Berlin* (1939), written by Shepard Traube, was "the first to include scenes in a concentration camp."[12] Rosten says *All Through the Night*'s success was indebted to Spigelgass wielding his "uncanny story sense."[13] No doubt the acting of Humphrey Bogart had something to do with it too. Concerning his wartime service, for which he volunteered, Spigelgass wrote blithely for *Who's Who* that "his Hollywood career was interrupted for four years" and that he "emerged from the Army a Lieutenant Colonel, having served in Washington, New York, the Aleutians and E.T.O. [the European theater of operations]."[14]

Spigelgass had his own Washington connections. His "fabulous sister," Beulah Roth,[15] wife of the photographer Sanford Roth, was "active in politics and was a speechwriter for Franklin D. Roosevelt and Adlai Stevenson."[16] Sanford Roth had a chain of women's clothing stores on the West Coast but withdrew from that lucrative business to be a photographer, in which he attained some success. After the war the couple spent time in Paris with others from the Hollywood clan. Claiming that she possessed "eyes like an owl and a nose like an eagle" was high praise from her brother—Beulah knew the ins and outs everywhere: where to eat, shop, and who was interesting to meet.[17] The siblings remained confidantes and collaborators throughout their lives.

Along with shaping the general character of the film program in its initial stages with Rosten, Spigelgass was critical in the efforts to mold the newsreels that were offered by the various companies and mined for use in countless government films. In addition to an unknown number of shorts, Spigelgass was at the head of filmmaking for a regular film series, the *Army-Navy Screen Magazine*, originally produced for servicemen. In addition to the *Screen Magazine*, there were related projects initially intended, exclusively, for military audiences, and almost all the broad governmental films as well as whatever came within its remit from studios, were cannibalized. One of the areas that was not often addressed by Rosten, however, was the division of films for strictly military versus civilian audiences. As mentioned previously, Rosten preferred that several films be made on the same topic or advanced through different genres and aimed at diverse target audiences. Rosten tended to think of movies as an instrument for influencing popular culture and consciousness generally. It is not surprising, then, that the *Why We Fight* series, and many other films originally made and shown for the armed forces, eventually reached general audiences far beyond the military—not only in the United States but abroad. Interestingly, when Lowell Mellett gave Spigelgass express permission to show a portion of *Why We Fight* "to the film department of the Comité National Français . . . for the officers and American sponsors of France Forever," he described it as "*your* Why We Fight series."[18] Mellett was fully aware that *Why We Fight* owed much to Spigelgass. Although the press release spelled Spigelgass's name incorrectly, it got the collective effort more or less straight: "Directed by Lieutenant Colonel Frank Capra, Lieutenant Colonel Anatole Litvak, Major Leonard Spiegelglass [*sic*], and the late Major Eric Knight, the film is a flaming indictment of the three Axis aggressors. These Hollywood experts drive home the indictment not by the use of far-fetched fiction but through the sound military strategy of letting the enemies condemn themselves."[19]

Despite dismissing his wartime service in three lines for his capsule biography for *Who's Who*, Spigelgass is more forthcoming in his autobiography, *Scuttle under the Bonnet* (1962), about his work with the US Army Signal Corps. Told under the guise of reminiscences during a trip to England and the Continent to purchase a Rolls Royce, it is a largely comedic take on his life. Yet, however instructive, it is far from a comprehensive, meticulous, or tell-all account. "I had an early draft number," Spigelgass recalled, "and, long before Pearl Harbor, I received my greetings and was ordered to report for a physical at a doctor's office on Pico Boulevard [Los Angeles] at seven o'clock of a February morning" in 1942. Admitting that he was a hypochondriac and his "medicine chest serves as a stockroom for Rexall," Spigelgass was classified as 4-F, meaning that he was unfit for military service, "on the official grounds that I was hopelessly neurotic. I could have told them that!" Spigelgass avers that he "grew even more neurotic about my nonparticipation in the war effort after Pearl Harbor and grasped Frank Capra's offer to work as a civilian on the Army Orientation Films, which he was making for General Osborn."[20]

Although Spigelgass clearly notes his subservience to Capra, and makes it sound as if Capra provided his entrée to wartime service, he was working closely with Rosten and Osborn before Capra came onto the scene. And it was Rosten who facilitated Spigelgass's entry into the army. "He kept nagging me," Rosten recalled. "Why couldn't I just pick up the phone and call General Marshall or Harry Hopkins and give him a commission?" After all, Rosten was not only Spigelgass's bosom friend but the Hollywood mole in the deepest recesses of Washington as well. Once in, under Capra, Spigelgass wrote, "a group of us prepared a number of scripts and the job was soon done, and I began to fret again. Instead of returning to Hollywood, I joined Leo Rosten in Lowell Mellett's Office of Facts and Figures, a government bureau that preceded O.W.I. as our war-information agency."[21] The chronology presented here by Spigelgass was jumbled, but few, except for Hollywood studio insiders, would have noticed. The earlier work Spigelgass was doing with Rosten was undercover.

"When Colonel Capra suggested I rejoin him to handle the Washington division of his film project," Spigelgass wrote, "I accepted avidly, and stationed in the Cooling Tower of the old Interior Building, busied myself with German and Japanese films, the business of involved government and civilian clearances, and the implementation of *the Capra program*." Spigelgass would never say publicly that it was a Rosten program too. It was, indeed, a complicated assignment. There had been a feverish debate within the US government about whether captured Axis footage should be used. Rosten, though, was never in doubt that anything available that might possibly assist the film work should be utilized. Spigelgass said he was fortunate that his "superior was General (then Colonel [Edward L.]) Munson, a man of rare understanding of the uses of film as a weapon. It was he who first noticed that my usefulness was somewhat impaired as a civilian, and suggested that I join the Army."[22] This version is completely at odds with Rosten's recollection.

> I laughed when I thought of the draft-board report," Spigelgass wrote. "But it was obviously lost in the mail because, in a matter of weeks, I was a captain, AUS, saluting on the streets of Washington, getting perfunctory training at Fort Mayer, and working day and night at a desk. In a month or two it appeared that Capra's whole unit, for reasons of table of organization, would be moved into the Signal Corps—and it was, except me. I remained with General Osborn and his Information and Education Branch, and was finally assigned to the Signal Corps Photographic Center [S.C.P.C.] in Astoria, Long Island, as the I. and E. representative on the Capra operation.[23]

In a field where credits are everything, Spigelgass offers them to Munson and Osborn, his Gentile military superiors, omitting Rosten and Manny [Emmanuel] Cohen. What appears in *Scuttle under the Bonnet* was probably a well-rehearsed narrative.

In a humorous but informative aside, Spigelgass, who even up to this point had been evasive, writes: "I hesitate to recount the history of the S.C.P.C., particularly in view of the fact that a number of us old veterans have an annual gin-rummy game, and, were I to make the most minute goof I would be laid wide open to the slings and arrows of Major Julian Blaustein, Major Daniel Taradash, Sergeant Herbert Baker, Lieutenant Stanley Kramer, Lieutenant Arthur Lewis, and Captain David Miller, all S.C.P.C. men, all distinguished filmmakers today, and certainly all expert marksmen-medal men when it comes to slings and arrows."[24] Spigelgass's recollection of their respective ranks was complicated. In one way, it was a joke—because they were such Hollywood guys. But they had all taken their wartime assignments with deadly seriousness and remained proud of having served. A description of Arthur Lewis could be applied to all of them: "He spent the Second World War in the US Army Signal Corps, largely making training, propaganda, and moral boosting films, as well as carrying out photographic assignments."[25] While all of them certainly were successful, only one among them, Stanley Kramer, is well-known, and Julian Blaustein has piqued academic interest.[26] Spigelgass later delineated another important cohort, including director Anatole Litvak. "I'll merely pencil in the fact that I represented General Osborn's interests with the *Army-Navy Screen Magazine*." Again, Spigelgass offers his place as a minor cog in the established hierarchy. "Officially, this project was described in these Army terms: 'The urgent need for presenting current information to the troops of the United States Army by means of motion pictures brought about the production of the *Army-Navy Screen Magazine*. The *Screen Magazine* was originated by Col. Frank Capra and Col. E. L. Munson, Jr., as a twenty-minute film subject to be released every two weeks, complementing the full-length orientation films, radio programs and publications of the Information Branch of the Army Moral Services Division.'"[27] A large share of its operating principles, however, had been set out by Rosten. "Facilities of the Army Signal Corps were made available, and Lt. Col. Emanuel Cohen, Maj. Leonard Spigelgass, Maj. Theodor Geisel and Capt. Ralph Dietrich were placed in charge of production."[28] Theodor Geisel would enjoy lasting fame as children's author Dr. Seuss. Perhaps the next most famous (unnamed) alumnus of this group is Mel Blanc, who voiced the animated portions of the show, notably the character of Private Snafu.

> The official history further records that the first issue was released on May 8, 1943, under its original title of *The War*. It was well received by an audience of several million men at naval and military installations both overseas and within the continental limits of the United States. The subject was welcomed so warmly by Navy personnel that active Navy participation in its production was requested. With the release of Issue No. 11 the title was changed from *The War* to

Army-Navy Screen Magazine and the production became a joint operation of the two forces. All film with any direct bearing on the war is made available to the editors of the *Screen Magazine*. *Screen Magazine* cameramen in the United States and in combat zones implement this footage. The total film is edited and produced for the single purpose of giving the American soldier and sailor objective current information on the breadth and character of the war we are fighting.[29]

Among the cameramen who had extraordinary impact on the overall character of their films were Jules Buck, serving under John Huston, L. Bennett ("Ebby") Fenberg with Garson Kanin, Philip Drell and Stanley Cortez with George Stevens, and Harold Tannenbaum with William Wyler.

Spigelgass wistfully recalls that "the men who worked on the *Army-Navy Screen Magazine* were about as dedicated a bunch of human beings as I've ever known—and my God, they were talented." The creative expression of their talent was encouraged because of the projected audience—servicemen—which meant that their films might be a little earthier and edgier than those for a general audience. "The three writers upon whom I most depended were Don Ettlinger (who had been a prominent screenwriter before the war), Teddy Mills (who joined Dave Garroway in the Chicago Television school and became a big wheel in NBC and subsequently married Genevieve," that is, the French actress who was known as Genevieve, "and John Cheever (whose novels and short stories you certainly know.)"[30] One film which illuminated the founding and operations of "the first motion picture unit of the Army Air Forces" based in Culver City, California,[31] mentions at the outset the "soldier-writers" whose work was fundamental. "On the West Coast we had Claude Binyon, the names of whose movies belong to history. We had others, too, helping us from time to time. Once we had William Sayoran, who wrote a piece on Army shoes that should belong to the literature of our time—and Irwin Shaw, Sidney Kingsley, Anatole Litvak, Arnaud d'Usseau, Jimmy Gow, Henry Berman, John Weaver, Irving Reis, Carl Foreman, Shepard Traube, and Gottfried Reinhardt."[32] There is little trace of some of these men, while the careers of others can be at least partially reconstructed.

"All of us, in various permutations and combinations," Spigelgass writes, "sat long hours in production rooms, viewing all the film pouring in from the fronts of the war, from all the services. We tried to assemble it into some kind of order."[33] It is possible to assign some credits to this work, as Spigelgass's personal clipping file is apparently selective with reviews mentioning particular episodes and segments of the *Screen Magazine*. A feature of the series "I Was There" is drawn from Rosten's plans for films based on soldiers' letters.[34] At least two of the segments involved Jewish servicemen: the former boxing champion Barney Ross, who enlisted in the army, and Meyer (aka "Mike") Levin, a pilot regarded as one of the earliest American heroes of the war.[35]

Barney Ross's presentation draws heavily on his background from a rough-and-tumble neighborhood on Chicago's South Side, which was a mild, ironic premonition of the kinds of conflicts he would encounter in Asia. "The roadwork on the island was nothing like the roadwork at Grossingers," the kosher Catskill mountain resort "where I used to train." And in comparison, "fightin' in the ring," Ross says, "was kids' stuff" compared with the trenches of Guadalcanal. When awarded the Silver Star for bravery, Ross modestly proclaimed that it belongs to his fellow soldiers, because without their collective effort his individual action would have been meaningless.

The show with Meyer (Mike) Levin, which is apparently lost, includes an interview shortly before his death in combat in February 1943. The story of Sergeant Levin had been critical to the widely related narrative of Colin P. Kelly Jr., "America's first widely-publicized air hero of World War II" who fell in combat. In the opening days of the US entry in the war, "Captain Kelly dived his early-type Flying Fortress on the Japanese battleship Haruna in Lingayen Gulf on December 10, 1941—for which he received the posthumous award of the Congressional Medal of Honor." Kelly managed to fly "the shot-up, burning plane back to within four miles of Clark Field, . . . then ordered the crew to jump." One of those who parachuted to safety was the bombardier, Sergeant Meyer Levin of Brooklyn. "Captain Kelly and the body of Staff Sgt. William J. Delehanty of Brooklyn, who had been killed by a Japanese shot, went down with the plane."[36]

Although the Pearl Harbor attack justified for many the American preparedness for war before December 1941, the story of Levin illustrated that being on war footing was beneficial and patriotic and helped mollify chatter that Jews were nefarious warmongers and would themselves shirk combat duty. Having joined up early was now something to be respected. "On his twenty-third birthday, in 1939, Meyer enlisted in the Army Air Corps. He served briefly at Fort Slocum and then went to Wheeler Field in Hawaii as an aviation mechanic. He entered a bombardier school, was transferred to the Philippines, and was at Clark Field 'on the day that will live in infamy.'" After being confirmed "a national hero" for his mission with Captain Kelly, "he served with General Douglas MacArthur on Corregidor, and later with the air forces based in Australia." Levin, an All-American boy and a Jew from Brooklyn, was recalled as "one of the most popular fellows at the post. The piano-playing, cigar-smoking Levin was always ready for fun and business."[37] Consistent with Rosten's notion of a blanket approach to media, a "Meyer Levin Day" was held in Brooklyn on October 26, 1942, when "the Brooklyn War Savings Staff of the

Treasury Department" staged a rally at Levin's parents' home.[38] Not surprisingly, after Levin was killed over the South Pacific "the names of Meyer Levin and George Washington" were "honored by 1,000 workers employed in the ten war plants in South Brooklyn" at what would have usually been a routine Presidents' Day event.[39]

The legend of Meyer Levin also was a key element of a short featuring singer extraordinaire Frank Sinatra, *The House I Live In* (presented by Frank Ross and Mervyn LeRoy, RKO, 1945), written by Albert Maltz. Taking an outside break for "a smoke" during a recording session, Sinatra chances upon a gang of kids about to beat up a Jewish boy. "What's it all about?" Frank asks. "We don't like his religion!" a kid pipes up. Frank calls the kids "Nazis," to which they take offense. He informs them that the father of the kid they were after had given blood that might have helped save one of the gang's injured fathers. "Would you have wanted him to die? Would your mom have wanted him to die?" "No!" the boy interjects. "Look fellas," Frank explains, "religion makes no difference—except maybe to a Nazi or somebody as stupid. Why, people all over the world worship God in many different ways. God created everybody. He didn't create one people better than another. Your blood's the same as mine, mine the same as his." Once he has the boys in the palm of his hand, he regales them with a story: "You guys remember Pearl Harbor? Well, the Japs socked us so it looked like we could never do anything about it. But a couple of days later something very important happened. Close your eyes and let me tell you about it. Go on, close your eyes, all of you, I want you to imagine it." The film audience sees a re-enactment on screen. "There was a Jap battleship, the Haruna. And one of our planes spotted it. Do you know how [hard it is] to bomb a battleship? It takes guts, and know-how, and teamwork. And our boys sure needed plenty of it, because that Jap was throwing up enough flak to get out and walk home on. But the pilot had only one thing on his mind: to get over that ship. And he did. And the bombardier pushed the button. A five-hundred-pound tomato smacked that Jap right in the middle." Again, the movie audiences didn't need their imaginations—they heard and saw it. "Yup, they sank it," Frank continued. "And every American threw his head back and felt much better. The pilot of that plane was named Colin Kelly, an American and Presbyterian. And you know who dropped the bombs? Meyer Levin, an American and a Jew. You think maybe they should have called the bombing off because they had different religions? Think about that fellas. Use your good American heads. Don't let anybody make suckers out of you."[40] It was another way of spreading the message in *Don't Be a Sucker* and several other films meant to undermine antisemitism and racism toward the end of the war.[41]

Although it might seem hackneyed even in the 1940s, Spigelgass and Rosten maintained that one of the best ways to fight antisemitism in America was to publicize the deeds of valiant Jewish servicemen in the US armed forces. They also sought to encourage racial tolerance, about which there was conflicting advice and motives, and support for women in the workforce and armed forces. From the very beginning, a number of stories in the *Army-Navy Screen Magazine* showed the importance of women's work in both the United States and Europe and even point out that a subgroup of Americans who might seem unlikely to be able to help the war effort—the blind—were making a stalwart contribution.[42]

Along with confronting prejudice on the home front in the United States, the *Army-Navy Screen Magazine* sought to assure the soldiers that their Allies, who were more foreign to them than the British and the Free French, were devoted to the same cause. Reflecting themes that would be repeated in the *Why We Fight* series, they presented Chinese combat flyers "somewhere in America" who were training in preparation for "the all-out war against Japan." Another early segment features battlefield letters of Soviet servicemen, demonstrating the commitment and sacrifice of their people toward "the defeat of Fascist Germany," which was spun into separate films and used for *Why We Fight*.[43]

A great deal of the screen magazine effort was devoted to helping soldiers contend with challenges in the field—from the complex, such as understanding the principles of flight for aircrews (drag, thrust, and gravity), to the simple, such as how an infantry soldier could preserve the leather of his boots (not to dry them out near a stove). The cartoon featuring "Private Snafu" was a regular part of their program. Rosten's suggestion for multiple treatments of the same issue even influenced the exploits of Private Snafu. At least two Snafu cartoons in the *Army-Navy Screen Magazine* took on the malaria menace. The first was characterized as "Malaria Mike" and the second, an edgier "Anopheles Annie"—resembling a prostitute. Malaria Mike is one of the few comic creations who was even more of a screwup than Snafu, perhaps to render the deadly insect a little less threatening, a menace that could be tamed if confronted intelligently. Likewise, there was more than one Private Snafu segment on the importance of soldiers not divulging any information about their whereabouts. The slogan "loose lips sink ships" was conveyed in many forms, but the Private Snafu episodes, which included spies who were stealth-Nazi buxom babes, were especially memorable.

Spigelgass described his team's work as trying "to make points in line with our directive." But they "were not too happy with the [quality of the] film" with which they were supplied from the theaters of war. "Some of it was magnificent; a great deal of it was repetitive and pedestrian. So I went to Washington and opened my Big Mouth."[44] This is how Spigelgass went from a combination of writing and editing to producing, directing, and editing. His initiative was a crucial part of the process of placing trained cameramen into the battlefields, which yielded superlative results."[45] John Gutmann, a refugee from Nazi Germany who would eventually gain fame as a San Francisco–based photographer, was first a still Signal Corps photographer before being assigned to the Pacific as part of a motion picture crew.[46] He probably was unaware that it was a Hollywood screenwriter who conceived this transition. In Spigelgass's terse rendition: "So Washington said: 'You think you can do it better?' So I stuttered something. So Washington ground orders through a mimeograph machine, and there I was at Fort Ord, California, in command of forty men, with three Signal Corps units still to join us, bound for . . ." Spigelgass, a 4-F, was off for the front, assuming that he might be sent to Guam. "But what I *really* thought was that I was involved in the highest military secrecy, that Secretary of War Stimson had sent us to the Pacific Coast to fool Göring, and that, in the dead of night, my unit would be sneaked back east, and we'd be sent to North Africa. Not a bit of it. We joined Amphibious Training Force No. 9, headed by General Corlett (of New Mexico), who, in turn, was under Admiral Rockwell, who was under Admiral Kinkaid. This was to be a Navy Show. But *what* show?"[47]

What Spigelgass does not share is the fact that he had been critical in the shaping of newsreel footage, under Rosten, since early in the war. Eventually he learned that he was going to Kiska, in Alaska. "We trained and equipped and waited and then, one day, all our gear was stuck in two trucks and I (along with Lieutenant Morse and Don Ettlinger) was in the first one, first row, first seat, in Alaskan jacket, helmet, carbine, and full battle dress." Spigelgass was perplexed: "there I was, with two truckloads of equipment and soldiers, and I hadn't the faintest notion where to put them." His description reads like a comedy screenplay: "At the waterfront there was a barrier bristling with sentries, and we stopped, and they saluted. I saluted back, briskly showed my papers, and they stood aside and let us through—the *last* thing I wanted. I didn't have the guts to ask where the ship was. Everybody *assumed* I knew; what the hell kind of commanding officer was I?"[48] He seems torn between wanting to take the credit he deserves but presenting himself as a bedazzled flunky who was just following orders.

After finally locating the vessel, through process of elimination, Spigelgass and his charges "sailed for Adak, and waited on Adak, and then came the day for the battle of Kiska." His autobiography includes an article by Grant MacDonald, an Associated Press photographer. "A darling friend sent me the clipping," Spigelgass writes. It begins with a note from his paper's editor: When

MacDonald, "who left the Seattle Bureau July 25, wrote a personal letter to his boss, Frank Gorrie, Seattle bureau chief, the Army censor attached this note: 'This is the best article yet written on the Kiska occupation. There is no objection to your printing such parts of it as you desire.' The censor." The letter follows.

> Back in Adak.—Dear Boss: Well, the Battle of Kiska is over. It was a clambake, but good. Secrecy was the word for days in advance. I was not able to send you any plans or information. Pictures of advance preparations were sent to Washington to be held until the story of Kiska was released there. If there had been a major battle, it would have been the most photographed one in history. There is quite an outfit from the Army under a Major S.—(Spigelglass) (spelling doubtful), who had a complete Hollywood camera outfit with him . . . including sound and cries of "Roll 'em!" "Cut!" "Action!" etc. . . . and all this made me very homesick. But not nearly as sick as Major S.—who shot thousands of feet of film on the preparations for the great battle, expecting to shoot the final super-stuff on Kiska as heroic American doughboys dashed ashore into the devastating machine-gun and mortar fire and the whirring blades of countless Eyemo cameras manned by other of our intrepid cameramen. All of this failed to materialize, and Major S.—is a very sad pigeon. His dreams of an Aleutian "Desert Victory" were shattered by those nasty little Nipos who took it on the lam, leaving the world a deserted Kiska to the now glumly silenced cries of Major S."[49]

Spigelgass demanded the last word on the subject. He wished to deprecate himself even further. "Now, see here, Mr. MacDonald. I'm not going to have you suggest that I was glum. I was hysterical with joy, because I am a devout coward, and don't let anybody ever tell you different. Nor am I a new coward. I was born with a yellow streak. It never shines as brightly as it does when I meet an official in uniform—police, fireman, postman, legionnaires, armed-forces or agricultural inspectors."[50] But both MacDonald and Spigelgass omit one of the most interesting parts of the story. Spigelgass and Don Ettlinger did capture a spectacular scene—of American soldiers being killed by "friendly fire," "and their film was later confiscated by embarrassed Army brass in Washington."[51] This is not the only work of Ettlinger's to have disappeared without a trace. It is difficult, if not impossible, to locate (or tie him to) the "secret" army training films for which he was responsible.[52]

What did survive, however, were Ettlinger's relationships with the men with whom he worked during wartime, such as John Cheever, Irwin Shaw, and Spigelgass.[53] The writing team of Ettlinger and Spigelgass produced *I Was a Male War Bride* (dir. Howard Hawks, 1949), although Ettlinger did not appear in the credits, and *Gypsy* (dir. Mervyn LeRoy, 1962). *Gypsy* is certainly the more highly regarded, but *I Was a Male War Bride* remains a surprisingly watchable and intelligent film that benefited from the combination of great acting by Cary Grant and Anne Sheridan, complemented by the inside scoop on military life as experienced by Spigelgass and Ettlinger. More than being topical, *I Was a Male War Bride* also helped to perpetuate the myth of the Second World War as the "Good War," with cooperation between the Allies as a key to success.

Screenwriter, novelist, and playwright Irwin Shaw contributed to Signal Corps film work in Los Angeles and Astoria before being assigned expressly to director George Stevens in the spring of 1943. Shaw would gain fame with the publication of a best-selling World War II novel, *The Young Lions*, in 1948. "In his quietly insistent way," Michael Shnayerson writes, "Stevens had gained permission to film the end of the Africa campaign, and tapped both Shaw and *New Yorker* writer Joel Sayre to help."[54] Sayre, like Shaw, had served as a Hollywood screenwriter, most famous for *Annie Oakley* (dir. George Stevens, 1935, with Barbara Stanwyck) and *Gunga Din* (dir. George Stevens, 1939), the latter of which was directed by Stevens. Sayre's father was a successful businessman, and his mother was "a photographer and interior decorator" in Columbus, Ohio. He had "attempted to enlist in the American army" in the First World War "but was refused because of his age. Fortified with a false certificate of birth, he succeeded in joining the Canadian Army and was sent to Siberia with its Expeditionary Force." After the war Sayre studied at Oxford University and later began, but did not complete, medical training in Heidelberg. In World War II, well past draft age, he was a reporter for *The New Yorker*, covering "the Persian Gulf Command which supplied the Soviet Union with munitions and other materials through Iran. As a correspondent he was present at the historic Tehran conference of 1943. His *New Yorker* articles were later reproduced in his book, *Persian Gulf Command: Some Marvels on the Road to Kazvin*. In 1945 the *New Yorker* sent him to Germany to cover the last phases of the war in Europe."[55] Sayre wrote a book based on his *New Yorker* pieces, *The House without a Roof* (1948), about a "mixed-race" family in the Third Reich, which probably was hard for many to understand. Having nearly disappeared, perhaps this book will be rediscovered, as have other challenging works on the Holocaust which defy simple categorization.[56] Somehow Sayre also managed to squeeze in the assignment to Stevens.

The plan was for Stevens's group to fly from Cairo by way of Brazil, but unforeseen events led to a "share of mishaps." General Montgomery's spectacular advance leading the British Eighth Army meant "the Tunisian campaign was nearly over by the time Shaw [Stevens, and Sayre] arrived in Cairo." While elated at the fortunes of the Allies, Stevens and Sayre were disappointed to have missed out on the "action." Shaw remained in Cairo and gained credentials as a reporter "for the newly started local edition of *Stars and Stripes*, the army's newspaper, and for the magazine *Yank*. Then, with journalistic carte blanche, he took a hot, slow train to Palestine, which was where Walter Bernstein found him. A fellow *New Yorker* writer who would go on to considerable success as a screenwriter (*The Front*, [dir. Martin Ritt, 1976]), Bernstein was now working for *Yank*."[57] It is said that the Palestine experience raised Shaw's ire at the plight of refugees who had tried to enter under the British Mandate.

By early June Stevens was in Algiers "to coordinate a documentary film recording the Allies' mop-up operations and the processing of 250,000 German prisoners. General Eisenhower, Shaw learned, was dissatisfied with the film record of the war thus far and had already tapped Stevens to put together a forty-five man Special Coverage Unit (SPECOU) in London to film the invasion of Europe—whenever, and wherever it came. The unit would be linked directly to the Supreme Headquarters, Allied Expeditionary Force (SHAEF), thus allowing the director ample supplies and, in effect, unlimited mobility." Shaw was shipped back to Astoria, then London, in January 1944, where he became part of "a British film unit making a three-reel documentary about the planning for D-Day," most likely with Anatole Litvak and/or Garson Kanin. Shaw also had a number of explicitly photographic duties. At this time Shaw was particularly close to Saroyan and famed war photographer Robert Capa. In contrast to Stevens, who missed the D-Day landing with most of his crew, and the group headed by Irving Reis on the destroyer *Algonquin*, which "remained well offshore," Capa was on one of the vessels that "discharged amphibious tankloads onto the beaches renamed for the invasion—Utah, Omaha, Gold, Sword." As is now legendary, as well as a matter of controversy, Capa "braved bullets at Omaha beach to gain priceless pictures, only to have his film ruined back in *Time-Life*'s London lab by an overly nervous lab assistant."[58] Those images that survived this mishap, though, are spectacular. In a devastating bizarre coincidence, the motion picture footage of Anatole Litvak from D-Day also was lost through a mishap. Despite the separation of Capa from his colleagues in this monumental moment, the intermingled experience of Shaw, Stevens, Sayre, and Capa reveals the extent to which Washington's Hollywood Jews were enmeshed in newspaper and magazine "print culture" as well as the still photography that came out of the war.

Shaw was given the critical duty, by Stevens, of liaison between the film unit and General George Patton's Twelfth Army. "Each evening in those first weeks after digging in," Shnayerson writes, "Shaw would take a jeep to headquarters and find out what troop movement or battle point should be covered the next day; often he ran into Capa on these errands, and the two eagerly swapped news," resulting in better and more extensive coverage. Later Shaw worked with cameraman Philip Drell, facing unexpected fire when they entered Paris—which was thought to be free of Nazi and Vichy French fighters. This was a death-defying adventure in itself. Escaping on foot, they "were forced to duck into a building that turned out to be the Comédie Française. In the lobby they came across a makeshift hospital, with the newly wounded being attended, for the most part, by beautiful actresses serving as nurses."[59]

However tempting it was to hunker down with the actresses, "Shaw and Drell returned to the jeep and drove toward another burst of fire, this one from the Chambre des Députés building on the Left Bank facing the Seine and one of its graceful bridges. From within, a diehard German contingent was firing mortar shells at regular intervals around the Place de la Concorde. A resourceful French officer on the other side of the bridge put a German prisoner with a white flag on top of a tank and got in it to drive across. To Shaw's amazement, Drell ran out ahead of the tank" to shoot photos. Drell's bounty included "the later famous images of French women with their skirts billowing in the breeze, hiding behind nearby monuments. When the mortar fire continued, the French officer abandoned the tank and ran the rest of the way toward the Chambre des Députés, accompanied by Drell." When it seemed that the enemy had spent their ammunition, "Shaw ventured out himself to discover that some four hundred Germans had surrendered, and that Drell had been the one who first came upon them. They had, in fact, tried to surrender to him, but Drell preferred to have them wait for the French officer to arrive, so he could photograph the occasion."[60] Drell's own account emphasizes the chaotic character of the scene and his befuddlement at having the large Nazi contingent attempt to surrender to him, which he referred to "as capitulation without glory." Drell also was one of a group of four, with George Stevens, who filmed the liberation of the Dachau camp with great sensitivity.[61]

As Mark Harris describes in *Five Came Back*, John Huston benefited enormously in his wartime work from the talent, courage, and possibly foolhardiness of photographer Jules Buck (1917–2001). Huston "described Buck as 'my one-man army throughout the war' and had requested him as a right-hand man as soon as Capra had told him to go to Italy."[62] James Agee, a writer in the same group as Buck and Huston, recalled that Huston "was spared an arm, leg or skull only by the grace of God and the horrified vigilance of Lt. Jules Buck."[63] A Saint Louis native, Buck's family moved to New York, where his father ran a cigar store on Broadway. Buck set out for Hollywood in the 1930s, where he worked mainly as a still photographer. He is now remembered for introducing actor Peter O'Toole to major motion pictures as well as for his vocal opposition to the anti-Communist hysteria of Hollywood's postwar period, which influenced his decision to leave the United States.

In the pressure cooker of battle conditions and the imperative to create movies that would immediately serve filmmaking needs on the home front, Huston was not always appreciative, and his frustration under fire exploded as antisemitic abuse leveled on Buck personally, which Huston soon regretted.[64] Ronald Bergan of the *Guardian* wrote that Buck shot "two of the finest and most powerful documentaries made during the war," directed by Huston (in which Spigelgass was also involved), *Report from the Aleutians* (1943) and *The Battle of San Pietro* (1945).[65] Critical evaluations of the latter, however, harshly criticized the extent to which it drew on recreations, which were presented as battle footage. Such commentary, however, underestimates the extent to which the film work during the war was regularly interspersed with stock footage and reenactments.[66] Although his movies were not notable for World War II themes, Buck produced a British television series in the late 1950s about the OSS (Office of Strategic Services) during the war, which realistically conveyed stories about the wartime espionage. There was no US equivalent of this popular and critically acclaimed show.

John Huston's filmmaking for the government extended beyond the Japanese and German defeats. One of his notable postwar movies, *Let There Be Light* (1946), detailed the treatment of soldiers who were admitted to Long Island's Mason General Hospital for psychiatric care. The film was not shown for some thirty years after its completion in 1948, having originally been shot in 1946. It was avant-garde in a number of respects: in its thoughtful, sympathetic handling of mental illness of various types and also in the racial integration of the patients and the facility.

It is no coincidence that Leo Rosten also had been deeply concerned with what would later be termed post-traumatic stress disorder, resisting the stigmatization of its victims as shown in his novel (1961) and film, *Captain Newman, M.D.* (dir. David Miller, 1963), starring Gregory Peck and Tony Curtis, which was set in 1944. Even as late as the 1960s, Rosten was driven by the idea that PTSD had not been understood and dealt with as was necessary, which had lasting repercussions. Its sufferers were not "oddballs, malingerers, and yellow-bellies." Although *Let There Be Light* was only shown to select audiences, its broad themes emerged in the screen version of *Captain Newman, M.D.*, which Rosten hoped would have made a much bigger impact.

The cinematography in *Let There Be Light*, by Stanley Cortez, was extraordinary. Cortez (born Stanislaus Kranz) was notorious for spending "most of his career at odds with the Hollywood system. His perfectionism, his insistence on making dramatic use of light, shade, and colour, but taking his time about it, may have turned off the major studios but has long been held in the highest esteem by other cinematographers and film historians."[67] Most likely the film was shown only for professional training purposes until the 1970s. Before turning to movies, Cortez worked in photographic portrait studios in New York, including that of Edward Steichen. He revisited the theme of psychological distress and therapy in *Three Faces of Eve* (1957). Predictably, though, the Hollywood film *Captain Newman, M.D.*, was not as racially integrated to the same degree as Huston's little-known masterpiece. It was, however, courageous enough to clearly label the bizarre orderly assistant to Gregory Peck's Dr. Newman, Tony Curtis, as Jewish, "Jackson Liebowitz." At the movie's end, during the hospital's Christmas assembly, Liebowitz leads a chorus of captured Italian prisoners of war in a rousing rendition of *Hava Negilah*—which they are told is a traditional "native American Indian" song and dance.

After Spigelgass's own operation in Kiska, he managed to get excellent film of the battle at Tarawa, which became an exceptionally good "I Was There" segment, and the work of photographer Norman Hatch was used in several other films. The opening scene of the episode was in "*The Army-Navy Screen Magazine* cutting room," where the combat film from "battlefronts all over the world" was turned into movies. Hatch had been among the first wave to go ashore in Tarawa, "armed with a pistol and a handcamera," and it was claimed that this film looked like it had been taken "from a gun sight."[68]

While Spigelgass remained mainly a writer, his *Screen Magazine* partner Stanley Kramer gained fame as a "message filmmaker" in the 1950s and 1960s, producing and directing movies with a "social bent." Through both his self-presentation and the way he was conveyed in the press, Kramer was identified "as a passionate Wunderkind, an independent producer eager to shake up the status quo with a string of socially conscious films in the early 1950s that raised many of the issues, like racial inequality and juvenile delinquency, that mainstream film companies were often too timid to explore. For instance, his acclaimed *High Noon* (dir. Fred Zinnemann, 1952), though a western, was actually a thinly veiled attack on the anti-Communist purges of the McCarthy era. He was also known for being economical, shooting polished-looking films on a budget only a fraction the size of that of most major films."[69] There was, it may be argued, a great amount of continuity between the themes of Kramer's wartime and postwar Hollywood creations. Those engaged in the wartime film projects were obliged to be "economical as well as efficient."[70]

They were devoted to not simply exploring problems in American society but to suggesting how such divisions could be overcome. Kramer's and Spigelgass's skill at improvising, of having those on their creative team pool their talents with little regard for tightly defined responsibilities, also contributed to Kramer's success at making important, widely respected, and popular movies at a much lower cost than normal. "In 1949 *Home of the Brave* [dir. Mark Robson] explored racial intolerance in the context of a war film. *Champion*, released the same year, was about destructive and unbridled ambition, personified in the film by Kirk Douglas as a doomed prizefighter. In 1950 *The Men* [dir. Fred Zinnemann], a tragic drama about (conventionally) wounded war veterans, introduced Marlon Brando to the screen." A central message of the latter film was embedded in the title: the movie attempted to portray the manliness of the disabled veterans, seeking to enjoy sports, such as wheelchair basketball, and continuing to pursue romance. It spoke of sympathy for the marginalized reminiscent of Wyler's *The Best Years of Our Lives* (1946). "*The Wild One*, also with Mr. Brando [dir. Laslo Benedek, 1953], was the first biker film and among the first to deal with juvenile delinquency, themes that spawned dozens of imitations."[71]

For those growing up in the 1950s through the 1970s, Kramer's movies, such as *The Defiant Ones* (1958), *Inherit the Wind* (1960), *Judgment at Nuremberg* (1961), and *Guess Who's Coming to Dinner* (1967) were pillars of liberal Americanism. *Judgment at Nuremberg* deals more graphically with the Holocaust, which was not yet well-known by that term, than any other major studio production, utilizing footage that had been compiled by Budd Schulberg and used in the Nuremberg trials.[72] *On the Beach* (1959), which would now be termed a postapocalyptic film about a submarine that had survived a nuclear war, predated Stanley Kubrick's *Dr. Strangelove* (1964). In Kramer's film the notion of international cooperation and compromise was stronger than the ideological challenge of Soviet Communism and gung-ho American anti-Communism.

Kramer was notorious for not addressing his own motives, failing to explain the rationale for tackling the subjects he did, "why he gravitated to socially conscious stories." Sometimes he would respond that he had come of age early in the administration of FDR, but he mainly deflected such questions by saying that he had not "bothered to give it any deep or prolonged thought."[73] He was asked so many times that this is unconvincing. His Second World War period, with Spigelgass and the men with whom he would continue to work, was a far more important incubator than he realized. And what he created in that time was much more consequential than he assumed. Before he became known as a socially conscious filmmaker, he was adroitly raising the consciousness of thousands, if not millions, of servicemen and women.

To a greater extent than their typical Hollywood directorial, writing, or cinematography vocations, those engaged in wartime film got their hands dirty and sometimes even placed themselves in the throes of battle. The intrepid nature of war photography was profoundly illustrated by the labor of William Wyler himself and his cameramen, including Harold Tannenbaum for the first incarnation of the movie *Memphis Belle*.[74] Wyler's recruitment of Tannenbaum also shows his insistence that accurate and compelling sound had to accompany the camerawork per se. Tannenbaum, most experienced as "a RKO sound man" who would be killed several months later, was brought in specifically at Wyler's request. They were joined by William Clothier and William Skall.[75] Following Rosten's lead yet again, Wyler's objectives in *Memphis Belle* had been influenced by Britain's *Target for Tonight* (dir. Harry Watt, 1941).[76] George Stevens wrote that "Wyler was a meticulous craftsman and a powerful storyteller, an artist who concealed the brushstrokes, never calling attention to himself. He used wide-angle lenses and pumped light into his sets to achieve great depth of focus—playing scenes that used the close foreground and deep background at the same time."[77] Wyler famously shot the film for *Memphis Belle* along with Clothier, Skall, and Tannenbaum and, ironically, lost much of his hearing in the process. Like Buck, Wyler's brushes with death most likely took a greater toll, in addition to the ear trouble, than he would have cared to admit.

While there can be no doubt of Wyler's courage and genius behind the lens, he could, however, have been more forthright in acknowledging the Hollywood expertise on which even he depended. He might have been more generous to screenwriter Julian Blaustein, who created a film about disabled veterans that drew his attention to Harold Russell for his classic *The Best Years of Our Lives* (1946). While the book on which the film was based, MacKinlay Kantor's *Glory for Me* (1945), had a "spastic," that is, a man who suffered epileptic seizures, Wyler nearly copied some key scenes from Blaustein's *Diary of a Sergeant* for *The Best Years of Our Lives*—such as Russell's help with getting into his pajamas and losing control of a cold bottle of milk. "While a staff producer at 20th Century-Fox," Larry Ceplair writes, Blaustein made "a film that challenged both the blacklist and conventional thinking about Native Americans, *Broken Arrow* [dir. Elmer Daves, 1950], as well as a film that was a powerful call for an end to war, *The Day the Earth Stood Still* [dir. Robert Wise, 1951], and *Storm Center* [dir. Daniel Taradash] (Columbia, 1956), from the script once known as *The Library*."[78]

Among the most illustrious of Rosten's and Spigelgass's intimates was Carl Foreman, who, like Ettlinger, is mainly uncredited for his US government film work.[79] A Chicagoan like Rosten, his career included stints in newspapers as well as writing fiction. After attending the University of Illinois and Northwestern University, he began law studies but did not complete a degree at John Marshall Law School, embarking on a Hollywood career in 1938. Continuing to write, he was a story analyst on the West Coast for several studios and worked as a film laboratory technician. In World War II he was assigned to director Frank Capra, officially making "orientation and training films." After the war he "began writing films for the producer-director" (and Signal Corps colleague), Stanley Kramer. Broad themes of tolerance for minorities and the handicapped informed his work.[80]

With sympathies on the left, Foreman felt pressured to swap "Hollywood for London after he appeared in 1951 before the House Committee on Un-American Activities and was named as an 'uncooperative witness' and was blacklisted." He was not initially credited for "the Academy Award-winning screenplay of the 1957 film *The Bridge on the River Kwai*, written with Michael Wilson. The script included Mr. Foreman's 'trademark'—characters named Baker, Grogan, and Weaver. At the time, the screenwriting credit and the Academy Award were given to Pierre Boulle, author of the novel." He was eventually awarded the credit and the Academy Award. Foreman's script for *High Noon* received an Academy Award nomination, as did "his scripts for *Champion*, *The Men*, *The Guns of Navarone* and *Young Winston*. Both the American and British screenwriters' guilds gave Foreman their Laurel Award for lifetime achievement. Before and after he left Hollywood, Foreman was involved with films based on social issues. He directed the antiwar film *The Victors* in 1963, and wrote scripts for *Home of the Brave*, about racial prejudice, and *The Men* [dir. Fred Zinnemann, 1950], about disabled veterans."[81] Foreman, along with Hebert Baker, joined their army buddy Stanley Kramer in a new film production company in 1947. Their work in Hollywood, proper, has become the grist of film studies, while the fruits of their highly consequential wartime service is in large part lost, forgotten, or, for reasons that were abundantly clear at the time, unattributed to Hollywood's Jewish denizens.

In the background to these figures, as has been demonstrated, was the largely secretive late 1930s and World War II work of Leo Rosten. Beginning in 1946, Rosten was under even deeper cover. "After the war," he said, returning to a year in Hollywood as a screenwriter, "I went into some very hush-hush work for a research agency affiliated with the Air Force, and then I never went back to movie work after that." (He did, in fact, return occasionally to

Hollywood from the 1960s on.) Rosten's association with the Air Force has thus far escaped historical attention. Afterward he "moved to New York, and then did a picture with Louie de Rochemont," *Walk East on Beacon* (1952), for which he wrote the original screenplay.[82] Perhaps Rosten's postwar espionage activity is disguised in his fictionalized movie and TV writing. He would come into the public eye mainly as a distinctly Jewish humorist.

4

Fathers and Sons, Home and Away

Jesse Lasky (1880–1958), later known as "Senior" to distinguish him from his son, established the Jesse L. Lasky Feature Play Company,[1] later the Famous Players–Lasky Hollywood studio.[2] The feisty Adolf Zukor (1873–1976) was president and Jesse Lasky, vice president in charge of production.[3] "From the beginning," according to Jesse Lasky Jr.'s telling, "it was my father's credo that 'the play was the thing.' The play, not the player, the story, not the star. Perhaps it was unfortunate that this concept was later eroded by the 'star system,' but another showman, a pint-sized Hungarian-born Jewish boxer with flat ears and a talent for survival," Zukor, "had a stronger conviction."[4] That company eventually was "swallowed" by Paramount, with Zukor riding high.[5] Lasky Sr. is not the best remembered film-industry pioneer, having gone bust after the Great Depression, heading a short-lived studio,[6] then working as an independent producer, mainly at Fox.[7] "Zukor and Lasky were dedicated men who would produce pictures that they thought should be done," Walter Wanger affirmed, "even though they weren't going to be profitable."[8]

On the one hand, Jesse Lasky Sr. is recalled as Hollywood's original mogul, while on the other hand, he frequently is omitted entirely when the origins of the movies are recounted.[9] Lasky's brother-in-law (until divorcing his sister, Blanche), the former glove cutter from Gloversville, NY, Sam Goldfish, who always had more in the bank than Lasky, would rename himself Samuel Goldwyn on the West Coast.[10] Goldwyn has not been ignored, then or now. "Sam was a master merchandiser," Lasky mused, "whether he was pushing a consignment of gloves or a motion picture not yet made by men who had never made one."[11] To insiders, though, Lasky Sr. was part of the woodwork. The barn-turned-museum commemorating the birth of the movies at the corner of Selma and Vine Streets was used by Lasky for making his first feature film, a western, *The Squaw Man* (1914), with Cecil B. DeMille. When they met in 1911, DeMille was a fledgling playwright and Lasky a grasping impresario.[12]

At Sam Goldfish's urging, and assuming that they would all go into the business together, motion pictures caught their fancy and the rest is history. "FLAGSTAFF NO GOOD FOR OUR PURPOSE," DeMille telegraphed Lasky, asking for "AUTHORITY TO RENT BARN IN PLACE CALLED HOLLYWOOD FOR SEVENTY-FIVE DOLLARS A MONTH." This was among the kernels of truth to the myth of the industry's founding.[13] Less famously, Lasky branched out to New York, establishing the Astoria Studios, the fortunes of which were erratic. "We made some pictures there with the New York stage stars, and also shifted West Coast stars to the Long Island studio occasionally to give them a change of environment and the stimulation of New York. Valentino made two of his pictures there." Still, "it was always a headache to the production department."[14]

Despite its mixed fortunes, at times a "corpse" in the eyes of Jesse Lasky Sr.,[15] the importance of Astoria Studios in American moviemaking is now part of the "film studies" landscape, thanks largely to the Marx Brothers having plied their antics there and more focused attention on director Walter Wanger.[16] And owing to the untiring and creative energy of curator Richard Koszarski, Kaufman-Astoria studios are known as a prime site where Second World War films were produced.[17] "The Astoria stages came to life again," Lasky Sr. writes, "with the advent of sound pictures and were very useful to us until we closed them once more in 1932. Then, during World War II, the Army took them over. My elder son, Jesse, Jr., was stationed there for a time, writing and supervising Army training films."[18] There are, however, obscured stories of wartime moviemaking and the Lasky family in Hollywood, Astoria (Queens, New York), and much further afield—from the backcountry of Tennessee to malaria-infested jungles of New Britain island—concerning their involvement in films that were tremendously important in their time. In part, Jesse Lasky Sr.'s autobiography, *I Blow My Own Horn* (1957), is animated by his desire to publicize his prescience before the Nazis launched World War II, especially in light of the supposed consensus among studio heads that war pictures were "out of date," sure to flop, and should be avoided.[19] He also wanted to make it known that his own boys had made notable sacrifices, and rather remarkable contributions, to the war effort.[20]

Lasky Sr. admitted to telling his own kids tall tales—the most colorful of which was that he had been a "Rough Rider" for Teddy Roosevelt. Having never been anywhere near San Juan Hill, he concocted this whopper when eight-year-old Jesse Jr. stumbled on a photo of his father in a "Rough Rider" uniform. Jesse Sr. did not want to tell the boy that he was in costume for a Vaudeville "military number" with his sister.[21] Lasky Sr. repeated and embellished the tale. So Jesse Jr. regaled his teachers and schoolmates with his dad's exploits, next steed over from Teddy Roosevelt. This led to embarrassment (a few degrees below scandal) when Jesse Jr. was asked to read an essay he wrote, featuring his dad's military exploits, before an assembly including Great War veterans at his school. Lasky Sr. felt pressured to come clean. He rationalized his "white lie" as similar to the stories that J. M. Barrie, author of *Peter Pan*, invented to entertain his grandchildren but conceded that it was rather self-serving.[22]

In light of this well-rehearsed family lore, Jesse Lasky Sr. was "astounded" in the late 1940s to learn that his granddaughter had never heard what his son, Jesse Lasky Jr., did during World War II. There was, after all, a vast gulf between his blowhard tales about charging San Juan Hill and the reticence of his son to talk about his harrowing experience in the Pacific.[23]

In *I Blow My Own Horn*, Lasky Sr. says that shortly after Jesse Jr. entered World War II military service in 1942, he was responsible for supervision of "as many as a hundred training film scripts at once in the old Famous Players–Lasky studio in Astoria" for the US Army Signal Corps, producing several himself. Thinking that he was capable of a more potent contribution, Lasky Jr. appealed to have his status changed to "active duty" in an overseas theater of battle, anticipating that he would be sent to Europe. "He served in New Britain, New Guinea, and the Philippines. In command of the photographic coverage of the Leyte invasion he insisted on putting himself in the first assault wave that went ashore on D-Day." This was not the invasion of Normandy, June 6, 1944 but, nevertheless, a hugely consequential, dangerous military engagement under General MacArthur. "I would never have known from his own lips how he compensated for my absence at San Juan Hill," Jesse Sr. wrote, "but Commander Robert E. Vining, whose ship he was on, was moved to send me a report of the landing, in which he stated: 'In a wide experience in this war, I have never seen displayed more sheer guts, more commendable courage, such cheerfulness and poise as Jesse exhibited. He was an inspiration to us all. . . . Never before have I come to have more sincere admiration for any man.'"[24] Returning to the world as seen through his granddaughter's eyes, Lasky Sr. wrote that someday she would possess "a Legion of Merit medal among her souvenirs, but she doesn't know it and hasn't seen it. 'What do you do for bedtime stories?' I asked my son. 'Peter Pan,' he grinned."[25]

The report of Jesse Jr.'s commander was accurate, and Lasky Sr. had more than ample grounds to *kvell*, to beam with pride about his son's courage. Lasky Jr. was, when given the chance, an exemplary soldier. But the proud papa neither knew nor understood that his son did not simply pivot from making movies about the war to fighting the war. Jesse Lasky Jr. applied his photographic, cinemagraphic, and overall Hollywood know-how to figuring out how to capture and present the kind of warfare in which the US armed forces were enjoined in the Pacific. It was precisely what was demanded by Spigelgass. This involved an unusual array of daunting challenges. Lasky Jr.'s preexisting relationships with Hollywood veterans, such as Robert Presnell Sr. and Jack Hively, resulted in significant collaborations informing and shaping the American public's information and opinions about the Pacific War.

Yet before his son, the war hero, devoted himself to the allied cause in the Astoria studio in 1942, and in the Pacific months later, Jesse Lasky Sr.—who had only playacted as a "Rough Rider"—was himself instrumental in Washington's efforts to generate enthusiasm, or at least to placate objections, for America's military engagement with fascism. A decade earlier, in 1919, Lasky Sr. had failed to secure film rights to the story of Sergeant Alvin C. York (1887–1964). York was a simple, backwoods American caught up in the draft; he had initially protested taking up arms in the Great War against any man, out of sincere Christian conviction—literally, in his mind, that "thou shalt not kill." Upon his discharge, York was decorated with the Medal of Honor, the United States' highest decoration for bravery. His was the ultimate "inspiring story of the conscientious objector turned war hero."[26] York eventually realized, through his experience in France during the First World War, that men may be justifiably compelled to fight, even kill, for the good of their nation and to defend their fellow countrymen. A true crack shot, he was said to have killed 25 Germans and taken 132 prisoners in the Battle of the Argonne, October 18, 1918.[27]

It was no coincidence that Leo Rosten, as head of the motion picture division of the Office of Facts and Figures, was able to use *Sergeant York*, starring Gary Cooper, as a prime filmic vehicle for setting the United States on war footing. Cooper received the Academy Award for Best Actor in 1941, and after the war began, Rosten had the greatest recruiting tool he could have imagined dropped into his lap.[28] *Sergeant York*, for Rosten, was a superb example of how a popular film could convey why men and their country must fight, in a way that was both clear and complex, reflecting a "maturity of consciousness."[29] *Sergeant York*, along with William Wyler's *Mrs. Miniver* (1942), set in 1939–41 Britain, were perhaps the most forceful portrayals of explicitly Christian soldiers fighting for ecumenical social justice.[30] A review of *Mrs. Miniver* in the *Catholic World* magazine lamented the "shame" that it had not been "some Catholic's privilege to have directed *Mrs. Miniver*," given that it won six Academy Awards. "Perhaps it was God's retort to anti-Semitism to have chosen William Wyler." Both President Roosevelt and Winston Churchill had their words appropriated in the dialogue and were involved in the film's production and promotion. *Mrs. Miniver*, Mark Harris writes, "became almost instantly a part of the narrative America told itself about the war."[31] "Churchill sent a telegram to studio head Louis B. Mayer that read: '*Mrs. Miniver* is propaganda worth 100 battleships.'"[32]

The motivation behind Lasky Sr.'s push for *Sergeant York* fit Rosten's objective ideally. Referring to the period shortly before the outbreak of World War II to the attack on Pearl Harbor, Jesse Lasky Jr. recalled that his father, "better than most," had "sensed the stillness before the gathering storm. Hollywoodites were like sleepers, unaware that the forces of their awakening were already in motion. Nobody, the Moguls insisted, wanted war films."[33] "The Moguls" comprised Lasky Sr.'s former cohort, to whom he was now something of an embarrassment, a has-been. The studio heads, according to Lasky Jr., contended that "patriotism hung like a dusty long rifle above the hearth. Nobody wanted old-fashioned, jingoistic nationalism! In vain Dad argued with the powers that were. The life of Sergeant York wasn't just a story of a war hero, it held the seed of self-questioning that many people would face if war should come again. York had been a pacifist, a religious conscientious objector. But in lone meditation on a Tennessee mountain top, he had sought and found his own answer—in his Bible."[34] "As tensions mounted in Europe," Michael Birdwell writes, "independent producer Jesse Lasky, who was then working at 20th Century-Fox, approached York in the fall of 1939 about making a film based on his life. York, when he reluctantly signed a contract in March of 1940, demanded that the film emphasize his struggles since the [First World] war, not his battlefield heroics. But in the course of his association with Lasky, the studio, and Harry Warner in particular, he slowly altered his views and the pacifist turned interventionist."[35]

While there was scant enthusiasm for *Sergeant York* until Lasky Sr. beat the drum, the idea that Hollywood was gun-shy when it came to war films in 1939–40 does not hold up.[36] Four of the other top-ten money-making films of 1941, along with *Sergeant York*, featured military or otherwise war-related themes: Charlie Chaplin's *The Great Dictator* (United Artists), *A Yank in the R. A. F.* (20th Century-Fox), *Dive Bomber* (Warner Bros.), and *Caught in the Draft* (Paramount).[37] Chaplin's *The Great Dictator*, the most critically acclaimed among the lot, was notoriously resisted by the major Hollywood studios,[38] and the ultra-light *Caught in the Draft* is one of the louder thuds of Bob Hope's movie career, which was infamous for one dud after another. But the cooperation between the studios and the US government that was essential for the production of *Dive Bomber* and *A Yank in the R. A. F.*, well before Pearl Harbor, underscored the superficiality, if not dishonesty, of government claims that it did not "produce" movies.[39] As a broadly appealing, generic justification for accepting one's call to duty, *Sergeant York* was in a class all its own.

There is no indication, though, of Rosten appreciating, or even knowing, the central role that Jesse Lasky Sr. played in bringing it to theater audiences.[40] It was welcomed and well treated as a Warner Bros.' picture, with Jack Warner pulling his weight to "obtain" Gary Cooper, who was under contract with Sam Goldwyn.[41] Of course Goldwyn was Lasky's former brother-in-law, and Lasky Sr. had girded himself "for a battle, but Sam assured me with a quizzical smile that he had no objection to loaning Gary Cooper to me for my picture." Goldwyn was notorious as "one of the toughest traders in the business," but on this occasion all the rivals made common cause.[42] And the fact that Goldwyn sought Bette Davis, a star under contract with Warners, for his property *The Little Foxes* helped grease the wheels.[43] Leo Rosten employed his own good offices to boost the fortunes of the film with glowing advance publicity.

For Lasky Sr., taking on Sergeant York was not a burst of pure Yankee patriotism, with a subtle Jewish subtext of angling to maneuver America into the war against the Nazis. Lasky Sr. also was "hunting for a story or theme important enough to serve for [his] second 'comeback' in the picture business."[44] In *I Blow My Own Horn*, Lasky Sr. writes that he sent a telegram to Alvin York, "asking him to meet me at his convenience to discuss 'a historical document of vital importance to the country in these troubled times.' Germany was on the loose and President Roosevelt had proclaimed a limited national emergency. Moved by my appeal to his patriotism, Sergeant York agreed to meet me."[45] That meeting did not elicit a positive response from York, but Lasky Sr. persisted. He returned to Tennessee a few weeks later and Lasky Sr. said he beseeched him: "'Sergeant, you risked your life for your country in the World War, and you'd do it again if your country needed you, wouldn't you?' He nodded slowly. 'Sergeant York,' I said in a melodramatic tremolo, 'that need exists right now, and I know you're going to give your life to your country—through the powerful medium of the screen. This country is in danger again and the people don't realize it. It's your patriotic duty to let your life serve as an example and the greatest lesson to American youth than can be told.' He looked puzzled. 'Maybe we do have something to talk about,' he conceded.'"[46]

Lasky Sr. did not bother to share that in his home, his family's "sleep was becoming more and more troubled by distant thunder—Nazi drums at vast torch-lighted gatherings, geographically far away but brought closer by newsreel scenes—gentle, elderly Jews, who should have been presiding over prayers in the light of religious candlesticks, being made to polish the pavements under the delighted scrutiny of brown-shirted, jack-booted bully boys. The horrors related by every arriving refugee were no longer bad dreams—or exaggerations."[47] The scenes to which the younger Lasky referred would have been fresh in his father's memory from both the violence following the Anschluss, Nazi Germany's annexation of Austria in March, and the wave of destruction unleashed on Germany's Jews, including the burning of the country's synagogues over November 9 and 10, 1938. But with his pitch for the good of the country, Lasky Sr.'s appeal helped prompt York to publicly support the controversial draft bill,[48] and his son, Alvin Jr., declared himself "ready to serve"—which was no small matter.[49] From the 1970s onward, the legend of Sergeant York swiftly faded from sight. But in 1964, his death was front-page news in America.

Sergeant York proved to be a smash hit. Besides it being a great story, Lasky Sr. attributed its success, in no small part, to John Huston, "who contributed some wonderful scenes including one where the sergeant went off to war."[50] Lasky Sr. expended magnanimous effort to make the movie authentic, even doing research himself in the backwoods of Tennessee. He had his son Billy capture a typical "turkey shoot" with his 16mm movie camera and shared it with director Howard Hawks in preproduction. Hawks was "intrigued by York's characteristic gesture of wetting his thumb and touching the sight of the rifle before aiming it. 'What's he doing?' Hawks asked me, and I explained that moistening the shiny gun sight reduced halation, or reflection from the sun, on it, permitting more accurate aiming of the old-fashioned rifle. Hawks established this habit early in the picture as a symbol of a perfect shot and a dead turkey, and for the telling dramatic effect in the subsequent battle sequences."[51] That particular gesture, which would probably have never come to mind without Lasky Sr.'s thick research, is indeed a memorable element of a film that holds up quite well. Despite York repeatedly calling him a "fat little Jew," Lasky Sr. let this roll off, and he did not comment on York's anti-Negro racism, which might have provoked an argument in a different context.[52]

A week after the premiere of the film in New York on July 2, 1941, which included a parade down Broadway, "the picture opened with great fanfare in Washington," including a parade with elected dignitaries. A reception hosted by FDR followed. "At the White House," Lasky Sr. recalls, "I winked at my old friend Steve Early, the presidential press secretary, who had once been in our employ at Paramount. We were shown into President Franklin D. Roosevelt's office. He greeted Sergeant York, Governor Cooper, and the others cordially. Then, turning to me and knitting his brows, he thundered in a voice of rebuke that shocked me numb, 'Lasky, I saw your picture last night and you made one unforgiveable mistake.' He paused for effect and with a roar of laughter added, 'You should have got old Cordell (Hull) to play himself.'" Later FDR turned to him and said, "'By the way, Lasky, did you ever find that scenario I sent you in 1923?' I had been praying fervently that he had forgotten. While Assistant Secretary of the Navy he had written a scenario for a film biography of John Paul Jones, called *I Have Just Begun to Fight*. He submitted it to the studio, and to our everlasting mortification, it disappeared without a trace. We were never able to track it down. I could only say, 'If we hadn't lost it, you might be a scenario writer now instead of President of the United States.'"[53] FDR's comfort, and familiarity with Hollywood's ins and outs, even its banter, was simply taken for granted.

Interestingly, Lasky Sr. followed this anecdote in *I Blow My Own Horn* with a typical Hollywood story: "I recently walked into a meeting of the Association of Motion Picture Producers and Frank Freeman greeted me with: 'Jesse, I was just telling the boys how I turned down *Sergeant York*.' His eyes gleamed with such pride that I felt like saying, 'That's no distinction—you were one of a mob.' I was deterred by reflecting that I have myself boasted about my stupidity in overlooking a Judy Garland, or passing up an *Alexander's Ragtime Band* [dir. Henry King, 1938]." "I guess we all like to identify ourselves with a smashing success," Lasky concluded, "if only by such a slight connection as letting it slip through our fingers."[54] But Lasky might have been referring to something beyond the standard Hollywood measurements of box office receipts and Academy Awards. He was, after all, on the right side of the argument, morally, pushing as hard as he did for *Sergeant York*.[55] (Not to mention that the president had asked him to produce something along these lines.)[56] And the setting was important: Roosevelt had famously originated the "association" of the motion picture producers when Lasky already was committed to US intervention. Freeman was among a small sub-minority of Baptists in the movie colony and would later be recognized for outstanding humanitarian work.[57] But he was not moved in 1939 by the Christian soldier's tale of Sergeant York for Hollywood fare as were Lasky, Warner, Goldwyn, and Rosten.

It is not surprising that in Jesse Lasky Sr.'s own account there is little sense of the extent to which the US Senate hearings weighed heavily on him.[58] "According to [Senator] Nye," historian Steven Carr writes, films such as *Sergeant York* (1941) "were 'all designed to drug the reason of the American people, set aflame their emotions, turn their hatred into a blaze, fill them with fear that Hitler will come over here and capture them, that he will steal their trade, that America must go into this war—to rouse them to a war hysteria.'"[59] As is well-known, the attack on Pearl Harbor and Germany's declaration of war on the United States stopped the Nye-Clark "warmongering" panel. "What was ironic about those hearings," Michael Birdwell astutely observes, was that they "*Could* have proven their allegation of warmongering against Warner Bros. if they had followed John T. Flynn's advice and had conducted a formal investigation. If they had subpoenaed studio records, production files, interoffice memoranda, or other documents currently housed at the Warner Bros. Archives, the committee would have had all the evidence it needed to prove that Warner Bros.—if not the whole industry by 1941—supported intervention."[60] The most explosive evidence, according to Birdwell, was a long memo of May 8, 1940, from Julien Josephson and Harry Chandler to Jesse Lasky Sr., in which "they openly discussed the propaganda elements inherent in *Sergeant York*. They wanted not only to fill audiences with patriotic pride, but also to illustrate the fact that war is sometimes necessary if liberty is to prevail."[61] But the remark cited by Chris Yogerst, of Lasky challenging the senators to subpoena him, seems to buttress his daughter-in-law's statement about the president asking him, in 1939, to send this precise message through the big screen.[62] Although they were clearly making the case for "intervention," there were no nefarious, self-interested motives from Lasky Sr. as a Hollywood man and a Jew. His actions were based on his accurate understanding that Hitlerism could not possibly coexist alongside a United States that was committed to democracy and the tolerance of Jews as rightful constituents of the nation. Leo Rosten was acutely aware that the term "propaganda," and even the appearance of it, was politically toxic,[63] but he himself had honed the character of scores of feature films in order to make its message as effective as possible.

Birdwell warns that "wide discrepancies exist between Lasky's version" of his interactions, in Tennessee, between York, his family, and friends, "and the story the records housed in Los Angeles and Tennessee reveal."[64] But what Lasky Sr. himself did *not* reveal, during his own lifetime—about his direct communication with the president in 1939—speaks volumes.

Around that time, according to Lasky Jr's account, he commenced to lead "a double life," about which his own father was apparently oblivious. "After a day of scriptwriting at MGM studio in Culver City, I would drive out the studio gate, the studio gate policeman would salute me respectfully and an hour later I would drive into the Los Angeles Armory, change into the suntans of a buck private in the 2nd Regiment California State Infantry, and salute the same studio gate guard who had meanwhile changed into the uniform of a Lieutenant!"[65] This notable dimension of Hollywood enjoining the war effort, before Pearl Harbor, was hushed up, on the same grounds that Washington did not want to publicize its formidable connection to studio insiders. The government was supposedly staying out of the movies. But the Hollywood crowd that volunteered for military service in fact undertook film work for the cause, which was not publicly acknowledged. This also was the setting for Jules Buck's foray into moviemaking for the government, before his famed and tempestuous pairing with John Huston.

Dipping his toe into the military at this point may have largely been a resurgence of Lasky Jr.'s boyhood fascination for military derring-do and adventurism. His exposure to the 2nd Regiment, though, seems to have endowed Lasky Jr. with something of an education in anti-fascism. It was loaded with émigrés, "refugees from every country in Europe, who had seen Nazism and Fascism in action. Some had already fought it. They knew, far better than we did, that this war would never be contained in continental boundaries."[66] The writers, especially, "were most alert to the gathering storms."[67] In terms of martial capabilities, Lasky Jr. opined that "seldom had a more motley crew been assembled in the name of home defense."[68] As a matter of fact, he may well have known that this was already a questionable statement. The "home defense" emerging in Britain was likewise a collection of such "motley crews." Some of the Los Angeles' regiment's film work was specifically to bring attention to the home front in the face of the Battle of Britain and the expected land invasion by the Nazis.[69] One of the most surprising bits of information in Lasky Jr.'s account is that he had "acquired a reserve commission as a Second Lieutenant in the US Army Signal Corps years earlier. I had applied to be activated and been turned down as too old, too inexperienced and too physically unfit. So I offered myself as a private to the 2nd California Infantry. I never heard of *them* ever turning anyone down."[70] We see that Lasky Jr.'s ties with the military were longer, more complex, and more extensive than any potted account reveals. He also may have been with the OSS, which would help to explain his near silence about his wartime service.

Lasky Jr.'s esteem for the military and those who served the US armed forces in particular predated his own involvement in "the good war" against fascism. There is only one instance in his autobiography, however, that is interlaced with scores of military-related persons, themes, and events, where a specific high honor of a soldier is mentioned: for Arthur Caesar (1892–1953), a Hollywood writer with over forty script credits, many of which were for films that are lost. Caesar was known to the Laskys from both the East and West Coasts. His family, like the Laskys, counted the Gershwins and Marx Brothers among their intimates. Arthur's younger brother, Irving, was a "Tin Pan Alley lyricist who put words to such enduring musical standards as 'Tea for Two,' 'Swanee,' 'Is It True What They Say About Dixie,' and 'Sometimes I'm Happy.'"[71] While Irving had over a dozen big song hits to his credit, Arthur had one film that gained notoriety, *Manhattan Melodrama* (dir. W. S. Van Dyk, 1934), which earned him an Oscar for "Best Writing, Original Story." But that wasn't what Jesse Lasky Jr. found memorable. Recalling Arthur Caesar during the 1930s,

Lasky Jr. remarked that Caesar was "a top writer of the day, who had won a Congressional Medal of Honor for courage in World War One." Years later he lunged "through a plate-glass window to attack single-handed an anti-Semitic meeting of the German-American Bund. The Los Angeles Police threw him in jail for disturbing the peace."[72] While Lasky Jr. admired his father for setting Sergeant York's story on the big screen, Arthur Caesar was to be praised and emulated for taking forceful, and possibly dangerous action, in his bold "lunge" for a just cause.

In the quip about his face-to-face with President Roosevelt, Lasky Sr. exposed a partial view of the hierarchy in the movie colony: those who supplied "scenarios,"—Hollywood's writers—with some exceptions, tended to be near the bottom, with the "true bottom" reserved for the studio "Reading Department."[73] Screen writers were noted for being paid (relatively) poorly and having the least secure positions in Hollywood. It is no mystery, then, that screenwriter Robert Presnell Sr. (1894–1969) is unmentioned in Jesse Lasky's Sr.'s autobiography, despite the fact that they were "good friends" and worked together extensively.[74] Presnell, like Rosten, Litvak, Spigelgass, and elder and younger Jesse Laskys, was one of the most significant interlocutors between Washington and Hollywood during World War II, making film from a far-flung environment that was extraordinarily ill-suited as a setting for war movies, whether they be documentaries or features, effective for the big screen.

Presnell also was known to Rosten. He was aware, precisely, of Presnell's wartime situation.[75] There is a good chance that Rosten was familiar with him from Chicago, Washington, and Hollywood. Twelve years older than Rosten, Presnell was born in Iowa and "raised in Cuba and the Philippines with his father, a Regular Army Surgeon."[76] Although not a career military man, Presnell saw military service at the Mexican border and in the Great War. Eventually settling in Chicago as a teenager, Presnell attended Lane Tech.[77] After graduating from the University of Chicago he worked as a journalist mainly for the Chicago *Evening Post* and *Tribune*. He served the *Tribune* as a reporter and foreign correspondent from 1919 to 1933. In addition to newspaper work he wrote plays and short stories. Presnell signed a contract with Lasky Sr. in 1928, "penning several scripts in New York before moving to the West Coast."[78]

With the title "scenarist" and having developed a specialty of "screen adaptions (usually in a collaborative environment), or as an occasional production supervisor/associate producer," Presnell worked during most of the 1930s for several studios in Hollywood, including Paramount, Warner Bros., MGM, RKO, Fox, and Universal. He wrote the story on which the classic Frank Capra film *Meet John Doe* (1941) was based, which won him an Oscar nomination.[79] *Meet John Doe* was, and is, regarded as one of Frank Capra's signature films, but Presnell was not, apparently, among Capra's intimates.[80]

Despite their documented collaboration, perhaps Lasky Sr. is silent about Presnell because Robert Presnell Jr. became an outspoken opponent of the post–World War II Hollywood "blacklist," and Presnell Sr. may well have harbored similar leftist sympathies. Presnell's conspicuous absence from Jesse Lasky Jr.'s autobiography, as well, may be telling. Describing himself as a "middle-of-the-roader," Lasky Jr. predictably denounced "the McCarthy witch-hunt, that miserably misguided purge on the part of a politico," Senator McCarthy, "sick with ambition."[81] Lasky Jr. soft-pedaled his association with Cecil B. DeMille, labeling him an "arch-Republican."[82] He was unabashed, though, in claiming affinity with Merian C. Cooper, who had produced, with Ernest Schoedsack,[83] "several films for my father's company, among the most important documentaries ever made."[84] Cooper proved to be one of McCarthy's staunchest supporters in Hollywood.[85] On the other side of the political spectrum, Presnell Sr. became a "film promotion officer" for the United Nations, but he does not seem to have had much of a tie to Hollywood after 1950.[86]

Perhaps Presnell Sr.'s familiarity with the Philippines, where he had spent part of his childhood, had something to do with his posting in the South Pacific. "During World War II, Presnell rose to the rank of lieutenant-colonel with the Signal Corps and became chief photography officer for combat films in the Southwest Pacific. His work was deemed of such importance that General Douglas MacArthur permitted him to attend military staff briefings." At least three children of Hollywood contemporaries served under Presnell Sr.'s command: Jesse Lasky Jr.; Bernard Small (1918–2003), the son of the outrageously prolific producer Edward Small (1891–1977), and Jack Hively (1910–95), a distinguished and popular director himself and the son of editor George Hively (1889–1950) as well as brother of George Hively Jr. (1933–2006), who made his career mainly in television.[87]

Because of the devastating surprise attack on Pearl Harbor, along with existing anti-Asian racism and conventional antiforeigner prejudice, it was not difficult for US government information providers, formal and informal, to paint the Japanese as America's lethal enemy. What proved daunting, though, was the effort to inform the public about the character of the conflict in the Pacific and, in particular, the jungle warfare in which US troops were engaged. In early January 1944, Presnell wrote to his superior, Lt. Col. H. W. Mixson, attempting to explain why it was so difficult to produce a movie about the war with the Japanese. First, he needed the appropriate manpower. "In trying to put together a picture of professional quality, it is necessary to have experienced craftsmen. Sgt. Small is not an editor. He would be considered an assistant cutter in Hollywood. He can handle film, cut and splice, physically. But the reasons for cutting here and not there, is an editor cutter's job and is only learned by years of doing it." Presnell Sr. was finding that many of the men who had been sent to him were mismatched to the roles to which they had been assigned. The exception was Jesse Lasky Jr.: "Lt. Lasky is burning the midnight oil on the narration which must be ready for each reel as it is dubbed."[88]

Presnell Sr. submitted extremely detailed reports that included not only criticism of the way things were proceeding but also constructive recommendations regarding how to conduct photographic work, writ large. The War Department had requested "the making of special motion picture productions in this area," the southwest Pacific, "for a possible release in the United States. These productions are to be of the documentary type such as *Desert Victory* (1943) and to tell the story of the manner in which the war is being waged here."[89] In an earlier secret memo, Presnell Sr. lamented that "for the size of the theater, the distances involved and the extent of the operations, the number of photographers [for] both still and motion pictures ... is pitifully small. ... The entire situation here reflects a lack of understanding of the importance of photographic coverage, as well as the service that could be rendered by a Photographic Company to the Theater Commander."[90] Despite desperate problems, under Presnell's command work progressed on the movie *Dexterity*, which was later renamed *Attack!*[91] *Dexterity* was a better, more appropriate and descriptive title, but it was replaced because it was the army's code word for the operation.[92]

The movie *Attack!* as it emerged was focused on "the invasion of New Britain Island." An unattributed prose narrative of the making of the film was most likely written by Presnell Sr. With him apparently as the guide, and with the names of key figures included, it is clear that Jews were far out of proportion to their numbers in the development of both still and motion picture photography in the Pacific theater. Jesse Lasky Jr. was the sparkplug. Many of the enlisted men behind the still photography, working with Australian Maurice Foster, were apparently Jews. Foster himself had produced, complementary to the work of Presnell, one of the most important photographic survey reports, replete with a host of critical, practical suggestions.[93] Presnell Sr., overall, was something akin to the director/producer, with Lasky Jr. as the chief "narrator," while it seemed that he undertook vast directorial work as well. The rough directing and writing roles needed an allowance for flexibility for the cameramen. Unlike Hollywood movie directors, Presnell Sr. did not "tell them what to shoot, deeming it inadvisable under combat conditions." Cameramen shot fifty-five thousand feet of film. "The staff worked as long as thirty-six hours at a stretch. Lt. Lasky wrote the narration. Col. Presnell and Lt. Geoffroy ran around to private homes [in

Sydney, Australia] and every possible source in search of records for appropriate music and for a sound track. Noises had to be simulated for rockets and liquid fire."[94] The production did not seem to be going well. "Abject depression gripped the staff. They were dissatisfied with *Dexterity* and with each other. Above all the faults they found with the picture they were making was this outstanding complaint—they felt *Dexterity* lacked action. Photographers had risked their lives in every engagement, and yet there was not one shot of the enemy, except dead or captured, there was not one sequence of a counter-charge, though many had taken place, there was not one sweeping wide-angle take of American troops attacking in a traditional manner." The landscape itself was inscrutable. "One fact became apparent—that jungle warfare, in its stark actuality is unphotogenic. A camera can seldom shoot more than a couple of yards ahead of its lens for foliage. There is no picturesque mass movement of troops in attack; patrols and the lone soldier carry the battle. The enemy is heard and felt but seldom seen in this combat of cover and concealment, and when he counter-attacks in force, he does it at night."[95] Without attaching its fortunes, come what may, to any one person, Presnell Sr. affirmed that the movie would sink or swim on the basis of what Lasky was bringing to the project. "If *Dexterity* was to be good, it must draw its worth from the story it told, from the feeling it carried, from the intelligence it could convey of what amphibious war in the jungle-pocked Southwest Pacific was like, and it could not be borne alone on the stirring spectacle of far-flung battle scenes."[96]

Presnell's crew came through with the goods. Covering the Gloucester Beach invasion, December 26,[97] Private Ira Rosenberg was armed with his personal Super Ikonta B (still) camera, with eighteen rolls of size 120 film, and for his 35mm Eyemo motion picture camera, about ten magazines.

> And then the rain started. It continued through a night of misery in which insects, flares from Japanese planes overhead, and continuous firing added to the torments of the photographers in their muddy fox holes. They placed their camera equipment on logs and covered it with a poncho. But the following morning inspection revealed that all but the K Eyemo and Private Rosenberg's Ikonta B were inoperative beyond emergency repair. The equipment was drenched and sand had blown into the lenses. (The best still pictures of the operation [were] obtained, not with Signal Corps equipment, but by Pvt. Rosenberg with his Ikonta.) Lt. Payne remained to direct Pvt. Rosenberg and Pfc [David] Silver in operating the two good cameras.[98]

David Silver had also been a very specific personnel request by Presnell, from the same group that included Allen H. Miner, who was a relative of Jesse

Lasky Jr.[99] Miner, who was a recent Yale graduate, became "a combat photographer during World War II, making newsreel footage of beachhead battles in the South Pacific. His camera recorded Gen. Douglas MacArthur's landing in the Philippines," directed by Lasky Jr. After the war, Miner mainly worked in television, with credits for *Wagon Train*, *Perry Mason*, and *The Untouchables*, and was a director for episodes of *Route 66*, *Mission: Impossible*, *Then Came Bronson*, *Dr. Kildare*, and *The Twilight Zone*.[100]

How good was *Dexterity*/*Attack!*? Robert B. Patterson, the undersecretary of war, informed Major General H. C. Ingles, the chief signal officer: "I showed the film *Dexterity* to the members of the House Military Affairs Committee this morning and they were all enthusiastic in their praise of it."[101] This was a not-quite-finished version of the film, most likely closest to *The Battle of New Britain*, which was reused for newsreels and appeared as at least two movies: *Attack in the Pacific* and *Attack! The Battle of New Britain* (1944).[102] "I myself believe it to be the best ground combat picture that has been made thus far. It is an excellent job for which you and the pictorial Division of the Signal Corps and the men who actually took the pictures deserve great credit. I trust that in the editing to be done on this picture a great deal of the grim stuff will be left in. I believe we should get the picture out promptly so that it will be given widespread distribution to the public."[103]

The film holds up well more than eighty years later. "This picture is dedicated," it proclaims, "to the officers and men you are about to see making the first landing on the Jap held island of New Britain. Particularly to those who lie beneath wooden crosses marking the road to Tokyo."[104] It is important to recall that at this point the United States expected the Pacific war to last much longer, culminating in a land invasion of Japan that would entail massive losses of lives. Surprisingly, anti-Japanese invective is relatively subtle. The environment itself is painted as the greatest obstacle. The one hundred thousand Japanese soldiers on New Britain were "expecting visitors." And "besides the Japs, there's always the jungle." Repeating the appeals of Presnell, Lasky's narration detailed the conditions: "Never before in history has a war on such scale been fought on such difficult battlefields. Looks pretty, doesn't it? Pretty as a picture in a prewar travel advertisement. But how is it to live in? Ask Joe Soldier. A jungle-clad paradise crawling with bugs, snakes, and lizards. Spiders. Ask him about sweating out a march through blazing equatorial heat. Ask him about the smell. That wet stench of the jungle. And don't let him forget to mention those tropical sunsets, bringing the malarial mosquito."[105] These lines were used in at least two of the film versions. The film shares many of the same features as the *Why We Fight* series and scores, if not hundreds, of other US films at the time, with maps clearly showing not just battle locales but also their relationship to one another in the Pacific theater and beyond. It illustrates and articulates what the soldiers in different settings were being asked to do, and why, and how they were being supported. It also showed the human cost, including some grisly images of men severely injured and killed in battle. The objective of vividly portraying the distinctive character of jungle warfare was definitely achieved.

Presnell Sr., who had exacting standards for himself, was able to put the work of his unit into context when he was apprised of what had been produced in the other battlefronts. In the spring of 1944 he was called back to the United States, most likely for planning involving the awaited invasion of Japan. "I discovered to my complete surprise while in Washington," Presnell Sr. wrote to Peter Keane, another Hollywood intimate whom he had recruited, "that all of the high-powered directors and cameramen they have sent to other theaters have turned in nothing of any great moment, at least nothing that tells a story in complete continuity as our picture does. This is the thing that aroused so much attention in Washington. They wanted to know how it had been done. On investigation I found that cameramen are not assigned to proper places or in the echelon of activity as we assigned them on the New Britain landing, but that they were doing it by hit and miss over there, which is the reason they are getting no coordinated results. There is some talk of shipping me over there to do the same thing. What a headache. Anyway I'm trying to stress the idea of planning an operation rather than trusting entirely to luck."[106]

Presnell Sr. did not fully appreciate the secret of his own success, what had made him and the execution of his project distinctive and, in so many ways, superior. He had come into the field with some standing, having been a military man in the US Army Reserve, even though his livelihood had been with the press and Hollywood. He also had more knowledge of the Philippines, through personal experience, than most of those who found themselves there. He meticulously sought to assemble a good team for film work, drawing from Hollywood itself, if at all possible. Although Jesse Lasky Jr. had held responsible positions in Astoria, he did not have anything approaching the military status to decide where he would be assigned for active service when he opted for an active battle front. He had imagined himself going to France, possibly because he spoke French.[107] But he wound up in the Philippines because Presnell Sr. suspected that he would be up for the challenge.

Besides underestimating his own ability to size up the situation and gather the squad fit to purpose, Presnell Sr. also seems to have underestimated how his personal personnel choices had a profound impact on how the film and production work was carried out. The young men he put in place, no matter their rank, were respected for their expertise and were able to call the shots to get the pictures they needed. For Presnell's "Stilwell" movie, realized as *The Stilwell Road* (1945), he was even more assertive in choosing his company, with a list that included commercial photographer Wilfrid Zogbaum, who would gain fame as a painter and sculptor.[108] Jesse Lasky Jr. recalled, in a rather humorous way, his surprise at issuing orders to superior officers—which were acted on with the greatest obedience. He was lower in rank, and he had to salute them first—but he was in charge. For a later engagement, Lasky Jr. recalled in his autobiography: "I was attached to the 96th Infantry, and embarrassingly in command of the combat photographic mission—embarrassingly, because my officers included ranks up to Lieutenant Colonels. I had to salute almost everyone before giving them orders."[109] Even before he was dispatched to the Philippines, Lasky Jr. was entrusted with decisions not necessarily corresponding to his rank.

In addition to giving Lasky Jr. the prerogative of control, Presnell Sr. worked assiduously with him on one extremely important administrative aspect of the *Dexterity* production: they were eventually allowed, after rather protracted efforts, to use "reconstructions," reenactments, and stock footage. The confidential memo, which Presnell Sr. took as his green light, stated: "In cases where it is impossible to photograph actual combat of important action in connection with making historical campaign pictures you are authorized to reenact such scenes. Plainly indicate on caption sheets such reenacted scenes.[110] There also was a starkly contradictory order passed, with no explanation, in January 1944: "The CinC directs that the historical campaign pictures be limited strictly to actual battle scenes without the reenactment of any action."[111] This was, apparently, ignored.

Presnell wrote expressly to Lt. Col. H. W. Mixson that "all scenes to be staged will be written [in] full by Lasky and shot from the script."[112] The use of reenactments was taken for granted in the *Why We Fight* series—yet Jules Buck was singled out and harshly disparaged for the practice in *The Battle of San Pietro* (dir. John Huston, 1945).[113] Presnell and Lasky Jr. knew that it would be impossible to craft a coherent story without adding elements from outside the context of the battle per se. This was neither dishonest nor duplicitous. The story was told both creatively and forthrightly. But the invasion footage itself would not have sufficed, which was apparent to Lasky Jr., especially as he was frantically writing the script. Immediately before the title credits appear for *Attack! The Battle for New Britain*, the titles announced: "The picture you are about to see is authentic in every detail. No scenes have been re-enacted or staged."[114] Throughout the war, the line between documentary and reenactment had been blurred beyond recognition. Most likely Presnell and Lasky Jr. would not have approved of this explicit opening statement. But the very style of the announcement reveals that it was a late addition, spliced in by someone, or some persons, other than the original filmmakers. Interestingly, after the opening narration, Presnell's *The Stilwell Road* adds the rejoinder: "Two close-ups of individuals have been re-enacted to permit live sound."[115] Although this was certainly true, there no doubt were other scenes in the film that did not precisely fit the narration.

Arguably the most dramatic moment of Lasky Jr.'s adventure on Cape Gloucester did not, however, find its way to the film. It was a result of his unit being a decoy designed by General MacArthur's strategy to keep the Japanese away from the major American landing site.

> Dug in on that fringe of jungle with our backs to the beaches, the 112th Cavalry seemed likely to follow in the footsteps of the defenders of the Alamo. Reinforcement was difficult to ferry over because the Japanese Imperial Air Force controlled the sky with swarms of Zeros. But rescue was on the way. A detachment of highly trained jungle fighters was filtered across from Finchhaven under cover of darkness. They landed behind us, passed through our lines and into the jungle. They worked round behind the Japanese positions and infiltrated them, which took the pressure off us and made life a lot easier for us all.[116]

Lasky Jr.'s mind raced back to Hollywood, not only because of the fast-moving, spectacular rescue of which he had been a beneficiary.

"How many times," he asked, "had I and other film people perpetuated the fable of embattled settlers rescued from Red Indians by the US Cavalry? That night our cliché came home to roost, for when the dawn rose over the Arawe we saw that our rescuers were in fact a detachment of American Indians, come to get the 112th Cavalry out of trouble. United by the common cause, they had come from a score of different tribes, many of whom were traditional enemies who did not even have a common tongue."[117] At this time Lasky Jr. had no inkling that military planners realized that the Navajo possessed specific cultural capital that could serve the US armed forces in an extraordinary way. American Indians were playing a large role in the war, overall. The tribe's language, high advisers in the military were advised, did not conform to known European models. This myth is not wildly exaggerated: the Navajo gave the Americans a communication barrier against the Axis that proved impenetrable. As we now know, code breaking and code making was a huge, if not decisive, dimension of the war effort.

"I resolved," Lasky Jr. firmly asserted, "that if I got out of New Britain I would never again write a scene in which the army arrived in the nick of time to save the settlers from the redskins. But the promise was broken on my first film after the war—*Unconquered*. It proves, I suppose, that nobody can trust a Hollywood promise."[118] *Unconquered* (dir. DeMille, 1947), starring Gary Cooper, did not just glorify the white man coming to the rescue. Owing more to Cecil B. DeMille than Lasky Jr., the film dripped with anti-Indian hatred. Perhaps Lasky Jr. took some solace from the fact that although *Unconquered* did well at the box office, the studio lost money on it because it was such a costly production.

A later film from the Philippines seems to be largely the work of Lasky, with which Presnell was uninvolved: *Brought to Action!* This was the operation, on the island of Leyte, to which Lasky Sr. had referred when his son was cited for bravery. It was called "the Second Battle of the Philippines," in October 1944, "meant to destroy Japanese bases, air and sea capacity," and to poise the US 3rd and 7th Fleets for what was assumed to be the impending invasion of Japan itself. The Japanese objective in this confrontation, which they were expecting, was for it to be "the final blow" delivered to the United States in the Pacific. The film was produced under the auspices of the OSS in cooperation with the US Navy. The qualifications at the beginning of the film titles were more reasonable than those in Lasky Jr. and Presnell Sr.'s earlier film: "This motion picture is based upon combat photography by [the] US Navy[,] US Marine Corps[,] US Coast Guard[,] US Army Signal Corps[, and] US Army Air Force" and "The Army-Navy Film is authentic." It served as an installment of the *Army-Navy Screen Magazine*, No. 46.

The quality of the film is similar to that of *Attack!* It tells the story well, but the action is even more dramatic, and the air and sea battles lend themselves far better to moviemaking. Although it was a resounding US victory, the movie ended on a melancholy note, warning that a huge part of the war lay in wait and that the sacrifices thus far had been acute. A plane is shown barely making it to the deck of an aircraft carrier. "For every victory men must die," intoned the voice-over. "It was battle-smashed planes like these that told the story of the victory eloquently. For there, in this plane damaged beyond repair, an American airman died at his battle station. His shipmates felt it fitting that he be buried this way." After a brief ceremony, the wreckage containing the deceased airman was pushed into the sea. "For now, let him be nameless. Let him be all the sons of America who had died for our cause. Let his death make that cause all the more precious to us, the living."[119] Lasky Jr. said little about this film, besides admitting that he had made it.[120]

An earlier picture, produced at the Astoria studios, that might have been supervised by Lasky Jr., *Life Line*, was a particularly effective complement to *Attack!* and *Brought to Action*. Written by Daniel Taradash, it was, in part, a newsreel of some of the early battles in the Philippines, mainly Rendova Island and Munda, "the Malta of the Pacific" in the Solomon Islands from June 30 to early August 1943.[121] Like Jules Buck and Lasky Jr., Taradash started his military service, voluntarily, before Pearl Harbor.[122] After the war began, he was called to active duty in the Signal Corps on "Special Orders" from the president.[123] Along with showing battle scenes, *Life Line* introduced viewers to the jungle environment and stressed that the sick and wounded needed exceptional resources, care, and attention. In addition to blood plasma, for which the public could contribute through blood banks, certain drugs were needed to treat the wounded and ill from that part of the Pacific theater. Taradash later recalled that he was "working with 'film' there," probably meaning editing, "which a writer would normally never get near in Hollywood."[124]

"Two battles were fought here," the narrator asserted. "One against the Japs. A second against another enemy: the swift approach of death. A new battle with medicine as ammunition, medical instruments as weapons. Here in the jungle one end of a life line from home. Morphine, atebrine, plasma, quinine sulfate, sulfa guanidine, sulfanilamide, bandages—wounds, infection." Broken bodies are shown being carried away. In addition to supporting the later films, and serving Rosten's aim of having a diverse range of media about any one subject, *Life Line* makes for an interesting comparison, cinematically. The narrator apologizes for the poor quality of the film work, attributing it to the unprecedented conditions. "Parts of this film are badly photographed. Some of it is underexposed, and there are light flashes. But forgive the cameramen. They were in danger of being killed."[125] The earlier and later films share, however, a sense of urgency and of drawing those distant, fellow Americans "carrying on in Pennsylvania, Illinois, New York" into the action as *their own* experience. The emphasis is in the narration. Taradash's commendation for *Life Line* was well deserved.[126] *Life Line* was the centerpiece of a highly successful fundraising and publicity campaign for the American Red Cross.[127] Compared to *Life Line*, the quality of the photography of *Attack!* and *Brought to Action* reveal, though, the extent to which the training scheme and hands-on approach of Lasky Jr. made a huge difference.

Certainly Presnell Sr. and Lasky Jr. were satisfied with *Attack!* and the various versions that followed. There is no record, however, of them being informed about the reception of the picture. In 1946, when the film was placed in the Museum of Modern Art in New York, Arthur Rosenheimer Jr., the assistant curator, shared his own insight with Presnell Sr. "It may interest and please you to know," he wrote, "that *Attack!* was extremely popular with the troops. I finished up the war by running a film library in Italy, and we were always able to judge the popularity of any particular subject by the number of times it was re-booked by any one outfit. *Attack!* was one of the few films (*San Pietro* and the VD subjects were the others) that was out every night. It is still a most impressive film."[128] The movie *Across the Pacific*, directed by John Huston and Vincent Sherman (1942), attempted to feature the Pacific theater for a *Casablanca* type film, even starring Humphrey Bogart, in a similar role to that of Rick Blaine, along with Sidney Greenstreet.[129] Little wonder that *Across the Pacific* is nearly forgotten. It's wooden and preachy compared with the fluid, subtle *Casablanca*. Explaining why America's part in the Pacific was significant was immeasurably better served by the unheralded effort of Lasky Jr.

Along with his insight about the popularity of *Attack!*, Rosenheimer was also in possession of an intriguing piece of misinformation about it. He had approached Presnell Sr. seeking "credits" for *Attack!* assuming that it was unusual for a film to have no information supplied concerning its origins and production, outside of its auspices of the US Army Signal Corps. Presnell Sr. politely enlightened Rosenheimer that he "was not surprised that credits are completely missing on *Attack!* as the War Department tried to maintain complete anonymity on all of its pictures." Of course this was not quite the case, as Capra and selected others did have their names in bold. "It was probably a good thing at the time," Presnell surmised. "But now that the war is over it is possible to tell who did what and how it was done. And some of these postwar notes should be very interesting for historians in the years to come."[130] Prennell's use of the word "tell" here is ambiguous: it could mean simple identification of those responsible, and/or "reveal," as information that was withheld earlier, for a purpose.

Presnell Sr. did, indeed, provide a valuable service by preserving his papers, which are not replicated, or even barely reflected, in official sources. He did not share with Rosenheimer what they both knew: that it might have looked off-putting if the names that appeared in the credits for War Department and US Army Signal Corps films revealed the extent to which they overlapped with Hollywood and with Hollywood's rather distinctive ethnic profile. Presnell Sr. danced around the issue, careful not to address it directly. "I was a little amused," he confided, "by the pencilled notation you spoke of to the effect that 'Colonel Calhoun made it.'" Possibly Rosenheimer or someone else from the museum had attempted to find out from the army who was responsible for the movie. "Just who Colonel Calhoun is I have no idea," Presnell Sr. volunteered. "Probably someone on the Public Relations staff in Washington. He certainly had nothing to do with the making of this picture at any time or at any place."[131] "Colonel Calhoun" sounds like the kind of name that could have been invented by Spigelgass and Rosten when they were pressed to name an author. It does not seem as if there were many exchanges such as that between Rosenheimer and Presnell, prompting an accounting for who, precisely, was responsible for what in the realm of wartime filmmaking. The vast majority of those involved, however, agreed with Presnell that it was the right thing to do at the time. Seventeen years later, in 1963, the Signal Corps was comfortable enough to dismiss the former policy on anonymity to allow the Hollywood Museum to use the information on credits given to it by Presnell. The head of the Signal Corps graciously admitted that the men identified by Presnell deserved mention. "In presenting his personal copies of these World War II documentaries, Colonel Presnell gave full credit for their production to the enlisted men and junior officers who photographed them in combat. Appropriate credit to them would be appreciated."[132]

In addition to supplying the print and list of production credits for *Attack!* to Hollywood's film museum, Presnell Sr. did the same for the second project for which he was chiefly responsible, *The Stilwell Road* (1945). Narrated by Ronald Reagan, the documentary about the China-Burma-India front, which was much less known than either the European or Pacific theaters, was nevertheless "the story of one of the great victories of World War II." It depicted what began with a "humiliating defeat," then "flaming courage, and hard won victory."[133] In numerous ways it follows the pattern set by Rosten, clearly illustrating the interconnectedness of disparate locales and the vital importance of logistics in the conduct of the war. More than sixty thousand men helped build the road itself, which mainly was used by the British, Indian, and Chinese (Nationalist) armies to ship supplies and troops from India to Burma. This was critical in keeping the Japanese from reaching the Indian subcontinent from the Pacific.

Although neither Russians nor the Soviet Union figured in the building of the Stilwell Road, they were essential to the story. The road built by the Chinese in 1937–38 was for the purpose of thwarting Japanese aggression along the former silk and jade route. They paved a modern roadway for "caravans of guns and fuel, ammunition and food, across the land bridge of Burma to China, to keep that country alive in its struggle against Japan—just as Russia had been kept alive in its battle against Germany by the land bridge of Iran. The Nazis tried to destroy that lifeline. But Iran was saved by the British at El Alamein and by the Russians at Stalingrad. China was not as fortunate. One month after Pearl Harbor the Japanese struck at the land bridge of Burma. This is the story of the destruction of that bridge"—which Stilwell, in the film, calls a "defeat that was humiliating as hell." It continues as the story of "the men who fought and died to build it, so that China could fight on."[134]

The task assigned to Stilwell was regarded as possibly "insurmountable."[135] The film underscored the uncompromising, tough-as-nails personality of

General Stilwell as the driving force of the mission's success. Yet Presnell Sr. also stressed that the key to the gargantuan effort to build the road was international cooperation. "You will see," the opening narration begins, "many battles and many stirring scenes, but more than anything else this is the story of Scots, Irish, English, Welsh, Australians, New Zealanders, Indians, Gurkhas, Burmese, Africans, Chinese, and Americans, and how they fought and planned side by side for a common objective, the achievement of total victory."[136] It could not have been accomplished without absolute coordination between very different nations and peoples in an extraordinarily democratic fashion. "Success was made possible only by the ability of men of all nations to work together," and "never was there such a polyglot army"—which might well have been true.[137] The "lesson" was hammered home: "Unless we, the free men of the world, learn the lesson that it teaches, we will never be able to maintain the peace, the freedom and the security for which all of us have fought."[138] Along with writing and producing for movies and television, nothing of which is especially memorable, Presnell was an ardently enthusiastic, moderately anti-Communist internationalist, becoming a "film promotion officer" for the United Nations, which was consistent with the *Stilwell Road* message.[139]

Rosten's agenda had also emphasized that winning the peace through internationalism was nearly as important as winning the war, so the movies marking the transition from wartime were of great consequence. One of the most important of these was a joint American and British effort distributed by Columbia Pictures, *The True Glory* (1945), produced by Britain's Captain Carol Reed and US Captain Garson Kanin, admittedly with "any number of talented assistants"—including, among others, Paddy Chayefsky, Peter Ustinov, and Claude Dauphin.[140] The movie covers the final stages of the war, mainly by following General Dwight D. Eisenhower. Its publicity explicitly related the human cost of the filming: of the "combat cameramen" from the Allied nations "who shot the film, thirty-two were killed, sixteen were reported missing, and one-thousand and ten were wounded. It is one of the most difficult collaborative efforts in movie history."[141] Reed and Kanin "had to reduce some 6,500,000 feet of shots to theatrical coherence (it runs eighty-four minutes), and to outline clearly the history of one of the world's major campaigns:" what started in Southampton and concluded in Berlin.[142] The film furthermore showcased the "comradeship and cooperation which war has taught," illustrating both the "teamwork among the men of many services and of several nations" as well as the stress on "ordinary servicemen"[143]—despite the overarching figure of General Dwight D. Eisenhower.

One of Spigelgass's most important projects, likewise, was undertaken during the transition from war to peace and was more at the behest of the United Nations than the US Army: the Academy Award–winning documentary *Seeds of Destiny* (dir. David Miller, 1946), for which he does not receive official credit.[144] The opening epigraph is Matthew 7:18: "A good tree cannot bring forth evil fruit, neither can a corrupt tree bring forth good fruit."[145] In a symposium in Spigelgass's honor and memory, David Miller wrote of "the deeply personal debt to Lennie which can never be fully repaid by an Army crew of 10 men—or by the millions of children all around the world whose lives have been saved through the efforts of an organization called 'UNRRA' the United Nations Relief and Rehabilitation Administration." Miller relates that "Lt. Colonel Spigelgass just happened to be in a general's office" when an "urgent request" to produce a film came in. It required a dramatization of the "desperate need for relief and rehabilitation of war-ravaged countries around the globe." He volunteered, equipped with the knowledge of how exactly to go about it. "His personal recommendations," Miller asserted, "were followed to the letter." The film *Seeds of Destiny* was a critical success and it also "raised hundreds of millions of dollars."[146] Written by Private Art Arthur, produced and directed by Maj. David Miller, it remains one of the most outstanding films on the state of post–Second World War Europe. It was produced as number 75 of the *Army-Navy Screen Magazine*.

Jesse Lasky Jr. might have guessed that a Hollywood gang comprised mainly of "members of the tribe" would frame their documentary with the New Testament, the gospel of Matthew. "I'd never been Bar Mitzvah," Lasky Jr. claimed, boasting of what an utterly non-Jewish Jew he was, "or even inside a synagogue, and in boarding school days been a leader of the Christian Endeavour Society."[147] Somehow, though, he managed to pick up enough Yiddish to know that getting paid *bubkas* (nothing) wasn't good.[148] Lasky Jr. mined a rich vein of humor and irony in being taken as a representative Jew, expert in Jewish matters—"the company Hebrew"—in some of the Hollywood productions in which he was involved, especially Cecil B. DeMille's blockbuster, *The Ten Commandments* (1956). "Once it was established in his mind that I was the unit Jew, however, DeMille would brook no protests."[149] True, he was born Jewish, but he had had absolutely no Jewish education, or even exposure to perfunctory "observance." Both his parents made concerted efforts, just short of converting to another faith, to distance themselves from any and all forms of institutional Judaism.[150] He was likely aware that Robert Presnell's son, yet another Hollywood writer, had a greater command and concern for explicitly Jewish issues than he did.

Sharing his father's passion for internationalism, Robert Presnell Jr. was sensitive to the plight of the oppressed as an activist in the human rights organization Amnesty International and SANE, dedicated to alerting Americans to the danger of the nuclear arms race.[151] In 1947 Presnell Jr. and his wife, Marsha Hunt,[152] joined the Committee for the First Amendment "along with other Hollywood figures such as John Huston, William Wyler, Humphrey Bogart, and Lauren Bacall. The group was founded as a way of supporting the Hollywood Ten, a group of writers and directors who refused to tell the House Committee on Un-American Affairs whether they were or had ever been Communist Party Members." In the mid-1950s, Presnell and Hunt traveled as emissaries of the United Nations, focusing on combating hunger and conflict resolution.[153] "Inexplicably," Marsha Hunt recalled some years later, "Robert was not blacklisted. I cannot tell you why. He was certainly more outspoken in his political pronouncements and outrage about what was going on, and enjoyed a good argument. He was without any kind of political discretion. And yet he kept working. Thank heaven. He was never a top-salary screenwriter, but he did work—and beautifully."[154]

Presnell Jr.'s liberal humanitarianism apparently influenced his choice of film projects. His decision in the late 1950s to tackle *Conspiracy of Hearts* (dir. Ralph Thomas, 1960), a film about Jewish children rescued by nuns in Italy during the Second World War, was unusual and is underappreciated as a significant treatment of the Holocaust. It was nominated for a Golden Globe for "best film promoting international understanding." Bosley Crowther, writing for the *New York Times*, found much to commend in the film, but reproached it for tugging on conventional heartstrings.[155] "The pathos of little children caught in the agony of war is always a solid staple of sentiment on the screen. It has been well and touchingly presented in any number of films. And it is offered again with deep compassion in *Conspiracy of Hearts*, a British film made on location in northern Italy." The sympathy for "Jewish orphans funneled into a reception camp in Italy in the later years of World War II—is combined with the further feeling that naturally generates toward gentle nuns doing courageous and charitable service in the name of God. The children are being smuggled out of the camp by nuns and hidden away in a convent until they can be passed along, presumably to Palestine. And the risks of the nuns in doing this humanitarian thing are the charge that explodes the melodrama in this emotion-laden film."[156]

Crowther judged *Conspiracy of Hearts* to be a rather "ordinary" movie, "in so far as artistry is concerned." He found it "contrived," "rather conventionally plotted, and a little too obviously 'performed.'" The script by Robert Presnell Jr. was too predictable: "There's the nun who resists the daring venture of smuggling children out of the camp, until her heart is captured by one of the saddest little girls. There's the novice with whom the nice Italian major is obviously in love. There's the iron-willed Nazi colonel and his brutal aide de camp. There's the radiant mother superior who has great daring and understands everything. There is also a bit of humorous by-play to go along with the poignant device of smuggling a rabbi into the convent to conduct Yom Kippur services for the orphaned children. The sisters are worried and reluctant lest this be a sacrilege. The mother superior has to instruct them on Jewish ritual. The homely humor is along this line. . . . The very material of the drama is sufficient to give it poignancy, and this is passed along in generous measure in this production from Betty E. Box."[157]

The stuff of the drama was certainly compelling, but Crowther—possibly because he prided himself as an opponent of expressly political films—did not recognize it for being pathbreaking. Despite its conventional aspects, *Conspiracy of Hearts* confronted Nazi antisemitism in a serious, historical, and sophisticated manner. Although it did not purport to be a true story, and the screenplay from which Presnell Jr. worked was set in a post–World War II displaced persons camp, not a concentration camp, it is in many respects remarkable and historically plausible.[158] The beginning blends newsreel coverage of the fall of Mussolini's regime in the summer of 1943 and the subsequent Nazi takeover into the film's fictional tale. To some extent it indulges the same cliché of blanket Italian resistance to the Nazis as displayed in *Life Is Beautiful* (dir. Roberto Benigni, 1997).[159] But it also shows Italians' willingness to comply with the Nazis, including turning on each other, and probes the range of opinions among the nuns concerning how putting themselves in danger for the sake of the Jewish children could be justified by their own faith. On the whole, it is much more realistic than fanciful or contrived. In contrast to Crowther's dismissal of the film's artistry, the juxtaposition of the Yom Kippur service and the simultaneous celebration of Mass by the nuns is cinematically brilliant. And the treatment of Judaism, at that time and place, is as good as it gets in the movies. Alas, it puts *The Ten Commandments* to shame on that score. Its American rights were bought by Paramount.

As often happens with movies, figuring out who is responsible for the script is convoluted, but Robert Presnell Jr. was most likely the screenwriter. Some believe that he was a "front" for the blacklisted Dalton Trumbo. The *Los Angeles Times* did not mention *Conspiracy of Hearts* in Presnell Jr.'s 1986 obituary.[160] The "story," that is, the work on which the script was based, was attributed to Dale Pitt (1931–2008). Pitt was a voluntary "front" for Adrian Scott (1911–72), a blacklisted writer who had written the story for television. The producer, Betty E. Box (1915–99), said it was a hard-fought struggle to get it made by the

Rank Organization (UK), where she was under contract. "They said, 'It's religion, it's nuns, it's wartime, who wants to know? Tell you what, make us another *Doctor* and you can do it!'" Box's *Doctor* films were comedies about medics in training, something like the much later American TV series *Scrubs* (created by Bill Lawrence, 2001–10). "And the interesting thing was," Box continued, "that that year in the UK the three top box-office films were the *Doctor* film (*Doctor in Love*), *Conspiracy of Hearts* and *Carry On (Constable*)."[161] *Conspiracy of Hearts*, then, more than held its own against proven low-brow comedic mainstays.

The making of *Conspiracy of Hearts* was embedded in an irony that probably would have been appreciated by Jesse Lasky Jr. had he known. Betty E. Box, who worked her way up through the movie business making "propaganda," training, and industrial films (the staple of the Hollywood writers during World War II) for Verity Films in Britain, owed her opportunity to being born Gentile. Historian Andrew Spicer writes that despite the immense demand for these kinds of wartime movies, "Verity had to vie with numerous other small documentary production companies in what was a highly competitive marketplace." Besides the commercial firms, "the government run Crown film unit, which had first pick of personnel, equipment and film stock was usually given the longer, more prestigious and generously funded commissions." Verity was not the most "polished" of the lot. Sydney Box, and by extension, his sister Betty, "benefited from Establishment prejudice. He wrote to [his wife] Muriel that the Air Ministry was willing to work with him because it was 'apparently looking for an extra company to add to their lists and they won't do business with Jews.'" Of course, this was beyond Box's control, and they themselves exhibited great "energy, organizational ability and skill in coordinating the efforts of a diverse range of people."[162] It helped, though, that they weren't named Lasky.

5

Hard-Boiled Hollywood Justice

While there is no firm evidence of friendship between them, Jesse Lasky Jr. had a soft spot for his slightly younger and more illustrious contemporary Budd Schulberg. Budd, like Jesse Jr., was born into show business aristocracy and was, by his own reckoning, "a Hollywood prince."[1] Budd's father Ben (also known as BP, 1892–1957) had worked as boss of production, one of two supervisors for Jesse Lasky Sr.'s Famous Players studio,[2] honing some Hollywood-hype gems ("America's Sweetheart" and "The 'It' Girl,'" to name but two) and with a slew of hits to his credit. The greatest boon to the company was that BP "touched off a cycle of gangster films by recommending that we buy the Ben Hecht story, *Underworld* [dir. Josef von Sternberg, 1927]," Jesse Lasky Sr. recalled in the 1940s. "It was so sordid and savage in content, so different from accepted film fare, that the sales heads were afraid that no amount of effort could drum up business for it. But the picture was one of the most tremendous hits we ever had." And "it was so widely imitated—and still is—that it would seem like a stereotype if you saw it now."[3] Despite being lauded for his moviemaking and promotional genius,[4] like Jesse Lasky Sr., Ben Schulberg died feeling neglected, dejected, disrespected, and poor by Hollywood standards.

Lasky Jr.'s spirited defense of Budd Schulberg was a backhanded way of defending himself against the charge that he owed his career to nepotism. Outside of the movie colony, Lasky Jr. opined: "Nepotism has been an honored tradition. Sons followed in their father's footsteps because they made loyal assistants and trustworthy successors; because, expected to carry on the job, they had assimilated it by association. But nepotism in show business has too often meant the abuse of opportunity through the misuse of influence."[5] From the 1920s to the 1950s, Hollywood's "ambivalent climate of sin and sanctity, public morality and private license for whatever morally destructive effect it had on the tycoons themselves, was frequently disastrous to their progeny. It would appear that the sons and daughters of the old film-makers had a higher proclivity to maladjustment than other offspring of success."[6] In large part due to the "ruthlessness" of their fathers, Lasky Jr. affirmed: "I've seen the neurotic wrecks, overdriven like engines unable to attain the high-speed ascendancies they thought their fathers demanded of them—because the fault was not always the father's, it was as often due to the son's inability to accept their own mediocrity."[7]

Yet "there were always outstanding exceptions. Budd Schulberg, son of the mighty BP [Ben Percival], became one of America's first-rank novelists, drawing on the experience of his own growth through the dream factory to write *What Makes Sammy Run?* and the immortal *The Disenchanted*."[8] Another screenwriter colleague, Val Lewton, Budd Schulberg's immediate boss at the David O. Selznick studios, said that Budd "impressed me as a young man of more than considerable talent, good character, and fine sense of knowing how to live in the world and get on with its peoples." Having begun modestly in the "story department," Budd Schulberg gained mounting acclaim "as both a novelist and a screenplay writer," according to Lewton. "This is a well-deserved success, because he is both hard-working and imaginative, a rare combination in a writer," which "has never for one moment gone to his head, or made him any less appreciative of other people's problems."[9] But Budd was one of Hollywood's bad boys, as the author of the exposé *What Makes Sammy Run?*—only slightly camouflaged fiction about the inner workings of the brutal studio system. Although Lasky Jr. did not follow his father's footsteps in every respect, he was a company man, beholden to Cecil B. DeMille and generally averse to rocking the movie industry's ship of state.[10] Lasky Jr.'s own autobiography is superficially cast as being critical of Hollywood, but the narrative reveals him as one of tinseltown's guardians.

Budd Schulberg was a more independent and tempestuous sort. He was a writer and a fighter. He boxed, a bit, and, at least for a while, toughed it out on the football team at Deerfield Academy, one of America's more sports-minded elite boarding schools. While thoughtful, he gave vent to his passions more exuberantly than most, even for Hollywood. Beyond the movies, he struck out into different realms. For several years, he was boxing editor for *Sports Illustrated*, one of the most important magazines on athletics and culture in general from the 1950s to the 1990s. Until the last decade of the twentieth century, one of the less known aspects of Budd Schulberg's career was the part he played at the end of the Second World War, and for the postwar Nuremberg Trial in particular.[11] Given his urge to lavish praise on Budd, Lasky Jr. probably would have added a line or two about Schulberg's postwar service to his character sketches (in his own memoir) had he known.[12] The fact that Budd Schulberg nabbed Leni Riefensthal for the US occupation forces would have been an irresistible tidbit.[13] Lasky Jr. might have found that feat even more remarkable than Schulberg winning an Academy Award for writing *On the Waterfront* (dir. Elia Kazan, 1954).

Lasky Jr. was probably aware, however, that Schulberg had contributed to the kind of films he had supervised in Astoria. But like the work of Anatole Litvak under Frank Capra and Jules Buck with John Huston, Budd Schulberg's World War II efforts, until the 1990s, were largely buried in the movies overseen by the famed directors George Stevens and John Ford.[14] Schulberg himself had been happy to officially bestow the credit for his work to John Ford for over forty years. But there is hardly any evidence of Ford's (or Stevens's) hand in Schulberg's frenetic 1945 endeavors,[15] except for Ford's wisdom of attaching him to his unit. Perhaps due in part to the emergence of the *History Channel*, with its incessant Second World War documentaries along with growing attention to the Holocaust, Budd Schulberg started speaking, writing, producing, and re-releasing films in his seventies related to his own military career. He began to see the complicated intermingling of his moviemaking and government service as personally and historically significant.[16]

Soon after World War II and the Nuremberg trials, Budd Schulberg did, thankfully, write with candor about his work while it was fresh in his mind, and he saved documents that might otherwise have been indefinitely sealed or lost to posterity. In the Charter of the International Military Tribunal, signed on August 8, 1945 (some three months after V-E, "victory in Europe," day), the Allies agreed "to bring charges against defendants for three crimes under international law—crimes against peace, war crimes, and crimes against humanity—as well as a fourth crime, conspiracy, which was a distinctive feature of Anglo-American law. Each of the Allies played a particular, pre-allotted role. The United States, with Robert Jackson as chief prosecutor, took responsibility for conspiracy, and the British, led by Hartley Showcross, for crimes against peace. The Soviets dealt with war crimes and crimes against humanity, as far [as] the Eastern Front was concerned, while the French took responsibility for these crimes for western Europe."[17] Incredibly, Budd Schulberg served the entire gamut of prosecution. The OSS, under whose auspices he worked, is hardly ever mentioned for its role at Nuremberg.

In an insider's Hollywood publication (1946), Schulberg solemnly proclaimed that "November 21 [1945] is a day none of us should forget." The "us" he addresses in the trade journal *The Screen Writer: A Publication of the Screen Writers Guild, Inc.*, are fellow Hollywood screenwriters. "That is the day," he continued, that Nazism went on trial before the first International Military Tribunal ever to sit in judgment on the crime of conspiring to wage war against peaceful nations. As Justice Robert H. Jackson rose to present the case of the United States against the twenty-one top-flight Nazis sitting in the box and the millions of lesser Nazis implicated in the crimes of the SS, the SA, and the General Staff, every one of us on Jackson's staff who had helped in even a small way to make possible this long-awaited event felt a sense of pride, an intimate association with history that was payment in full for all the disappointments, all the snafus, redtape and organizational cul-de-sacs inevitable in setting up almost overnight an international system of social and military justice. And when Jackson, in that inspiring first-salvo promised the defendants that he would prove his case not only with documents and witnesses but by the aid of motion pictures that would convict the Nazi leaders out of their own mouths, all of us who had concentrated on this phase of Operation Justice felt far more compensated than if we had just heard that we had all won Academy Awards and had our salaries doubled.[18]

Justice Jackson's pronouncement of the use of film at the trial was not as full-throated as Schulberg's account attests, but it did have its place. Emphasizing the centrality of teamwork in the mission he headed, Schulberg related his experience concerning the appropriation and use of the Nazi's motion pictures and photographs for the Nuremberg trial.[19] The official commendation awarded to Lt. Budd W. Schulberg, USNR [United States Naval Reserve], April 3, 1946, reads:

For meritorious service rendered the Office of Strategic Services and this unit [the United States Naval Reserve] from 15 July 1945 to 25 November 1945, Lieutenant (j.g) Schulberg, a member of the Field Photographic Branch, with tireless devotion to duty, great vision and initiative, directed the collection, under the most difficult conditions, of vast quantities of photographic evidence of German war guilt and crimes against humanity. The evidence, which includes tens of millions of feet of motion picture film, not only assisted materially in the prosecution of major war criminals but also has tremendous value for the United States Government intelligence and research agencies for the establishment of a permanent photographic record of European political and military developments during the past two critical decades.[20]

While this distills Schulberg's OSS activity fairly well, the term "collection" is misleading. Schulberg not only tracked down, collected, and compiled but immediately set about interpreting it for use by the International Military Tribunal at Nuremberg as well. This work was rendered even more difficult because prosecutors changed their minds, midstream, about what they wanted and what they wanted left out. Budd Schulberg was, in fact, the chief producer-director-editor of the "one-hour presentation of Nazi atrocities" screened to such dramatic effect in the proceedings. Schulberg himself gave greatest credit for this "compilation" to two colleagues: Com. Ray Kellogg (1905–76), whom he had known when Kellogg was with the 20th Century Fox Special Effects Department and who was "acting chief of our unit in [John] Ford's absence,"[21] and lawyer Com. James Britt Donovan (1916–70), who was general counsel for the OSS.[22] (James Britt Donovan was no relation to General William Donovan, whom both men served.) It was James Donovan, among Justice Robert H. Jackson's staff, who was most focused on seeing that "the power of motion pictures were employed for the first time in any major trial."[23] Kellogg mainly edited the film, and Donovan shaped it in such a way as to fit the judicial arguments. Ray Kellogg would be best remembered, though, for masterminding the gust of air from a New York subway grate (on a Hollywood lot) that sent Marilyn Monroe's dress aflutter in *The Seven Year Itch* (dir. Billy Wilder, 1955). Donovan is now mainly recalled through the character played by Tom Hanks in the movie *Bridge of Spies* (dir. Steven Spielberg, 2015). Donovan was noted for brilliantly negotiating the 1962 exchange of captured American pilot Francis Gary Powers for the Soviet spy, Rudolf Abel (William August Fischer), who were then literally traded across a fog-covered bridge.

Kellogg has been given supervisory credit for the one-reel film *That Justice Be Done* (1945), also attributed to George Stevens as director, which was produced as the Nuremberg trial was getting underway.[24] It was presented as an overview of how justice was to be administered in former Nazi Europe toward those who were accused war criminals. The film was unmistakably drawn from the work of Schulberg's unit and most likely written by Schulberg and actor/director Irving Pichel (1891–1954). Although specific information is difficult to pin down, Pichel is said to have "directed several anti-Nazi and pro-British films in the years before the United States entered World War II and directed a fictionalized feature about the OSS itself (*O.S.S.*, 1946)."[25]

It was a matter of military protocol, and an act of Hollywood graciousness, too, for Schulberg to specifically name the members of his team who he knew were unlikely to receive any public recognition. In early July 1945 Schulberg wrote, "As we made plans for our own little D-Day," to gather the film evidence, "our invasion force consisted of myself, Lt. Com. Jack Munroe, Svengali-like-ex-Movietone front-man, who wore a watch inscribed 'to Stinky from Doris' (Duke), [and] Ensign John Bott, a happy-go-lucky Connecticut lad not yet recovered from a demoralizing case of CBI." "CBI" was the acronym for the China-Burma-India theater, as previously discussed, which was infamous as a Sisyphean mission. He also thanked Dr. Carl Jacoby, a German Jewish refugee lawyer, "Magda Policek, an Austrian refugee who spoke a handful of languages, Susan Shestopel, a pint-sized Russian dynamo who had worked for the Soviet newsreel service, cutters Joe Zigman, CPO [Chief Petty Officers] Bob Parrish and Bob Webb, a Sgt. Smith, an earnest speed-writing expert, Sgt. Robert Hiden, a civilian interior decorator metamorphosed through the exigencies of war into an excellent cross-filer, and my brother, Staff Sgt. Stuart Schulberg, an ex-newspaperman drafted from the Marine Corps."[26] Schulberg's younger brother Stuart (1922–79) was the intellectual of the family, having begun college at the University of Chicago, dropping out to join the Marines, and landing in the early OSS. He too had a hand in the family trade of moviemaking, even as a teenager in boarding school, and Stuart Schulberg would have a profound impact on the evolving depth of critical news reporting in a distinguished career for NBC Television news.[27]

Budd Schulberg's article also mentions "two Marine Majors" he does not name, who apparently were there to provide extra muscle, if necessary. Their "lack of knowledge of Nazi history and motion picture technique was supposed to have been compensated for by FBI and counter-intelligence experience."[28] They did, indeed, put their special skills to work. "They had proceeded us to Europe by several weeks and upon our arrival reported triumphantly the discovery of an important cache of secret film they had uncovered" by strong-arming an exhibitor, who "directed them to an abandoned church outside of Munich."[29] But this tale within a tale did not end so gloriously. "Sgt. Schulberg, leading a field team that tracked down this and others of the Majors' leads, succeeded in finding the abandoned church, and indeed it had been turned into an improvised film storehouse. But what the well-meaning officers had neglected to learn was that the film consisted of nothing but dupe-negative's stock!"[30] Budd Schulberg's unit also had a number of former-Nazi informers, the most important of whom was Walter Rode, who told them that "the largest secret vault of the German Film Archive was in the shaft of a granite quarry just outside the village of Reudersdorf, about thirty miles east of Berlin, in the Soviet zone."[31] Rode seems to have promoted himself as a bigger fish than he actually was in the orbit of Goebbels.

Schulberg's second precedent-setting contribution to the Nuremberg trial was its less heralded "four-hour Conspiracy film." This was a motion picture indictment of Nazism by means of National Socialism's self-presentation—using only footage that the Nazis themselves had shot. The film emphasized that their ascension to power, launch of the Second World War, invasion of neutral countries, and methods of maintaining control and suppressing their enemies (and innocents) had abrogated the basic comprehension of justice, law, and order in the modern world.[32] Neither of these film projects could possibly have materialized without the talented, high-energy, and fiercely devoted crew behind them, all of whom Schulberg was keen to acknowledge. But it was Budd Schulberg, as his military superiors duly noted, who spearheaded the whole operation. Like the role played by Jesse Lasky Jr. in the Pacific, Schulberg understood, but never fully articulated, that all the film products had to be "scripted" in order to flow and make sense, a task he himself largely undertook.

It was not only Schulberg's military rank and assignment but also his status as Hollywood royalty and his youthful mastery of nearly every phase of moviemaking that made him so attractive to the Soviets and former Nazis who helped him scoop up the Nazi film legacy. Former Nazi archenemies, Soviet allies (since June 1941) who were expected to be belligerent and obfuscating, and others with whom he was engaged turned out to be extraordinarily forthcoming in granting requests that issued directly from Budd Schulberg. Some were "personal friends" from the film world.[33] The impulse of those who were associated in any way with the movies to cozy up to a Hollywood scion proved to be immeasurably useful to the Nuremberg prosecutors. Budd Schulberg was not an actor, by trade, but he knew how to play the part he had designed and assigned to himself with great panache.

In addition to the films that were presented at the trial, his efforts brought forth a mountain of additional motion picture film and still photographs submitted as evidence to the tribunal, accompanied by concise but remarkably informative guides. Budd's brother, Stuart, who began even earlier in the OSS, was part of a team that discovered and analyzed thousands of Nazi still photographs, but these were not determined to be immediately applicable to the Nuremberg prosecutors.[34] At the "Reich Film Archive at Hauhausen, south of Munich, approximately 100,000 ft of Nazi propaganda film, film records of scientific experiments, and other material as yet unidentified has been procured by Lt. Max Loeb and Sgt. Stuart Schulberg, Field Photographic Branch, OSS," Budd Schulberg detailed in his "Progress Report" of September 11, 1945. It comprises a capsule history of Nazi film itself. The tribunal and its legal staff could not possibly have had time to seriously consider, or even superficially view, this mass of material collected and incredibly well analyzed by Budd Schulberg and his team over an absurdly brief period. Perhaps the justices apprised themselves of Schulberg's analyses, or were informed of them in a secondhand, legal memo style, focused as they were on simply having film as part of the courtroom presentation.

Budd Schulberg's personal politics also were part of what motivated him to render superlative service in the interest of the Nuremberg Tribunal. Before the war's end, his actions as a soldier would have been extraordinary enough—helping to capture the city of Münster and uncovering critical evidence, on the spot, leading to the destruction of the famed "Bridge at Remagen"—resulting in high decorations.[35] After Germany surrendered, Schulberg was swiftly reassigned to Berlin. The Europe that had been devastated by the Nazis, and Jews who had been literally annihilated, needed a champion, and his time had come. How could he resist "Operation Justice"? For this kind of work, he had no expectation that his name would ever be in lights. The anonymity with which most government film activity was done, as opposed to Hollywood glare, might have made it an even more enticing mission.

The Nazis had used the movies, and used them well, to do their bidding. In 1945 Schulberg fleshed this out and assisted justice to take its course—in part through understanding the role that film had played in Nazism. Even before the United States formally entered World War II in 1941, "Hitler, Mussolini, Franco and Hirohito's heavy hitters turned our values inside out," Schulberg recalled in 1981. "War per se was no longer the enemy. Wars of aggression were upon us now and could only be countered by wars of liberation. Virtually overnight, we pacifists became interventionists. We joined Bundles for Britain and backed Administration support of the Allies. Only the doctrinaire Left and the Lindbergh isolationists clung to neutrality. If ever there was a war between good and evil, this seemed to be it."[36] His writing colleague and supervisor, Val Lewton from the David O. Selznick Productions story department, believed that "Schulberg's ready sympathy and feeling for the underprivileged has begotten on his part a democratic viewpoint which is apparent in all of his writings and in most of his conversations on these subjects."[37] Such ideals are apparent in many of his films.[38]

For Budd Schulberg there was, as well, a personal dimension to Nazi Germany's assault on the Jews. He makes no mention of, say, relatives of his in Germany or elsewhere in Europe being under threat or attack. But Nazi antisemitism hit home. The Nazis charged that Hollywood's moguls, invariably Jewish, were all corrupt and degenerate, peddling pornography to the world and "hate films" [Hetzfilme] against Germany.[39] Nazis and their sympathizers also launched a campaign of Jew hatred specifically on Los Angeles and among the non-Jewish employees in the movie industry. As part of the "divide and conquer" strategy that so animated Leo Rosten, the German American, pro-Nazi "Bund" posed as a "Hollywood union" that could expose the Jewish moguls' animus to their Gentile workforce, even if it meant undermining their own studios.[40] One of the 1939 American Nazi leaflets that Schulberg kept in his own records is titled "Suicide of the Hollywood Motion Picture Industry." It charged that

> UNEMPLOYMENT in the Motion Picture industry is reaching TREMENDOUS PROPORTIONS. Not more than 50% of the capacity personnel is working today. Thousands of cinema technicians, actors and extras are wondering: Why They Are Out of Jobs. These American workers are DEMANDING TO KNOW the true reasons for this ALARMING CONDITION whereby their families are on the verge of STARVATION, while the JEWISH MONOPOLY of the Motion Picture Industry BRAZENLY DISCHARGES NON-JEWISH MEN AND WOMEN and replaces them with refugee JEWS FROM Europe.
> ASK the Jew Motion Picture Producers.
> ASK the Jew-controlled publicity staffs of the Studios.
> ASK the Jew Motion Picture publications.
> ASK the Jew writers of ANTI-American propaganda pictures.
> ASK the Jew actors themselves.
> ASK the Jew-controlled Hollywood anti-Nazi League.
> WHY THEY ARE ENGAGED, day and night, in spreading VICIOUS, UN-AMERICAN propaganda of insult and hate, in order to satisfy JEWS who have been thrown out of Europe, and to antagonize FRIENDLY, ANTI-JEWISH Governments in stirring up INTERNATIONAL WAR for Jewish Vengeance and Profit.[41]

Don't Be a Sucker (1943), a US Army Signal Corps film produced by crews under the likes of Jesse Lasky Jr. and Leonard Spigelgass, uses this familiar cadence of the charges by a mean-spirited, bigoted speaker on a soapbox, but arguing more generically against foreigners, Negroes, Freemasons, and Jews, claiming that he himself is "a *real* American."[42]

Citing as its source *The Hollywood Reporter* newspaper, the handbill further alleged that the movie industry had lost (in an unspecified period) $37 million, which

> probably does not concern the Jew producers who STILL receive their royal salaries and their MILLION DOLLAR BONUSES. They STILL get their 100% even though only 50% of the capacity personnel is needed. BUT . . . this great loss DOES CONCERN the great army of UNEMPLOYED MOTION PICTURE actors, technicians, and extras, whose talents and abilities are MAINLY responsible for whatever success has been achieved by the industry.[43]

While many Angelenos and Gentiles working in the movie colony may have shared some of these antisemitic sentiments, most of those with any sense of the business knew that the studios embodied heated rivalries and were much more complex. And not all the movie companies were run by Jews. The movement favoring intervention in Europe was not of one piece and was complicated by the willingness of a number of studios to maintain business abroad, including with Nazi Germany.[44] Warner Bros. was the chief exception.[45] Threatening violence on the Jews among Hollywood's elite was, in fact, part of an explicit, sustained Nazi effort, which local Jews were compelled to countermand.[46]

Budd Schulberg also knew that the Nazis' polemics against Hollywood drew on his own writing. Included in his own archive was a clipping from the *Berliner Illustrierte Zeitung* from 1942, which included an excerpt from a German translation of *What Makes Sammy Run?* The short article introducing the selection asserted:

> An American wrote this novel which appeared a few months ago. It is a popular historical and political document of the period prior to the war. An all-knowing individual describes Hollywood, the film metropolis, also as the center of pro-war agitation in the USA. The cunning business spirit of the American film industry, run by Jews, is embodied in one of its underlings who has become a great master at exploiting the efforts of others, the greedy, insolent Sammy Glick. He began as a messenger boy for a New York newspaper.[47]

We do not know if the Nazi use of *What Makes Sammy Run?* for its antisemitic and anti-Hollywood vitriol dismayed Schulberg. The Nazis and others wishing to exploit Schulberg's novel as anti-Jewish ammunition could never admit, however, that the studio system also had fostered, and to some extent permitted, this kind of stinging dissent, rising as it did to a bestseller. While Sammy was definitely a Jewish "type," so was the narrator who was trying to understand him, Al Mannheim, and one of the many whom Sammy would use and climb over to make his way, the earnest Julian Blumberg. "And there were many Julian Blumbergs in the world," thinks Mannheim in the novel. "Jews without money, without push, without plots, without any of the characteristics which such experts on genetics as Adolf Hitler, Henry Ford and Father Coughlin try to tell us are racial traits."[48]

Bennett Cerf (1898–1971), the head of Random House, wrote a letter of recommendation for Schulberg in January 1943 as he was attempting to gain a commission in the Marine Corps. He affirmed that Schulberg was "the finest kind of officer material, particularly if his assignment is to have anything to do with writing or public relations."[49] Cerf gained lasting fame for publishing an unexpurgated edition of James Joyce's *Ulysses* (1922) and cultivating a down-to-earth, jocular public image.

Schulberg also emphasized, in his pitch to the Marines, his "interest in foreign affairs," complemented by "a fair knowledge of Spanish and German." He had "travelled through Italy, France, Germany, England, Poland, Czechoslovakia, Russia, and Japan and spent six months collaborating on the first anti-fascist films to be procured in Mexico." He also published fiction while serving as an "official correspondent" for *The Saturday Evening Post* and *Colliers*.[50] Although he does not appear in the credits, Schulberg may have been referring to work with Max Aub (Max Aub Mohrenwitz, 1903–72), in the reference to anti-fascist filmmaking. Aub was a writer, journalist, and actor born in France who made his post–World War II career mainly in Mexico and had earlier served as attaché for cultural affairs at the Spanish Republic Consulate in Paris. After the fall of France, Aub was sent to a Vichy-run concentration camp in Djelfa, Algeria.[51] Schulberg added that he had "followed the development of international affairs with keen interest and supplemented first-hand knowledge of foreghn [*sic*] countries with extensive reading."[52]

Many believe that the caustic nature of *What Makes Sammy Run?* led Schulberg to be "shunned" by the Hollywood studios.[53] This was never quite the case. Insiders knew that his father had been treated miserably, and that BP was far from a monster by Hollywood standards. He was not only a decent fellow but also a political liberal among studio chiefs who were mainly conservative and Republican. But perhaps more important: Budd Schulberg's *What Makes Sammy Run?*, although fiction, was plausible. Hollywood honchos, while making themselves and "stars" obscenely wealthy, treated many in their midst abominably. The main problem with *What Makes Sammy Run?* for the Hollywood set was that it was written by someone who really knew the score. They suspected who was behind the fictional characters. It confirmed much of what Hollywood's fiercest critics had been saying for years. So when Budd Schulberg presented his resume for placement in the Field Photographic Branch of the OSS he was able to confidently affirm that he had "been employed as a screen writer by Selznick International Pic., Samuel Goldwyn, and RKO."[54] He had enemies, and many in the movie colony thought that *Sammy* went too far. But overall, he was one of its bright boys.

Another letter written for Schulberg's desired Marine Corps commission came from Lowell Mellett, then chief of the Bureau of Motion Pictures of the Office of War Information Mellett wrote that "personal contact with Mr. Schulberg has resulted in a very favorable opinion of his intelligence, sincerity, breadth of view and loyalty." In other words, he was not a spoiled Hollywood brat. "Beyond that I know, as a result of my continuing relationship with the motion picture industry, the very high esteem in which he is generally held."[55] By that time Mellett had probably become familiar with Schulberg through his (supposedly) anonymous film work in New York and around the country. But most likely Mellett's recommendation was informed by, and came at the prompting of, Leo Rosten. He was no studio insider himself.

Schulberg eventually was awarded a commission, but it was with the United States Naval Reserve and attached to the OSS, not the Marine Corps.[56] Upon hearing that Schulberg was available, John Ford approached him "about joining the OSS Naval Unit he was forming." Contrary to the notion that the furor over *Sammy* made him unattractive, Schulberg believed that he "was in demand because [his] first novel, *What Makes Sammy Run?*, was a surprise success that year."[57] Schulberg underwent "regular Naval training as an Ensign at Fort Schuyler" in the Bronx and reported to Ford at his Washington headquarters. Initially, he "wrote documentary films on Pearl Harbor and battles in the Pacific for public exhibition."[58]

Only recently has Budd Schulberg been given a credit for the screenplay for the so-called docudrama, *December 7*,[59] a movie that incorporated some real footage about the bombing of Pearl Harbor and its monumental consequences.[60] It seems that Robert Presnell urgently contributed photographic work while the film was in production, which Mark Harris depicts as one of the most chaotic movie-salvage operations of the war.[61] Schulberg did a mop-up job, apparently the final rewrite, which not only helped to save the project but also won a 1944 Oscar for the US Navy as the Best Documentary Short Subject.

Schulberg did not bother to record the titles of his wartime films. The only other government film that may definitively be traced to Schulberg, beyond *December 7* and the Nuremberg movies, is a short, *That Men May Fight* (1943 or 1944), about the US Navy's Women's Reserve corps, known as the WAVES (Women Accepted for Volunteer Emergency Service). It relates the kinds of roles the women had on base, mainly shot in San Diego, and the movie also was meant to serve as a vehicle for recruitment.[62]

The special assistant to the director of the WAVES, Frances Rich, made a point to congratulate Schulberg on his effort. Lieutenant Rich, like Schulberg, also was a Hollywood kid, the daughter of actress Irene Rich (1891–1988). "From the beginning," Rich informed Schulberg, "I have felt the enthusiasm of all of you in assisting to put this little film together in one piece and to make it as good as possible." She gave her colleague the kind of specific feedback she knew would please him. "It was shown here in the Bureau of Personnel on Tuesday and the committee was unanimously delighted with it. I simply want to voice my appreciation to you for your great help in writing the dialogue and at the same time simplifying it. It is really a charming movie and my only hope is now that we may be able to work on another one soon, for there is no unit like Commander Ford's unit for photography, you know that."[63] Both Rich and Schulberg "worshipped" John Ford, which also describes Jules Buck's lifetime regard for John Huston.[64] *That Men May Fight* is a sweet, lively, informative film, and even a touch irreverent. Frances Rich herself was an actress but especially accomplished as a sculptor.[65]

In addition to film work, Schulberg might also have been involved in producing illustrative materials about the war, such as "Newsmaps," large posters that would have been hung in military bases or at home in community centers, schools, and churches.[66] Mainly, though, he was assigned to training, orientation, and recruitment films, working from diverse military bases, New York, Washington, and Los Angeles before being shipped off to Europe. He was good at it and, importantly, was able to work fast, with limited means, and without much direction. But he felt that he could be doing more of substance for the war effort.

The first substantial approach to Schulberg about preparing a "film on the subject of war crimes" in 1945 came from Gordon Dean (1905–58). Dean, a formidable lawyer, was a lieutenant in the Intelligence Branch, having been assigned as an assistant to Supreme Court Justice Robert H. Jackson, chief United States counsel in the prosecution of the major Nazi war criminals at Nuremberg. His remit was "public relations for the trials."[67] It is not entirely clear where the tie between "public relations" and film work originated, even though film would provide a striking public face for the proceedings of the international tribunal. Born in Seattle, Washington, Dean was an undergraduate at California's University of the Redlands. While a student he was a reporter for the Pasadena *Evening Post* and *Star News*, going on to study law at the University of Southern California.[68] As a practicing criminal lawyer he never completely left the newspaper and public relations fold, and his Washington, DC, firm was known for work with Hollywood.[69] Dean was aware that movies had been important to the Nazis and had a general sense that they should play a part in Nuremberg. In his article "The Celluloid Noose," Bud Schulberg, though, gives himself credit for explicitly "suggesting that we could screen and break-down all film on the Nazi period already collected and organize a search through Europe for secret and previously undiscovered Nazi films,"[70] which was indeed a pathbreaking, perhaps startling, proposal.

After conferring with a group that included Schulberg, Gordon Dean's refined instructions to him were complicated. "We are engaged in providing a pattern," Dean wrote in a confidential letter of June 2, 1945. "By a series of shots," he repeated, "we can indicate that out of all the individual instances of murder, thievery, butchery, persecution, we are building a mosaic, that each atrocity fits somehow into a chart of the major Nazi crime." These should include "incidents, individuals, and groups." "This is important because memories are short and it must always be clear not only for contemporary consumers but for future generations just exactly what was done." The "major messages" could be compressed into "one reel without giving the effect of being disjointed or unconnected. In other words, one message flows pretty naturally into another. I told you that these ideas would be very rough and very informal, and simply for the purpose of starting our thinking on a script."[71] Dean's request for "one reel" probably raised eyebrows. In filmmaking, nothing happens "naturally" but, rather, is the result of painstaking directing, writing, and editing. But it helped that Dean had some sense of how movies worked.

Schulberg started his "quest" in New York.[72] He began with "the impressive stock library of Fox Movietone news with one of our cutters, Joe Zigman, a hulking Brooklyn boy who looked incongruous in his tight-fitting sailor suit," another Naval Reserve man.[73] Zigman (1916–96) would go on to work extensively with Budd's brother Stuart in film and television, including editing Stuart's 1948 film, *Nuremberg*.[74] Budd Schulberg's second close collaborator at this stage was "Dr. Karl Jacoby, our technical expert, a public prosecutor in Berlin before 1933 who had somehow maneuvered his way out of Germany in the summer of 1941." Jacoby

> would grow so excited when recognizing an early and incriminating shot of Goering or Hess that he would grab the lethargic but ever patient Joe around the neck, shouting 'Stop! Stop! There he is!' often grabbing the controls of the moviola himself, inevitably knotting the film and causing endless delay. In spite of these minor disturbances, we managed to screen approximately 20,000 feet a day, stopping, rerunning and translating until at the end of two weeks we had boiled down several hundred thousand feet to 65,000 which we analyzed and cataloged. Much of this was later discarded as we came across even more incriminating material, but it was from this initial screening that we found such items as Goering's speech as Minister of Interior for Prussia before the Nazis ascent to power, threatening to "wipe Germany clean with an iron brush of every kind of opposition," Goebbels exhortation to the SA on the morning of the first organized anti-semitic riot and the first of the great book-burnings.[75]

Interestingly, one of the major missteps of the Nuremberg tribunal was to find the SA, along with the High Command of the German military, innocent of all charges. Although the SA leader, Ernst Röhm, had lost his very life in his power struggle with Hitler and Himmler, the murderous SA, too, should have been found guilty of high crimes.[76]

The Fox Movietone collection only ran up to September 1939. "But fortunately [the] OSS, through connections in Switzerland, Portugal, Spain and other neutral countries, had been receiving their official German newsreel *Wochenschau* regularly throughout the war." Schulberg's team was able, therefore "to document Nazi aggression from the first strike across the Polish frontier (beautifully covered by *Wochenschau* cameramen with close shots of Wehrmacht soldiers ripping the Polish Insignia off the border gates) until the August 1, 1944, edition, in which Major Rehman, Hitler Jugend alumnus credited with putting down the July 20 Putsch screams at his company of Wehrmacht Honor Guards that they are not merely soldiers but *political* soldiers who must take their orders directly from Der Fuhrer [sic] and his deputies, thereby indicating the split beginning to separate some of the German high command from their Nazi partners."[77] Such details demonstrate the photographic crew's adherence to the developing conduct of the trial, in which charges were leveled against individuals and distinct Nazi organizations.

Along with what they gleaned from newsreel footage, Schulberg, Zigman, and Jacoby turned to selections "from Nazi documentary films, some of which had already been analyzed by the OSS Film Library group, while others were obtained from the Museum of Modern Art and the Alien Property Custodian, which had confiscated Nazi propaganda films showing in Yorkville [New York, which had a large German-American community] and other German communities at the outbreak of the war."[78] These would, Schulberg stated in his progress report of September 11, 1945, "substantiate the broad charges of conspiracy to seize and hold power illegally in Germany through terror and persecution, as well as the master plan of world domination."[79] "One of the most edifying of these [documentary films] was the 11-reel Leni Riefenstahl epic, *The Triumph of the Will* [1935]." In his report to his superiors, Schulberg specified that *Der Triumph des Willens*, produced and directed by Riefenstahl, "by the order of Der Fuehrer," covered the Nuremberg Nazi Party Congress of 1934, hence, it might have special resonance for the trial that was being held in Nuremberg. "Its dominant themes are the Leadership Principle, the unity of the Army, Party and State, the military preparedness of quasi-military organizations like the SA, the SS, the Deutsche Arbeits Front, the Hitler Jugend, the Flieger Corps, as well as the growing strength of the Wehrmacht and the unbreakable loyalty of the SA under Victor Lutze, despite the purge of Roehm and other SA leaders the summer before. Hans Frank, Rudolph Hess and other leaders reiterate the pledge 'Our Fuehrer is our supreme judge,'"[80] to which Schulberg later added, a "somewhat novel interpretation of justice."[81]

He explained that "besides the eleven-reel German version, exactly as released to the German people, in Germany and other countries with large

German-speaking communities (including the USA) this Branch has produced a four (4) reel (38-minute) edited version [of *Triumph of the Will*] with English commentary. Both versions will be available at Nuremberg."[82] The edited version might have been mainly for the use of Jackson's staff, or possibly with an eye to showings for select audiences in the United States and Europe. Later, though, the remit for Schulberg's group would be confined to film confiscated in Germany exclusively—no matter where it was produced. The 1945 short version of *Triumph of the Will*, with commentary, which would have been excellent for use in university courses, seems to have vanished.

Schulberg and his unit were unable, up to this point, to find two additional films by Riefenstahl that they thought would be significant, *Der Sieg des Glaubens* (The Victory of Faith, 1933) and *Tag der Freiheit* (Day of Freedom, 1935), despite conducting an "extensive search in the United States, in London, and in and around Berlin."[83] Efforts were underway to canvass Switzerland and other neutral countries. Getting his hands on these films was a prime motivation for Schulberg to track down Leni Riefenstahl himself. Although he chose to omit any further discussion of Riefenstahl from the 1946 "Celluloid Noose" article as well as his lengthy Progress Report to (General) Donovan and other superiors,[84] Leni Riefenstahl was not simply the creator of an important Nazi film to Schulberg.

In a 1999 interview, Schulberg recalled that one of his "more ironic tasks" in this period "was to locate famed documentary filmmaker Leni Riefenstahl."[85] In 1946 he wrote about the experience for *The Saturday Evening Post* in an article titled "The Nazi Pin-Up Girl."[86] "Even before the Nazi party came to power in Germany," Schulberg had explained in his Progress Report, "it revealed a profound understanding of the use and influence of motion picture propaganda. Adolf Hitler and Joseph Goebbels were both extremely aware of the value of this medium in winning the German people to their cause, and as early as 1927 Nazi Party Congresses and public gatherings were being photographed by Party cameramen."[87] In "The Celluloid Noose," Schulberg mentioned, in passing, that he "had helped organize a boycott of Riefenstahl when she visited [Hollywood] in 1939,"[88] and he stated a little more emphatically in "The Nazi Pin-Up Girl" that he had done his "bit to help launch a boycott against Miss Riefenstahl upon her visit to Hollywood."[89]

In the 1999 conversation, Schulberg stressed that he had never believed "her claims that she was 'apolitical' and ignorant of what Hitler and the Nazis were up to," including what would come to be known as the Holocaust. After locating her in Kitzbuhel, Austria, in the Tyrolian Alps, Schulberg said he "took her to Nuremberg as a material witness."[90] While more or less true, the actual encounter between Schulberg and Riefenstahl was a Hollywood tale in itself,[91] but it has only rarely been commented on in the torrent of writing about Riefenstahl's life and work, despite Schulberg's *Saturday Evening Post* piece.

In the endeavor to find, talk to, and possibly "capture" Riefenstahl, Schulberg had a number of intermingled objectives. First, he simply wished to find her—which was not so easily done. Riefenstahl herself, far from naive, suspected that she might be called as a material witness to the upcoming trial, perhaps prosecuted herself. She was wary of the C.I.C., the US Army Counterintelligence force, discovering her address.[92] Schulberg also, as mentioned, wished to obtain, for his unit's haul, copies of the two missing films that she had directed. His hunch that they were legally and historically significant would only be realized long after his quest, as both were only discovered and brought to public attention some fifty years later. When he had a chance to observe Riefenstahl's den, one of the first things Schulberg noticed was the conspicuous absence of *Triumph des Willens*, *Der Sieg des Glaubens*, and *Tag der Freiheit* in her (otherwise complete) set of "leatherbound scenarios," the shooting scripts for her films.[93] If these movies were not in her possession, he would ask her where they might be found, and he would also use that line of questioning to mine her for information about the existence of other Nazi films that had escaped them. One of the purposes of interviewing her was also to determine precisely how she fit into the Nazi moviemaking enterprise. Schulberg wanted to know, in as much depth as possible, about her relationship with Adolf Hitler. In a way, it was prurient: like countless others, he was curious if the rumor were true, that she had been Hitler's girlfriend or mistress. But Schulberg also was inquisitive about her role in Nazi filmmaking, beyond the movies to her credit. What was her part in Nazism, writ large? And last, but far from least, was the question that consumed a large portion of their encounter: her thought and actions about antisemitism and the Jews. Some of this part of the conversation was omitted from Schulberg's confidential "Intelligence Report" on his meeting, but it appeared in "The Nazi Pin-Up Girl" article and seems highly plausible.[94]

It is something of a stretch to say that Schulberg caught or apprehended Riefenstahl. She had been located at the close of the war, questioned, and released as being harmless. It was not widely known, though, that she returned to one of her previous addresses in Austria. A US Army official who dealt with her, Col. Milton H. Medenbach (1907–2007), a career army man, was said to have "never heard of Leni Riefenstahl" before and prided himself on being sympathetic to Germans who lived through Nazism.[95] After graduating from Johns Hopkins University in 1929, Medenbach studied at the University of Marburg in 1929–30 and the Konsularakademie in Vienna the next year.[96] Fluent in German, he apparently was in a civilian administrative position when he dismissed Riefenstahl as "a woman in distress, disheveled but handsome and, in spite of fatigue and agitation, capable of charm. The United States Army, he informed her, [at that time] temporarily requisitioned her house at the suggestion of Kitzbühel's mayor. But her mother was safe," living in the nearby estate of the former Nazi foreigner minister, Joachim von Ribbentrop.[97] Ribbentrop, on October 16, 1946, would be the first of the Nuremberg defendants to be executed by hanging.

US military authorities did not, however, seem to care much about her whereabouts or status. The official intelligence report states that she was "arrested by American troops in her house in Kitzbuhel, where she has been living and working for years."[98] A quite substantial report on her was filed after her interrogation, in German, by Hans Wallenberg and Ernest Langendorf, German-born US Army officers, which even dealt fairly well with the issue of antisemitism.[99] Langendorf was a Social Democrat who had fled the Third Reich in its early days for the United States, and Wallenberg, defined as a Jew by the Nazis, also had the good fortune to flee. But they did not seem to appreciate the critical role that Riefenstahl had played in Nazi film, and Langendorf became quite friendly with her, following the lead of Medenbach.[100]

Schulberg himself may have helped cover up the sloppiness of the army and OSS.[101] Perhaps he was concerned that John Ford might face scrutiny if word got out that he had let Leni Riefenstahl fall through the cracks. Schulberg was far from alone in thinking that she was a big player and that letting her off was a mistake. So Schulberg did, in fact, through truly imaginative sleuthing, track her down, with the ultimate result that from then on she was not quite the free bird she might otherwise have been. Although Schulberg did not acquire the two films he sought, he learned that *Der Sieg des Glaubens* was "a four-reel documentary film of the 5th Parteitag Congress in Nuremberg in September 1933 and that *Tag der Freiheit* was a short documentary film about the Wehrmacht, made in 1935.[102] He wanted to see if these were as incriminating, fitting the tribunal's objectives, as the *Triumph des Willens* and *Olympia* (1938) movies. It seems, though, that he also was very interested in simply talking to her, to see what she thought about the role she played in fabricating the legend of Hitler's savior-like leadership. He, too, was intrigued to find out if she had been a lover of Hitler, a rumor, now discredited, that was very much alive in the 1940s.

Leni Riefenstahl proceeded to talk at length with Schulberg. She tried to ingratiate herself. Most likely, he was among the few Jews with whom she had spoken in years. She probably would not have been able to recognize him by sight, and there is no indication whether he used his real name or an alias. Believing that she had already received her *Persilschein*, the German slang for a document attesting to one's innocence for wrongdoing in the Third Reich, Riefenstahl attempted to use the interview to cleanse her reputation as far as antisemitism was concerned. The central ploy that Schulberg invented was effective. But his Jewishness and his "Hollywood-ness" mattered a lot. He left it to his *Saturday Evening Post* readers to use their imaginations about this. In his official report he adds a parenthetical note that "Riefenstahl believes that I am collecting these films for the US Government film archives and Major Finke or any other officer following up this lead should maintain this cover."[103]

When Riefenstahl realized he was an officer who had made a protracted effort to find her, she protested that she had been "cleared." She produced a document that affirmed her being "released without prejudice by the 7th Army G2."[104] Schulberg knew she had so far not been identified as a leading Nazi figure: "After two arrests" she was "cleared by both US Army and French Army authorities. Her home is in a French-occupied territory and the French seem reluctant to let her cross into other Allied zones."[105] He told her that he was representing an official body in the United States that aspired to have a complete collection of her films—hence his request for the other "political" films she had directed. "'I'm not CIC,' I told her. He was with 'Intelligence,' and she feared that he was from the Counterintelligence Corps of the US Army. "'I'm from the National Film Archives in Washington. We want a complete library of your documentaries for our files. So far we have all but two.' (Frighten her or flatter her, my instructions had been. Whichever seems the best to get her working for us.)"[106] It was a measure of both. But he also charmed her, and she thought she'd be able to charm him as she had Medenbach and others.

Riefenstahl bought the ruse, or at least she accepted it enough to keep talking. "The fear went out of her face," Schulberg recalled. "She took my hand and pressed it impulsively—'(impulsively),' the stage direction would have indicated—and turned to her little husband."[107] "'*Liebling*, just think, he's come all the way from Berlin to talk about my films!' She turned back to me happily."[108] The term of endearment she uttered, "*Liebling*," was directed at her husband, who was disparaged by Schulberg as a bit player. Her own charm offensive, just short of the batting of eyelashes, was launched on Schulberg. "'Would you like some tea? And some little cakes? I wish we could offer you more but . . . (sighing bravely) . . . these French take everything.'" She was in the French zone of occupation, which made finding her more difficult and entailed some problems in appropriating film from that area. "Then, to 'liebling' again," Riefenstahl said: "'Ask Paula to bring us some tea and Kuchen,' and she waved him off to the kitchen. 'I think this is so exciting,' she said, turning to me eagerly again, *her hand happening to drop against mine,*

'Your wanting my pictures. Tell me, which ones have you already?'" She was impressed that the names of her films were on the tip of his tongue.[109]

When Schulberg pronounced the title, in English, she would make a brief comment and supply the German, chatting about the films in which she had starred, *The White Hell of Pitz Palü* (dir. Arnold Fanck and G. W. Pabst, 1929) and *SOS Iceberg* (dir. Tay Garnett, 1933), and those that she had herself directed, *The Blue Light* (1932) and the *1936 Olympics*. "'I cut every foot of that myself,' she said," speaking of the Olympics film, "liking this game more and more. 'It took me three years. Translated into sixteen different languages.'"

> "And *The Triumph of the Will*," I said. *Her hand moved away from me and the intense brown eyes that could be warm and beguiling became aloof and suspicious.* "Why do you want that one?" she said. "Well, after all, it is a great documentary," I said. "The photography. The use of music." She felt a little better. "Exactly," she said. "That's the way I meant it. Not propaganda but, after all, a Party Congress in Nurnberg, the speeches, the ceremony, the great demonstrations in the Stadium, it was something important happening, whether you were for it or not. As an artist, I only wanted to show what was happening, to catch the spirit of it." "You certainly succeeded in doing that," I said. "The trouble with me is," she said, with an air of self-critical candor, "I just can't do anything badly." Paula arrived with the tea, and some very tasty little cakes. Leni smiled at me, watching my reaction. We were just a couple of artists, Leni and I, sipping tea in her cozy Bavarian chalet. "And after all, if it was propaganda, it certainly wouldn't have won a prize from the French Government in 1937," Leni added.[110]

She instructed her husband to fetch "the certificate from the Paris Exhibition for the Lieutenant." Schulberg then stated: "So now the only films of yours we are missing are 'Victory of Faith' and 'Day of Freedom,'" which prompted an exaggerated frown from Leni. "Oh, those. Those are nothing. They really won't interest you."[111]

When pressed, she said that "Victory of Faith," *Der Sieg des Glaubens*, "was just a short on the first Party Congress after Hitler came to power. It was just something I had to do. And it was on such short notice all I could do was a rush job. After all, when the head of a state orders you to make a film . . ."[112] But there was quite a story about that movie, of which she gave no hint. It is now regarded as "of great historic interest because it shows Adolf Hitler and Ernst Röhm on close and intimate terms, before Röhm was shot on the orders of Hitler on 'the Night of the Long Knives' in July 1934." Schulberg had almost no chance of finding it, as "all known copies of the film were destroyed on Hitler's orders, and it was considered lost until a copy turned up in the 1990s in the U.K."[113] Besides clearly showing Hitler and Röhm to be extremely chummy, which they were, the film also might have been removed for being a tad homoerotic, with numerous up-close focuses on teenage Hitler Youth boys. The movie should be recalled as furthermore significant because *Triumph des Willens* "was conceived, in part, to replace *Sieg des Glaubens*."[114]

Schulberg then mentioned "Day of Freedom," prompting Leni to dismiss it as "just a little picture I had to make for the Wehrmacht in 1935." She added that Werner Von Blomberg, Hitler's minister of defense, "didn't think there was enough about the Army in 'The Triumph of the Will,' it was just a little tribute I had to make for the Army to keep them quiet. It wouldn't interest you, really."[115] *Tag der Freiheit-Unsere Wehrmacht* (1935) ("Day of Freedom-Our Army") does, it is generally agreed, owe its origins to German Army officials feeling slighted in *Triumph of the Will*, although Riefenstahl's more subtle military chic in her other Nazi-era films were at least as effective at flaunting weaponry. Von Blomberg's fall from Hitler's grace, along with Werner von Fritsch, was not nearly as spectacular as the public murder of Röhm. But it was crucial in Nazism's history because it eased Hitler's assumption of more direct control of the military and bestowed greater power to the SS. So there was a reason why *Tag der Freiheit* would not have been a regime favorite. That film, too, was long lost—until the 1970s, when an "incomplete print" was recovered.[116]

Schulberg did not think to ask if these might have been suppressed by the Nazis. Hitler was her patron and fan, but even Riefenstahl's films were subject to the changing breezes in National Socialism—who was in and who was out. Discredited officials featured in a film meant it would be removed. This was the kind of technique attributed to Stalinism when airbrushed photos were circulated that had earlier shown the leader and others with those later deemed to be traitors. Schulberg's crew found one film produced under Nazi auspices, *Jahre der Entscheidung* ("Year of Decision"), that was known to have been "withdrawn" and that had an "interesting history." It was produced by Carl Junghans, the former film coordinator of the German Communist Party.[117] "Although under the titular supervision of Goebbels," Schulberg related, "Junghans succeeded in turning this film into subtle anti-Nazi propaganda by quoting a pre-1933 speech of Goebbels that stated that Nazi leaders were men of the people who would not seek luxury and special privileges once they were in power. The contrast between this pledge and the actual conditions once the Nazi regime was installed was apparently so glaring that Hitler ordered this film withdrawn after three hundred copies had been released."[118] According to one of their informants, Junghans had "fled to France."[119] He made his way to the United States, returning to Germany in 1963, in large part living off the revival of his social-realist film of 1929, *So ist das Leben/Takovy je zivot* (*That's the Way Life Is*), about the tragic life of a washerwoman.[120]

The insight into the *Jahre der Entscheidung* movie, and Junghan's fate, came from a Dr. Mueller, who Schulberg describes as a film director from Austria, former head of the Rex-Film studios in Berlin, who was now assisting the OSS. Mueller also informed the unit that the (unseen or missing) movie *Opfer der Vergangenheit* (dir. Gernot Bock-Stieber and Kurt Botner, 1937) ("Victims of the Past"), which he mistranslated as "The Sacrifice of Passover," an expressly antisemitic film, was "so violent in its presentation of 'Jewish atrocities' that people in the audience have fainted."[121] He misrepresented its character. This was about the Nazi so-called "euthanasia" program, to justify the state's taking of lives deemed "unworthy of life."

But with the subtitle *Die Sünde wider Blut und Rasse* ("The Sin against Blood and Race"), it did include expressly antisemitic scenes. It purported to show that Jews had the greatest guilt for begetting a large portion of the incurably disabled and mentally ill people, for whom, the narrator argued, "the German people" had to shoulder the burden. *Opfer der Vergangenheit* is a thoroughly sickening film, however mis-recalled by Mueller.[122]

The Psychological Warfare Division of the Supreme Headquarters of the Allied Expeditionary Force also viewed hundreds of German films and understandably called attention to the inhumanity of *Ich Klage An* ("I Accuse") (dir. Wolfgang Liebeneiner, 1941). This was a less gruesome, subtler presentation of the idea of "mercy killing."[123] The Nazi "euthanasia" program was mentioned in the Nuremberg indictment, but it took historians decades to realize its essential relationship to the genocide of European Jewry, in large measure by poison gas, beginning in 1941.[124] Mueller was one of Schulberg's chief sources in his quest for an explicit Nazi film depicting atrocities perpetrated on Jews, which never was found.

Schulberg did not bother to ask Riefenstahl if she had any knowledge of the atrocity film, which he had heard described by at least two separate Nazi informants. Mueller, contradicting another voluntary witness, said that the "atrocity film" "was not produced by the SS, since they had no motion picture branch of their own, but by the Hitler Youth 'Filmstette.' [sic] He stated definitively to Lt. Schulberg and Mr. [Fred] Stalder [a Swiss OSS man], that this film was made under the direction of Hans Schoenmetzler, Berlin-Halensee Kuno-Fischerstrasse, with the cooperation of Herrn Weidemann and Gunther Kauffmann, both believed to be in Berlin at the present time," September 1945. "The cameramen," that is, the men who filmed the atrocities, "are said to be Captain Typke and Unter-offizier Mensing. Authority for these allegations is based on statements of an employee of Dr. Mueller's, Hern Martin Mehls, Ber N 20, Uferstrasse 17, former combat photographer, who claims to have first-hand knowledge of this film and of the participation of the abovementioned people." Mueller was judged to be "a sincere anti-Nazi and that his information is relatively accurate. A further search for this 'Gruelfilme' [atrocity film] as well as for the personalities said to be involved with its production, will be intensified upon the return of Lt. Colonel Downs and Lt. Schulberg to Berlin on or before 17 September 1945."[125]

In all his published, unpublished, and recorded recollections, Schulberg does not do justice to the intensity with which he pursued his attempt to locate this particular film, which most certainly had existed and had been shown to selected Nazi audiences. Although there was more than enough material evidence of the annihilation of Europe's Jews, including film of the "liberated" concentration camps, he wanted desperately to get his hands on the Nazis' own film proof of its horrific crimes.

Despite Riefenstahl's brush-off of *Tag der Freiheit* and *Sieg des Glaubens* as immaterial, Schulberg nevertheless plowed ahead, making it clear he considered these necessary for his archival collection task. He asked if she had prints in her possession, which she emphatically denied. She enthusiastically volunteered that the only film she had in hand was "my beautiful *Tiefland*," "an idyllic love story" that she claimed transcended politics and expressed "the real Leni Riefenstahl, like *The Blue Light*, or the Olympic Film, the poetry of motion, the poetry of mountains and meadows. The film of pure art."[126] Schulberg clearly was not interested in indulging her about *Tiefland* and tried again: "Where do you think I could find these Wehrmacht and Party Congress films?"[127] Now he was getting somewhere. "'Well, if we must talk about such things,' Leni's expression seemed to say, 'Just before the war ended, an agent came to see me from the Propaganda Ministry. He was collecting all government films and hiding them in a tunnel in a mountain somewhere in the Italian Tirol. Near Balzano, I think.'"[128] This was a truly important piece of information, and before he departed, she provided precise directions.

Riefenstahl was no doubt wary of giving the Allies something they did not possess that might incriminate her. But she also was keen to spark a relationship with Schulberg because he was obviously well connected in the film world, even if she was oblivious to the fact that he was a Hollywood prince in a US Navy uniform. He proved, though, that he was a "somebody" in the motion picture trade. Although Schulberg was hoping that she would be more forthright, the fact that she gave him her time and attention, and any information at all, was significant. We have no idea how she would have responded if her interlocutor was someone outside the film industry. With Schulberg, she could not plead that she was just an apolitical artist, a formerly affluent German woman in distress due to the exigencies of the war. Although the excursion to the tunnel repository she identified turned out mostly disappointing, and the team had heard elsewhere about it, it was nevertheless a piece of valuable information. It helped to confirm that there was a lot of film they might never find, and that much of it had been deliberately destroyed.

Riefenstahl's "little husband" then appeared with the Paris Exhibition diploma, which, however real, Schulberg thought had rewarded "her cinematic deification of the Nazi Gang."[129] She saw it as disproving any notion that *Triumph des Willens* presented a threat to anyone, but the "jury" of the festival was exclusively right-wing.[130] "Leni ran her hand around the edge of the certificate fondly. 'In Paris I was given an ovation. They treated me marvelously in London, too. That's the way art should be, international.'"[131] Again, Schulberg was not going to let her determine the course of the interview, which Riefenstahl still did not quite realize was more of an interrogation. To this day, though, critics are divided over to what extent Riefenstahl's work should be regarded as universal, even brilliantly transcending borders and conventions, versus the extent to which it is largely claptrap with overheated techniques, reliant on hackneyed, chauvinistic, and racist tropes. Internationalism and nationalism were not necessarily mutually exclusive, and the internationalism of sport, for instance, did not preclude the Olympic movement and other bodies from being antisemitic, racist, and favoring right-wing, authoritarian regimes as well as prone to corruption.[132] Likewise, a number of international organizations dealing with issues of law and order, and (supposedly) the overall betterment of lives of women and children, had distinct class and race biases, along with antisemitism, and the arts world was certainly comparable.[133]

Schulberg cleverly used this, though, as a segue to one of the major topics he wished to engage: her relationship with Adolf Hitler. He told her that he "had never been able to think of the Führer as an advocate of that sort of thing," that is, "internationalism," however vaguely, as seeing nations on par with each other in his comprehension of art and aesthetics.[134] Hitler's Germany, conceived as the Aryan ideal, was to reign supreme in a well-defined hierarchy, subjecting most of the world's nations to conquest, utter destruction, slavery, or subservience, at best.

Riefenstahl believed that she could score some points. "'Oh, but Hitler had a tremendous interest in art, he was very artistic himself and sensitive,' Leni explained. 'He liked to encourage creative people—and not only Germans. There were many intellectuals who appreciated this. Knut Hamsun, Sacha Guitry.'"[135] Hamsun (1859–1952) was, and still is, regarded as a trendsetting and talented writer but tainted by racism and his explicit support for Hitler and Nazism.[136] Sacha Guitry (1885–1957), whose acting career flourished on stage and screen in Vichy France, was accused but cleared of being a Nazi collaborator. His national loyalties were complicated. Riefenstahl's (likely accurate) report that Hitler had "encouraged" Guitry would have been enough to raise suspicions. She thought, though, that such figures might impress Schulberg. But the name-dropping also revealed that her familiarity with Hitler's thinking on such matters was intimate. "You must have known Hitler very well," Schulberg interjected. Interrogation about her relationship to Hitler was nothing new. This was one of the first questions Leni faced when she arrived in the United States in 1938,[137] which she brusquely rebuffed. To Schulberg, however, she was circumspect but still effusive. "'Oh, not nearly so well as people think,' Leni said. 'It's all been so terribly exaggerated. Just because I saw him a few times alone . . .' 'How did you meet him?' 'Well, it was in 1932,' Leni said. 'He invited me to come to his apartment in Berlin. He wanted to tell me how much he admired my mountain pictures.'"[138] Schulberg, the Hollywood guy, knew that a powerful man summoning an actress to his apartment, well, meant something.

As a man who so loved both the mountains and motion pictures, Riefenstahl gushed, "my work appealed to him very much. 'Miss Riefenstahl,' he said to me, 'very soon now, in a year or two, I'm going to be the Leader of Germany. And when I do, I want you to make pictures just for me, just about me, and the movement." According to Schulberg, Leni told Hitler "'that this was a big order.' After all, she had to be true to her art. She could only make pictures she felt a deep urge to make." Schulberg then asked: How did Hitler respond? "He was very understanding," said Leni. "You know he wasn't at all the way people thought he was. I never heard him loud and unreasonable. He had a very gentle manner. He listened carefully to everything you said, even though he seemed to know everything you were going to say. He was so intuitive." In the midst of what Schulberg describes, sardonically, as "a communion of souls," Hitler implored Leni "to join the Party. And the conversation that ensued, according to Leni, went something like this."[139]

Budd Schulberg, the screenwriter, was admitting to some artistic license. But it is a thoroughly plausible reconstruction, with a Humphrey-Bogart-style narration. "'Leni,' Adolf said, 'you love Germany, you love the mountains, you love the outdoor life, I think you belong to the Partei.' 'No, Adolf, I can't,' Leni said. 'I am an artist. An artist is a free spirit, not a joiner of organizations.'" Hitler, quite accurately, specified that his movement had no shortage of intellectuals and artists. Leni nevertheless protested that, "besides not liking to join organizations," there were some aspects of the Nazi program with which she disagreed. "'Like what, Leni?' Adolf said, his intuitive, sensitive brown eyes staring gently into Leni's innocent, artistic brown ones. 'Well, this matter of the Jews,' Leni said."[140]

Schulberg did not have to raise it. Riefenstahl thought that she could redeem herself, and lift some of the blame from Hitler in the bargain. But rather than defusing the issue of her own antisemitism, she only confirmed what had long been known, that the persecution of the Jews did not terribly bother her. Her attempt at rationalization, a rather pathetic apologia, did not sit well with Schulberg. Continuing the reported conversation, Leni contended that Hitler was "reasonable" about Jews, "not really anti-Semitic, just pro-Aryan." In the film industry, "for instance," there simply were too many of them, Hitler explained. "'Motion pictures are dominated by Jews. That's why there is so much anti-Semitism. But if we reduced the number of Jews in the film industry, say by 50%, can't you see how there would be that much less feeling against them from the Aryan film people?' Miss Riefenstahl, it appears, even though she has the poetic, unsystematized mind of the artist, had to admit the logic of this."[141] She wished to emphasize that this "was really true."[142]

Thinking that showing Hitler as a dispassionate observer of the German film scene would solicit sympathy for both her and Hitler, she reiterated that "there were so many Jews in the film industry before 1933. You can see how that might have been a bad thing—for the Jews themselves, I mean?" No, Schulberg did not see the logic. Why should the number of Jews in the movie business translate into being a "bad thing" for them? Schulberg chose not to push it. "'What was the other point on which you and Hitler disagreed?' I wanted to know."[143] "'Well, I have always been a pacifist,' Leni said. 'I didn't see why there had to be so much militarism. That's what I told him. I had heard people say that he wanted Germany to fight another war.'" Returning to the Adolf/Leni dialogue: "'But I am a pacifist, too,' Adolf told Leni. 'That is why I am for a strong Germany. So no country will ever attack us again.'"[144]

Schulberg asked if she found this credible. "'Well, everybody believed him,' Leni told me. 'If you listened to him you couldn't help believing him. He sounded so good, so idealistic, so sincere. The only way I can explain it is that there must have been a demon inside him, something hidden inside him that nobody else could see.' 'Do you think it's so hidden that you can't see it in *Mein Kampf*?' I asked."[145] The next scene seemed particularly well rehearsed.

"She gave me a coy smile. 'Would you believe it, I've never read it,' she said. 'I started to once, but . . . well I'm just not interested in politics.' (*Which Actress Do You Believe Dept*: Dolly Haas, Austrian refugee actress, describing her meeting with Leni Riefenstahl in Switzerland in 1933: 'Leni said all her leftist ideas were completely changed by reading *Mein Kampf*.')"[146] This was a freighted reference: Dolly Haas (1910–94) was a Hamburg-born, much-respected actress on stage and screen, who had left Germany without pressure when Hitler assumed power. Raised both in England and Germany, she was not Jewish and was principled and highly intelligent. Yes, she was the kind of person to be trusted.[147]

"'But the concentration camps,' I said. 'Even in Thirty-Three there was Dachau, there was Oranienberg.' Leni shook her head. 'I had no idea,' she said. 'We never heard.'"[148] Riefenstahl herself claimed that when she came to Los Angeles in 1939 she had no inkling of violence against the Jews—which is patently absurd, given that *Kristallnacht*, the Night of the Broken Glass, which occurred over November 9/10, 1938, was front-page news everywhere.[149] Seven months earlier, in March 1938, and well before the start of her American tour, violent antisemitic demonstrations and the burning of synagogues erupted across Austria upon the *Anschluss*.

Perhaps because he was so disgusted by her remark, Schulberg bluntly asked: "Were you really Hitler's mistress?" Rather than a simple "no," she was again coy, portraying herself as morally and intellectually superior to Eva Braun. "'Of course not,' Leni said. 'I wasn't his type. I'm too strong, too positive. He liked soft, cow-like women, like Eva Braun. All the time that people were saying I was Hitler's girl, it was really Eva.' 'What made people think you were?'"

She chalked it up to "jealousy" and a failure to understand Hitler's sense of her importance as an artist. "Because I could always get in to see him alone. I couldn't stand talking to him with all those adjutants and SS around. So I'd ask Hitler to send everybody away. And once or twice we were seen out together—when my films opened, for instance, but that was purely professional, there was nothing personal about it. He just respected me as an artist." She alleged that "the SS and Goebbels hated me because I could go over their heads. When I started to film the Olympic Games, for instance, I had so many fights with Goebbels he threatened to take me off the picture and put another director in my place." So she appealed to the Führer himself "and told him how I felt and how much it meant to me and I would never make another picture unless Goebbels would leave me alone."[150] The rest was history. She was able to make her movies owing to the intervention of Hitler despite infuriating his henchmen.

Resuming his Sam Spade–like narrator mode, Schulberg comments: "And once more Hitler the gentle, Hitler the wise, told Leni he understood. After all, he was an artist, too. Goebbels was advised that Riefenstahl was to be made the one exception to his general control of all film production." But she remained, in her own mind, a victim of the Third Reich. Complaining about being a misunderstood genius, subject to vile mistreatment, was old hat and would persist into her later years. Upon her return to Europe in 1939, "she objected strenuously to 'being trailed continuously by two detectives'" while in Hollywood, "who she said had been paid by an American anti-Nazi organization. She asserted that they not only interfered in her walks about Hollywood but 'were actually rude to me a couple of times.'" How could they! "Another thing she said she did not like," the press reported, "was an alleged order from studio executives prohibiting their stars from talking to her."[151] After her arguments with Goebbels while filming the 1936 Olympics, Riefenstahl told Schulberg that she became "the victim of the Goebbels propaganda machine. She was forced to undergo such familiar Nazi tortures as being deprived of all publicity in Goebbels's newspapers. 'He never mentioned me again,' Leni says bitterly. 'I was even afraid he might put me in a concentration camp.' 'But why should you be afraid of concentration camps?' I said. 'After all, you hadn't heard of them.'"[152]

Now she was forced to beat a clumsy retreat. "'Oh, I knew there were some,' Leni said. 'But I had no idea what they were really like, how terrible they were, until I saw some of your pictures after the war.'" She was referring to photographs and films of the liberation of the camps, of the wreckage of mass atrocities. "You have no idea how little we heard about these things. It just didn't seem possible. When I went to America in 1939," actually, arriving November 3 or 4, 1938, "some reporters in New York asked me what I thought of the persecution of the Jews in Germany and I said as far as I knew it was just foreign propaganda. When I got to Hollywood there was a boycott against me."[153] The timing here is important. Although there had been countless anti-Jewish actions from 1933 to 1938, and thousands of antisemitic signs throughout the country, Kristallnacht happened between her stops in New York and Los Angeles. "Only a few realized that I didn't come as a propaganda agent at all—in fact, Goebbels tried to stop me from coming—Winnie Sheehan and Maritz and Sigrid Gurie, they were very kind." "Winnie," Winfield Sheehan (1883–1945), was then an independent producer, having been chief of production at Fox from 1926 to 1935, with five nominations and an Oscar for *Calvacade* (dir. Frank Lloyd, 1933), which won "Best Picture" in 1932–33.[154] Sigrid Gurie (1911–69), the "Norwegian Garbo" (but born in Brooklyn), is a little-remembered actress. Ironically, she is mainly recalled because of her brother, Knut Haukelid, a leader of the anti-Nazi resistance in Norway and "one of the commandos who helped cripple Nazi Germany's atomic weapons program in Norway."[155]

In this interview, Riefenstahl did not, however, mention the most famous person she met in Hollywood, Walt Disney. (Or else Schulberg chose to keep quiet.) Possibly she refrained from name-dropping Disney, despite his renown, because he was widely reputed to be one of the few antisemitic studio heads in Hollywood. In a Viennese movie magazine interview (from Paris) soon after her return from the United States, she denounced "the opposition of the Hollywood film-Jews who used every means at their disposal against her." "I visited

New York, Washington, Chicago, and Los Angeles. With a single exception, namely Hollywood," she felt welcomed "with open arms." There she faced the "German-hating and Jewish-American film industry." But in Hollywood, too, there was "a notable exception, which deserves to be highlighted. Walt Disney, the creator of the *Snow White* film [dir. David Hand et al, 1937], received me very warmly and took me around his extensive studios—even showing me his latest work. It was also gratifying to see how decent Americans distanced themselves from the Jewish agitation."[156] Schulberg was aware, though, that Disney put these prejudices behind him in turning his studio over to the war effort.

Disney might have defended himself by saying that his studio always welcomed foreign visitors and by citing the example of his graciousness in hosting Sidney Bernstein from London in 1936. It was well known that Bernstein had come to the United States for the express purpose of generating enthusiasm for anti-Nazi pictures and had a special "obligation," prompting the meeting with Walt Disney. Bernstein wished to introduce, to Disney, "the works of his eccentric and brilliant colour film-maker friend, Len Lye." Lye, from New Zealand, had been taken into Bernstein's Bloomsbury Film Society, which supported his work. "Sidney showed Disney two experimental reels of *Tusalava* and *Kaleidoscope* he had brought with him, and the American was highly impressed."[157] Although Len Lye does not seem to have found a place in the history of *Fantasia* (dir. James Algar et al., 1940), a look at his animated films suggest that Lye, and the "Gasparcolor" process he used, deserve greater credit for *Fantasia* than has been accorded.

It was a lie, then, for Riefenstahl to say she "couldn't even get into a studio." It was not one of the companies, though, Leni sought. "I felt very badly. When I got back to Germany I asked one of Hitler's adjutants, 'Is it really true, all these things they say in America are happening to the Jews here?' 'Yes, it's absolutely true, Leni,' he said. I'll never forget how stunned I was."[158] She thought that that should settle it. "She paused a moment and offered me a cookie. 'Perhaps a little more hot tea?'" She asked her husband to get the servant and "turned to me with her best smile again. 'Have you any idea if I'm on the blacklist or not?'"[159] This was what she wanted most from Schulberg. Leni most likely thought that her cooperation, up to that point, might change a negative verdict that already had been lodged against her. She also felt that she had explained away any possible taint of antisemitism.

Schulberg told her he "hadn't seen the list" but that he "rather imagined she was on it. 'Yes, I suppose so,' she said, 'Oh, if only I could do something, if I could just not be Leni Riefenstahl any more—as long as I could go on making pictures. Do you suppose they would boycott my new picture in America—it's just a pure film, a sweet story with not one word of dialogue in the entire first reel—a pastorale.'" There was no reason to give her false hopes. "It would be boycotted in America," he said. Riefenstahl seemed resigned: "'Yes, I suppose so,' said Leni. 'I don't know what I'm going to do. Maybe France, if I wait, a year perhaps, things may change.'" Schulberg assumed it would be possible for her to continue work in Germany. "Won't you be able to show it here?" Her response probably needed more explanation for his *Saturday Evening Post* audience. "'Oh no,' she said. 'I was never a Nazi, but the concentration camp Germans will be in power, I think they are liable to misunderstand. Yes, I am sure they will.'"[160] She was speaking about opponents of the Nazis, such as the Communists, Social Democrats, and maybe even Jews who might return—that is, those who she knew had been in the Nazi concentration camps. After that, she provided him with detailed directions, of "how to find the tunnel in Balzano, where the missing films were supposed be."[161] Predictably, she did not reveal the location where she knew her more recent film work on *Tiefland* was stored.[162]

Following Schulberg out to his car, she said: "'If there's any other way I can help you, please let me know. . . . And if there's any way you could do something about that blacklist . . .' 'Sorry,' I replied, 'That's ICS, Information Control Service. Not my department.'" That may have been so, but Schulberg was, nevertheless, in a position to negotiate her disposition. Leni had not, in total, helped her case. "Her smile disappeared, and then, as she came closer, her face became suddenly animated again. There was something queer about the smile, it was intimate and appealing and yet clearly designing. That must have been the way she looked at Hitler when she wanted to make Goebbels back down to her, I thought. 'Would you be able to give us a can of gas?' she said. 'We have a car but the French won't give us any.'" Schulberg recalls that he "thought of the places that car must have gone," to Hitler's Berlin headquarters, to his retreat at Berchtesgaden, on carefree visits to Italy, France, and Greece. "'Sorry,' I said, 'it's not allowed.' 'Just one litre, so we can get into town and back?' 'Not allowed,' I said. Suddenly the smile faded, leaving her face unmasked and hard and heavy with self-pity. As I drove down the hill I saw her walking slowly back into her big three-story house, back to her well-trained Mr. Jacobs, her well-trained servants, and the stubborn ghosts of the Third Reich who insisted on being part of the family."[163]

Schulberg left his encounter with Leni Riefenstahl embittered—not simply because he did not receive the films he had come for but also because she was so adamant to deny that she had known about, or had anything to do with, the immense unsavory dimensions of Nazism, including its persecution and annihilation of the Jews. She wanted to be seen as the leading artist of National

Socialism but assume no responsibility for the consequences of its actions. Although not to the same degree as America's movie colony, Germany's film industry, too, had counted a disproportionate number of Jews before 1933,[164] many of whom Schulberg knew as émigrés and refugees in Los Angeles and New York. Riefenstahl could not possibly have been in the dark.

As depressing as was the experience with Leni Riefenstahl, Schulberg's relationship with another movie trade insider was surprising, and in some ways great fun. The Soviet officer in charge of the Third Reich's film archive in Babelsberg was a Major Gregory Arinarius. Outside of Schulberg's account, this major is so elusive that one might think that Schulberg the screenwriter imagined him.[165] Schulberg relates that he "explained his mission" to Arinarius and "asked for permission to make prints of the entire Nazi period from those in his control."[166] As expected, the major was cautious. "Arinarius, a tall, thin ascetic looking intellectual, studied me a little suspiciously, I thought. 'What is a naval officer doing looking for films in Germany?' he wanted to know. 'Well, it is a little hard to explain,' I said, 'but I belong to a Photographic Naval Unit headed by Captain John Ford which has been put in charge of photographic evidence for the Nuremberg trial.'"[167] Schulberg was a little short on the truth, not identifying himself as being with the OSS, but Arinarius, probably N.K.V.D., the state security service of the USSR, would have assumed so.[168]

"'John Ford, the director?' Arinarius said. 'Yes,' I said. 'You've heard of him?' 'In my book on the history of motion pictures,' Arinarius said, 'I give Ford two chapters. *The Iron Horse* [1924] is still one of my favorite pictures.' To tell the truth," Schulberg confessed, "I had forgotten what pictures Ford had made in the silent days, but Arinarius knew them all. Here in the Russian zone on the outskirts of Berlin I had run into Ford's greatest and surely most erudite fan."[169] In their developing relationship, Arinarius learned of Schulberg's own background, which would strengthen their bond.

He duly listed director Ford's legendary filmography: "*Dawn Patrol* [sic, 1938], *Young Mr. Lincoln* [1939], *The Informer* [1935], *Stage Coach* [1939], *Long Voyage Home* [1940], *The Grapes of Wrath* [1940], *How Green Was My Valley?* [1941]. . . . Arinarius continued, 'Every one of these pictures I have analyzed in my book.' He smiled at me for the first time. 'Tell me, will John Ford (he pronounced it as one word *Djonford*) be coming over to take charge personally?'"[170] John Ford's relationship with the operations of Schulberg's unit was hands-off, to the extreme. "At that moment I had no idea whether Jack was in Hollywood, Washington, or in China with [General] Wedemeyer. 'Oh yes, we expect him over any time now,' I said."[171] Schulberg's wish, as they say, was now the Soviet major's command.

The next day, Schulberg's first three hours were spent "talking, or rather, listening to him discuss Hollywood. For at least three quarters of an hour he analyzed the humor of Mack Sennett and how it has influenced all subsequent Hollywood comedy, even the contemporary work of Walt Disney. He compared Ford with other outstanding directors, Capra, Wyler, McCarey . . . ; he knew them all. But when he really endeared himself to me (and to all brother Screen Writers I'm sure) was when, in discussing *Casablanca*, he said: 'Let me see, that was written by the brothers Epstein, was it not.'"[172] This was not as simple as it sounds. For many years a rather heated controversy ensued concerning the attribution for that film, and to Schulberg, he got it right.[173] Now the love affair was (nearly) mutual. "Arinarius then proceeded to cite screen credits of every prominent picture released in the last five years. It's part of his job in civilian life, he told me, as professor of motion picture history at the Cinematic Institute in Moscow. As an alternate member of the SWG [Screen Writer's Guild] Board in absentia, and this is a very small voice indeed, I vote one complimentary subscription for Major Arinarius to our Guild's magazine *The Screen Writer*."[174] While a light aside to the *Saturday Evening Post* readership, this was a gesture of warmth. "Before you publish your next book," I told him, "you should come to Hollywood and do some of your research right in the studios." "Oh no I mustn't," Arinarius said. "I've found so much new material here in Berlin I've had to postpone publication six months. If I went to Hollywood I'd have to postpone six years!"[175] Schulberg's suggestion, inferring an invitation, of sorts, was not bestowed on Leni Riefenstahl, but it likely was what she had expected.

As sparkling and enjoyable as was his encounter with Arinarius, the culmination was a crushing blow. Schulberg and Arinarius were informed by the long-term caretaker at the Babelsberg archive that "Goebbels' outfit had come out there personally, just before the Russians entered the city, and burned the top secret films which included the SS murders of Jews and Poles, photographed by special SS film units."[176] As much as there was a confessional aspect to "The Celluloid Noose," Schulberg did not share the depth of his grave disappointment. He attempted to make the most of it. "We did receive from Arinarius however all the newsreel photographs we needed for our chronological record of the Nazis in power. In another bunker we found biographical material on all the Nazi leaders, including a two-reel monologue by Rosenberg describing in detail the formation of the Nazi party, the abortive attempt to seize power in 1925 [*sic*] and the ten-year struggle that ended with Hitler's assuming dictatorial power from the Reichstag in 1933."[177] These were, indeed, important. It showed that Arinarius understood the stakes and was willing to help, as much as possible. "This film, to which Jackson referred in his opening address, was used to introduce the four-hour documentary on *The Nazi Conspiracy to Seize Power and Wage Aggressive War*, supplementing Counts One and Two of the Allies' Indictment."[178]

Trawling through what was available, the crew sorted through only "a fraction" of the remaining archive. Arinarius "was completely sympathetic to our mission," Schulberg said, "but he could not throw open all the bunkers to us without the permission of his colonel."[179] Despite obvious differences in perspective and agenda, the officers saw themselves as working toward a common goal: making the most vivid case possible against National Socialism. The colonel, Kaleeshkin,[180] was an even more convivial, colorful character. A creative organizer in Schulberg's unit, Jack Munroe, prepared "a lavish dinner" flowing with vodka and "repeated toasts to Soviet-American friendship" in order to woo Kaleeshkin.[181]

The crowd for the banquet included "the Colonel, Major Arinarius, Major [Yuri] Viergang and several other Russian officers we had not expected. With a perfectly straight face, Munroe went to the piano and played *Song of the Plains*." That would be like a Soviet officer belting out a rendition of *God Bless America* followed by the Marine Corps anthem. "After a half dozen cocktails toasting each other, Stalin, Truman, lasting friendship etc. and etc., we sat down to dinner. We arose about one o'clock in the morning, with the Colonel finishing the last of our wine and promising to send us a case of his own Caucasian wine in the morning. Then we staggered over to the other house to run the July 20th film which the Soviet officers had never seen and a print of which they were anxious to obtain. The five-reel film was run one reel at a time, with a ten-minute intermission for refreshments. At three o'clock in the morning the Colonel, who everyone said was a member of the NKVD, was dancing in the street with one of our WAC [War Activities Committee] interpreters. 'We must work closer together,' he said happily has he and his staff drove off just as the sun was coming up over the Wann-See."[182]

With the colonel's approval in hand, Schulberg's unit "carried film out of the bunkers until it grew dark. All in all, the Russians had given us more than 200,000 feet of secret Nazi Party and Propaganda Ministry films. Our toasts, thrown out upon the vodka, had brought results. Among the films obtained that day were every single Party Day Congress from the very first one in 1923 in which Himmler and Hess appeared with Hitler in short Bavarian pants looking like Hitler Jugend. There was also a Party film on the 1932 election, with SA men patrolling the streets and an SA machine gun unit lined up outside a trade-union headquarters."[183] Although it was not the atrocity film he had sought, Schulberg was particularly satisfied that the haul unearthed "another valuable document, marked Geheim-Oberkammando" (Secret, by order of the High Command). He described it as "a horrendous two-reel film depicting the rounding up of the Jews in the Warsaw Ghetto and their inevitable burial in mass graves. German thoroughness is seen in its most frightening aspect in one shot in which a uniformed Waffen SS cameraman can be seen at the bottom of a mass grave getting a reverse shot as naked, emaciated bodies, including those of small children and infants, come hurtling toward him."[184]

Decades later, in May 1973, Schulberg felt compelled to revisit his meeting with Leni Riefenstahl, at a moment when she was basking in a great deal of attention, if not adulation. Nevertheless, she portrayed herself as a victim of a "continuing predicament" led by film people who were unjustly hostile to her. She identified Budd Schulberg "as a leader of the 'Hate Leni' cult" in a report that appeared in *Variety*. In response, Schulberg, in a letter to the editor of *Variety*, asserted that "Leni Riefenstahl gives me far too much credit when she attributes to me the leadership for the 'persisting "Hate Leni" cult.'" When I took her into custody, in accordance with my orders, she not only assured me that she had many enemies among the Nazis, but also that she had many friends in Hollywood. She saw me, of course, only as an American officer, and it did not occur to her that I might also be a member of the American film community."[185] Perhaps Schulberg's memory had failed him: this does not square with his own account. Her behavior toward him followed from his enticing appeal for the preservation and glorification of her films. And his name was certainly known to those in the movies. The discussion between them, reported by Schulberg in at least two versions, attests to her believing that there was some kind of common ground between them, and her cloying gestures were motivated by the thought that he may have had the power to help her.

Schulberg also related, in the letter to *Variety*, that "she told me of the wonderful party that Hal Roach had given her during her visit to Hollywood in the middle '30s [*sic*]. I remembered, but did not feel it necessary, to tell her that the 'wonderful party' had been bitterly resented by Hollywood's anti-Nazi community, and that a widespread boycott led by anti-Nazi stars and directors involved an overwhelming majority of the leading Hollywood personalities.[186] They set up a telephone campaign, urging other celebrated invitees not to attend the reception for Riefenstahl. As a result, her reception was a fiasco." Schulberg does not assume credit for her being shunned. "I was only a young Hollywood writer at the time." Worse, in fact. In the early 1930s his father found himself on the outs at Paramount, with the company even declining to distribute his films in 1937. B. P. Schulberg was not completely outcast but, rather, in Hollywood's equivalent of the wilderness until signing with Columbia Pictures in 1940. So when Riefenstahl hit the town in 1939, Budd Schulberg, no matter his reputation as a bright boy, was two years out of college, and a lightweight as far as Hollywood was concerned. "I would like to think that I was the leader of the 'Hate Leni' movement, but, in all modesty, several hundred of Hollywood's best known artists led the demonstration against Riefenstahl." Few of them would be able to forgive her for her "cinematic glorification" of Adolf Hitler.[187] (This was before *Kristallnacht*, when the dimensions of the Holocaust were unimaginable.) Budd Schulberg was not in a frame of mind to forgive and forget when he graced her doorway in 1945, and Riefenstahl herself thought that her unmatched artistry would trump any politically based reservations against her.[188] There is a good chance she learned about his article about her in *The Saturday Evening Post* when Schulberg quipped that earlier "I had done my bit to help launch a boycott against Miss Riefenstahl upon her visit to Hollywood."[189] In her eyes, he was "wanting in gallantry," a cad, or worse.[190] Budd Schulberg had correctly feared that Leni Riefenstahl would be "a strenuous advocate for her rehabilitation."[191] Perhaps he had had some influence in what Steven Bach, Riefenstahl's biographer, sees as "the most crippling blow," which was the seizure of her bank accounts by the French.[192] Schulberg might have taken some solace in her eventually being "pronounced a Nazi sympathizer by the Allies" and, despite incessantly promoting and reinventing herself, never again assuming a success from the commanding position of movie director.[193]

Leni Riefenstahl's memoir is rife with self-serving omissions, half-truths, and outright lies. Her account of the brief time spent with Walt Disney in Hollywood in 1938, nonetheless, is reasonably accurate.[194] On her personal studio tour she recalled that Disney previewed his major work in progress, Mickey Mouse as "the sorcerer's apprentice," which became a signature chapter of *Fantasia*, his blockbuster of 1941.[195] It was a fortuitous common ground. The tale developed by Disney was partly based on a ballad by Goethe, *Der Zauberlehrling* (1797), which Riefenstahl might have known.[196] Disney's earlier feature-length cartoon, which she adored, was *Snow White and the Seven Dwarfs*. It derived from a Grimm Brothers folktale and was a big hit in Germany. "By her own account," Riefenstahl's most astute biographer, Steven Bach, writes, "nothing in or out of school so preoccupied her as fairy tales. Germany was the home of the Brothers Grimm, of course, but subscribing to a fantasy journal called *Once Upon a Time* at fifteen, as Leni did, suggests fixation rather than pastime, and the predilection for fairy tales and myths would survive and flourish."[197]

Although she prided herself on being strong-willed and independent minded, Leni Riefenstahl could be seen as a sorcerer's apprentice to her friend, fellow artist, and idol, Adolf Hitler. But unlike Mickey's bewitched water-carrying brooms, her incantations did not seem to go berserk. She made the Führer himself descend from the clouds to lead the Nuremberg rally. She made white, athletic bodies glisten, without being overtly sexy or sweaty. Enamored of her Führer, she shared his inclinations almost totally, and her work complemented how Hitler cast himself in mesmerizing, minutely choreographed spectacles. To Schulberg, this must have consequences.

The sorcerer in Disney's tale to whom Mickey was beholden in *Fantasia* was not a lovable, wizened Merlin but an ugly, forbidding character—bearing marked resemblance to the antisemitic caricatures of peddlers in Disney's early films. Walt Disney, to his credit, threw the full weight of his formidable studio, which was extremely well-suited to the task, into making and enhancing wartime films for the government and the armed forces when asked in 1942. Donald Duck may have been second fiddle to Disney's Mickey, but he was an American darling, therefore an important government spokesman, quacky voice and all. In *The New Spirit* (dirs. Wilfred Jackson and Ben Sharpsteen, uncredited, 1942), Donald vividly made the case that Americans could "fight the Axis with their taxes, . . . taxes, to bury the Axis." Disney got on just fine with Rosten.[198] The constructive collaboration between Disney's character, Donald Duck, and FDR's (Jewish) Secretary of the Treasury Henry Morgenthau Jr. became legendary: "Donald Duck made good in such a big way as one of Mr. Morgenthau's minions in 1942, that the Secretary of the Treasury drafted him again as a tax expert in 1943. The Technicolor short, *Spirit of '43* [dir. Jack King, uncredited], produced by Walt Disney for the US Treasury, was so widely distributed and exhibited through the War Activities Committee, that at least part of the gloom inherent in the ides of March," that is, when Americans prepare their taxes, "was dissipated by Donald's good humored decision to use his taxes to help smash the Axis. Thus, the people's medium once again was used to impress upon people throughout the nation the importance of cheerful, prompt payment of taxes to help win a people's war."[199] We will never know, though, to what extent Donald's selflessness for the cause was driven by peer pressure from Porky Pig, Bugs Bunny, and Daffy Duck from the stable of Leon Schlesinger at Warner Bros.[200] Bugs Bunny, in fact, had beaten Donald to the punch in *Any Bonds Today?* (Warner Bros. & US Treasury Dept., Defense Savings Staff, 1942), when "Defense Bonds" were transformed into "War Bonds."[201] If he could have, Joe McCarthy probably would have hauled the Looney Tunes' cast, too, before his investigation's committee as premature anti-fascists.

But in late 1938, whether he was sincere or not, Walt Disney demonstrated to Leni Riefenstahl that there were "good" Americans, "authentic" Americans, who respected what Hitler was doing in Germany. It is not known if Disney articulated a distaste for "the Jewish element," as did Leni while being interrogated in the ruins of the Third Reich.[202] But by merely inviting her to his studio, and spending time with her, Disney was making a show of his disagreement with those who boycotted Leni Riefenstahl, as they had also, a year earlier, refused to entertain and promote the aspirations of Mussolini's son Vittorio.[203] After the Second World War, Walt Disney, along with (nearly) everyone else in Hollywood, was immeasurably more sensitive to deploying mean-spirited stereotypes against Jews that might be understood as calls to hatred and incitement to violence. Although they were handled less crudely after 1945, women and black people (in Disney productions and beyond) remained subject to patronizing attitudes that would take decades to shake off, an effort that is far from completion into the third decade of the twenty-first century. A process was set in motion (pictures), though, in which it became "routine to reject racism, sexism, homophobia, or ethnocentrism."[204] This became part of the unarticulated formula, allowing for exceptions, for determining what makes a film great.

6

Reckonings—or Not

Along with the films that Budd Schulberg's unit unearthed in 1945, Nazi motion pictures were sent to them from other intelligence groups, including the Psychological Warfare Division of the Supreme Headquarters of the Allied Expeditionary Force (SHAEF) in London.[1] The SHAEF was established in February 1944, but Rosten had been in London for longer than the previous year. Although not officially part of the OSS, Rosten had a hand in such efforts, as he remained central to the "continuing information campaigns" with the aim of presenting the twelve-year history of the Third Reich in order "to emphasize the whole record of Nazi aggression and the Nazi threat to us and the world."[2] He was, at that time, "a civilian, in an officer's uniform, with the lofty rank of colonel ('assimilated')," on the SHAEF staff headed by General Dwight D. Eisenhower.[3] The Psychological Warfare Division material, too, comprised part of the evidence and shaped the case against the accused in Nuremberg. The work of Schulberg's people was expedited because these movies were grouped, with reports, including suggestions as to which films were "closely associated with the most aggressive and abusive policies of the Third Reich."[4]

In his Progress Report, Schulberg confessed that he could not possibly name each of the German features this branch had "screened or reviewed." But Schulberg cherry-picked fourteen of the 300 hour-plus movies and 150 shorts, which he himself believed "to be the most indicative of the close connection *between the German film industry* and the aggressive and repressive policies of the Third Reich."[5] Schulberg's list integrated the most egregious antisemitic films with the savage, ultranationalist productions of the Nazis, assuming that the campaign against the Jews would be prominent in exhibiting the Nazis' crimes against humanity. Shortly before the start of the International Tribunal, pieces of these films were incorporated into the US government/OSS newsreel, *That*

Justice Be Done (dir. George Stevens, 1945), which also served as an introduction for the public of what to expect from the Nuremberg proceedings.

Predictably, *Jud Süß* (*Jew Süss*, dir. Veit Harlan, 1940) is high on the list. Schulberg describes it as "an anti-Semitic tract, in a historical setting, purporting to be the biography of a wealthy, grasping Jew who gains power in Wuertemberg, exercises tyrannical control over the population, ravishes and murders a woman who refuses to become his mistress, which so stirs the population that they rise in revolt. Suess is hanged and his fellow Jews are driven back into the Ghetto from whence they had emerged during Suess's tyrannical reign."[6] Schulberg might have said much more. The story for the film was appropriated from a book by a famed German Jewish writer, Lion Feuchtwanger, who escaped to Hollywood after having been interned as an "alien" in interwar France and a concentration camp under the Vichy regime.[7] But departing from Feuchtwanger's historical novel, "a subtle and complex" tale of a court Jew in the eighteenth century was transformed into "a violently ant-Jewish motion picture."[8] It is not known if Schulberg heard that Ferdinand Marian (1902–46), the talented actor who played Süss, was profoundly distressed about being assigned the role, or that the director's ex-wife, Dora Gerson (1899–1943), was murdered at Auschwitz. Leaving aside its subject matter, Schulberg likely was aware that there were some in the film world who thought it a stunning movie, perhaps the finest produced under the Nazis. Veit "was tried twice after the war on charges of crimes against humanity but was acquitted in both trials."[9]

Schulberg's unit did not locate all the Nazi films that historians and critics would later deem to be the most potently antisemitic.[10] In retrospect, it seems odd that the film *Kolberg* (1945), also written and directed by Veit Harlan, escaped their grasp, which had prompted this statement by Goebbels: "Gentlemen, in a hundred years still another color film will portray the terrible days we are undergoing now. Do you want to play a role in that film which will let you live again in a hundred years? Every one of you has the opportunity today to choose the person he wishes to be in a hundred years. I can assure you that it will be a tremendous film, exciting and beautiful, and worth holding steady for. Don't give up!"[11] Perhaps Schulberg's group missed it because it was finished too late to have had much of an impact on the German public. "Using a historical event from the Napoleonic wars, the film was supposed to teach the populace to defend their town and country at whatever cost, and to die rather than surrender. As the film only came out in the beginning of 1945 when most cinemas were destroyed, it did not reach its public."[12] *Kolberg*, in the understated evaluation of Peter Paret, "is not among the major successes of the German motion-picture industry during the Third Reich."[13] There is a chance the choppy editing and poor quality of the *Agfacolor* process, which was supposed to be a selling point, relegated it to Schulberg's dustbin. Yet the sheer manpower and money that went into the making of *Kolberg*, at such a late stage of the war, might have strengthened the case for how seriously the Nazis took their movies.

Schulberg rightly argued for the importance of the notorious Nazi pseudo-documentary, *Der ewige Jude* (*The Eternal Jew*, dir. Fritz Hippler). His unit was not, however, able to discern who, exactly, was responsible for it beyond the Nazi Party film division.[14] Dr. Mueller said that "this film was shown to the public in 1942, but had to be withdrawn because of the unfavorable reaction of German audiences."[15] Although the former Nazi informants no doubt provided a lot of useful information, for the most part Schulberg's OSS team attempted to determine, for themselves, the relative significance of movies and those behind them. Clearly, Leni Riefenstahl was Public Enemy Number One in this regard. There is a chance that her name-dropping during the session with Schulberg might have backfired. Some of the individuals Schulberg singles out for culpability were her close personal friends, such as actor Emil Jannings,[16] or those who had been working with Riefenstahl up to the end of the war, such as screenwriter Gerhard Menzel.[17]

Schulberg knew that the American film industry, which he himself lambasted in *What Makes Sammy Run?*, had enthusiastically accommodated the interests of the US government and military during wartime, and in doing so, was overwhelmingly on the side of democracy, the tolerance of diverse races and religions, and a broad internationalism. Schulberg himself had helped to restrain the anti-Japanese viciousness in the Academy-Award-winning *December 7*. That film could not have been more explicit in its call for a United Nations to assume the lead in world governance and peacekeeping.[18]

The German films that Schulberg underscored, in the context of the Nuremberg trial objectives, were those that were vehemently anti-British, anti-French, anti-Polish, and anti-Russian as well as those expressly hostile to mentally and physically handicapped people and European Jews. Each had been crafted to justify extraordinary destructiveness beyond conventional military objectives and transcended even wartime extremes of national solidarity and security concerns.[19] These movies were, Schulberg knew for certain, of a different order from what Hollywood and its associates were producing, even allowing for expected excesses of national chauvinism. Movie studios everywhere made wretched films that often were fused with native, brutal triumphalism over imagined internal and external foes. But the Nazified studios had produced a new genre, investing a fortune in condoning and glorifying mass violence and wanton destruction with real-life consequences. These could not be dismissed for serving rational notions of national defense or promoting territorial compensation for past injustices. They demanded immediate death to persons, peoples, and nations that were not constituted as military adversaries.

Although he did not explain his criteria, Schulberg apparently seized on the films that had consumed big budgets and had attracted the leading actors to starring roles. In addition, he selected the movies dealing primarily with Jews, therefore axiomatically antisemitic in Nazi discourse. Overall, outside of the Riefenstahl films, *Ohm Kruger* (1941), directed by Hans Steinhoff (1882–1945) and starring Emil Jannings (1884–1950), was at the top of his list.[20] According to Schulberg's capsule, it displays "anti-British propaganda, in which the British are depicted as ruthless, cynical conquerors, who rape, pillage, set up concentration camps and shoot defenseless women. Juxtoposed [sic] to Cecil Rhodes and Kitchener is the German leader Kruger, whose dying prophecy is that one day a great nation will arise to repay 'Perfidious Albion' for all the suffering she has inflicted on mankind."[21] This was a box-office smash in Nazi Germany, despite the fact that its director, Steinhoff, was regarded as among the least talented and most obnoxious of his peers. He was the kind of person who owed his success, in great part, to Jews being thrown out of the profession.

Ohm Kruger also may have come in first on Budd Schulberg's list of evil Nazi films owing to Emil Jannings having been its star, with Jannings also credited as a producer and artistic director.[22] Having started his career in Germany, Emil Jannings, in the silent days, had also made it in Hollywood, winning the first Academy Award for Best Actor for his part in *The Way of All Flesh* (dir. Victor Fleming, 1927). In Schulberg's opinion, he was more than a gifted actor. He regarded *Der letzte Mann* (dir. F. W. Murnau, 1924, released in the United States and Britain as *The Last Laugh*), in which Jannings appeared in almost every scene of the film, as a "masterpiece."[23] Jannings also happened to be a "foreign import" of his father, BP.[24] The youthful Budd Schulberg himself advised his father to take a chance on an early scenario draft of the eventual *Way of All Flesh* with Jannings as its star, about which Adolf Zukor, the head of Paramount pictures, and his chief financier, Otto Kahn, lacked confidence.[25] As the Oscar demonstrated, it was a good call, and Jannings went on to further Hollywood success.

Emil Jannings's career had intertwined with that of actress Marlene Dietrich (1901–92) and director Josef von Sternberg (1894–1969), also hailing from Central Europe. In contrast to Jannings, they remained sincerely beloved to the Schulbergs. Dietrich, famously, championed the plight of refugees from Nazism, good causes generally, and played opposite Spencer Tracy in *Judgment at Nuremberg* (dir. Stanley Kramer, 1961). That film focused on Allied proceedings that followed the main international tribunal for which the photographic unit's efforts were dedicated. Interestingly, Joe Sternberg served in the US Army Signal Corps in World War I making training films.[26] Emil Jannings had starred in Sternberg's *The Last Command* (1928), and he helped to launch Dietrich's career, somewhat inadvertently in 1930 in his role as a pathetic suitor in *The Blue Angel*.

But in contrast to most of his fellow Hollywood Germans, Jannings decided to return to Germany for good, saying that performing in English "in the new talkies was too much of a challenge."[27] "So he came to say goodbye with a fervent avowal of love for all the Schulbergs and an open invitation for us to be his houseguests whenever we came to Germany," Budd Schulberg wrote in his memoir. "After all, Emil insisted, he was a *landsman*, or at least a *half-landsman*, having been born in Brooklyn of a Jewish mother who took him to Europe when he was still a child."[28] There is now broad agreement that Jannings was born in Switzerland, but his origins remain murky. In Hollywood he was happy to pass himself off as half-Jewish.

"Yet when Hitler and his Brown Shirts came to power," Schulberg asserts, "and Jannings's professional status if not his life was endangered, he went to court and became a certified member of the Master Race by declaring that he had been born out of wedlock to an Aryan maid in the Jannings' household. Which prompted father to say, 'I've known a lot of bastards in this business, but this is the first time I ever heard of anyone going to court to make it official.'"[29] Similar to his origins, the end of Jannings's career is cloudy. He reportedly was "blacklisted" by the Allies, but there are conflicting accounts that US authorities sought to have him rehabilitated.

Some of the Nazi anti-Polish films were even more caustic than those demonizing Britain, France, and the Soviet Union. One of the most bloodthirsty was *Feinde* ("Enemies," 1940), number 5 on Schulberg's list, directed by V. Tourjansky. Tourjansky, a Russian who supported the antirevolutionary and antisemitic Whites, chalked up some success in Hollywood before returning to Europe, voluntarily joining the UFA-Film studio in 1936 when it was firmly under Goebbels control.[30] The anti-Polish fare not only presented hyperdistorted historical interpretations but fabricated outright lies about the danger to their persons and property that ethnic Germans had faced in Poland. Schulberg was probably correct in thinking that the anti-Polish invective helped to animate the Nazi drive to the east in the interest of acquiring *Lebensraum*, or "space to live." Nazi films also made no bones about the fact that acquiring territory and exploiting local populations meant "revenues" for those at home.[31]

Heimkehr (dir. Gustav Ucicky, 1941) is a turgid, melodramatic, and sprawling ode to German ultranationalism and, particularly, a justification for Germany conquering Poland in the name of granting its ethnic German inhabitants, although a small minority, life in a German-dominated environment. Katie Trumpener writes that the film

> offers a pretext not only for Germany's occupation of Poland but for its dismantling of the Polish film industry. Shot partly in occupied Poland, *Homecoming* cast Polish actors as the film's villains. The Polish resistance retaliated after 1941 by assassinating the Warsaw actor and collaborator who had helped Ucicky with casting. In reprisal the Germans executed twenty-one Polish hostages and sent several prominent Polish actors and directors to Auschwitz (where they were soon joined by mass transports of Polish Jews).[32]

After the German defeat, "the Allied Occupation" (specifically Schulberg's unit) "and then the West German government banned Ucicky's film." Most of the Polish actors in the movie, who were still alive in 1947 and could be apprehended, received prison sentences by "a Polish tribunal." As of 2024, *Heimkehr* "remains banned in Germany, and thus is seldom discussed, despite its incendiary subject."[33]

While Jews are stereotypically portrayed in several scenes, *Heimkehr* is more vociferously anti-Polish than antisemitic. The Polish anti-German outrages depicted in the film, which replicated what the Nazis were doing to Jews, are the kinds of incidents that William L. Shirer, as a journalist, found baseless.[34] The less bombastic anti-Jewishness of the film, however, might have contributed to Schulberg taking such umbrage.

Rather than the incessant, crude stereotypes of *Der ewige Jude*, as a vehicle for shaping opinion *Heimkehr* was possibly more effective. In an early scene, the heroine Maria Thomas, played by Paula Wessely (1907–2000), considers buying a scarf from a Jewish merchant she passes in an open market. She is polite to him but doesn't purchase the scarf she handled, and he mutters abuse on her as she departs. In another scene, a German-language school is shut down, vandalized, and its books are set on fire. Jews, both secularized and traditional, take part and approvingly look on.

In the initial stages of preparations for the trial, Schulberg and his colleagues had watched American newsreel footage from Germany, none of which was used. "It was the cavalier treatment" of the antisemitic book burnings "by the Hearst Metrotone News, incidentally, that crystallized for me the spiritual bankruptcy of *our* newsreels" up to 1939, Schulberg wrote. "The book-burning, for instance, which can truly be said to have set the world on fire, is accompanied by carefree *It's a Hot Time in the Old Time* [sic, *Town*] *Tonight* music, with a racy, happy-go-lucky narration by Lowell Thomas that begins, 'Well, looks like these young Heidelberg students are having a hot time for themselves tonight . . .' and continues in this tone, a simple simon describing a world tragedy in the jocular terms of an apple-ducking contest."[35] Leonard Spigelgass and his colleagues expended great effort to assure that a replay of this kind of callousness in newsreels would never be repeated.

Especially in the last third of *Heimkehr*, Maria delivers a number of soliloquies. Toward the movie's conclusion, she wistfully proclaims her vision of Poland under Germany, "that surrounding us will be the sound of German, . . . and when you come into a shop somebody there speaks neither Yiddish, nor Polish, but instead (*sondern*) German. And not only the whole village will be German, but all around."[36] Despite Wessely's reputation as the highest paid Nazi actress, her postwar ban from filmmaking lasted only three years, and she became a producer in addition to acting. Only confirming suspicions about her personal politics and lack of remorse, Wessely starred in an antihomosexual movie, *Anders als du und ich* ("Different from You and Me," released with the English title *Bewildered Youth*) (1957), directed by Veit Harlan, the previously mentioned director of *Kolberg* and *Jud Süß*. This film, supposedly, was intended to loosen the West German criminalization of homosexuality. But it was so contradictory that it is now regarded as expressly antihomosexual. Schulberg, however, refrained from comment on any individual actors in his survey (except for Jannings), but when big stars appeared in the Nazis' most hate-mongering productions, he noted it. Schulberg did not seem, however, well acquainted with the actresses,[37] and possibly he regarded them as beholden to Nazi Party and studio bosses.

Schulberg is sure to have noticed a minutely choreographed key scene in *Heimkehr*. In the eastern Polish town square, the lead couple happily look forward to a temporary respite from their high-minded nationalist fieldwork to attend a cinema matinee.[38] It's fully packed. Not surprisingly, a Hollywood film is on, a Jeanette McDonald and Nelson Eddy musical. First, they sit through an American-style, Polish language newsreel. One of the events shown, after tidbits from a cheesy American beauty pageant, is a speech by the (former) Polish prime minister, Felicjan Slawoj Skladkowski, addressing a military formation, concluding with the singing of the Polish national anthem, "Dabrowski's Mazurka" ("Poland Is Not Yet Lost"). This brings the bulk of the movie audience to its feet, boisterously joining in the singing. Our good Germans in the movie audience reluctantly stand, with heads down, not singing, which raises the ire of the crowd, and a violent riot ensues. It is a foretaste of the gruesome, merciless deaths of pure, valiant Germans.

The setting of these events is not random. The cinema, the "Grand Kino Lucky," is revealed as a decadent space, its newsreel spotlighting the scantily clad American girls and encouraging Polish nationalists to flout their chauvinism and intolerance. It is also made clear, in more than a single scene, that the movie house is part of an industry that shows movies from Fox and MGM, Metro-Goldwyn-Mayer. MGM also was said to stand for "Means Great Movies" as well as "*Mayers Gantse Mishpokhe*," or "Mayer's entire family" in Yiddishized Hollywood lore. (Similarly, Gaumont-British was called *Gaumont-Yiddish*.) After the Germans are assaulted, the owner of the theater invites the patrons back in, including those who abused the good Germans, and informs them that this showing is on him. Perhaps this was not what captured the attention of Budd Schulberg, the Hollywood prince. But the alleged complicity of American movie studios and their Polish accomplices, in the mix of motives compelling Germans to conquer and destroy Poland, was quite a confection. And *Heimkehr* was, in its context, one of the better told and more effective tales of the Nazis.

Schulberg's summary of *Heimkehr* related that the film "deals with the alleged cruelties perpetrated by the Poles on the Germans. Germany goes to war to save its 'Volksgenossen' who are just about to be ruthlessly executed by the Poles when the Fuehrer's Stukas and tanks come to the rescue. The PWD report comments: '. . . it can not be doubted that many Germans felt justified to commit their barbarous crimes during the occupation of Poland after the (Ucicky and Menzel invented) atrocities."[39] "Hitler initiated World War II," a historian writes, "with an act of unprovoked aggression, bolstered by projection and lies concerning a border incident the regime had fabricated. It followed months of propaganda blaming Poland for the war Hitler was planning to start. Hitler claimed that Polish troops had engaged in an unprovoked armed assault on a German radio station at Gleiwitz in Upper Silesia. In fact, the faked 'attack' was carried out by SS troops; the bodies of Polish concentration camp prisoners who had been killed by lethal injection and then shot were left lying at that site."[40] With these events clearly in mind, Schulberg repeated the claim of his London colleagues that "we strongly feel that the producer (Ucicky) and the author (Menzel) of this film should be on the list of war criminals.—(a report to this effect has been made to Intelligence P.W.D.)."[41]

Discussions may have followed about which of the well-known actors and directors named should be pursued for prosecution, but Gerhard Menzel (1894–1966) and Gustav Ucicky (1898–1961) were the only movie people to be deemed "war criminals" in Schulberg's "Progress Report."[42] "As late as 1940," despite throwing in his lot with the Nazified Wien-Film company, Gustav Ucicky remained "a respected name" to some critics because of his film *Mutterliebe* (*A Mother's Love*, 1939), for which Gerhard Menzel cowrote the screenplay.[43] While that film was an ardent endorsement of the generic conservative (and Nazi) slogan of "Kinder, Küche, Kirche," it had none of the violence of their wartime productions.

Neither Menzel nor Ucicky, however, suffered more than a brief hiatus from filmmaking after the German defeat. Ucicky is now best known not for his Nazi filmography—but as an illegitimate offspring of painter Gustav Klimt; Ucicky was eventually able to claim a number of his father's works. After Ucicky's death in 1961, his wife established a foundation that has made an effort to "resolve the provenance" of the works, that is, to discover their previous owners and make some effort at compensation. Many of Klimt's paintings were owned by Jews and then, after 1933, sold under pressure or looted by the Nazis.[44] Ucicky's descendants, though, have reaped a fortune by "sharing" auction proceeds.[45]

Schulberg's intention to bring the German film industry to account was beyond his control and not consistently followed through. "Whatever one's views from an ethical or a pragmatic perspective," Mary Fulbrook writes, "there is a related paradox. The familiar narrative about public debates and cultural representations in West Germany is one of 'facing up to the past' ever more openly and honestly over time, yet this narrative is almost entirely at odds with the actual records of justice in the courtroom, as well as the stories told in the privacy of the home. In none of the Third Reich successor states," East and West Germany, later unified Germany, "were the problems of state-ordained mass violence dealt with adequately through the legal process."[46] Many of the actors and directors Schulberg identified, such as Hans Schweikart, Willie Birgel, Paul Hartmann, Arthur Maria Rabenalt, Harald Paulsen, Heinz Paul, Alfred Bittins, and Svend Noldan, had two or three years away from film work. Hans Steinhoff was killed in a plane crash in 1945, and one of the few others not to enjoy a thriving post–Second World War career was Karl Ritter (1888–1977). Ritter, an early and deeply committed Nazi, was the director of *Kadetten* (1939), which "depicts the cruelty of the Russians when they enter the war against Frederick the Great."[47] This obviously was produced when the brief Nazi-Soviet Nonaggression Pact seemed inconceivable. Ritter also directed *Über alles in der Welt* (1941), which showed German bomber crews cheering when ordered to bomb Warsaw, and "mocking" the efforts of the Free French, the Free Austrians, and the Allied Air Force.[48] Perhaps as a result of Schulberg's constructive if not uproarious engagement with his Soviet counterparts, Ritter was apprehended, tried, and found guilty of being a Nazi "fellow traveler" (*Mitläufer*) by the Soviets. He managed, though, to flee to Argentina in 1947, returning to West Germany and free to work as he pleased since the 1950s.[49]

But the ground laid by Schulberg's unit, in such a brief space of time, for the purpose of serving the main Nuremberg proceedings with film evidence was extraordinary. "The IMT [International Military Tribunal] had grand aims" historian Mary Fulbrook astutely observes: "In effect, it served not only to try individual defendants but also to *display* the extraordinary scope of Nazi atrocities. Devastating evidence was presented across a wide range of areas. *It often is said that the genocide of the Jews did not figure prominently at this time, and certainly the word Holocaust was not as yet current, but there was a full awareness of the enormity of crimes against the Jews.*"[50] Schulberg also may be seen as remarkable, among US government officials, in recognizing the significance of antisemitism and the annihilation of European Jewry as inextricably linked with Nazi aggression and colonization and as a unifying force for National Socialism as well as a consistently vital element in Nazi propaganda.[51] Among those who comprised the Washington-Hollywood connection, Budd Schulberg and his brother Stuart, under the auspices of the OSS, most pointedly engaged the annihilation of European Jewry, although terms such as genocide and the Holocaust were not yet common.

The efforts of the brothers Schulberg emerged in the wake of the war, partly through the film that was unearthed in Germany's rubble as well as that shot by Allied cameramen among the liberators of the death camps. That these films were shocking no doubt contributed to the early postwar compilation movies of Stuart Schulberg and Sidney Bernstein being shelved for decades. But they also were probably sidelined owing to their Jewish centeredness. Authorities in the United States and Britain—not only the Soviet Union—were wary of showing how much Nazi energy was disproportionately expended on persecuting and murdering Jews. In the USSR and the United States, decision-makers in these matters included Jews. Even retrospectively, they did not want the world war to be perceived as a Jewish war, especially given that there were already strident voices in the United States and Britain claiming that it had been a mistake to accept the Soviets as an ally.[52]

Schulberg's obsession with locating Nazi films of anti-Jewish atrocities points to a problem faced by Rosten and Spigelgass that they had a hard time articulating. It was difficult to deal, in film news reports and features, with the plight of European Jewry during wartime because they had little to hang it on, pictorially. What would be the basis, photographically, of such a story? Interestingly, it seems that Rosten might have had a hand in setting the stage for the work of Schulberg's crew. As early as 1943, he was assigned, with his British counterpart, to determine how war criminals were to be treated at the close of hostilities.[53] This was intertwined with his high-level role in shaping European opinion with an eye to the future. Rosten's people had to turn to other means besides film to tell the story of mass atrocities, as was attempted through the "Lidice" presentations that focused on the killing of Reinhard Heydrich by

Czech partisans, followed by the Nazi mass murder of civilians, including numerous women and children, as a supposed "response."[54] In confronting what was happening to Jews, Rosten maintained that film and other media had to be scrupulous to avoid spreading "rumors."[55] He also may have been wary about giving away information that had been gleaned through intelligence, such as code breaking, of which he was no doubt aware.[56] For the American Jewish Congress, Lowell Mellett and Nelson Poynter were the officials to whom they turned in hopes that a feature film or documentary would focus attention on the Jewish catastrophe. Mellett's response, claiming that such a course of action could be detrimental to Jewry, left them frustrated and perplexed.[57] There is little doubt that the advice he received also was animated by the unarticulated fear of giving credence to any suspicion that the Second World War was, in any respect, undertaken for a Jewish cause.

To the extent that Rosten, Spigelgass, and the other Hollywood Jews may have had some, however limited, scope for doing something to relieve the plight of Jews: this might be seen in their consistent advocacy, when given a chance, of opening up a major western front well before D-Day in 1944.[58] They also were extremely supportive of the Soviet Union as an ally,[59] a role that Anatole Litvak, Michael Curtiz, Albert Maltz, and others took on with great aplomb. But unlike Schulberg, they hardly ever concerned themselves directly with the catastrophe being faced by Europe's Jews.[60]

This does not mean, however, that those who comprised the Hollywood-Washington nexus were oblivious to antisemitism. They worked assiduously to root it out in the US armed forces and American society in total. Perhaps most importantly and effectively, they helped to staunch the impression that FDR had "dragged the nation into war," which harbored unmistakable antisemitic undertones.[61] They self-consciously fostered the myth of racial and religious harmony, which they hoped would become a self-fulfilling prophecy, as was perhaps most clearly evident in the body of work of Robert Rossen, Daniel Taradash, and Stanley Kramer. These ideals reflected, in fact, what many Jewish American servicemen lived and felt, which was also shared, to a great extent, on the home front. They were part of the country, and even appreciated. This was most in evidence when the parents of servicemen who happened to be first-generation Americans, including "Jewish heroes" killed in action, were presented to the public.[62] Military service was a leveler, and the greatest cause imaginable, in which Jewish interests were at one with the nation.

The unwieldy production of American film attempted to show how anti-Jewish prejudice would not be tolerated in the evolving wartime ethos of the Allies. Perhaps nothing illustrates this more succinctly than the Frank Sinatra short, *The House I Live In* (dir. Mervyn LeRoy, 1945), for which the title song concludes: "All races and religions, that's America to me." One of the writers of *The House I Live In*, Albert Maltz, was screenwriter of *Destination Tokyo* (1943) and the Academy Award–nominated *Pride of the Marines* (dir. Delmer Daves, 1945). Like the story-within-a-story of Meyer Levin in *The House I Live In*, the center of *Pride of the Marines* is a classic buddy tale, in which the two buddies, Al Schmid, played by John Garfield, and Lee Diamond, played by Dane Clark, are portrayed as all-American while being recognizably Gentile and Jew. The third of their tight-knit unit, Johnny Rivers, was played by Anthony Caruso, who would easily have been identified as Italian. Johnny appears only briefly, because he was killed in the Battle of the Tenaru River on Guadalcanal, August 21, 1942, which is vividly portrayed. Lee was wounded in the arm, and Schmid was nearly blinded by a Japanese hand grenade. In this case, softly ethnic German and Jewish friendship is just as important as the love story between Schmid and his hometown sweetheart, Eleanor Parker as Ruth Hartley.

Maltz's own tale would not close with a satisfying Hollywood sunset. Born into a wealthy family, Maltz studied at Columbia University followed by the Yale School of Drama. He became interested in Marxism and joined the Communist Party. He courted controversy by calling on fellow Communists not to impugn the quality of their writing for their cause in *The New Masses* in 1946, which has been grist for quasi-Talmudic disputations ever since.[63] Along with screenwriting, he was author of a novel, *The Cross and the Arrow* (1944) about internal resistance to the Nazis, showing that not all Germans had been true believers in Hitler.[64] "In the latter half of the nineteen-twenties," Maltz writes, concerning the family of the village doctor who tends to the protagonist in the novel's beginning, "the activities of the growing Hitler movement began to intrude into their sheltered life. Zoder [the doctor] read the leaflets mailed so regularly to his home; invariably he used them to light his stove. He didn't like the violence of the Nazi creed, he despised the absurdity of its racism, and he felt certain that no intelligent person would adhere for long to a movement so stupid. Even later, when the Nazis grew powerful, Zoder was still not frightened. If Hitler ever did become Chancellor, he told his wife, Germany would nevertheless continue on its democratic way. No one could turn a society on its head. That was unthinkable."[65]

Rosten most likely was involved in *The Cross and the Arrow* being produced in a special edition and given to US servicemen in Europe. Prior to *The Pride of the Marines*, Maltz cowrote (with Elliot Paul) the English-language subtitles of a Soviet war film, *Moscow Strikes Back* (dirs. Leonid Varnlmov and Ilya Kopalin), which received an Academy Award for Best Documentary in 1942. Upon his death in 1985, the *Los Angeles Times* wrote that Maltz was "one of the

'Hollywood 10' whose careers were overshadowed if not eclipsed by their refusal to betray their friends and principles by testifying before the House Un-American Activities Committee in 1947." Maltz was "found guilty of contempt of Congress and spent ten months in prison for refusing on constitutional grounds to answer questions about alleged Communist infiltration and influence of the motion picture industry. The ten, plus more than two hundred other lesser-known Hollywood figures, were blacklisted and denied work in the film industry for decades afterward. Friends said that during his last months, Maltz worked ten to twelve hours a day to finish his last novel, a long and serious work entitled *Bel Canto* based on the French Resistance movement during World War II."[66] The fate of Albert Maltz is part of the reason why the story told here is not better known.[67] Many of those who were hounded, if they were able to work in film, fled abroad. This was an age when the trans-Atlantic trade in film and television, from Britain and Europe to America, was not nearly as lively as it would later become.

Jesse Lasky Jr., who should have been given a pass due to his association with DeMille, was nevertheless "called up before HUAC and questioned as to whether he was a member of the Communist Party." He was accused of having attended a suspicious event with Dorothy Parker. He answered truthfully that he had not. He was not questioned any further when it was discovered that the very day he was supposedly hobnobbing with Parker and the reds Lasky had been filming a landing of General Douglas Macarthur in the Pacific.[68]

Leo Rosten and Leonard Spigelgass, while generally "liberal," clearly cast their lot with those who chose to play it safe in the witch hunts. Budd Schulberg's ambivalence, in light of his earlier flirtation with radicalism, has been revisited a number of times.[69] He never had been much of a follower of any political camp since his youth, and he was embittered by the Communist Party's attempt to interfere with his writing of *What Makes Sammy Run?* But those who found themselves shunned by Hollywood or were more deeply affected than others by the recriminations were not only split between those persecuted and those not. The men who had so loyally served their country through film work, with a kind of solidarity that would have been comical in their prewar studios, were often bitterly divided through the excesses of the Cold War. The fierce enmity against those who abetted the cause of Joseph McCarthy, or remained silent when colleagues were unfairly defamed, was fueled because so many of the accused had given their all for the American cause. Some, like Maltz, were specifically used by Rosten, Capra, Mellett, and Poynter for their familiarity with the Soviet Union, writing the script for *Mission to Moscow*.[70] In 1943 Jesse Lasky Sr. wrote to his son that *Mission to Moscow* was certain to "cause considerable controversy" but that it was "the most courageous film ever produced."[71] Talents like Maltz were desperately needed to explain to the Americans that the Russians were now their friends, that the Soviet Union should be embraced as an ally, and to tell compelling stories such as the Soviets' monumental victories over the Nazis. It is estimated that there were around twenty feature films "with a clear pro-Soviet message" between 1942 and 1944 as well as several short films and segments of series such as *The Army-Navy Screen Magazine*.[72]

Jules Buck was never a Communist, nor expressly pro-Soviet, but he found he could no longer countenance the mean-spirited climate, and the accompanying dishonesty, of Hollywood under McCarthyism in the 1950s. He was one of the movie men who had been crucial in elevating the quality of wartime cinematography and moviemaking overall. Buck famously endured a tumultuous relationship with John Huston, and he was one of the few film professionals castigated for using reenactments in *The Battle of San Pietro*. Buck and Huston were "unjustly accused of having faked the battle footage," but Huston suffered few ill effects.[73] The use of "reenactments" and shots from other times and locales was, however, a standard practice, especially as the category of "documentary" film was barely defined. This was in full view in the case of *December 7*, an Academy Award–winning documentary, which has "Uncle Sam" and his "Conscience" as lead characters.

After 1945 Jules Buck continued his Hollywood filmmaking and worked with Jules Dassin (1911–2008) as associate producer on *Brute Force* (1947) and *The Naked City* (1948). Dassin had been a Communist, leaving the party after the announcement of the Nazi-Soviet pact in 1941. This was enough, though, for him to be implicated by the House Un-American Activities Committee in 1951, which derailed his career.[74] During the war, Dassin directed *Reunion in France* (1942), a star vehicle for John Wayne and Joan Crawford, with a Casablanca-like storyline, and *Nazi Agent* (1942), about a set of German twins representing good versus evil, which was in production before the Americans officially entered the war. His wartime work probably included being an assistant director for Garson Kanin. Dassin left the United States for France in 1953.[75]

In the late 1940s, Jules Buck joined John Huston and Sam Spiegel to create Horizon Pictures, for which the first project was Huston's *We Were Strangers* (1949). Following that, Buck joined Darryl Zanuck at 20th Century Fox, producing *Treasure of the Golden Condor* (dir. Delmer Daves, 1953) and *Love Nest* (dir. Joseph M. Newman, 1951). "Although he was not blacklisted, Mr. Buck left Hollywood in 1952 in protest against political repression," such as that experienced by Dassin.[76] "Jules was not a Communist," his daughter, Joan Juliet Buck, writes. "He had the American mistrust of socialism, but he knew that every American had the right to his beliefs. His friend Philip Dunne founded the Committee for the First Amendment to protest the first witch hunt. Jules joined at once."[77] Dunne (1908–92), "a leading screenwriter and founder of the Screen Writers Guild," had served as the head of production for the Motion Picture Bureau of the Office of War Information during the Second World War.[78] He was one of the writers of *A Salute to France* (1944), an exceptionally good film directed by Garson Kanin and Jean Renoir, which helped to convince American soldiers why it was important to fight for the liberation of France—despite its crushing defeat and collaborationist regime eager to do the Nazis' bidding.[79] Leo Rosten also had been deeply involved. He coordinated the effort to bolster support for the French in the transition to peacetime, writing an unattributed (at the time) guide for overcoming ill feelings about the French.[80]

After relocating himself and his family to France, Jules Buck enhanced the comedic worldliness of Americans by arranging, with his brother-in-law Don Getz, the American distribution of Jacques Tati's movies.[81] In 1959, after seeing Peter O'Toole on the West End stage, Buck hired him to appear in *The Day They Robbed the Bank of England* (dir. John Guillermin, 1960), which led to O'Toole being cast in the title role of *Lawrence of Arabia* (dir. David Lean, 1962). Later Buck and O'Toole joined forces in their own production company. In addition to movies, Buck produced a television series in Britain, *O.S.S.* (1957), about an intrepid American agent operating in Nazi-occupied France. "With his wife, Joyce, he returned to Los Angeles in 1980. After his wife died in 1996, he moved to Paris, where he lived with his daughter, Joan Juliet Buck, who was then editor of French *Vogue*."[82] Buck never told his daughter, or anyone else, precisely what he had done to merit a Purple Heart.[83]

Jules Buck may have supported neither Communism nor socialism, but he and his "tribe" were in favor of a joined-up world without chauvinism, generally liberal and humanitarian, and vehemently anti-racist. In a sea of ironies, Howard Koch, who had been a screenwriter for *Sergeant York* and *Casablanca*, was blacklisted in the 1950s, "at least partly because he had written *Mission to Moscow*. Asked how he knew his Hollywood career had ended, he answered, 'The phone stopped ringing.' He and his wife moved to England, where he worked on screenplays under pseudonyms," returning to the United States after some five years.[84] A similar fate befell director Lewis Milestone (1895–1980). Milestone, who gained experience with training films for the US Army Signal Corps immediately after the Great War, directed *The North Star* (1943), the underappreciated *Edge of Darkness* (1943), and *A Walk in the Sun* (1945), written by Robert Rossen. Few would have disagreed that films such as *Mission to Moscow* were "a necessity in time of war." But "the witch hunt that followed," exacerbated by "paranoia and uncertainty, left a great scar on the history of the American society of the 1950s."[85] It could barely go unnoticed that many of the accused happened to be Jews. One of the reasons why it would be problematic to accord Leo Rosten and Leonard Spigelgass a heroic stature is that they were very aware that Hollywood professionals like Koch, Milestone, Rossen, and others were being severely punished, and lives were ruined, because they had done what was asked of them during World War II. Rosten and Spigelgass were, after all, among the individuals best situated to testify on their behalf but remained silent on this front. Few took notice of Rosten's rare public statements about the mindlessness of accusations of "propagandizing."[86]

As post-1945 winds of change brought the demand for Black civil rights to public attention, Rosten, Spigelgass, and the other wartime filmmakers also could be challenged for not focusing greater efforts on ameliorating anti-Black racism during wartime. There were, as to be expected, a few efforts to publicize "heroic" Negroes,[87] and Rosten strongly asserted that there was a "great need for more honest portrayal of the negro and his problem at this time."[88] But like their difficulties in presenting the story of Nazi antisemitism, it seemed that they lacked film material as the basis for a story. "There are, obviously, great difficulties in the way of a film specifically directed to negroes or specially concerned with the negro problem."[89] Rosten did say what was well known: that "negroes" were, until very late in the war, segregated into subsidiary services roles in the US armed forces.[90] He added, parenthetically, that "We are, you remember, planning a short based on Joe Louis," the Black boxing legend, "and the Army; and Frank Capra outlined an excellent film which he is planning to do as part of his series."[91] This materialized as a recruitment film, *The Negro Soldier* (dir. Stuart Heisler, 1944), but it was not officially part of the *Why We Fight* series.[92] It may be argued, though, that emphasis on Nazism's institution of slavery as one of its greatest evils was a means of addressing the historical persecution and dispossession of America's black population.[93] Certainly efforts were made, such as a short on "Negro colleges in wartime," even though stereotypes were far from overcome.[94] Arnaud d'Usseau, another scriptwriter in Spigelgass's cohort during the war, one of the few African Americans, wrote a long-running Broadway play, *Deep Are the Roots* (1945), with James Gow. This was a "drama about a black Army officer who returns to the South after World War II, becomes the head of a school and falls in love with the daughter of a retired Senator."[95] The greatest objective for the Hollywood-Washington crew during the war was to create and maintain cohesion and solidarity in the United States itself more or less in its 1941 form.[96] They were much more progressive in their internationalism than their anti-racism.

The work for which Leo Rosten is best known, *Joys of Yiddish* (1968), can be seen as a way of joining the chorus, of claiming and enhancing multiculturalism—integrating Yiddish into America. It was the polar opposite of what the heroine in *Heimkehr* was decrying: that American culture is made all the more rich and interesting by being interspersed with Yiddish. And Yiddish must be seen as inextricable from its base in the German language, its abundance of Hebraisms, and countless words derived from other languages, including Turkish and Arabic. It also was a way of dealing with the Holocaust—partly restoring the lost culture—from which Rosten studiously maintained a distance during his vital government service.[97]

Certainly in the 1960s and 1970s, especially in the wake of the television miniseries *Holocaust* (1978), questions would have arisen for Rosten: if you worked for the government during the war, what did you know, and what did you do about the Jews? Eventually the question would be asked: What did you do about the Holocaust? Some individuals might have even recalled appealing to Rosten to bring attention to the Jewish plight, only to be shunted to his assistant, who was said to "specialize in minority group problems."[98]

Rosten and Spigelgass could claim, to their credit, that their own movie *All Through the Night* (1942), for which Spigelgass and Rosten wrote the story and Spigelgass shared screenwriting credit, had the first Hollywood mention of a concentration camp. None other than Humphrey Bogart sounded the alarm: the Nazis were "criminals, murderers," unlike any other threat to the country and the world. They were already sowing "disruption and dissension," and conquest of the United States was part of the plan for world domination. The best comic turn is when Phil Silvers, playing an unnamed waiter with poor eyesight, becomes the most effective fighter in a brawl against the (American) Nazis. When a man comes near him, he says "Heil." And if the guy raises his arm and responds "Heil Hitler!" Phil bashes him in the head with a club. But despite sharing several cast members with *Casablanca*, *All Through the Night* was not a film that would make much of a difference. The anti-Nazi message may have been confusing because the main plot device was an attempt to blow up a battleship in the New York harbor. By the time of its release, even the ambition of such an attack by Nazi accomplices in New York was a pale imitation of the reality of Pearl Harbor.

It is worth considering what makes *All Through the Night*, in the long run, not terribly successful. It is hardly ever shown or broadcast, versus *Casablanca*, which is among the most seen and feted films of all time. *All Through the Night* did decently at the box office and with the critics. But to many Americans from the 1950s to the present, it would strike some discordant notes. Besides being filled with glib, mainly Irish stereotyped characters and lines—taken for granted at the time—there are two aspects that sharply differentiate it from *Casablanca*. Bogart's Nick in *Casablanca* is more subdued than his character of "Gloves" Donahue in *All Through the Night*. "Gloves" strikes, with a closed fist, the costar and love interest, Leda Hamilton, played by Kaaren Verne. The blow to the "dame" is to knock her out, to get her out of the way for her own good at that moment. He does, though, apologize later, and she's more than understanding. Still, Bogart delivering a punch to the head, to a woman, is strange and shocking. Hitting women, though, was typical in movies up to that time. In William Wyler's British melodrama *Mrs. Miniver* (dir. William Wyler, 1942), when Walter Pigeon's Clem Miniver learns that his wife (played by Greer Garson), in his absence while he was shuttling soldiers from Dunkirk, has single-handedly subdued an armed German airman slaps her quite sharply on the behind. But in the context, it is after Mrs. Miniver has proven that she was the "tough" of the family.

Another aspect of *All Through the Night* that would be unpalatable to post–World War II audiences is the treatment of the shoeshine "boy"/valet, "Deacon," also (inexplicably) called "Saratoga" by Gloves. He is a pop-eyed, all-too-eager-to-please Black man. Although Rick (in *Casablanca*) gets angry with "Sam, the 'Negro' musician," played by Arthur "Dooley" Wilson, it is their ease with one another and warm relationship that predominates, even though Rick is Sam's employer.[99] "Sam helps to propel the film forward," Noah Isenberg writes, "his deep voice conveying an abundance of grace and humanity, his gimlet eyes leading the viewer to understand the full significance of Ilse's return. He's a genuine friend to Rick, his sole traveling companion, and the one character who tries to shield him from pain, offering to get drunk and go fishing with him to avoid the torturous revisiting of his love affair. He's also the friend who, in the Paris flashback, breaks the news of Ilsa's rejection."[100]

That Dooley's "Sam" is "deep and complex" is the antithesis of "Deacon," the dopey manservant played by Sam McDaniel in *All Through the Night*. While there is an intimation of more of a history and substance behind "Deacon," when he mentions that he had been a soldier fighting Germans in France, he plays the fool in a quick exchange with a minor (white) character, Annabelle. Annabelle has just married Barney, a second-tier underling of "Gloves." Barney wants to leave for his honeymoon, but Gloves insists that Barney must stick with his crew. In a huff, Annabelle, left alone with Deacon, exclaims: "Married twenty minutes. And already I'm a widow." To which Deacon replies, his face taking up most of the screen: "Don'sha worry, Miss. Things ain't always as black as dey looks." While it may be argued that such depictions had come long before and would outlast this particular character in *All Through the Night*, from the 1970s onward it makes for cringeworthy viewing. Robert Rossen's film about corruption in boxing, *Body and Soul* (1947), included a Black supporting character, Canada Lee playing boxer Ben Chaplin, who was treated abysmally by the promoters but stood up for himself and the ideal of the "fair fight." The film's protagonist, Jewish actor John Garfield playing a Jewish fighter, Charley Davis, is inspired to challenge a rigged match when his friend Chimen reminds him how much he means to fellow Jews, especially in light of Hitler having tried to destroy them. Both Rossen and Lee, a professional boxer and civil rights activist, were victimized by the "blacklisting" of the 1950s.[101]

One of the lessons that Rosten and Spigelgass's cohort would impart, in large measure, in their wartime work is to "treat others as you would wish to be treated yourself." One could trace this to the sage Hillel in the Talmud, Jesus in the Gospel, and Immanuel Kant's "categorical imperative" to regard all people as "ends" and never as "means." In the kind of movies that were churned out by Americans during the war, gratuitous violence, and humiliating discrimination based solely on ethnic and racial markers were reserved for the Axis. They defined their own country and its people against such "Nazi" ways of thinking and acting.

It would mainly be Black people themselves who would do the most to alter deeply ingrained, prejudiced attitudes about race in American films. The wartime film enterprise, however, helped to pave the way for such changes. Before Harry Truman's integration of the US armed forces, there probably wasn't even a discussion about whether to include a Negro boy as a character in the pithy, liberal short *The House I Live In* (1945), even though Frank Sinatra spoke pointedly against judging people on the basis of "race and religion." "Negros," though, had been included among those targeted as unfairly maligned in two of the most explicitly anti-racist "government" films, *Don't Be a Sucker* and *Twenty-Seven Soldiers*.

And in *The Pride of the Marines* (1945), the Black train porter (played by the uncredited George Reed) is depicted as a wise, elderly soul—who also had served in World War I. The movie takes pains, though, to lambast antisemitism as well as prejudice against Mexicans. A major objective of *Pride of the Marines* was to engender compassion for disabled war veterans, such as the blinded protagonist Al Schmid, in hopes that they would get the support needed to effect their integration into society as much as possible. Although it served as good press, actor John Garfield, who played Schmid, had met and befriended the real Schmid "well before there were plans to make a movie of his life," and he spent a few weeks with Schmid and his wife in preparing for the role.[102] No doubt this contributed to the verdict of the *New York Times* film critic who wrote of *Pride of the Marines* that "the vital and delicate subject of the rehabilitation of wounded men—a subject which has broad implications to civilians as well as to service men today—is treated with uncommon compassion, understanding, and dignity, as well as with absorbing human interest."[103] The producer, Jerry Wald—thought to be one of the models of Schulberg's *Sammy*—was among Leo Rosten's closest colleagues, to whom he had earlier imparted meticulous advice about how to make movies fit for the purpose of supporting US war aims.[104] Wald took these to heart in *Pride of the Marines*, which originally had been titled *The Love of Ours*.[105]

Whatever the failings of *All Though the Night*, Rosten, Spigelgass, and the rest had more than a satisfactory answer about not answering, more affirmatively, to both anti-Black racism and the yet-unnamed Holocaust: they were providing a means of cohesion that could not be taken for granted. They served the president and first lady, who knew and appreciated Hollywood and were truly at home with Jews—despite their patrician upbringing. For quite understandable reasons, Jews themselves were instrumental in the Jewish story being subsumed in the dramatic whole of the myths and realities of "The Good War."[106] On the other hand, there was greater political and cultural engagement with antisemitism by the United States during and after the war through film than many have contended. Jewish questions were handled directly and in understated and coded ways that nonetheless fostered non-Jews' solidarity with Jews. Despite antisemitism within the United States armed forces and society at large, and lingering suspicions about ties between Jews and Hollywood, the industry's Jews punched way above their weight for the war effort. They had always taken pride in their work, seeking "to make good pictures,"[107] and the US role in the war endowed it with significance that affected them deeply.[108] They helped keep the United States, at home and its troops in the field, at one with the cause and feeling mutually accountable to each other. And their work extended to using movies to ensure that the peace would hold firm, justice would be done, and the world would be a better place, however corny that might sound.

Epilogue

In 1947 Leo Rosten identified himself as having been "the chief" of the Motion Picture Bureau of the US National Defense Advisory Commission.[1] Formed in May 1940, the administration deemed it a successor of the Council of National Defense, an obscure agency created during the First World War. In early January 1941, "an administrative order of the President (6 F.R. 192) provided that the activities and agencies of the Advisory Commission, which had absorbed the functions of the Council, should henceforth be coordinated through the Office for Emergency Management, which was established within the Executive Office of the President. The last meeting of the Advisory Commission was on October 22, 1941." If recognized at all, this commission is seen as having been superseded by the Office of Scientific Research and Development in 1941. Yet the National Defense Advisory Commission, later a "committee," maintained an advisory role.[2] The clout reserved and asserted by its members, into the war years and beyond, is an open question.

Leo Rosten, for one, didn't just fade away. His appointment to this position in 1940 by FDR was a strong signal, in terms of where the president placed his trust and confidence.[3] But Rosten's name appears nowhere in official publications concerning this commission (or committee). He remained one of Roosevelt's key men dealing with motion pictures. Hundreds of documents, many of which have been cited in this book, attest to Rosten's function as a "chief" in coordinating Washington's connection to Hollywood. It's a fitting, if somewhat impolitic title, as so many from tinseltown were "members of the tribe."

At first it would be a fraught mission for Rosten. With the notable exception of the Schulbergs, the Laskys, Walter Wanger, and the Warners, most of Hollywood's moguls, in contrast to actors, writers, cameramen, and (most) directors, were not so keen on FDR. Up to December 7, 1941, critics of FDR in Congress seethed with indignation that Hollywood was abetting the president's "interventionist" inclination. Which it was. Barring Cecil B. DeMille, Hollywood's heavyweights had generally refrained from vilifying Roosevelt as did the staunch Republicans and conservatives. The president was attempting to bring the country out of the Depression, its worst crisis since the Civil War. And before Pearl Harbor, FDR seemed willing to assist those worldwide who were suffering from, or threatened by, the yoke of tyranny, in the face of home-grown isolationists who counted Charles Lindbergh as their champion.[4] The power of Lindbergh, a historian has recently argued, was diminished as a result of the strengthening of public ardor for *Sergeant York*—the person and the movie.[5]

To those who were in the first wave of expeditionary forces to be sent overseas in 1941 (such as my own father), FDR wrote a brief but powerful message: "You are a soldier of the United States Army. You have embarked for distant places where the war is being fought. Upon the outcome depends the freedom of your lives: the freedom of the lives of those you love—your fellow citizens—your people. *Never were the enemies of freedom more tyrannical, more arrogant, more brutal.* Yours is a God-fearing, proud, courageous people, which, throughout its history, has put its freedom under God before all other purposes. We who stay at home have our duties to perform—duties owed in many parts to you. You will be supported by the whole force and power of this Nation. The victory you will win will be a victory *of all the people*—common to *them all.* You bear with you the hope, the confidence, the gratitude and the prayers of your family, your fellow-citizens, and your President."[6]

While the president's wishes were heartfelt, not all his claims about his own nation could hold up to scrutiny. Despite the attack on Pearl Harbor, there were many Americans who, along with a large share of the press corps, did not trust FDR.[7] Despite Hitler having declared war on the United States, many felt that there was insufficient justification for America being in Europe, particularly so soon after the last conflict—which had supposedly been "the war to end all wars."

President Roosevelt, his administration, and the military needed help to turn the solidarity he exalted from wishful thinking into a resilient reality. He needed storytellers and artists to describe, to the soldiers, what they might face and, to those at home, what was going on in the far-flung, complicated jumble of theaters that comprised the Second World War. FDR could not risk being seen, or even suspected, of being chummy with these lead tacticians who happened to be Jews. While movies were not the only wellsprings of information and cohesion, they were hugely popular. These young and not-so-young (mainly Jewish) Hollywood guys professed and embodied "an honest interest in the medium."[8] "Pictures are more than a great business," proclaimed Irving

Thalberg, the closest Hollywood would come to a local saint. "They're a social responsibility."[9] A feeling of mutual accountability and national responsibility was intensified with the rise of fascism, even though many Hollywood bosses contended until December 1941 that "no matter what we think of those countries personally, we're still maintaining diplomatic relations, we're still trying to do business with them."[10]

But modern societies, from the 1930s on, could only wage total war with the help of movies. FDR himself, as a young man, was keen to get into film, a goal that was shared by thousands, if not millions, of his fellow Americans. After war in Europe was ignited by Hitler, and especially after the fall of France, the president knew that, as commander in chief, to make Hollywood his helpmate he needed to engage those who were already in its inner organs. Among the young men with whom he was well acquainted, who were deep in the *kishkes* of Hollywood, was a certain Leo Rosten. Rosten was a favorite of Roosevelt's beloved "brain trust" stalwart, Louis Brownlow—who himself never sought a spotlight. FDR, prizing able administrators, also valued the crafts of cinematography, scriptwriting, editing, and creating musical scores. He knew that those who made movies were not a representative cross section of America. Eleanor Roosevelt was probably one of a select few who found Louis B. Mayer, "the industry's most powerful figure," "extremely cordial and kind" on a visit to his studio in March 1938.[11] Hollywood's ranks, while not exclusive, were heavily weighted to a less-than-disciplined tribe, first- and second-generation American Jews, and a number of émigrés and refugees.[12] Their European coreligionists happened to be the focus of sizzling hatred of America's enemy, Germany, and Jews in the United States were themselves demeaned by large patches of FDR's own constituency. "The domestic fascists," the historian William E. Leuchtenberg writes, "execrated Franklin Roosevelt and the 'Jew Deal.'"[13]

Less than two months into the war, Nazi Germany heated up a propaganda campaign in America, claiming that the president was "entering into a partnership with the Jews of the world to defend Jewish aspirations and to fight in distant regions for Jewish aims."[14] FDR took pains not to lend such charges credence, but he needed the Hollywood Jews. He also liked them, and he relished working and playing with them. Roosevelt was sophisticated enough to know that no matter how intelligent people are, they need stories. And they might have to be told hard truths, complex matters that ultimately would benefit them. FDR did not believe in the myth of objectivity, as it applied to the news and newsreels in particular. He did not trust that truth and goodness were certain to win out. He would have heartily agreed with the words of Jules Buck, whom he probably knew through his cousin Kermit: "You can't capture reality. You have to shape it."[15] Although he was not explicitly referring to his Second World War role, Leo Rosten dismissed the idea that "facts speak for themselves" as a vacuous myth. "Facts don't speak at all. Facts are entirely and utterly meaningless until they are arranged and structured and patterned."[16] The work of Jules Buck, Rosten, Lasky Jr., Taradash, Cukor, Kanin, and others, along with the five biggest name directors, helped assure that the Second World War was experienced as "The Good War" to the mass of Americans.

At the war's end, Budd Schulberg played an extraordinary role in showing how the Nazis, with the help of their own movies, had attempted to dominate Europe with no thought to the humanity of the nations and people they had vanquished. Photographs and motion picture film conveyed the unspeakable aftermath of the Holocaust, and crimes against humanity were vividly accorded a place in the courtroom as never before. Despite the unprecedented tyranny of the Allies' adversaries, ideas were promulgated in American film of according justice and generosity to the defeated, through movies such as *Battle of Peace* (1945) and *The Pale Horseman* (dir. Irving Jacoby, 1946).[17] Precisely following the advice of Donald Slesinger, *The Pale Horseman* was done in both 35mm and 16mm, showing that it was intended for theaters and small communities far and wide. The short, *Battle of Peace*, for which there is no credit given except to the US Army Signal Corps, underscored the city of Cologne, "as each edition of the Army's German language newspaper hit the street, it talked of the rebuilding life of the city, the things inside the Germans, the other part of the MG's [Military government's] double job," along with tending to its cleanup and restoration of normal industry and functions.

> Half a million Germans read it every day. Although they suspected it as propaganda, they could look around and see what it talked about, see what the propaganda meant—what the military government had already done. They could see Corpus Christi celebrated in front of their exquisite cathedral for the first time in fourteen years. MG's doing—the battle of the peace. They could see Jewish people standing again in their temples. Buildings ruined not by war, but by the Nazis. They could see human beings raised again to honor and citizenship and freedom of religion under God—the things Americans had died in battle to bring back—the things MG was bringing back, the battle of the peace.[18]

The film closes with the title "Army-Navy Screen Magazine/The End/Issue No. 66." No names are given. Among those who would have filled conventional credits are Leonard Spigelgass, Julian Blaustein, Anthony Veiller, Daniel Taradash, Herbert Baker, Stanley Kramer, Arthur Lewis, David Miller, Don Ettinger, Teddy Mills, John Cheever, Claude Binyon, William Soroyan, Irwin

Shaw, Sidney Kingsley, Anatole Litvak, Arnaud d'Usseau, Jimmy Gow, Henry Berman, John Weaver, Irving Reis, Carl Foreman, Shepard Traube, and Gottfried Reinhardt.[19]

The fact that so much of the world loved Hollywood was the result of the fantasies it spun but also because it was terrific at what it did. The men (and occasional women, besides actresses) who had accumulated the usual Hollywood credits before going unnamed while in the US armed forces understood the innermost workings of the movies. Budd Schulberg conceived of using the Nazi's own movies against them to achieve justice. In contrast to Leni Riefenstahl's earlier interrogators, Schulberg realized that Riefenstahl had been one of the most significant proponents of Nazism. But as talented as were those who remained to make films for Hitler and Goebbels, one would be hard-pressed to find any semblance, in their camp, of the humor, warmth, grace, deft touches, and self-deprecation that accompanied the telling of stories on the part of the Washington-Hollywood nexus.

Many of the American wartime films, even on mundane subjects, are surprisingly watchable over seventy years later. Despite shying away from dealing with Nazi anti-Jewish persecution as it was happening, the careers of many of these filmmakers interwove abiding concern for racial and religious prejudice as well as wide varieties of wartime trauma and physical disabilities among soldiers and civilians that had only rarely been addressed in popular culture. They also sought to render, in film, a commitment to the idea of a harmonious Europe in the postwar world, which would be enmeshed with a multireligious and multiracial United States and would inherently respect Jews and Judaism. Movies, in total, would never be the same.

The Hollywood-Washington cohort was in thrall of the brilliance of Frank Capra, John Huston, John Ford, and George Stevens. Given the breadth and depth of what was asked of the highest level directors, it was critical that their underlings consistently made good quality, creative, and captivating movies.[20] The hyperenergetic and multifaceted efforts of Jules Buck, Jesse Lasky Jr., Daniel Taradash, Leonard Spigelgass, and Budd Schulberg at creating meaningful film, under intense pressure, is remarkable. The war, in and of itself, was not presented as "a virtue in American World War II film; it is, to use a recurring word, a job."[21] They accomplished their goal of teaching servicemen how to do their tasks, keeping them abreast of why they were significant and their role in the greater scheme of the war. They entertained and informed the public with an exceptional degree of honesty and integrity.

It was a milieu in which Albert Maltz, with pronounced leftist sympathies, could produce a Hollywood love letter to the US Marines Corps, in *Pride of the Marines*. And that movie contained explicit, not merely symbolic, rejoinders that Jews, Mexicans, and the physically handicapped must be treated fairly—which had not been the rule before the war. The general principle was to ensure the treatment for others that you would wish for yourself. Negroes, too, in their terms, were to be shown respect. The Hollywood tribe and those animated by its vision would help to create a world order, expressed through film, that would never permit another Hitler to rise. The Jewish members of the loose filmmaking detachments—although not always acknowledged for being leaders—fostered solidarity between Americans themselves and with the wider world without forcing conformity. They celebrated the differences and decency that they believed were hallmarks of America. Even before the US entry into the war, Hollywood overall sought to portray what one historian has called "fundamental distinctions between democracy and dictatorship."[22] They did so, both before and during the war, in tandem with the Roosevelt administration to a much greater extent than anyone was aware. An official US wartime publication, *Movies at War*, reported that of the approximately 200,000 people who were "employed in the various branches of the motion picture industry" in 1941, 78,808 of them, almost 40 percent, were serving in the armed forces by 1943.[23] There was never an estimate of how many of these were applying their Hollywood skills for the war effort.

Although the Washington-Hollywood guys never articulated it in such terms, they espoused and helped to fashion a distinct form of "public diplomacy," or perhaps more fittingly, "screen democracy."[24] Rosten himself suggested that the film work he coordinated, in service to FDR and the US government during World War II, was worthy of a scholarly reckoning. "Somebody could do a good study on it," he said in 1959.[25] Hollywood, the second major focus of Rosten's academic research (after studying the Washington press corps), had never been, and would never be, the bastion of the best and the brightest—unlike the wise souls he so admired who were summoned by Roosevelt for his "Brain Trust" and his "anonymous assistants."[26] Although the same could be said for Washington, Hollywood's ranks would invariably include "phonies, mediocrities, and good men who have lost their way," Budd Schulberg wrote as a young man. "But there is something that draws you there that you should not be ashamed of."[27] Concurring with Leo Rosten, FDR's movie gang scoffed at the "inept dichotomy of 'entertainment versus propaganda,'" which "made it difficult for Hollywood to defend the continuing broadening of subject matter which the movies were compelled to undertake,"[28] especially as the war was underway. Yet it is safe to assume that the Washington-Hollywood cohort was satisfied with what was accomplished. In an article, "The Myths We Live By" (1965), Rosten wrote: "The purpose of life is not to be happy. It is to be useful, to be honorable. It is to be compassionate. It is to *matter*, to have it make some difference that you lived."[29] But Rosten also admitted that "people love their work in the movies," even if it's "exhausting."[30]

This book began with a vignette of Harpo Marx accompanying President Roosevelt at an intimate yet important film screening. Watching the first of the "Why We Fight" series with Harry Hopkins, Alexander Woollcott, and FDR, Harpo helped initiate a dramatic shift in the movies that were presented to the American public. Harpo, apparently, kept this completely to himself.

It was not, however, the sole instance when the president warmly confided in his beloved Harpo. At the time of the 1944 Republican National Convention, June 30, Harpo wrote to FDR:

My dear Mr. President,

I listened to Governor [Earl] Warren's address outlining the Republican platform and he stressed three points. 1. Win the war, 2. Bring back the boys, 3. Get them jobs.
   I wonder if he thinks the Democratic platform is
   1. Lose the war, 2. Keep the boys over there, 3. Don't give them any jobs.

                                      My best to you always,
                                      Harpistically yours,
                                      (Herbert Swope gave me that word.)
                                      (signed)
                                      Harpo Marx

Barely a week later, July 7, 1944, the President wrote back.

Dear Harpo:

Thanks for your nice letter of the thirtieth. I'll bet if you tried to, you could play those six lines on your harp beautifully.
   It was good to hear from you.

                                      sincerely yours
                                      (signed)
                                      FRANKLIN D. ROOSEVELT[31]

Those discussed here were happy to have put their know-how to good use—sitting cheek by jowl with the president watching movies, staffing official and unofficial offices in Washington and Hollywood, shooting and editing film in the European theaters of war and jungle battlefields of the Pacific, and scouring burnt-out film depositories in defeated Germany. They were thrilled to have had the opportunity do what they loved at such a consequential moment. Rosten, Spigelgass, Slesinger, Litvak, Presnell, the Laskys, Schulberg, and company did indeed matter during the Second World War and its immediate aftermath. But they rarely talked about it. After all, it was the time of their service.

Notes

Preface and Acknowledgments

1. Letter from John Gutmann to Petra Benteler, June 21, 1989, AG:173: 6/23, business: Benteler-Morgan Galleries, 1989–90, Center for Creative Photography archives, University of Arizona, Tucson, Arizona.

2. Clayton D. Laurie, *The Propaganda Warriors: America's Crusade Against Nazi Germany* (Lawrence: University Press of Kansas, 1996), 118, 181.

3. Leo Rosten, *The Joys of Yiddish: A Relaxed Lexicon of Yiddish, Hebrew and Yinglish Words Often Encountered in English . . . from the Days of the Bible to Those of the Beatnik* (New York: McGraw-Hill, 1968).

4. Judith E. Doneson, *The Holocaust in American Film* (Philadelphia: The Jewish Publication Society, 1987).

5. Miriam Hansen, *Babel and Babylon: Spectatorship in American Silent Film* (Cambridge, MA: Harvard University Press, 1991).

Introduction

1. James M. Myers, *The Bureau of Motion Pictures: Its Influence on Film Content during World War II: The Reasons for Its Failure* (Lewiston, NY: Edwin Mellen Press, 1998), 171–78. "Roosevelt," along with "Churchill, Stalin, Mussolini, and Hitler had personal projectionists and private screening rooms for nightly viewing of dramatic and documentary films" (John Whiteclay Chambers II and David Culbert, "Introduction," in *World War II, Film, and History*, ed. John Whiteclay Chambers II and David Culbert [Oxford: Oxford University Press, 1996], 4). See also Thomas William Bohn, *An Historical and Descriptive Analysis of the "Why We Fight" Series* (New York: Arno Press, 1995).

2. Leo C. Rosten to H. L. McClinton, February 17, 1942, RG 208, Office of War Information, NC-148, Entry 294, Box No. 1554, File "R", National Archives and Records Administration (hereafter NARA), College Park, MD.

3. "Oral History interview[s] with Leo Calvin Rosten, [June and July] 1959 [transcription]," interviewed by Joan and Robert Franklin, Popular Arts Project, 55–57 and 2196–98, Columbia University Library, New York. Neal Gabler, in *An Empire of Their Own*, refers to this interview, and several scholars have cited Gabler's citations concerning movie producers. To the best of my knowledge, no other scholar has consulted

the entirety of this important interview. It was conducted in two parts, the first in June 1959 and the second in July 1959. The pages on the typescript (101 pages) have two sets of numbers, both of which will be cited here. See Neal Gabler, *An Empire of Their Own: How the Jews Invented Hollywood* (New York: Crown, 1988), 121, 209, 259, 302.

4. Myers, *Motion Pictures*, 172. Osborn's name is spelled "Osborne" by Myers, Leonard Spigelgass, and others.

5. Myers, *Motion Pictures*, 172–73.

6. See Mary Gelsey Samuelson, "The Patriotic Play: Roosevelt, Antitrust, and the War Activities Committee of the Motion Picture Industry" (PhD dissertation, University of California, Los Angeles, 2014), 118–21, for an alternate perspective. Samuelson's dissertation is a legal, administrative, and financial analysis of these relationships.

7. Samuelson, *"The Patriotic Play,"* 198.

8. See Allan M. Winkler, *The Politics of Propaganda: The Office of War Information, 1942–1945* (New Haven, CT: Yale University Press, 1978), 22–24, 29, 57–60. There is no indication of the significance of Leo Rosten and his work for the film division of the Office of Facts and Figures. The entirety of the Office of Facts and Figures is judged here as "unsuccessful," 24, 29.

9. Memorandum from Donald Slesinger to Milton Eisenhower, circulated by Leo Rosten, June 29, 1942, Organization, 1942–43, RG 208, Office of War Information, Records of the Office of the Director, Records of the Director. 1942–45, File M-O, Box 3, NARA.

10. Samuelson, *"The Patriotic Play,"* ii, 285.

11. Samuelson, *"The Patriotic Play,"* 256–57.

12. Rosten, *"Oral History,"* 54–55 and 2195–96.

13. The absence of Leo Rosten from the well-researched books of Thomas Doherty, *Projections of War: Hollywood, American Culture, and World War II* (New York: Columbia University Press, 1993), and James Myers may be due to Rosten's correspondence being classified until a very late date.

14. This is rarely noticed. It is mentioned in a footnote in Myers, *Motion Pictures*, n. 53, 185–86.

15. Kathryn Cramer Brownell, *Showbiz Politics: Hollywood in American Political Life* (Chapel Hill: University of North Carolina Press, 2014), 34, 45; Samuelson, *"The Patriotic Play,"* 76–81, 97, 102–3, 105–6, 113, 258–61, 263–64, 283–84.

16. Harpo Marx with Rowland Barber, *Harpo Speaks!*, new ed. (1962; repr., Lanham, MD: Limelight, 2017), 179.

17. Myers, *Motion Pictures*, 185–86, n. 53.

18. On Harpo's popularity and reputation at the time, see Oscar Levant, *A Smattering of Ignorance* (Garden City, NY: Garden City Publishing, 1940), 53–85, passim.

19. Levant, *A Smattering of Ignorance*, 65.

20. Simon Louvish, *Monkey Business: The Lives and Legends of the Marx Brothers* (London: Faber & Faber, 1999), 141–48, passim.

21. Generally reliable, *The Marx Brothers Encyclopedia* by Glenn Mitchell (London: B. T. Batsford, 1996) has little on the family's political activity.

22. Cf. Samuelson, *"The Patriotic Play,"* 287–88, 299–301, 306, 366, 375, 384.

23. Brownell, *Showbiz Politics*, 51–55.

24. Levant, *A Smattering of Ignorance*, 66.

25. Marx with Rowland Barber, *Harpo Speaks*, 13.
26. Doherty, *Projections of War*, 40.
27. Leonard Spigelgass, *The Scuttle under the Bonnet* (Garden City, NY: Doubleday, 1962), 164–65; Leo Rosten to Robert Taplinger, March 23, 1942, G 208, Office of War Information, NC-148, Entry 294, Box No. 1554, File "T," NARA.
28. "Marshall Is Dead in Capital at 78; World War Chief; a Nobel Laureate. Eisenhower Mourns Passing of Former Secretary of State," *New York Times*, October 17, 1959, 1.
29. Samuelson, *"The Patriotic Play,"* 333.
30. "Frederick Osborn, 91, a General, 91, Dies," *New York Times*, January 7, 1981, Section B, 12.
31. Rosten, "Oral History,", 70–75 and 2211–16.
32. Spigelgass, *Bonnet*, 163–66, 109.
33. "Federal 'War' Film Held 4th Term Bid. Senator Holman Also Charges That OWI Magazine Booms Roosevelt for 1944. Demands Investigation. Article in PM Says Close Associates of President Expect Him to Run Again," *New York Times*, February 9, 1943, 21.
34. In 1943, in a Truman Committee hearing, "Sen. Ralph O. Brewster (R-Maine) was concerned about Litvak's commission in the Army Signal Corps because the Russian-born director of *Confessions of a Nazi Spy* (1939) was a naturalized American citizen. 'So recently a convert to Americanism was not a particularly happy selection unless your talent was considerably exhausted.' Brewster informed Under Secretary of War Robert P. Patterson, 'You could use somewhat more seasoned citizens.'" Doherty, *Projections of War*, 191.
35. Samuelson, *"The Patriotic Play,"* 155–60, 173–85.
36. Pat Silver-Lasky, *Hollywood Royalty: A Family in Films* (Albany, GA: BearManor Media, undated [2017]), 211.
37. Jesse Lasky with Don Weldon, *I Blow My Own Horn* (London: Victor Gollancz, 1957), 261.
38. Nancy Snow, "Confessions of a Hollywood Propagandist: Harry Warner, FDR, and Celluloid Persuasion," accessed May 24, 2021, https://www.researchgate.net/publication/275833924_Confessions_of_a_Hollywood_Propagandist_Harry_Warner_FDR_and_Celluloid_Persuasion; see also Harvey Cohen, "The Warner Brothers and Franklin Delano Roosevelt: Connections and Collaborations," working paper, Kings College London, accessed May 24, 2021, https://kclpure.kcl.ac.uk/portal/en/publications/the-warner-brothers-and-franklin-delano-roosevelt(fe2bbee8-dcc2-4f27-85e4-eb375c040381).html.
39. Michael E. Birdwell, *Celluloid Soldiers: The Warner Bros. Campaign against Nazism* (New York: New York University Press, 1999), 15, 44.
40. Walter Wanger (oral history interview), in *The Real Tinsel*, ed. Bernard Rosenberg and Harry Silverstein (London: Collier-Macmillan, 1970), 90. See also Richard Brody, "The Hollywood Movie Made for F.D.R.'s Inauguration," *New Yorker*, January 20, 2013; Matthew Bernstein, *Walter Wanger: Hollywood Independent* (Berkeley: University of California Press, 1994).
41. Leo Rosten "became friends with Wanger in the early 1940s." Bernstein, *Walter Wanger*, 8.

42. Leo C. Rosten, "Movies and Propaganda," in *Annals of the American Academy of Political and Social Science* 254 (November 1947): 124.

43. Samuelson, *"The Patriotic Play,"* 277–80.

44. Rosten, *"Oral History,"* 55 and 2196.

45. Matthew Josephson, "Profiles: Production Man-I," March 8, 1941, *New Yorker*, 23.

46. Rosten, *"Oral History,"* 55 and 2196.

47. Rosten, *"Oral History,"* 55–56 and 2196–97, (emphasis added).

48. Rosten, *"Oral History,"* 56–58 and 2197–99, (emphasis added).

49. Rosten, *"Oral History,"* 58 and 2199.

50. Rosten, *"Oral History,"* 26 and 2167.

51. Rosten, *"Oral History,"* 26 and 2167.

52. Steven Alan Carr, *Hollywood and Anti-Semitism: A Cultural History up to World War II* (New York: Cambridge University Press, 2001), 228–37.

53. Rosten, *"Oral History,"* 37 and 2178.

54. Rosten, *"Oral History,"* 40–41 and 2181–82.

55. Rosten, *"Oral History,"* 46–52 and 2187–94.

56. Rosten, "Movies and Propaganda," 117; also cited in Brownell, *Showbiz Politics*, 103. See also Bernstein, *Walter Wanger*, 138, with Wanger expressing the same view.

57. Rosten, *"Oral History,"* 3–4, 18 and 2144–45, 2159.

58. Rosten, *"Oral History,"* 77 and 2218. Rosten is recognized as a foundational historian and analyst of the Washington press corps in the most recent, authoritative work on the press in the Cold War: Kathryn McGarr, *City of Newsmen: Public Lies and Professional Secrets in Cold War Washington* (Chicago: University of Chicago Press, 2022), 38, 251 n. 91, 263 n. 6.

59. Leo Rosten's and Budd Schulberg's perspectives and roles illuminated here are largely consistent with the incisive argument of Lary May, *The Big Tomorrow: Hollywood and the Politics of the American Way* (Chicago: University of Chicago Press, 2000).

60. *Fellow Americans*, Garson Kanin, dir., 1942, Office for Emergency Management Film Unit, The War Activities Committee of the Motion Picture Industry, accessed June 8, 2021, https://www.youtube.com/watch?v=j8UJ1DrNkQI.

61. *Ring of Street* (dir. Garson Kanin, 1942), Office for Emergency Management, accessed June 8, 2021, https://www.youtube.com/watch?v=GbUSESVr_p8. The composer for this film was Morton Gould.

62. "War Comes to America," segment of *Why We Fight*, 1942, Director: Anatole Litvak; Producer: US Army Signal Corps; Producer: Frank R. Capra; Writer, Anthony Veiller; Writer [composer] Dmitri Tiomkin; Film | Accession Number: 1994.119.1 | RG Number: RG-60.1111 | Film ID: 931, United States Holocaust Memorial Museum (hereafter USHMM), accessed June 8, 2021, digitized at https://collections.ushmm.org/search/catalog/irn1000874.

63. Cf. David Thomson, *Warner Bros.: The Making of an American Movie Studio* (New Haven, CT: Yale University Press, 2017). There is sparse reference here to the Warners' close relationship with FDR, except for the contention that the president had "pressured" Jack Warner "personally" to make *Mission to Moscow* (dir. Michael Curtiz, 1943) to support the wartime alliance with the Soviet Union, 149.

64. "Federal 'War' Film Held 4th Term Bid. Senator Holman Also Charges That OWI Magazine Booms Roosevelt for 1944. Demands Investigation. Article in PM Says Close Associates of President Expect Him to Run Again," *New York Times*, February 9, 1943, 21; Carr, *Hollywood and Anti-Semitism*, 238–50.

65. Many insights of Kathryn McGarr regarding how the Washington press corps, in the Cold War, was critical to an "information economy operated through public lies and private understandings" is helpful in understanding Rosten's effectiveness. See McGarr, *City of Newsmen*, 1.

66. During his military training beginning the summer of 1941, Kanin corresponded, regularly, with comedian Phil Silvers. The letters are really funny. Ruth Gordon, Garson Kanin Collection, Box 14, Folder 16, Silvers, Phil, February 19, 1942, July 10, 1942, Library of Congress, Washington, DC (hereafter LOC).

67. Cf. Doherty, *Projections of War*, 135–39, 62, 147–48, 255–59. Prior to 1993 Budd Schulberg was not credited for writing the movie *December 7* (1943).

68. Scott Spector, "Was the Third Reich Movie-Made? Interdisciplinarity and the Reframing of 'Ideology,'" *American Historical Review* 106, no. 2 (April 2001): 460–84.

69. Cf. Doherty, *Projections of War*, 16–35. Kanin's filmmaking for the US government was facilitated by Robert Sherwood, also a stalwart of the Algonquin Roundtable, well before Sherwood officially assumed a position for the Office of War Information. See Garson Kanin, Box 1, Folder 4, General Correspondence, Sherwood, Robert, 1941–51; Sherwood to Kanin, July 14, 1941, Kanin to Sherwood, August 1, 1941, LOC. See also Brownell, *Showbiz Politics*, who also discusses Sherwood as a speechwriter for FDR, 46.

70. Correspondence of Rosten indicates that he had a hand in the theatrical distribution of films done under Frank Capra's supervision beyond *Why We Fight*. See especially Leo C. Rosten to William B. Lewis, April 13, 1943, RG 208, Office of War Information, NC-148, Entry E-75, l-Z, Box No. 233, NARA.

71. In his study of the movies, Rosten repeatedly stressed the extent to which filmmakers had university-level education. Leo C. Rosten, *Hollywood: The Movie Colony, The Movie Makers* (New York: Arno Press, 1970), 58–59, 267–68, 288–89, 320–21, 335–36.

72. Rosten, *Hollywood*, 24.

73. Thomas Doherty, *Hollywood's Censor: Joseph L. Breen and the Production Code Administration* (New York: Columbia University Press, 2007); Carr, *Hollywood and Anti-Semitism*, 130–31. Doherty builds substantially on the work of scholars such as Gregory Black, *Hollywood Censored: Morality Codes, Catholics, and the Movies* (Cambridge: Cambridge University Press, 1994), and Frank Walsh, *Sin and Censorship: The Catholic Church and the Motion Picture Industry* (New Haven, CT: Yale University Press, 1996).

74. Rosten, *Hollywood*, 53.

75. Thomas Schatz, *The Genius of the System: Hollywood Filmmaking in the Studio* (New York: Pantheon Books, 1988), 8–9, quoted in Samuelson, "The Patriotic Play," 137.

76. Rosten, *Hollywood*, 38.

77. Chris Simmons, "Celluloid Deliverance, Marquee-Lit Promised Land: East European Judaism, Yiddish Theater and the Mogul's Hollywood" (unpublished Master's seminar paper, University of Chicago, 1998), 28.

78. Rosten, *Hollywood*, 317.

79. Rosten, *Hollywood*, 7.

80. Rosten, *Hollywood*, 3.
81. Rosten, *Hollywood*, 6.
82. Rosten, *Hollywood*, 3.
83. Rosten, *Hollywood*, 27, 61.
84. Rosten, *Hollywood*, 262.
85. Rosten, *Hollywood*, 27, 61.
86. Rosten, *Hollywood*, 17, note at bottom.
87. Budd Schulberg, *Moving Pictures: Memories of a Hollywood Prince* (London: Souvenir Press, 1982), 115.
88. "Louis B. Mayer to Pay $3,250,000 to Wife Who Divorces Film Producer After 43 Years" (AP), *New York Times*, April 29, 1947, 29.
89. Samuelson, *"The Patriotic Play,"* 256.
90. Rosten, *Hollywood*, 242.
91. Samuelson, *"The Patriotic Play,"* 138; Rosten, *Hollywood*, 242–45.
92. Richard deCordova, *Picture Personalities: The Emergence of the Star System* (Urbana: University of Illinois Press, 2001).
93. Rosten, *Hollywood*, 30.
94. Rosten, *Hollywood*, 162.
95. Samuelson, *"The Patriotic Play,"* 256.
96. Samuelson, *"The Patriotic Play,"* 2 (emphasis added).
97. Samuelson, *"The Patriotic Play,"* 5.
98. Rosten, *Hollywood*, 70.
99. Samuelson, *"The Patriotic Play,"* 8.
100. Rosten, *Hollywood*, 133.
101. Samuelson, *"The Patriotic Play,"* 10.
102. Samuelson, *"The Patriotic Play,"* 99–101, 109.
103. Rachel Maddow, *Prequel: An American Fight Against Fascism* [large-print edition] (New York: Random House, 2023), 207.
104. Samuelson, *"The Patriotic Play,"* 78.
105. Vincent Brook, *Driven to Darkness: Jewish Émigré Directors and the Rise of Film Noir* (Piscataway, NJ: Rutgers University Press, 2009), 1.
106. This serves as the opening epigraph in Chris Yogerst, *Hollywood Hates Hitler! Jew-Baiting, Anti-Nazism, and the Senate Investigation into Warmongering in Motion Pictures* (Jackson: University Press of Mississippi, 2020).
107. Rosten, *Hollywood*, v.
108. Rosten, *Hollywood*, 21, 56–57, 67, 69, 178.
109. Rosten, *Hollywood*, vi.
110. Rosten, *Hollywood*, 18.
111. Rosten, *Hollywood*, 21.
112. George L. Mosse, *The Crisis of German Ideology* (New York: Grosset & Dunlap, 1964).
113. Rosten, *Hollywood*, 56–57.
114. Noah Isenberg, *We'll Always Have Casablanca: The Life, Legend, and Afterlife of Hollywood's Most Beloved Movie* (New York: W. W. Norton, 2017).
115. Rosten, *Hollywood*, 287–88.
116. Rosten, *Hollywood*, 77.

117. Rosten, *Hollywood*, 154.
118. Rosten, *Hollywood*, 144–51, 158.
119. Rosten, *Hollywood*, 141–51.
120. Rosten, *Hollywood*, 154 (emphasis added).
121. Chris Yogerst, *Hollywood Hates Hitler!*
122. Maddow, *Prequel*. Rachel Maddow clearly gives credit to historians Steven J. Ross, Charles R. Gallagher, Bradley W. Hart, and Nancy Beck Young for the foundations of her survey, xv.
123. Rosten, *Hollywood*, 77–78.
124. Rosten, *Hollywood*, 77–78.
125. Samuelson, "The Patriotic Play," 9–10, 11, 19, 21–25, 45.
126. Samuelson, "The Patriotic Play," 64–71, 67–68, 275–76.
127. Samuelson, "The Patriotic Play," 73–75, 274.
128. Rosten, *Hollywood*, 262.
129. Samuelson, "The Patriotic Play," 103, 118, 130.
130. Cf. Samuelson, "The Patriotic Play," 118–31, 359–60. *The March of Time* newsreel, *Main Street on the March* (dir. Edward Cahn, 1941) was credited as written by Karl Kamb, but much of it seems to be the work of Rosten. An MGM film, it was in production before Pearl Harbor.
131. Mark Harris, *Pictures at a Revolution: Five Movies and the Birth of the New Hollywood* (New York: Penguin, 1989).
132. Mark Harris, *Five Came Back: A Story of Hollywood and the Second World War* (New York: Penguin, 2015), 366–77, 413–18.
133. "When G.I. Johnny Comes Home Again" (noveltoon), directed by Seymour Kneitel, Famous Studios [later Telefilm Associates, Paramount Pictures], February 2, 1945; accessed May 24, 2024, https://www.youtube.com/watch?v=oJEY7RZNTjo.
134. "Richard Maibaum: A Pretense of Seriousness," interview by Pat McGilligan, in *Backstory: Interviews with Screenwriters of Hollywood's Golden Age* (Berkeley: University of California Press, 1986), 279. Richard Brooks made documentaries within the Marine Corps Photographic Section, including *Battle of Iwo Jima, Guadalcanal*, and *The Marianas Islands*. See "Richard Brooks: The Professional," interview by Pat McGilligan, in *Backstory 2: Interviews with Screenwriters of the 1940s and 1950s* (Berkeley: University of California Press, 1991), 29.
135. *Twenty-Seven Soldiers*, produced by the Army Pictorial Service, Signal Corps, accessed May 25, 2024, https://www.youtube.com/watch?v=3RLi1W_6uDo.
136. "[Memo] SECRET, November 25, 1944, SUBJECT: Report on SWPA, TO: Signal Officer, Headquarters, Pacific Ocean Area," in correspondence between Robert Presnell and Robert Capa, Robert R. Presnell Sr. Coll. [Collection], Folder 76, Signal Corps, Margaret Herrick Library, Academy of Motion Picture Arts and Sciences, Los Angeles (hereafter Herrick).
137. Lee Carruthers, "Modulations of the Shot: The Quiet Film Style of George Cukor in *What Price Hollywood, Born Yesterday, Sylvia Scarlett*, and *My Fair Lady*," in *George Cukor: Hollywood Master*, ed. Murray Pomerance and R. Burton Palmer (Edinburgh: Edinburgh University Press, 2015), 81–82; Elyce Rae Helford, *What Price Hollywood? Gender and Sex in the Films of George Cukor* (Lexington: University Press of Kentucky, 2020), 159.

138. Rosten, *"Oral History,"* 15 and 2156.

139. Rosten, *"Oral History,"* 80 and 2221.

140. Cf. Doherty, *Projections of War*, 25, 36–59, 60, 79–83.

141. McGarrr, *City of Newsmen*, 1, 38, 251, 263.

142. On the often-overlooked Anthony Veiller, see Harris, *Five Came Back*, 247–52, 262–64.

143. Helford, *What Price Hollywood?*, 1. Helford is speaking of Cukor, generally.

144. Yogerst, *Hollwood Hates Hitler!*; Guiliana Muscio, *Hollywood's New Deal* (Philadelphia: Temple University Press, 1996), 137–40.

145. Victor S. Navasky, *Naming Names: Historical Perspectives* (London: John Calder, 1982), 110.

146. Incredibly, there is not a single mention of Leo Rosten in Patrick McGilligan and Paul Buhle, eds., *Tender Comrades: A Backstory of the Hollywood Blacklist* (New York: St Martin' Griffin, 1997), a very substantial volume; Larry Ceplair and Steven Englund, *The Inquisition in Hollywood: Politics and the Film Community, 1930–1960* (Urbana: University of Illinois Press, 2003), 21.

147. Chris Yogerst, *Hollywood Hates Hitler!* Yogerst juxtaposes Alvin York, as a hero, with Charles Lindbergh, 37–40.

148. Christian Delage, "The Judicial Construction of the Genocide of the Jews at Nuremberg: Witnesses on Stand and Screen," in *Holocaust and Justice: Representation and Historiography of the Holocaust in Post-War Trials*, ed. David Bankier and Dan Michman (Jerusalem: Yad Vashem; New York: Berghahn Books, 2010), 107.

149. Here, and throughout this book, I am massively indebted to David Shneer, *Through Soviet Jewish Eyes: Photography, War, and the Holocaust* (New Brunswick, NJ: Rutgers University Press, 2011).

150. Ceplair and Englund, *The Inquisition*, 59, 67, 378, 423, 436, 447.

151. Cf. Doherty, *Projections of War*, 205–26.

152. See "4 Days of Films Recalls Army's Astoria Studio," *New York Times*, October 29, 1982, C8; Richard Koszarski, "Subway Commandos: Hollywood Filmmakers at the Signal Corps Photographic Center, *Film History* 14 (2002): 296–315; Koszarski, *Hollywood on the Hudson: Film and Television in New York from Griffith to Sarnoff* (New Brunswick, NJ: Rutgers University Press, 2008); Koszarski, *The Astoria Studio and Its Fabulous Films: A Picture History with 227 Stills and Photographs* (New York: Published in association with the Astoria Motion Picture and Television Foundation by Dover Publications, 1983).

153. Rosten, *"Oral History,"* 52 and 2193.

Chapter 1. Launching Countercurrents

1. See Stanley Karnow, *Vietnam: A History*, 2nd rev. and updated ed. (New York: Penguin, 1997).

2. Sabine Hake, *Popular Cinema of the Third Reich* (Austin: University of Texas Press, 2001).

3. In one of the most recent academic studies of Adolf Hitler, Brendan Simms observes that Hitler regarded American popular music, especially jazz, as more of a cultural threat to Germany than Hollywood films. See Brendan Simms, *Hitler: A Global Biography* (New York: Basic Books, 2019), 156.

4. Ben Kenigsberg, "Review: 'Hitler's Hollywood' Unearths the Cinema of the Third Reich," in *New York Times*, April 11, 2018, Section C, 4; Eric Rentschler, "The Legacy of Nazi Cinema: *Triumph of the Will* and *Jew Süss* Revisited," in *The Arts in Nazi Germany: Continuity, Conformity, Change*, ed. Jonathan Huener and Francis R. Nicosia (New York: Berghahn Books, 2009).

5. Budd Schulberg is one of the more thoroughly treated figures in Victor Navasky's *Naming Names*, a classic study of the House Committee on Un-American Activities, but there is no mention of his significant World War II activity (239–46). In contrast, Christian Delage, in a capsule of Schulberg's career notes that "during World War II, he was on active duty in the Field Photographic Branch. In 1945, he worked on the editing of the film evidence to be shown at Nuremberg, 'The Nazi Plan.'" See Delage, "The Judicial Construction," 107.

6. Yogerst, *Hollywood Hates Hitler!* (Budd Schulberg, however, does not appear in his account); Carr, *Hollywood and Anti-Semitism*.

7. Steven Ross, *Hitler in Los Angeles: How Jews Foiled Nazi Plots Against Hollywood and America* (New York: Bloomsbury, 2017); Laura B. Rosenzweig, *Hollywood's Spies: The Undercover Surveillance of Nazis in Los Angeles* (New York: New York University Press, 2017).

8. Cf. Ben Urwand, *The Collaboration: Hollywood's Pact with Hitler* (Cambridge, MA: Belknap Press of Harvard University Press, 2013).

9. Carr, *Hollywood and Anti-Semitism*; Brownell, *Showbiz Politics*; Myers, *Motion Pictures*; Winkler, *Politics of Propaganda*; Michael E. Birdwell, *Celluloid Soldiers*; Thomas Patrick Doherty, *Hollywood's Censor: Joseph I. Breen and the Production Code Administration* (New York: Columbia University Press, 2007); Doherty, *Hollywood and Hitler, 1933–1939* (New York: Columbia University Press, 2013).

10. Quoted in Myers, *Motion Pictures*, from *OWI American Handbook* (Washington: Public Affairs Press, 1945), 55–56.

11. Letter from Jesse L. Lasky Jr. to Jesse L. Lasky (father), May 13, 1942, quoted in Silver-Lasky, *Hollywood Royalty*, 222. While stationed and working at Camp Tyson, Tennesse, Lasky Jr. was officially part of the "Publications Division," revealing the mixing of print and other media work.

12. Letter from Jesse L. Lasky to Bess Lasky (mother), June 12, 1942, in Silver-Lasky, *Hollywood Royalty*, 224–25.

13. Letter from Jesse L. Lasky Jr. to Jesse L. Lasky (father), May 13, 1942, quoted in Silver-Lasky, *Hollywood Royalty*, 222.

14. Silver-Lasky, *Hollywood Royalty*, 230.

15. Bernard Feins to Daniel Taradash, April 5, 1943, Daniel Taradash Papers, f. 350 Feins, Bernie, Herrick.

16. Bernard Feins to Daniel Taradash, April 10, 1943, Daniel Taradash Papers, f. 350 Feins, Bernie, Herrick.

17. Andrew Sarris's classic, *The American Cinema*, pays little attention to the films made during the war on war themes despite noting the dozens produced. See Andrew Sarris, *The American Cinema: Directors and Directions, 1929–1968* (New York: Da Capo Press, 1996).

18. Jesse Lasky Jr. to Bess Lasky, September 9, 1942, in Silver-Lasky, *Hollywood Royalty*, 241–42.

19. See "Pacifists at War," posted on June 2, 2015, by Indiana University Libraries Moving Image Archive, https://blogs.libraries.indiana.edu/filmarch/tag/war-activities-committee-of-the-motion-picture-industry/; see Doherty, *Projections of War*, 60, 79–83, 315, 42–53.

20. Isenberg, *We'll Always Have Casablanca*, 189; on the Production Code Administration and Joseph Breen, see 165–76.

21. Yogerst, *Hollywood Hates Hitler!*, 7.

22. George Dugan, "Francis S. Harmon, 82, Executive of YMCA and Film Association," in *New York Times*, April 28, 1977, 38.

23. Myers, in *Motion Pictures*, shows how this was imposed and how it attempted to function during wartime.

24. For the period immediately before the US entry into World War II, see also David Welky, *The Moguls and the Dictators: Hollywood and the Coming of World War II* (Baltimore: Johns Hopkins University Press, 2008). Up to 1939, see Doherty, *Hollywood and Hitler*; and May, *The Big Tomorrow*.

25. Tracy Campbell, *The Year of Peril: America in 1942* (New Haven, CT: Yale University Press, 2020).

26. See Mark Harris, *Pictures at a Revolution: Five Movies and the Birth of the New Hollywood* (New York: Penguin, 2009), 19, 393, 323, 337.

27. Andrew Sarris deploys this term as demeaning to Stanley Kramer (see *The American Cinema*, 260).

28. Michael Renov and Vincent Brook, "Editorial Introduction," in *From Shtetl to Stardom: Jews and Hollywood*, ed. Steven J. Ross, Michael Renov, Vincent Brook, and Lisa Ansell (West Lafayette, IN: Purdue University Press, 2017), ix.

29. Gabler, *An Empire of Their Own*.

30. For general background, see Wheeler Winston Dixon, ed., *American Cinema of the 1940s: Themes and Variations* (New Brunswick, NJ: Rutgers University Press, 2006).

31. Harris, *Five Came Back*.

32. See Steven Ross, *Hitler in Los Angeles*. The appearance of Urwand's *The Collaboration: Hollywood's Pact with Hitler* ignited great controversy but is deeply flawed, with a highly tendentious thesis. See, in comparison, Doherty, *Hollywood and Hitler*, Yogerst, *Hollywood Hates Hitler!*, Brownell, *Showbiz Politics*, and May, *The Big Tomorrow*.

33. To the best of my knowledge there is no comprehensive biography of Leo Rosten. The most extensive analysis appears to be in Armin Paul Frank, *Off-Canon Pleasures: A Case Study and a Perspective* (Göttingen: University of Göttingen, 2011), which centers on Rosten's book, *The Education of Hyman Kaplan* (1937), published under the pseudonym Leonard Q. Ross, and Archibald MacLeish's radio play, *Air Raid* (1938). Frank does not investigate the real-life relationship between them.

34. Rosten, *"Oral History,"* 56–58, 2197–99.

35. Carr, *Hollywood and Anti-Semitism*, 228–29; Yogerst, *Hollywood Hates Hitler!*, 27, 51, 20.

36. Yogerst, *Hollywood Hates Hitler!*, 27, 37–38. In July 1941, General Richardson was transferred to a more conventional "field" assignment. See Charles Hurd, "Shifts 20 Generals to Vitalize Army; Marshall Installs Younger Men in Numerous Important Posts and Commands; Airman Gets Caribbean; Andrews Wins Key Promotion—Devers Gets Armored Force—Richardson Transferred," *New York Times*, July 17, 1941, 8.

37. For instance, Spigelgass is now mainly recalled for a bit part in the anti-Communist hysteria. See Navasky, *Naming Names*, 175, 176; and Litvak is missing from Sarris's *American Cinema*.

38. Frank S. Nugent, "The Screen. In 'Mayerling' at the Filmarte, a New Solution of the Celebrated Habsburg Mystery is Offered," *New York Times*, September 14, 1937, 27.

39. "Anatole Litvak Dies at 72; Directed 'The Snake Pit,'" *New York Times*, December 17, 1974, 40; Murray Schumach, "Bergman Flouts Contract Axiom. Signs to Star in Film of New Sagan Novel without Any Fuss or Conditions," *New York Times*, December 11, 1959, 39.

40. "Chaplin Is Called For Movie Inquiry; Senators Will Ask Testimony on 'The Great Dictator,'" *New York Times*, September 14, 1941, 41.

41. Welky, *The Moguls*, 289.

42. Welky, *The Moguls*, 333. Interestingly, there is no mention at all of Nelson Poynter in Welky's work.

43. Samuelson, *"The Patriotic Play,"* 300, 367.

44. It is furthermore telling that neither Mellett nor Poynter are mentioned in Doherty, *Hollywood and Hitler*.

45. Myers's study, *Motion Pictures*, is mainly on the attempted management of content in wartime film, in which Rosten is totally absent. The files, however, were possibly still classified when Myers conducted his research. It is appropriate that Yogerst's *Hollywood Hates Hitler!* Includes only a passing reference to the Bureau of Motion Pictures (170) and no mention of either Mellett or Poynter.

46. Carr, *Hollywood and Anti-Semitism*, 224–27.

47. Carr, *Hollywood and Anti-Semitism*, 225–28.

48. Nicholas Beck, *Budd Schulberg: A Bio-Bibliography* (Lanham, MD and London: Scarecrow, 2001), 39, note 2; Budd Schulberg, "Nazi Pin-Up Girl," Folder 41, WWII: "Nazi Pin-Up Girl," by Budd Schulberg, Budd Schulberg Collection, Special Collections, Dartmouth College, Hanover, NH (hereafter SCD), 2.

49. A 1943 training film of George Cukor, *Resistance and Ohms Law*, which he considered "fascinating," and another shot at the Merchant Seamen Canteen cannot be located. See George Cukor to Elsa Schroeder, undated [April 1943], and April 18, 1943, George Cukor Papers, Box 61, Folder 865, Herrick; Taylor Mills to Fredrica Barach, June 23, 1944, RG 208, Office of War Information, NC-148, Entry 288, Box No. 1531, Folder "Merchant Marine," NARA.

50. As noted earlier, Rosten noted the high educational qualifications of filmmakers. Rosten, *Hollywood*, 58–59, 267–68, 288–89, 320–21, 335–36.

51. Spigelgass, *Bonnet*, 109.

52. Andrew Sarris, "The Rise and Fall of the Film Director," in *Hollywood Voices: Interviews with Film Directors*, ed. Andrew Sarris (London: Secker & Warburg, 1971), 7.

53. The workings of the Hays Office, Production Code Administration will not be addressed here; for an excellent recent summary and analysis, see Isenberg, *We'll Always Have Casablanca*, 165–69, 173–78, 182–88. Perhaps surprisingly, concern over censorship is hardly in evidence in the correspondence.

54. Yogerst, *Hollywood Hates Hitler!*

55. Silver-Lasky, *Hollywood Royalty*, 211.

56. Yogerst, *Hollywood Hates Hitler!*, 76.

57. Carr, *Hollywood and Anti-Semitism*, 158–59, 254–55, 274–75; Maddow, *Prequel*, 205–24; Dixon, "Introduction: Movies and the 1940s," *American Cinema of the 1940s*, 1.

58. Doherty, *Projections of War*, 40.

59. Rosten, "Movies and Propaganda," 120.

60. Studs Terkel, *"The Good War": An Oral History of World War II* (New York: New Press, 1984).

61. "Julian Blaustein, 82, Film Producer, Dies," *New York Times*, June 22, 1995, Section B, 6; "Julian Blaustein," *Variety*, June 26, 1995. See, for example, C. Gerald Fraser, "Shepard Traube, 76, Is Dead; Stage Producer and Director," *New York Times*, July 25, 1983: "During World War II, Mr. Traube was an officer in the Army Signal Corps." On Traube, see Carr, *Hollywood and Anti-Semitism*, 150–51.

62. Caroline Moorehead, *Sidney Bernstein: A Biography* (London: Jonathan Cape, 1984).

63. Typescript of letter from Robert Riskin to Messrs. Sherwood, Gamblet, Jackson Feby [February] 24, 1944, Riskin, Robert file, Box 2, RG 208, Office of War Information, Records of the History, Name File [Sidney Bernstein]. 1944, Box 1, Entry 6D, confidential memo, [dated on bottom] 18.5.44, NARA.

64. "German Concentration Camps Factual Survey," Production Credits, accessed May 28, 2021, https://www.iwm.org.uk/sites/default/files/public-document/Production_Credits_0.pdf.

65. "German Concentration Camps Factual Survey Film," accessed March 2, 2020, https://www.iwm.org.uk/partnerships/german-concentration-camps-factual-survey. An unfinished version of *German Concentration Camps* was aired on both the BBC and PBS several times throughout the 1980s and 1990s.

66. Doherty, *Hollywood and Hitler*, 78–95.

67. Thompson and Dixie L. Harris, *The Signal Corps: The Outcome (Mid-1943 through 1945)* (Washington, DC: Office of the Chief of Military History, 1966); George Raynor Thompson and Dixie L. Harris, "Army Photography at Home and Overseas," in *United States Army in World War II: The Technical Services* (Washington, DC: Office of the Chief of Military History, 1970), 540–79.

68. Yogerst, *Hollywood Hates Hitler!*, xiv.

69. Jeffrey Herf, *The Jewish Enemy: Nazi Propaganda during World War II and the Holocaust* (Cambridge, MA: The Belknap Press of Harvard University Press, 2006).

70. Michael Berkowitz, *The Crime of My Very Existence: Nazism and the Myth of Jewish Criminality* (Berkeley: University of California Press, 2007).

71. W. B. Lewis to Leonard Spigelgass, May 10, 1942, memo concerning *Citizens Handbook for War*, RG 208, Office of War Information, NC-148, Entry 294, Box No. 1554, File LEONARD SPIGELGASS (Official), NARA.

72. The significance of Wyler's Jewishness is treated in depth, with nuance and sensitivity, in Harris, *Five Who Came Back*.

73. Michael S. Shull and David E. Wilt, *Doing Their Bit: Wartime American Animated Short Films, 1939–1945* (Jefferson, NC: McFarland, 2004), 2–10, 71–160.

74. "Any Bonds Today?" Warner Bros. & U.S. Treasury Dept. Defense Savings Staff (cartoon), released in December 1941, with Bugs Bunny dressed as Uncle Sam. The number was based on the act of Barry Wood and a song by Irving Berlin; accessed May 25, 2024, https://www.youtube.com/watch?v=Z6Wo2xGN6kk.

75. Todd James Pierce, "In Defense of Walt: Walt Disney and Anti-Semitism," Disney History Institute, accessed June 19, 2021, http://www.disneyhistoryinstitute.com/2014/02/in-defense-of-walt-walt-disney-and-anti.html.

76. Rosten, *"Oral History,"* 59 and 2200.

77. Michelangelo Capua, *Anatole Litvak: The Life and Films* (Jefferson, NC: McFarland & Co., 2015).

78. Leo Rosten to William B. Lewis, April 3, 1942, RG 208, Office of War Information, NC-148, Entry 294, Box No. 1554, File "R"; Press clipping from *New York Herald-Tribune* 5/12 [43], 24, "Army Releases 'Prelude to War' Film to Public, Facts of Dictators Will Be Shown to Civilians Here for the First Time," NARA.

79. Myers's main point in relating this episode is to examine if the content of the film had been checked by US government authorities, and to comment on the supposed competition between "government" and "studio" films. Myers, *Motion Pictures*, 172–75, 185–86 n. 53.

80. R. Barton Palmer, "The Furthest Side of Paradise: *Two-Faced Woman, A Woman's Face, Hot Spell, Wild Is the Wind*, and *Winged Victory*," in *George Cukor: Hollywood Master*, ed. Murray Pomerance and R. Barton Palmer (Edinburgh: Edinburgh University Press, 2015), 171.

81. Cf. Harris, *Five Came Back*, 425–26.

82. "*Welcome Home*-script," Project 12.903, The Returning Soldier[:] *Welcome Home*, Daniel Taradash Papers, f. 176, Herrick.

83. One of the First Lady's contacts at Warner Bros. was Dr. Herman Lissauer, who had a career in the rabbinate before becoming head of the research department at the studio. Eleanor Roosevelt, "My Day" newspaper column, March 19, 1938, the Eleanor Roosevelt Papers, digital edition, accessed May 30, 2020, https://www2.gwu.edu/~erpapers/myday/displaydoc.cfm?_y=1938&_f=md054905.

84. Certificate for service, Research Council of the Academy of Motion Picture Arts & Sciences, private collection, Joan Juliet Buck.

85. Yogerst, *Hollywood Hates Hitler!*, 17–18.

86. Bernstein, *Walter Wanger*.

87. Yogerst, *Hollywood Hates Hitler!*, 38–39, 66.

88. Moorehead, *Bernstein*, 133–34; 139–41. For instance, Bernstein brought *Target for Tonight* (1942) to the attention to Harry Warner. It appears that Leo Rosten and Sidney Bernstein served together in London when the Psychological Warfare Branch of the Office of War Information and American strategic services was attached to the British Psychological Warfare Branch (Moorehead, *Bernstein*, 151). In December 1943, this was put under the command of the SHAEF, the Supreme Headquarters Allied Expeditionary Force, headed by General Eisenhower, and after April 11, 1944, Bernstein "supervised all film operations for PWD—anonymously." Moorehead, *Bernstein*, 158–59.

89. Taylor Mills to Fredrica Barach, June 23, 1944, attached note, RG 208, Office of War Information, NC-148, Entry 288, Box No. 1531, Folder "Merchant Marine," NARA.

90. S. J. Perelman's *The Dream Department: Humorous Sketches* was published as a pocket-size "Armed Services Edition," No. 2, undated [1943]. Number 1 was Mark Twain, *The Mysterious Stranger*.

91. An attempt to turn *H*y*m*a*n K*a*p*l*a*n* into a Broadway musical in 1968, however, was an utter bust. See "Oscar Brand Returns to Hyman Kaplan," *New York*

Times, February 11, 1990, Section 12LI, 13. In the early 1990s I enjoyed the great pleasure of Oscar Brand's company in the basement of the former Hadassah headquarters when I was doing research and he was planning Hadassah's annual variety show.

92. Leo Rosten to Rachel Ehrlich, May 20, 1964, Box 5, Papers of Rachel Ehrlich, RG1300, YIVO archives, Center for Jewish History, New York.

93. One of the few preserved "oral history" interviews of Rosten is more in the form of a lecture on the history of the movies, including some personal reflections. Rosten, "Oral History." He does not, however, always speak honestly and directly about his relationship with FDR and wartime work.

94. "ENSIGN BUDD WILSON SCHULBERG, USNR," [one-page CV], Folder 2, WWII: Resume, 1942, SCD.

95. Navasky, *Naming Names*, 239, 241; see also McGilligan and Buhle, *Tender Comrades*, 44–45, 417–19, 530–35.

96. Navasky, *Naming Names*, 377.

97. Best known as the single-edition work, Rosten, *Hollywood*.

98. See Carr, *Hollywood and Anti-Semitism*, 228–44, for the best analysis of Rosten's work and impact before 1941.

99. Leo Rosten, *The Many Worlds of L*E*O R*O*S*T*E*N; Stories, Humor, Social Commentary, Travelogues, Satire, Memoirs, Profiles, and Sundry Entertainments Never Before Published; with a Special Introd., Background Notes, Revelations and Confessions, All Hand-Written and Themselves Worth the Price of Admission* (New York: Harper & Row, 1964), 119–20.

100. Rosten, *Many Worlds*, 119–20.

101. Rosten, *Many*, 119–20.

102. Rosten, *Many Worlds*, 119–20.

103. Myers, *Motion Picture*, 208–9. See also McGarr, *City of Newsmen*.

104. Interestingly, the published book and the dissertation are one and the same, apparently permitted (then) by the University of Chicago: Leo Rosten, *The Washington Correspondents* (New York: Harcourt, Brace, 1937).

105. Leo C. Rosten, "President Roosevelt and the Washington Correspondents," *The Public Opinion Quarterly* 1, no. 1 (January 1937): 38–39.

106. Leo Rosten, *People I Have Loved, Known, or Admired* (New York: McGraw-Hill, 1970), 224. Rosten married a fellow graduate student at the University of Chicago, Priscilla Mead (1911–59), who was the sister of anthropologist Margaret Mead. She committed suicide after divorcing Rosten in 1959, which could also be a reason why Rosten rarely wrote about his own life. See Jill Franks, *Islands and the Modernists: The Allure of Isolation in Art, Literature, and Science* (Jefferson, NC: McFarland, 2006), 201.

107. Rosten, *People I Have Loved*, 224.

108. See "Roosevelt's Appointment of Mellett," in Myers, *Motion Picture*, 208–9. Without the connection to Rosten, the appointment makes little sense.

109. 111-Executive Order 8922 Establishing the Office of Facts and Figures, October 24, 1941, Franklin D. Roosevelt, XXXII President of the United States, The American Presidency Project, accessed June 3, 2020, http://www.presidency.ucsb.edu/ws/?pid=16024.

110. Clayton D. Laurie, *The Propaganda Warriors: America's Crusade Against Nazi Germany* (Lawrence: University Press of Kansas, 1996), 118.

111. Leo Rosten, "The Great Berlin Caper," in *Passions & Prejudices: Or, Some of My Best Friends Are People* (New York: McGraw-Hill, 1978), 168–72.

112. Rosten, "The Great Berlin Caper," *Passions & Prejudices*, 168.

113. Rosten, "The Great Berlin Caper," *Passions & Prejudices*, 168.

114. Rosten, "The Great Berlin Caper," *Passions & Prejudices*, 168.

115. "Hitler and Goering Warn Europe Races 'Red Peril,'" *New York Times*, January 31, 1943, 1, 40.

116. It was announced the day before that Hitler would not be speaking. Rather than saying there was anything wrong with Hitler, the choice of Goebbels and Goering was presented as a gesture of modesty given the grave situation that Germans were facing in the heat of total war. Guido Enernis, "Hitler Will Not Speak to Germany Today, Anniversary Plan Indicates" (byline Berne, Switzerland, January 29), *New York Times*, January 30, 1943, 1, 2.

117. James MacDonald, "Two Blows in Day; British Fliers Hit Nazi Capital Just at Talks by Goering, Goebbels. Foes Confusion Heard. Sounds of Raid Come Over the Reich Radio—Only One of Mosquito Planes Lost," *New York Times*, January 31, 1943, 1, 40.

118. Rosten, "The Great Berlin Caper," *Passions & Prejudices*, 172.

119. "Dix Ans Apres" and "Tandis que la R.A.F bombardait Berlin. Goering et Goebbels Ont Annonce le "Sacrifice Total," *France*, no. 755, 1. Next to the article in the French paper was an item about President Roosevelt's sixty-first birthday, noting that he had received a telegram from General de Gaulle.

120. David Shneer, *Through Soviet Jewish Eyes: Photography, War, and the Holocaust* (New Brunswick, NJ: Rutgers University Press, 2011).

121. Myers, *Motion Picture*, 123–25; see also K. R. M. Short, "Hollywood Fights Anti-Semitism, 1940–1945," in *Film & Radio Propaganda in World War II* (London: Croom Helm, 1983), 146, 156–59

122. Short, "Hollywood Fights Anti-Semitism," *Film & Radio Propaganda*, 146.

123. Peter Hayes, *Why? Explaining the Holocaust* (New York: W. W. Norton, 2017), 267; Richard Breitman and Allan J. Lichtman, *FDR and the Jews* (Cambridge, MA: Harvard University Press, 2013), 317.

124. Hayes, *Why?* 267.

125. Campbell, *The Year of Peril*.

126. Correspondence with Leonard V. Finder, July 19, 1943, and Leonard Farbstein, December 23, 1942, and February 10, 1943, File F, RG 208, Office of War Information, NC-1458, Entry E-75, A-H, Box No. 232, Leo Rosten, NARA.

127. Christof Decker, "Imaging Axis Terror: War Propaganda and the 1943 The Nature of the Enemy Exhibition at Rockefeller Center," *Imaging the Scenes of War: Aesthetic Crossovers in American Visual Culture* (Bielefeld: Transcript Verlag, 2022), 35–60, 41–42.

128. "Many See Exhibits of War's Horrors. Tableaux in Rockefeller Center Depict Six Phases of 'The Nature of the Enemy,' Maimed Victim Speaks, Editor Who Lost Feet as Result of Japanese Imprisonment and Others Voice Warning," *New York Times*, May 18, 1943, Section Amusements, 19.

129. See Wojciech Rappak, *Karski's Reports: The Story and the History* (PhD dissertation, University College London, 2021).

130. "The Nature of the Enemy" in *New York Times*, August 28, 1943, 10.

131. *Don't Be a Sucker*, 1945, accessed April 7, 2020, https://collections.ushmm.org/search/catalog/irn1001130. See Thomas Cripps, *Making Movies Black: The Hollywood Message Movie from World War II to the Civil Rights Era* (New York: Oxford University Press, 1993); Kathleen M. German, *Promises of Citizenship: Film Recruitment of African Americans in World War II* (Oxford: University Press of Mississippi, 2017).

132. Leo Rosten to Henwar Rodakiewicz, May 1, 1942, RG 208, Office of War Information, NC-148, Entry 294, Box No. 1554, File "R," NARA.

133. Walter Laqueur, *The Terrible Secret: An Investigation into the Suppression of Information about Hitler's "Final Solution"* (London: Weidenfeld and Nicolson, 1980).

134. Carr, *Hollywood and Anti-Semitism*.

135. See Thomas Doherty, *Show Trial: Hollywood, HUAC, and the Birth of the Blacklist* (New York: Columbia University Press, 2018).

136. Leo Rosten, memo to James Allen, January 2, 1943, "Suggestions for J. Edgar Hoover Speech on National Network," [for] January 30, 1943, 10:45 PM, RG 208, Office of War Information, NC-1458, Entry E-75, A-H, Box No. 232, Leo Rosten, NARA.

137. Rosten's relationship with J. Edgar Hoover would continue. He wrote *Walk on East Beacon* (1952), "a screenplay based on J. Edgar Hoover's accounts of the nationwide F.B.I. offensive against Communist espionage in the United States," produced by Louis De Rochemont ("Of Local Origin," *New York Times*, May 16, 1951, A47).

Chapter 2. Artful Dodges

1. In June 1942, Leo Rosten sent no fewer than a dozen memos to Nelson Poynter, the official liaison between the War Department and Hollywood, many with extremely detailed plans for film work and related media. It is clear that everything raised was meant to be enacted, or at least attempted (RG 208, Office of War Information, Entry 264, NC-148, Box No. 1444, File Copies Rosten Memos to Poynter, NARA). In directing joint United States and British efforts, his language was more diplomatic—"The enclosed memorandum is intended solely for suggestive purposes"—but he was, again, giving orders. See, for example, Leo Rosten to David Bowes-Lyon, November 4, 1942, RG 208, Office of War Information, NC-1458, Entry E-75, A-H, Box No. 232, Leo Rosten, File "B," NARA. See also Rosten, "Oral History," 54–60 and 2195–2201.

2. "Rialto Gossip. Noel Coward Won't Bring His New Plays Here Until War Ends," *New York Times*, May 23, 1943, Section Drama, 1: "Dr. Leo Rosten, perhaps better known as Leonard Q. Ross, and his collaborator, Charles Rabiner, have finished the first act of their dramatization of Dr. Rosten's 'The Education of Hyman Kaplan . . .'"

3. Carr, *Hollywood and Anti-Semitism*, 231.

4. I found only one instance where Rosten was challenged, by Harold Jacobs—"I agree with most of what Rosten says—but not all." Harold Jacobs to Lowell Mellett, SUBJECT: LEO ROSTEN'S NEWSREEL COMMENT OF JUNE 10, JUNE 13, 1942, in which Mellett seems to sympathize with Jacobs, RG 208, Office of War Information, Entry 264, NC-148, Box No. 1435, File "Jacobs, Harold"—newsreel critiques, File "J," NARA.

5. Leo Rosten to William Lewis, [undated most likely March or April 1942], RG 208, Office of War Information, NC-148, Entry 294, Box No. 1554, File "R," NARA.

6. Charles Hurd, "Shifts 20 Generals to Vitalize Army; Marshall Installs Younger Men in Numerous Important Posts and Commands; Airman Gets Caribbean; Andrews Wins Key Promotion—Devers Gets Armored Force—Richardson Transferred," July 17, 1941, *New York Times*, 8.

7. Thomas Brady, "Films for Defense," *New York Times*, December 1, 1940, Section X, 4.

8. Thomas Brady, "Films for Defense," *New York Times*, December 1, 1940, Section X, 4.

9. Thomas Brady, "Films for Defense," *New York Times*, December 1, 1940, Section X, 4.

10. Thomas Brady, "Films for Defense," *New York Times*, December 1, 1940, Section X, 4.

11. Rosten, *Many Worlds*, "about the author" blurb. This was close, but did not precisely match the description given for the academic political science journal in 1947; see Rosten, "Movies and Propaganda," 124.

12. Carr, *Hollywood and Anti-Semitism*, 185–89.

13. Archibald MacLeish et al., *The Jews of America, by the editors of Fortune* (New York: Random House, 1936).

14. MacLeish, *The Jews of America*, 50.

15. MacLeish, *The Jews of America*, 41, 59.

16. Winkler, *Politics of Propaganda*, 58.

17. Memo from Leo C. Rosten to Col. W. M. Wright, May 27, 1942, File "WRIGHT, Col. Wm. Mason [Jr.]," RG 208, Office of War Information, NC-148, Entry 294, Box No. 1554, NARA.

18. Archibald MacLeish, *Land of the Free* (New York: Harcourt, Brace, 1938), 89.

19. Winkler, *Politics of Propaganda*, 22–27, 29, 57–63.

20. Leo Rosten, "A Letter to My Readers," in *The Leo Rosten Bedside Book. Stories, Humour, Social Commentary, Travelogues, Satire, Memoirs, Profiles—& Sundry Entertainments Never Before Published, with a Special Introduction, Background Notes, Revelations and Confessions, Hand-Written and Themselves Worth the Price of Aadmission* (London: Gollancz, 1965), ix. Published in the United States as *The Many Worlds of Leo Rosten*.

21. Harold Jacobs, Newsreel Critique, Week Ending December 19, CONFIDENTIAL, following Progress Report, Bureau of Motion Pictures, Office of War Information, Week ending December 18, 1942, Confidential, I. Production Division, II. Creative Division., III. Newsreel Division, IV. Educational Division, V. Research Division, 1, RG 208, Office of War Information, NC-148, Entry 264, Box No. 1436, NARA (emphasis added).

22. This might have influenced the enlistment of Donald Duck to help Morgenthau with the war bond drive. See epilogue.

23. Harold Jacobs, Newsreel Critique, Week Ending December 19, CONFIDENTIAL, 1, following Progress Report, Bureau of Motion Pictures, Office of War Information, Week ending December 18, 1942, Confidential, I. Production Division, II. Creative Division., III. Newsreel Division, IV. Educational Division, V. Research Division, 1, RG 208, Office of War Information, NC-148, Entry 264, Box No. 1436, NARA.

24. Leo Rosten to Robert Spencer Carr, February 13, 1942, RG 208, Office of War Information, NC-148, Entry 295, Box No. 1555, File "B," NARA.

25. Mordecai Lee, "Working for Goodwill: Journalist Lowell Mellett," an extended version of "Working for Goodwill: Journalist Lowell Mellett," published in *Traces of Indiana and Midwestern History* (Quarterly of the Indiana Historical Society) 27, no. 4 (Fall 2015): 46–55, available at https://cpb-us-w2.wpmucdn.com/sites.uwm.edu/dist/9/86/files/2016/06/Mellett-article-long-vers-2k33mtz.pdf, 1; see also "Lowell Mellett, Ex-U.S. Aide, Dies. Administrative Assistant to President Roosevelt, 1940–1944, Was a Former Newspaper Editor," *New York Times*, April 7, 1960, 35.

26. Leo Rosten to Robert Spencer Carr, February 13, 1942, RG 208, Office of War Information, NC-148, Entry 295, Box No. 1555, File "B," NARA (emphasis added).

27. Allen Rivkin to Leo Rosten, March 2, 1942, RG 208, Office of War Information, NC-148, Entry 294, Box No. 1554, File "R," NARA.

28. Memo from Leo Rosten to Frank Capra, March 9, 1942; RG 208, Office of War Information, NC-148, Entry 294, Box No. 1554, File "R," NARA.

29. Frank Capra to Leo Rosten, March 11, 1942, RG 208, Office of War Information, NC-148, Entry 294, Box No. 1554, File "R," NARA.

30. Richard Fleischer, *Out of the Inkwell: Max Fleischer and the Animation Revolution* (Lexington: University Press of Kentucky, 2005), 125.

31. Leo C. Rosten to H. L. McClinton, February 17, 1942, RG 208, Office of War Information, NC-148, Entry 294, Box No. 1554, File "R," NARA.

32. Leo C. Rosten to H. L. McClinton, February 17, 1942, RG 208, Office of War Information, NC-148, Entry 294, Box No. 1554, File "R," NARA.

33. Samuelson, *"The Patriotic Play,"* 297–98. See https://www.youtube.com/watch?v=pmyxOXvdAgY, accessed January 12, 2024. *Main Street on the March* also stresses the togetherness of those of different religious faith and races. The credits say "original story and screenplay by Karl Kamb," but this is highly questionable. Kamb (1903–88) was later a writer for *Main Street After Dark* (1945), a very different type of film.

34. Myers, *Motion Pictures*, 53.

35. Leo Rosten to Albert E. Sindlinger, May 12, 1942, RG 208, Office of War Information, NC-148, Entry 295, Box No. 155, File "H"; long memo about the work of Rosten and Spigelgass up to June 1942 [to] Mr. John Baker, June 2, 1942, Report for May [1942], RG 208, Office of War Information, NC-148, Entry 295, Box No. 1555, File "B," NARA.

36. Thomas F. Brady, "Of Local Origin," *New York Times*, May 16, 1951; "'Walk East on Beacon,' a Louis de Rochemont Production, Is New Bill at Victoria," *New York Times*, May 29, 1952, 17; see https://www.imdb.com/title/tt0045309/fullcredits?ref_=tt_ov_wr#writers/, accessed March 8, 2020.

37. Rodney Hill and Gene D. Phillips, entry for "de Rochemont, Richard," *The Encyclopedia of Stanley Kubrick* (New York: Checkmark Books, 2002), available at http://stanley_kubrick.enacademic.com/45/de_Rochemont_Richard.

38. Leo Rosten to Albert E. Sindlinger, May 12, 1942, RG 208, Office of War Information, NC-148, Entry 295, Box No. 155, File "H," NARA.

39. Leo C. Rosten to William B. Lewis, February 17, 1942, RG 208, Office of War Information, NC-148, Entry 294, Box No. 154, File "R," NARA.

40. "William B. Lewis, Headed Ad Agency," *New York Times*, February 26, 1975, 42.

41. Leo C. Rosten to William B. Lewis, February 17, 1942, RG 208, Office of War Information, NC-148, Entry 294, Box No. 1554, File "R," NARA.

42. Leo C. Rosten to William B. Lewis, February 17, 1942, RG 208, Office of War Information, NC-148, Entry 294, Box No. 1554, File "R," NARA.

43. Leo C. Rosten to John R. Fleming, RG 208, Office of War Information, NC-148, Entry 294, Box No. 1554, File "R," NARA.

44. Leo C. Rosten to John R. Fleming, 1–2, RG 208, Office of War Information, NC-148, Entry 294, Box No. 1554, File "R," NARA.

45. Leo C. Rosten to John R. Fleming, 2, RG 208, Office of War Information, NC-148, Entry 294, Box No. 1554, File "R," NARA.

46. Leo Rosten to Jack Chertok, Metro-Goldwyn-Mayer, Culver City, California, April 30, 1942, RG 208, Office of War Information, NC-148, Entry 294, Box No. 1554, File "The Boys Write Home," NARA.

47. Rosten, "Oral History."

48. Letter writing was the central device in the film written by Budd Schulberg, *That Men May Fight* (1943 or 1944), about the US Navy's Women's Reserve Corps. See below, as well as *Pride of the Marines* (1945). The producer of *Pride of the Marines*, Jerry Wald, took extensive advice from Rosten, which he followed closely.

49. Leo Rosten, MEMORANDUM RE: Newsreel Presentation of the Statement on the Rubber Situation, February 14, 1942, RG 208, Office of War Information, NC-148, Entry 294, Box No. 1554, File "R," NARA.

50. Patrick McGilligan, *George Cukor: A Double Life* (Minneapolis: University of Minnesota Press, 2013), 172.

51. WAR DEPARTMENT REPORT [unattributed], [in pencil, dated ca. April 1943], under heading "Colonel Lawton," RG 208, Office of War Information, Entry 264, NC-148, Box No. 1436, NARA.

52. Helford, *What Price Hollywood?*

53. Leo Rosten, MEMORANDUM RE: Newsreel Presentation of the Statement on the Rubber Situation, February 14, 1942, RG 208, Office of War Information, NC-148, Entry 294, Box No. 1554, File "R," NARA.

54. Leo Rosten, MEMORANDUM RE: Newsreel Presentation of the Statement on the Rubber Situation, February 14, 1942, RG 208, Office of War Information, NC-148, Entry 294, Box No. 1554, File "R," NARA.

55. George H. Roeder Jr., *The Censored War: American Visual Experience during World War Two* (New Haven, CT: Yale University Press, 1993), 18, 163.

56. Reihold Wagnleitner, *Coca-Colonization and the Cold War: The Cultural Mission in the United States after the Second World War*, trans. Diana Wolf (Chapel Hill: University of North Carolina Press, 1994), 237; Doherty, *Projections of War*, 25, 36–59, 60, 79–83.

57. Glenn Fowler, "Leo Hurwitz, 81, Blacklisted Maker of Documentaries," *New York Times*, January 19, 1991, Section 1, 18.

58. Alfred Stieglitz/Georgia O'Keeffe Archive, YCAL MSS 85, Series I, Alfred Stieglitz: Correspondence, Box 41, Folders 979 to 998, Folder 987, Rodakiewicz, Henwar/1032–42 n.d., Rodakiewicz to Stieglitz, January 12, 1932; January 7, 1939; June 9, 1940, Beinecke Library, Yale University.

59. "George A. Barnes, Federal Aide, 55. Ex-Newsman in Capital Dies—Also Served with U.N.," *New York Times*, January 11, 1965, 45.

60. Leo Rosten to Henwar Rodakiewicz, April 24, 1942, RG 208, Office of War Information, NC-148, Entry 294, Box No. 1554, File "R," NARA.

61. Leo Rosten to Henwar Rodakiewicz, May 15, 1942, RG 208, Office of War Information, NC-148, Entry 294, Box No. 1554, File "R," NARA.

62. Rodakiewicz to Rosten, April 27, 1942, RG 208, Office of War Information, NC-148, Entry 294, Box No. 1554, File "R," NARA.

63. "Arch A. Mercey, Author, Executive at Merkle Press," *Washington Post*, November 1, 1980.

64. Rodakiewicz to Rosten, April 27, 1942, RG 208, Office of War Information, NC-148, Entry 294, Box No. 1554, File "R," NARA (emphasis added).

65. Rodakiewicz to Rosten, April 27, 1942, 2, RG 208, Office of War Information, NC-148, Entry 294, Box No. 1554, File "R," NARA.

66. "It May Interest You to Know," in *Health and Physical Education* 13, no. 5 (May 1942): 311.

67. Leo Rosten to Henwar Rodakiewicz, May 15, 1942, RG 208, Office of War Information, NC-148, Entry 294, Box No. 1554, File "R," NARA (emphasis added).

68. Rodakiewicz to Rosten, April 27, 1942, RG 208, Office of War Information, NC-148, Entry 294, Box No. 1554, File "R," NARA (emphasis added).

69. Rodakiewicz to Rosten, April 27, 1942, RG 208, Office of War Information, NC-148, Entry 294, Box No. 1554, File "R," NARA.

70. Rodakiewicz to Leo Rosten, April 27, 1942, RG 208, Office of War Information, NC-148, Entry 294, Box No. 1554, File "R," NARA.

71. In the archives, and retrospectively, Slesinger's name has two different spellings: "Sch" and "Sl." This probably has led to some confusion and lack of attention to his role.

72. "Donald Slesinger, a Psychologist and Ex-Law School Dean, Is Dead," *New York Times*, October 14, 1977, 28.

73. "Stephen Slesinger, TV Film Producer," *New York Times*, December 18, 1953, 29.

74. Jewish Women's Archive. "Tess Slesinger," accessed May 9, 2020, https://jwa.org/people/slesinger-tess.

75. Moorehead, *Bernstein*, 109.

76. Donald Slesinger to Leo Rosten, March 21, 1942, 1, RG 208, Office of War Information, NC-148, Entry 295, Box No. 1555, File "B," NARA.

77. Donald Slesinger to Leo Rosten, March 21, 1942, 1, RG 208, Office of War Information, NC-148, Entry 295, Box No. 1555, File "B," NARA.

78. Donald Slesinger to Leo Rosten, March 21, 1942, 2, RG 208, Office of War Information, NC-148, Entry 295, Box No. 1555, File "B," NARA.

79. Donald Slesinger to Leo Rosten, March 21, 1942, 2, RG 208, Office of War Information, NC-148, Entry 295, Box No. 1555, File "B," NARA.

80. Donald Slesinger to Leo Rosten, March 21, 1942, 3, RG 208, Office of War Information, NC-148, Entry 295, Box No. 1555, File "B," NARA (emphasis added).

81. Donald Slesinger to Leo Rosten, March 21, 1942, 2, RG 208, Office of War Information, NC-148, Entry 295, Box No. 1555, File "B," NARA (emphasis added).

82. Donald Slesinger to Leo Rosten, March 21, 1942, 3, RG 208, Office of War Information, NC-148, Entry 295, Box No. 1555, File "B," NARA.

83. Donald Slesinger to Leo Rosten, March 21, 1942, 4, RG 208, Office of War Information, NC-148, Entry 295, Box No. 1555, File "B," NARA.

84. Donald Slesinger to Leo Rosten, March 21, 1942, 4, RG 208, Office of War Information, NC-148, Entry 295, Box No. 1555, File "B," NARA.

85. R. R. Ford to Leo Rosten, March 17, 1942, 1, RG 208, Office of War Information, NC-148, Entry 295, Box No. 1555, File "B," NARA.

86. R. R. Ford to Leo Rosten, March 17, 1942, 1, RG 208, Office of War Information, NC-148, Entry 295, Box No. 1555, File "B," NARA.

87. R. R. Ford to Leo Rosten, March 17, 1942, 3, RG 208, Office of War Information, NC-148, Entry 295, Box No. 1555, File "B," NARA.

88. R. R. Ford to Leo Rosten, March 17, 1942, 4, RG 208, Office of War Information, NC-148, Entry 295, Box No. 1555, File "B," NARA.

89. FILMS FROM BRITAIN . . . CIVIL DEFENCE (Second Edition) [flyer, marked up by Leo Rosten], RG 208, Office of War Information, NC-148, Entry 295, Box No. 1555, File "B," NARA.

90. FILMS FROM BRITAIN . . . CIVIL DEFENCE (Second Edition) [flyer, marked up by Leo Rosten], RG 208, Office of War Information, NC-148, Entry 295, Box No. 1555, File "B," NARA.

91. Leo Rosten to C. M. Vandeburg, CC'd to Archibald MacLeish and William B. Lewis, May 21, 1942, RG 208, Office of War Information, NC-148, Entry 294, Box No. 1554, File "Vandeberg [sic], Clyde," NARA.

92. Leo Rosten to Jerry Wald, February 25, 1942, 1, RG 208, Office of War Information, NC-148, Entry 294, Box No. 1554, File "W," NARA.

93. Leo Rosten to Jerry Wald, February 25, 1942, 1, RG 208, Office of War Information, NC-148, Entry 294, Box No. 1554, File "W," NARA (emphasis added).

94. Leo Rosten to Jerry Wald, February 25, 1942, 2, RG 208, Office of War Information, NC-148, Entry 294, Box No. 1554, File "W," NARA.

95. Leo Rosten to Jerry Wald, February 25, 1942, 2, RG 208, Office of War Information, NC-148, Entry 294, Box No. 1554, File "W," NARA.

96. Birdwell, *Celluloid Soldiers*, 23.

97. Jerry Wald to Leo Rosten, March 17, 1942, RG 208, Office of War Information, NC-148, Entry 294, Box No. 1554, File "W," NARA.

98. Memo from Leo C. Rosten to Col. W. M. Wright, May 27, 1942, RG 208, Office of War Information, NC-148, Entry 294, Box No. 1554, File "WRIGHT, Col. Wm. Mason [Jr.]," NARA.

99. Collier (Collie) Young to Leo Rosten, April 28, 1942, RG 208, Office of War Information, NC-148, Entry 294, Box No. 1554, File "Y," NARA.

100. The response followed a long consultation with Leonard Spigelgass. Leo Rosten to Collier Young, May 14, 1942, RG 208, Office of War Information, NC-148, Entry 294, Box No. 1554, File "Y," NARA.

101. Robert S. Taplinger to Leo Rosten, March 19, 1942, RG 208, Office of War Information, NC-148, Entry 294, Box No. 1554, File "T," NARA.

102. Robert S. Taplinger to Leo Rosten, March 19, 1942, RG 208, Office of War Information, NC-148, Entry 294, Box No. 1554, File "T," NARA (emphasis added).

103. "Nate Spingold, 72, Film Official, Dies. Vice President of Columbia, a Former Newsman, Was Collector, Art Patron," *New York Times*, 77.

104. Leo Rosten to Allen Grover, "THE INVADERS," February 20, 1942, RG 208, Office of War Information, NC-148, Entry 294, Box No. 1554, file: "The Invaders," NARA.

105. Leo Rosten to Allen Grover, April 30, 1942, RG 208, Office of War Information, NC-148, Entry 294, Box No. 1554, File "The Invaders," NARA.

106. Leo Rosten to Robert Taplinger, March 23, 1942, RG 208, Office of War Information, NC-148, Entry 294, Box No. 1554, File "T," NARA.

107. "R. S. Taplinger, 66, of Publicity Unit. Rogers, Cowan President Dies—Active in Films," *New York Times*, November 25, 1975, 40.

Chapter 3. Credit(s) Where Credit Is Due?

1. Rosten, *"Oral History,"* 45, 72 and 2186, 2123. See entry for "Swerling, Jo (Joseph)," in Ephraim Katz, *The International Film Encyclopedia* (New York: Macmillan, 1980), 1115; see also Joseph Horowitz, *"On My Way": The Untold Story of Rouben Mamoulian, George Gershwin, and "Porgy and Bess"* (New York: W. W. Norton, 2013).

2. I have found no information concerning Presnell's religious or ethnic background.

3. Ronald Bergan, "Jules Buck: Film Producer behind Peter O'Toole's Rise to Screen Stardom," in *Guardian*, July 23, 2001; Joan Juliet Buck, *The Price of Illusion: A Memoir* (New York: Atria, 2017), 38.

4. Harris, *Five Came Back*, deals with Wyler extensively, 425–35, 49–52.

5. Leonard Spigelgass, Notes explaining reimbursements for official travel, including meetings concerning the United Nations, June 12–15, 1942, RG 208, Office of War Information, NC-148, Entry 294, Box No. 1554, File LEONARD SPIGELGASS (Official); Leo Rosten to John R. Fleming, February 14, 1942, RG 208, Office of War Information, NC-148, Entry 294, Box No. 1554, File "R," NARA.

6. See especially Welky, *The Moguls*.

7. The exception is Spigelgass, *Bonnet*.

8. Koszarski, "Subway Commandos," 296–315.

9. Budd Schulberg, "The Celluloid Noose" (1946), typescript photocopy, published in *The Screen Writer: A Publication of the Screen Writers Guild, Inc.* (August 1946), 1, Folder 39, WWII: "The Celluloid Noose," SCD.

10. LEONARD SPIGELGASS BIOGRAPHY, Box 1, Folder 18, Special Collections, Ohio State University, Columbus.

11. Leo Rosten, "Leonard Spigelgass: 26 November 1908–15 February 1985," *WGAw* [Writer's Guild America West] *News*, April 1985, 20.

12. Carr, *Hollywood and Anti-Semitism*, 150–51.

13. Leo Rosten, "Leonard Spigelgass: 26 November 1908–15 February 1985," *WGAw* [Writer's Guild America West] *News*, April 1985, 20.

14. LEONARD SPIGELGASS BIOGRAPHY, Box 1, Folder 18, Special Collections, Ohio State University, Columbus.

15. Spigelgass, *Bonnet*, 36.

16. "Obituaries: Leonard Spigelgass," *Variety*, February 19, 1985, 26.

17. Spigelgass, *Bonnet*, 35.

18. "Army Releases 'Prelude to War' to Public. Facts of Dictators Will Be Shown to Civilians Here for the First Time," *NY Herald Tribune*, December 5, 1943, from clip-

pings file, RG 208, Office of War Information, Records of the Office of the Director, RECORDS OF THE DIRECTOR, 1942–45, M-O, Box 3, NARA; Lowell Mellett to Leonard Spigelgass, June 12, 1943, RG 208, Office of War Information, Entry 264, NC-148, Box No. 1445, File SL (beginning SL), NARA (emphasis added).

19. "Army Releases 'Prelude to War' to Public. Facts of Dictators Will Be Shown to Civilians Here for the First Time," *NY Herald Tribune*, December 5, 1943, from clippings file, RG 208, Office of War Information, Records of the Office of the Director, RECORDS OF THE DIRECTOR, 1942–45, M-O, Box 3, NARA.

20. Spigelgass, *Bonnet*, 164.
21. Spigelgass, *Bonnet*, 164–65.
22. Spigelgass, *Bonnet*, 165 (emphasis added).
23. Spigelgass, *Bonnet*, 165.
24. Spigelgass, *Bonnet*, 165.
25. "Arthur Lewis," *Telegraph* [London], July 29, 2006.
26. Larry Ceplair, "Julian Blaustein: An Unusual Movie Producer in Cold War Hollywood," *Film History* 21, no. 3 (2009): 257–75.
27. Spigelgass, *Bonnet*, 166.
28. Spigelgass, *Bonnet*, 166.
29. Quoted in Spigelgass, *Bonnet*, 166.
30. Spigelgass, *Bonnet*, 166.
31. The film has the same name: *The First Motion Picture Unit of the Army Air Forces* (1943); see also Richard O'Connor, AAF [Army Air Forces staff unit] [untitled article], *Flying*, April 1945, 54.
32. Spigelgass, *Bonnet*, 167.
33. Spigelgass, *Bonnet*, 167.
34. "Army-Navy Screen Magazine. A pictorial report from all fronts for Service Men and Women. Program. Thursday, February 17, 1944," Folder 1, Box 1, Claude Binyon Papers, US, Mss 168AN, Wisconsin Historical Society Archives, Madison, Wisconsin (hereafter WHS); Leo Rosten to Lt. Col. W. M. Wright, May 1, 1942, RG 208, Office of War Information, NC-148, Entry 294, Box No. 1554, File "The Boys Write Home," NARA.
35. This Meyer Levin should not be confused with the (older) novelist and playwright of the same name (1905–81), who wrote a play based on the diary of Anne Frank.
36. "Body of Colin Kelly Believed at Manila," *New York Times*, January 26, 1946, 7; "Sergt. Levin, Brooklyn Hero of Air, Killed in Action in South Pacific. As Bombadier for Capt. Colin Kelly He Hit Battleship Harauna—On Fifty Missions—Won Coveted Decorations," *New York Times*, February 19, 1943, 7; "Russian-Born Gold Star Parents 'Proud' They Gave Son to U.S. Defense Chiefs Hail Attitude of Brooklyn Couple at Presentation of Oil Portrait of Pacific Hero to Symington," *New York Times*, November 10, 1948, 31.
37. "Sergt. Levin, Brooklyn Hero of Air, Killed in Action in South Pacific. As Bombadier for Capt. Colin Kelly He Hit Battleship Harauna—On Fifty Missions—Won Coveted Decorations," *New York Times*, February 19, 1943, 7.
38. "Sunday 'Meyer Levin Day.' War Savings Staff to Hold Rally at Brooklyn Home of Air Hero," *New York Times*, October 26, 1942, 22.

39. "Sergt. Levin, Brooklyn Hero of Air, Killed in Action in South Pacific. As Bombadier for Capt. Colin Kelly He Hit Battleship Harauna—On Fifty Missions—Won Coveted Decorations," *New York Times*, February 19, 1943, 7.

40. *The House I Live In*, accessed April 7, 2020, https://www.youtube.com/watch?v=ovwHkbIwEfU; see also, accessed April 7, 2020, https://www.loc.gov/item/mbrs0 0009167/.

41. *Don't Be a Sucker*, 1945, accessed April 7, 2020, https://collections.ushmm.org/search/catalog/irn1001130. See Cripps, *Making Movies Black*, and German, *Promises of Citizenship*.

42. "Army-Navy Screen Magazine. A pictorial report from all fronts for Service Men and Women. Program. Thursday, February 17, 1944," Folder 1, Box 1, Claude Binyon Papers, US, Mss 168AN, WHS.

43. *Army-Navy Screen Magazine*, 2. Issue No. 7—released July 31, 1943, in "Army-Navy Screen Magazine. A pictorial report from all fronts for Service Men and Women. Program. Thursday, February 17, 1944," Folder 1, Box 1, Claude Binyon Papers, US, Mss 168AN, WHS.

44. Spigelgass, *Bonnet*, 167.

45. Spigelgass, *Bonnet*, 167.

46. John Gutmann to Petra Benteler, June 21, 1989, AG: 173: 6/23 BUSINESS: Benteler-Morgan Galleries, 1989–90, Center for Creative Photography, University of Arizona, Tucson, AZ.

47. Spigelgass, *Bonnet*, 167.

48. Spigelgass, *Bonnet*, 167–68.

49. Spigelgass, *Bonnet*, 168–69.

50. Spigelgass, *Bonnet*, 169.

51. Doug Galloway, "Don Ettlinger," *Variety*, August 30, 2000.

52. Dinitia Smith, "Don Ettlinger, 86, Who Wrote for Film, Theater and Television," *New York Times*, August 13, 2000, 40.

53. Doug Galloway, "Don Ettlinger," *Variety*, August 30, 2000.

54. Michael Shnayerson, *Irwin Shaw: A Biography* (New York: G. Putnam's Sons, 1989), 120.

55. "Biographical/Historical Information," Joel Sayre Papers, 1918–79, Mss Col 6135, New York Public Library Archives and Manuscripts.

56. J. Sayre, *The House without a Roof* (New York: Farrar, 1948). It was translated into French, but it is held by a small number of libraries and few copies are in circulation.

57. Shnayerson, *Irwin Shaw*, 122.

58. Shnayerson, *Irwin Shaw*, 136.

59. Shnayerson, *Irwin Shaw*, 141.

60. Shnayerson, *Irwin Shaw*, 141.

61. Oral history interview with Philip Drell, February 10, 1984, RG 50.031*0010, USHMM.

62. Harris, *Five Came Back*, 265.

63. Mel Gussow, "Jules Buck, 83, Film Producer and Battlefield Cameraman," *New York Times*, July 26, 2001, Section B, 9.

64. Harris, *Five Came Back*, 269.

65. Ronald Bergan, "Jules Buck: Film Producer behind Peter O'Toole's Rise to Screen Stardom," *Guardian*, July 23, 2001.

66. It was approved, secretly, as a matter of policy in Robert Presnell to H. W. Mixson, January 5, 1944, Robert R. Presnell Sr. Collection, Folder 74, Signal Corps, Herrick.

67. Allen Eyles, "Obituary: Stanley Cortez," *Independent* [London], January 22, 1998.

68. *Army-Navy Screen Magazine*, Tarawa—Issue No. 21—Released Feb. 12, 1944: "A 22-year-old Marine combat photographer, the first man to take a camera in with the leading forces of an attack, talks about his work on Tarawa, the bloodiest of all Marine Corps operations," "Army-Navy Screen Magazine. A pictorial report from all fronts for Service Men and Women. Program. Thursday, February 17, 1944," Folder 1, Box 1, Claude Binyon Papers, US, Mss 168AN, WHS.

69. Rick Lyman, "Stanley Kramer, Filmmaker with Social Bent, Dies at 87," *New York Times*, February 21, 2001, Section A, 1. Stanley Kramer was an uncredited producer of *High Noon*.

70. *The First Motion Picture Unit of the Army Air Forces* (1943); Shnayerson, *Irwin Shaw*, 118–19.

71. Rick Lyman, "Stanley Kramer, Filmmaker with Social Bent, Dies at 87," *New York Times*, February 21, 2001, Section A, 1.

72. "German Concentration Camps Factual Survey Film," accessed March 11, 2020, https://www.iwm.org.uk/partnerships/german-concentration-camps-factual-survey; and see chapter 4.

73. Rick Lyman, "Stanley Kramer, Filmmaker with Social Bent, Dies at 87," *New York Times*, February 21, 2001, Section A, 1.

74. This is treated in depth in Harris, *Five Came Back*.

75. Jan Herman, *A Talent for Trouble: The Life of Hollywood's Most Acclaimed Director, William Wyler* (New York: G. P. Putnam's Sons, 1995), 245.

76. Herman, *William Wyler*, 246–47.

77. George Stevens Jr., *Conversations with the Great Moviemakers of Hollywood's Golden Age at the American Film Institute* (New York: Vintage, 2007), 204.

78. Larry Ceplair, "Julian Blaustein: An Unusual Movie Producer in Cold War Hollywood," *Film History* 21, no. 3 (2009): 257.

79. Navasky, *Naming Names*, 154–64, 379–80.

80. Jon Pareles, "Carl Foreman, Producer and 'River Kwai' Screenwriter, Dies," *New York Times*, June 27, 1984, Section 1, 24.

81. Jon Pareles, "Carl Foreman, Producer and 'River Kwai' Screenwriter, Dies," *New York Times*, June 27, 1984, Section 1, 24.

82. Rosten, *"Oral History,"* 60 and 2201.

Chapter 4. Fathers and Sons, Home and Away

1. Lasky, *I Blow My Own Horn*, 92.

2. Silver-Lasky, *Hollywood Royalty*, ix–x.

3. Adolf Zukor (1873–1976) founded Famous Players earlier. Lasky, *I Blow My Own Horn*, 122.

4. Jesse L. Lasky Jr., *Whatever Happened to Hollywood?* (London: W. H. Allen, 1973), 6.

5. Lasky, *I Blow My Own Horn*, 121.
6. Pickford-Lasky Productions, Inc., existed for less than a year, 1935–3/6.
7. Lasky, *I Blow My Own Horn*, 245.
8. "Walter Wanger" (oral history), in *The Real Tinsel*, ed. Bernard Rosenberg and Harry Silverstein (London: Collier-Macmillan, 1970), 84.
9. An exception, which deals with Jesse Lasky Sr. in depth, is Birdwell, *Celluloid Soldiers*.
10. Lasky, *I Blow My Own Horn*, 89.
11. Lasky, *I Blow My Own Horn*, 93.
12. Lasky, *I Blow My Own Horn*, 88.
13. Lasky, *I Blow My Own Horn*, 92–95.
14. Lasky, *I Blow My Own Horn*, 194.
15. Lasky, *I Blow My Own Horn*, 197.
16. Lasky Jr., *Whatever Happened*, 40.
17. Koszarski, "Subway Commandos," 296–315; Koszarski, *Hollywood on the Hudson*; Koszarski, *The Astoria Studio*.
18. Lasky, *I Blow My Own Horn*, 197.
19. Lasky Jr., *Whatever Happened*, 192. Cf. Yogerst, *Hollywood Hates Hitler!*, 76, 27, 104.
20. While in the army during World War II, Billy Lasky, Jesse Lasky Jr.'s brother, "made an important mosquito survey singlehanded, trapping and identifying twenty-nine thousand mosquitoes and eight thousand larvae of eighteen varieties, and published a paper in a scientific journal on the work." Lasky, *I Blow My Own Horn*, 238.
21. Lasky, *I Blow My Own Horn*, 61.
22. Lasky, *I Blow My Own Horn*, 204.
23. Lasky, *I Blow My Own Horn*, 203–4.
24. Lasky, *I Blow My Own Horn*, 204.
25. Lasky, *I Blow My Own Horn*, 204.
26. Lasky, *I Blow My Own Horn*, 252.
27. "Sergeant York, War Hero, Dies; Killed 25 German and Captured 132 in Argonne Battle," *New York Times*, September 3, 1964, 1. Later research confirmed the accuracy of the legend. Shells were found fired from his Springfield rifle and Colt .45 sidearm, along with German ammunition that had never been fired. Craig S. Smith, "Proof Offered of Sergeant York's War Exploits," *New York Times/International Herald Tribune*, October 26, 2006. The subject is dealt with extensively in Birdwell, *Celluloid Soldiers* (up through 1999).
28. Clippings, including reviews from the *Washington Post*, February 24, 1942, praising *Captains of the Clouds*, *Sergeant York*, and *All Through the Night*, most likely indicating that Rosten had something to do with the review(s). RG 208, Office of War Information, NC-148, Entry 295, Box No. 1555, NARA.
29. Leo Rosten to Jerry Wald, February 25, 1942, 2, RG 208, Office of War Information, NC-148, Entry 294, Box No. 1554, File "W," NARA.
30. Harris, *Five Came Back*, 122.
31. Harris, *Five Came Back*, 138, 139.
32. Emily Yellin, *Our Mothers' War: American Women at Home and at the Front during World War II* (New York: Free Press, 2004), 100. *Mrs. Miniver* was so much a part

of American culture, up through the 1960s, that Laura Petrie (played by Mary Tyler Moore) referred to it in an episode of *The Dick Van Dyke Show*, "Long Night's Journey Into Day," 1966.

33. Lasky Jr., *Whatever Happened*, 192.
34. Lasky Jr., *Whatever Happened*, 192.
35. Birdwell, *Celluloid Soldiers*, 2, 101–5, 116–17. In Birdwell's excellent account, there is, however, no mention of the direct communication between FDR and Jesse Lasky.
36. Yogerst, *Hollywood Hates Hitler!*, 23–32.
37. "Film Money-Makers Selected by Variety. 'Sergeant York' Top Picture, Gary Cooper Leading Star," *New York Times*, December 31, 1941, Section Amusements, 21.
38. David Robinson, *Chaplin: His Life and Art* (New York: McGraw-Hill, 1985).
39. Thomas Brady, "Films for Defense," *New York Times*, December 1, 1940, Section X, 4.
40. The Lasky connection was newsworthy; see "Sergeant York in Films. To Be Lasky[s'] Technical Adviser in Picture Based on His Life" (AP), *New York Times*, March 24, 1940, 33; see also Mark Harris, *Five Came Back*, 83–84.
41. Lasky, *I Blow My Own Horn*, 258–59.
42. Lasky, *I Blow My Own Horn*, 259.
43. Lasky Jr., *Whatever Happened*, 192.
44. Lasky, *I Blow My Own Horn*, 253.
45. Lasky, *I Blow My Own Horn*, 253.
46. Lasky, *I Blow My Own Horn*, 254.
47. Lasky Jr., *Whatever Happened*, 115.
48. "Sergeant York for Draft," *New York Times*, August 23, 1940, 9.
49. "Sergeant York's Son 'Ready,'" *New York Times*, September 14, 1939, 12.
50. Lasky, *I Blow My Own Horn*, 259.
51. Lasky, *I Blow My Own Horn*, 258.
52. Harris, *Five Came Back*, 84; *Whatever Happened*, 116.
53. Lasky, *I Blow My Own Horn*, 261–62.
54. Lasky, *I Blow My Own Horn*, 262.
55. Yogerst, *Hollywood Hates Hitler!*, 143, xvi–xvii, 138–40.
56. Silver-Lasky, *Hollywood Royalty*, 211.
57. "Y. F. Freeman Dies, Movie Executive," *Atlanta Constitution*, February 7, 1969, 41.
58. Carr, *Hollywood and Anti-Semitism*, 242; Yogerst, *Hollywood Hates Hitler!*, 76.
59. Carr, *Hollywood and Anti-Semitism*, 242.
60. Birdwell, *Celluloid Soldiers*, 172.
61. Birdwell, *Celluloid Soldiers*, 172.
62. Yogerst, *Hollywood Hates Hitler!*, 76.
63. *Rosten, "Oral History,"* 55 and 2196.
64. Birdwell, *Celluloid Soldiers*, 207, n. 77.
65. Lasky Jr., *Whatever Happened*, 193.
66. Lasky Jr., *Whatever Happened*, 193.
67. Lasky Jr., *Whatever Happened*, 97.
68. Lasky Jr., *Whatever Happened*, 194.

69. Photos, private collection, Joan Juliet Buck.

70. Lasky Jr., *Whatever Happened*, 194.

71. Richard Severo, "Irving Caesar, Lyricist of Timeless Hits Like 'Tea for Two,' Dies at 101," *New York Times*, December 18, 1996, Section B, 13.

72. Lasky Jr., *Whatever Happened*, 97.

73. Lasky Jr., *Whatever Happened*, 62.

74. I. S. Mowis, "Robert Presnell Sr.," IMDb, accessed March 31, 2020, https://www.imdb.com/name/nm0696190/bio?ref_=nm_ov_bio_sm. Presnell appears frequently, however, in Silver-Lasky, *Hollywood Royalty*.

75. Leo Rosten to Michael (Mike) Blankfort, June 13, 1942, RG 208, Office of War Information, NC-148, Entry 295, Box No. 155, NARA.

76. CV, undated, of Robert R. Presnell, Robert R. Presnell Sr. Coll., Folder 6, Attack!, Herrick.

77. Lane Tech was then a mechanically and practically oriented public school, which was and remains—although now a college preparatory, comprehensive high school—among the more impressive public secondary schools in the United States. See https://lanetech.org/about/history/ (accessed April 1, 2020).

78. I. S. Mowis, "Robert Presnell Sr.," IMDb, accessed March 31, 2020, https://www.imdb.com/name/nm0696190/bio?ref_=nm_ov_bio_sm.

79. I. S. Mowis, "Robert Presnell Sr.," IMDb, accessed March 31, 2020, https://www.imdb.com/name/nm0696190/bio?ref_=nm_ov_bio_sm.

80. See Joseph McBride, *Frankly: Unmasking Frank Capra* (Springville, UT: Vervanté, 2019); Leland Pogue, *Frank Capra: Interviews* (Oxford: University of Mississippi Press, 2004).

81. Lasky Jr., *Whatever Happened*, 118.

82. Lasky Jr., *Whatever Happened*, 117.

83. Silver-Lasky, *Hollywood Royalty*, 82–83, 300.

84. Lasky Jr., *Whatever Happened*, 205.

85. Some believe it is fitting that Cooper's first name is misspelled as "Meriam" on his Hollywood Walk of Fame "star."

86. I. S. Mowis, "Robert Presnell Sr.," IMDb, accessed March 31, 2020, https://www.imdb.com/name/nm0696190/bio?ref_=nm_ov_bio_sm.

87. Jon C. Hopwood, "Edward Small: Biography," IMDb, accessed March 31, 2020, https://www.imdb.com/name/nm0806448/bio?ref_=nm_ov_bio_sm; I. S. Mowis, "Robert Presnell Sr.," IMDb, accessed March 31, 2020, https://www.imdb.com/name/nm0696190/bio?ref_=nm_ov_bio_sm.

88. Robert R. Presnell, Lt. Col. Signal Corps, to Lt. Col. H. W. Mixson, Advance Photo Laboratory, January 17, 1944, Robert R. Presnell Sr. Coll., Folder "Dexterity," Herrick.

89. Robert R. Presnell to Office of the Chief Signal Officer, August 15, 1943, Folder "Dexterity," Herrick.

90. Robert R. Presnell to Office of the Chief Signal Officer, July 17, 1943, Folder "Dexterity," Herrick.

91. "DEXTERITY" [typescript], Folder 3, Attack!, Robert R. Presnell Sr. Coll., Herrick.

92. Ira H. Genet, MEMORANDUM FOR ARMY PICTORIAL SERVICE, March 24, 1944, Folder 5, Robert R. Presnell Sr. Coll., Herrick.

93. "The Dexterity Production. An Official History of a Signal Corps Motion Picture. Prepared by the US Army Signal Corps. Southwest Pacific Area," 28, Robert R. Presnell Sr. Coll., Folder 4, Herrick.

94. "The Dexterity Production. An Official History of a Signal Corps Motion Picture. Prepared by the US Army Signal Corps. Southwest Pacific Area," 28, Robert R. Presnell Sr. Coll., Folder 4, Herrick.

95. "The Dexterity Production. An Official History of a Signal Corps Motion Picture. Prepared by the US Army Signal Corps. Southwest Pacific Area," 28, Robert R. Presnell Sr. Coll., Folder 4, Herrick.

96. "The Dexterity Production. An Official History of a Signal Corps Motion Picture. Prepared by the US Army Signal Corps. Southwest Pacific Area," 28, Robert R. Presnell Sr. Coll., Folder 4, Herrick.

97. "PHOTOGRAPHIC COMBAT COVERAGE OF DEXTERITY OPERATION" attached to "The Dexterity Production. An Official History of a Signal Corps Motion Picture. Prepared by the US Army Signal Corps. Southwest Pacific Area," 28, Robert R. Presnell Sr. Coll., Folder 4, Herrick.

98. "The Dexterity Production. An Official History of a Signal Corps Motion Picture. Prepared by the US Army Signal Corps. Southwest Pacific Area," 28, Robert R. Presnell Sr. Coll., Folder 4, Herrick.

99. Orders, 15th December 1943, [signed by] J. L. Schwering, 1st Lt. A.G.D. Ass't Adjutant General, [apparently from Presnell, Folder 5, Attack!], Robert R. Presnell Sr. Coll., Herrick. I have been unable to locate any information about this David Silver.

100. "Allen H. Miner, 86; TV and Film Writer, Director, and Producer," *Los Angeles Times*, January 16, 2004.

101. Robert P. Patterson to Major General H. C. Ingles, undated, Robert R. Presnell Sr. Coll., Folder 6, Attack!, Herrick.

102. *The American Film Institute Catalog of Motion Pictures Produced in the United States, F4 1. Feature Films, 1941–1950*, vol. 4 (Berkeley: University of California Press, 1999), 120–21.

103. Robert P. Patterson to Major General H. C. Ingles, undated, Robert R. Presnell Sr. Coll., Folder 6, Attack!, Herrick.

104. The narration is transcribed from *Attack! The Battle for New Britain*, accessed April 3, 2020, https://www.youtube.com/watch?v=nEaXOXbS9TE.

105. The narration from *Attack! The Battle for New Britain*, accessed April 3, 2020, https://www.youtube.com/watch?v=nEaXOXbS9TE.

106. Presnell to First Lt. Peter Keane, March 20, 1944, Robert Presnell Sr. Coll., Folder 5, Attack!, Herrick.

107. Lasky Jr., *Whatever Happened*, 203.

108. Robert Presnell, MEMORANDUM to Captain Waldo Drake, USN, August 7, 1944, Herrick.

109. Lasky Jr., *Whatever Happened*, 207.

110. CONFIDENTIAL [undated] memo from "Washington" TO: GHQ SWPA [South West Pacific Area] (FOR SIGNALS); see also SPSFA Memo from Milton R. Krims, Captain, Air Corps Commanding, November, 22 1943, Subject: Combined activities of the Army Air Force and the Signal Corps in the making of a motion

picture, To: Lt. Col. Robert Presnell, Robert S. Presnell Sr. Coll., Folder 74, Signal Corps, Herrick.

111. In Robert S. Presnell Sr. Coll., Folder 74, Signal Corps, Herrick.

112. Presnell to Lt. Col. H. W. Mixson, [marked] SECRET, January 5, 1944, 2, Robert R. Presnell Sr. Coll., Folder 74, Signal Corps, Herrick.

113. Harris, *Five Came Back*, 280.

114. Pre-title announcement, *Attack! The Battle for New Britain*, accessed April 3, 2020, https://www.youtube.com/watch?v=nEaXOXbS9TE.

115. *The Stilwell Road*, produced by the Army Pictorial Service, Signal Corps, accessed April 3, 2020, https://youtube.com/watch?v=TVyLkG7RXiw.

116. Lasky Jr., *Whatever Happened*, 207.

117. Lasky Jr., *Whatever Happened*, 207.

118. Lasky Jr., *Whatever Happened*, 207.

119. *Brought to Action!*, produced by the Office of Strategic Services and the US Navy (no further credits are on the IMDB or BFI databases), accessed April 4, 2020, https://www.youtube.com/watch?v=1uCgyRoI8Yc.

120. Lasky Jr., *Whatever Happened*, 207.

121. "LIFELINE-script," Project 3720, "LIFELINE," prepared by Signal Corps Photographic Center [and] prepared for Industrial Services Division, Bureau of Public Relations, September 29, 1943, Herrick.

122. Certificate that Daniel Taradash honorably served in the Active Federal Service in the Army of the US from May 23, 1941, to October 23, 1941, Daniel Taradash Papers, f. 578, United States Army, Herrick.

123. "Special Orders Number 244," delivered by R. E. McLoughlin, Major, Signal Corps, Adjutant, by command of Brigadier General Van Deusen, September 6, 1942, Daniel Taradash Papers, f. 578, United States Army, Herrick.

124. "Daniel Taradash: Triumph and Chaos," interview by David Thompson, in *Backstory 2: Interviews with Screenwriters of the 1940s and 1950s*, ed. Pat McGilligan (Berkeley: University of California Press, 1991), 314.

125. *Life Line* (US Army Signal Corps,1944), identified as War Film 10, Daniel Taradash Papers, f. 578, United States Army, Herrick; see *Lifeline, 1944*, accessed April 7, 2020, https://www.youtube.com/watch?v=8Q3ECoDMhtQ.

126. Memo from Kenneth MacKenna, Capt. Signal Corps, Project Officer, January 6, 1944, Daniel Taradash Papers, f. 578, United States Army, Herrick.

127. "RED CROSS 1944 WAR FUND OF GREATER NEW YORK, Hotel Commodore Grand Ballroom, Friday, Feburary 25, 1944," in "LIFELINE-programs," Daniel Taradash Papers, f. 107, United States Army, Herrick.

128. Arthur Rosenheimer Jr., Museum of Modern Art, NY, to Robert Presnell, September 5, 1946, Robert R. Presnell Sr. Coll., Folder 6, Attack!, Herrick.

129. Leo Rosten recognized *Casablanca*, with which he was apparently not involved, as a great boon to his efforts. See Ulric Bell to Robert Riskin, December 9, 1942, RG 208, Records of the Office of War Information, Records of the Office of the Director, M-O, Box 3, File Motion Pictures-Prelude to War 1942–3, NARA. Bell here was clearly continuing the work of Rosten. Rosten did not, however, recognize the significance, it seems, of another important and successful movie as complementary to his work, *Mrs. Miniver*, directed by William Wyler (1942) (see Welky, *The Moguls*, 323–24). For

a sense of why *Mrs. Miniver* was strongly rejected by many Americans, see Robert Fyne, *The Hollywood Propaganda of World War II* (Metuchen, NJ: Scarecrow, 1994), 198.

130. Presnell to Arthur Rosenheimer, August 23, 1946, Robert R. Presnell Sr. Coll., Folder 6, Attack!, Herrick.

131. Presnell to Arthur Rosenheimer, August 23, 1946, Robert R. Presnell Sr. Coll., Folder 6, Attack!, Herrick.

132. F. K. Tourtellotte, Colonel Sig C, Executive, MEMO FOR THE HOLLYWOOD MUSEUM, November 27, 1963, Robert R. Presnell Sr. Coll., Folder 6, Attack!, Herrick.

133. *The Stilwell Road* (1945), accessed April 5, 2020, https://www.youtube.com/watch?v=TVyLkG7RXiw.

134. *The Stilwell Road* (1945), accessed April 5, 2020, https://www.youtube.com/watch?v=TVyLkG7RXiw.

135. *The Stilwell Road* (1945), accessed April 5, 2020, https://www.youtube.com/watch?v=TVyLkG7RXiw.

136. *The Stilwell Road* (1945), accessed April 5, 2020, https://www.youtube.com/watch?v=TVyLkG7RXiw.

137. *The Stilwell Road* (1945), accessed April 5, 2020, https://www.youtube.com/watch?v=TVyLkG7RXiw.

138. *The Stilwell Road* (1945), accessed April 5, 2020, https://www.youtube.com/watch?v=TVyLkG7RXiw.

139. I. S. Mowis, "Robert Presnell Sr.," IMDb, accessed March 31, 2020, https://www.imdb.com/name/nm0696190/bio?ref_=nm_ov_bio_sm.

140. "Cinema. The New Pictures," TIME, September 17, 1945 [clipping], Garson Kanin, Production File, Films, "The True Glory," printed matter, manuscript collection, LOC.

141. "Cinema. The New Pictures," TIME, September 17, 1945 [clipping], Garson Kanin, Production File, Films, "The True Glory," printed matter, manuscript collection, LOC.

142. "Cinema. The New Pictures," TIME, September 17, 1945 [clipping], Garson Kanin, Production File, Films, "The True Glory," printed matter, manuscript collection, LOC.

143. "Cinema. The New Pictures," TIME, September 17, 1945 [clipping], Garson Kanin, Production File, Films, "The True Glory," printed matter, manuscript collection, LOC.

144. *Seeds of Destiny* (1946); also *Army-Navy Screen Magazine*, No. 75, 1946, attributed to Department of Defense, Department of the Army, and War Department, accessed April 5, 2020, https://youtube.com/watch?v=S9F1LEAHOhM

145. *Seeds of Destiny* (1946).

146. David Miller, "Leonard Spigelgass: November 26, 1908–February 15, 1985," *WGAw* [Writer's Guild America West] *News*, April 1985, 19.

147. Lasky Jr., *Whatever Happened*, 262–63.

148. Lasky Jr., *Whatever Happened*, 111.

149. Lasky Jr., *Whatever Happened*, 262–63.

150. Lasky Jr., *Whatever Happened*, 263.

151. "Screenwriter Robert Presnell Jr. Dies at Age 71," *Los Angeles Times*, June 17, 1986.

152. Doherty, *Show Trial*, 93, 250, 313; Wendell Jamieson, "Marsha Hunt, Actress Turned Activist at Home and Abroad, Is Dead at 104," *New York Times*, September 11, 2022, Section A, 23.

153. See peoplepill.com/people/Robert-presnell-jr/ (accessed April 5, 2020).

154. Marsha Hunt interview by Glenn Lovell, in McGilligan and Buhle, *Tender Comrades*, 324.

155. Crowther often did not appreciate or recognize important developments in film. See Mark Harris, *Pictures at a Revolution*, 338–44, 371, 380.

156. Bosley Crowther, "Screen: Valiant Nuns. 'Conspiracy of Hearts' at Two Theaters," *New York Times*, April 8, 1960, 24.

157. Bosley Crowther, "Screen: Valiant Nuns. 'Conspiracy of Hearts' at Two Theaters," *New York Times*, April 8, 1960, 24.

158. Lasky Jr. was one of the group of writers for an Italian film set in a displaced persons camp, *Donne senza nome* (Women without names), 1949; Lasky Jr., *Whatever Happened*, 242. It did not focus on Jews or antisemitism.

159. Ruth Ben-Ghiat, "The Secret Histories of Roberto Benigni's 'Life Is Beautiful,'" in *Jews in Italy under Fascist and Nazi Rule, 1922–1945*, ed. Joshua D. Zimmerman (New York: Cambridge University Press, 2005), 330–349.

160. "Screenwriter Robert Presnell Jr. Dies at Age 71," *Los Angeles Times*, June 17, 1986. The IMDb and British Film Institute (BFI) database credits Presnell for the screenplay and does not mention Trumbo.

161. Tom Vallance, "Obituary: Betty Box," *Independent*, January 18, 1999.

162. Andrew Spicer, *Sydney Box* (Manchester: Manchester University Press, 2006), 21.

Chapter 5. Hard-Boiled Hollywood Justice

1. See Budd Schulberg, *Moving Pictures: Memories of a Hollywood Prince* (New York: Stein and Day, 1981).

2. Lasky, *I Blow My Own Horn*, 129–30.

3. Lasky, *I Blow My Own Horn*, 206.

4. Lasky, *I Blow My Own Horn*, 143.

5. Lasky Jr., *Whatever Happened*, 91.

6. Lasky Jr., *Whatever Happened*, 86–87.

7. Lasky Jr., *Whatever Happened*, 90–91.

8. Lasky Jr., *Whatever Happened*, 90–91.

9. Val Lewton, April 13, 1943, letter of reference for Budd Schulberg's Marine Corps commission, Folder 8, WWII: Report for duty documents and information for Seymour W. Schulberg, 1943–45, Manuscript MS-978, SCD.

10. There is at least one report of anti-Nazi activity being run out of DeMille's office; see "Charles Bennett: First-Class Constructionist, Interview by Pat McGilligan," in *Backstory*, 38–40.

11. Delage, "The Judicial Construction." Works that treat this subject that are foundational and offer alternative perspectives include John J. Michalczyk, *Filming the End of the Holocaust: Allied Documentaries, Nuremberg, and the Liberation of the Concentration Camps* (London: Bloomsbury Academic, 2014), 86–87, 132; Christian Delage, *Caught on Camera: Film in the Courtroom from the Nuremberg Trials to the Trials of the Khmer Rouge,*

ed. and trans. Ralph Schoolcraft and Mary Byrd Kelly (Philadelphia: University of Pennsylvania Press, 2013); Kevin Patrick Reynolds, *That Justice Be Seen: The American Prosecution's Use of Film at the Nuremberg International Military Tribunal* (DPhil thesis, University of Sussex, September 2011); Kathy Lee Peiss, *Information Hunters: When Librarians, Soldiers, and Spies Banded Together in World War II Europe* (New York: Oxford University Press, 2020); Justin Hart, *Empire of Ideas: The Origins of Public Diplomacy and the Transformation of U.S. Foreign Policy* (Oxford: Oxford University Press, 2013).

12. Lasky Jr., *Whatever Happened*, 97.

13. "American Intelligence Report on Leni Riefenstahl, May 30th, 1945," Folder 52, WWII: "American Intelligence Report on Leni Riefenstahl—May 30, 1945, printed publication, undated; Schulberg, "Nazi Pin-Up Girl," Folder 41, WWII: "Nazi Pin-Up Girl," SCD.

14. Harris, *Five Came Back*, 376–77.

15. Harris, *Five Came Back*, 376–77.

16. Schulberg also helped secure a place for himself by donating his private papers, including several boxes saved from his wartime and postwar service, to Dartmouth College, his alma mater, and recording lengthy interviews for the United States Holocaust Memorial Museum.

17. Mary Fulbrook, *Reckonings: Legacies of Nazi Persecution and the Quest for Justice* (Oxford: Oxford University Press, 2018), 213. For a later historical study of the Soviet Union and the Nuremberg trials, see Francine Hirsch, *Soviet Judgment at Nuremberg: A New History of the International Military Tribunal after World War II* (Oxford: Oxford University Press, 2020).

18. Budd Schulberg, "The Celluloid Noose" (1946), typescript photocopy; published in *The Screen Writer: A Publication of the Screen Writers Guild, Inc.* (August 1946), 1, Folder 39, WWII: "The Celluloid Noose," SCD.

19. See Simon Willmetts, *In Secrecy's Shadow: The OSS and CIA in Hollywood Cinema 1941–1979* (Edinburgh: Edinburgh University Press, 2016), 56–63.

20. John Macgruder, Brig. General, USA [United States Army], Director, "Commendation given to Lt. Budd W. Schulberg, USNR, 1946," Folder 23, WWII, Budd Schulberg Papers, 1913–2014, SCD.

21. Schulberg, "The Celluloid Noose" (1946), 1, Folder 39, WWII: "The Celluloid Noose," SCD, 5.

22. Schulberg, "The Celluloid Noose" (1946), 1, Folder 39, WWII: "The Celluloid Noose," SCD, 5, 18. James Britt Donovan was not a relative of William Joseph Donovan, one of the founding figures of the OSS.

23. Schulberg, "The Celluloid Noose" (1946), 1, Folder 39, WWII: "The Celluloid Noose," SCD, 20.

24. *That Justice Be Done* (1945), accessed May 1, 2020, http://imdb.com/title/tt0362236/plotsummary?ref_=tt+ov=pl; available at "Nazi justice and Allied justice contrasted," Film/Accession Number: 1994.119.1/RG Number: RG-60.2252/Film ID: 858, accessed May 1, 2020, http://collections.ushmm.org/search/catalog/irn1000185.

25. "Irving Pichel, Biography," accessed May 1, 2020, http://imdb.com/name/nm0681635/bio?ref_=nm_ov_bio_sm.

26. Schulberg, "The Celluloid Noose" (1946), 1, Folder 39, WWII: "The Celluloid Noose," SCD, 5. On another dimension of the unit's work: "While our cutters, half

American Navy, half German UFA, assembled this material which the translators and analysts were annotating, the search for other films continued. In Munich my brother uncovered not only the entire Heinrich Hoffmann film library, but Hitler's old friend Hoffmann himself. Like all the other Germans we encountered, Hoffmann was perfectly willing to lend his services to the Allied cause, even though in this case he was helping us tighten the noose around his own son-in-law, Baldur Von Schirach, one of the 21 defendants. Hoffmann's excellent library, his cooperation and Sgt. Schulberg's diligence produced one of the major contributions to photographic evidence at Nuremberg." Schulberg, "The Celluloid Noose" (1946), 1, Folder 39, WWII: "The Celluloid Noose," SCD, 16.

27. Tom Mascaro, *Into the Fray: How NBC's Washington Documentary Unit Reinvented the News* (Washington, DC: Potomac Books, 2012), 13–14.

28. Schulberg, "The Celluloid Noose" (1946), 1, Folder 39, WWII: "The Celluloid Noose," SCD, 5–6.

29. Schulberg, "The Celluloid Noose" (1946), 1, Folder 39, WWII: "The Celluloid Noose," SCD, 6.

30. Schulberg, "The Celluloid Noose" (1946), 1, Folder 39, WWII: "The Celluloid Noose," SCD, 6.

31. Schulberg, "The Celluloid Noose" (1946), 1, Folder 39, WWII: "The Celluloid Noose," SCD, 6.

32. These films should not be confused with a documentary written and directed by Stuart Schulberg, Bud's brother, about the Nuremberg trial, which aired in 1948 and was rereleased in 2009. The work of Budd Schulberg, discussed in this chapter, was used in the 1948 film, and Stuart Schulberg contributed substantially to the trial and the film work of his brother. Some of the reports on the restoration and rerelease of the 1948 film *Nuremberg* as *Nuremberg: Its Lesson for Today* conflate the histories of these different projects. See A. O. Scott, "Movie Review: Nuremberg: Rare Scenes Re-Emerge from Nuremberg Trials," *New York Times*, September 29, 2010, Section C, 6. The *New York Times* on October 5, 2010, admitted a number of mistakes in the original review. The effort of Stuart Schulberg's daughter, Sandra, with filmmaker Josh Waletzky, to present this film and contextualize it is highly commendable; see the filmmaker's site, accessed April 16, 2020, http://www.nurembergfilm.org/. See also Tom Stockman, "Nuremberg: Its Lesson for Today—The Review," We Are Movie Geeks website, accessed April 16, 2020, http://wearemoviegeeks.com/2012/01/nuremberg-its-lesson-for-today-the-review/; Padrig Belton, "Lesson for Today: The Restoration of a Documentary about the Nuremberg Trials—63 Years after It Was Filmed," Frieze [online] Magazine, accessed April 16, 2020, https://frieze.com/article/lesson-today.

33. Lt. Schulberg, USNR, to Cmdr. Donovan, Cmdr. Kellogg, Major Finke, Report on field trip Nov. 4–8, 9, 1945, 5, Folder 15, WWII: Memorandum to Cmdrs. Donovan, Kellogg and Major Finke from Budd Schulberg regarding Leni Riefenstahl interview, 1945, SCD: "Mr. Winston, a person[al] friend of mine, is in charge of editing the weekly ICD newsreel. He has collected Wochenschau newsreels from 1933–1945 (1934 excepted) and is now listing those he considers of greatest importance. He is willing to help our project in any way possible. Items we are lacking can be checked with him. If he has them, he will knock off prints for us."

34. LT. (jg) [also j.g., for "junior grade"] S.W. Schulberg, USNR, Project Supervisor, Photographic Evidence Div., Field Photographic Branch, OSS, MEMORANDUM, TO: U.S. CHIEF OF COUNSEL, COMD'R J. DONAVAN, COL. STOREY, COL. GILL, COL. BROSS, COL. GABLE, COL. KAPLAN, AND FIELD PHOTOGRAPHIC BRANCH, WASHINGTON, DC, SUBJECT: Progress Report, 19, Folder 11, WWII: Memorandum: Progress Report regarding film and recording procurement, OSS, War Crimes Photographic Report with German list of films, 1945, SCD. This document also is available online from the General William Donovan collection at Cornell University, accessed April 17, 2020, lawcollections.library.cornell.edu/Nuremberg/catalog/nur:02024.

35. Budd Schulberg to Ellen Harrington, July 1, 1994; Budd Schulberg to Ruda Dauphin, July 1, 1994; both Folder 43, WWII: Correspondence, 1980–94, SCD.

36. Budd Schulberg, "Our War—World War II," typescript carbon, undated, 2, published in "Ideas: Books," *Newsday*, December 6, 1981, 6–7, Folder 40, WWII: "Our World War II" by Budd Schulberg, SCD. Most likely the piece appeared for the 40th anniversary of Pearl Harbor.

37. Val Lewton, April 13, 1943, letter of reference for Budd Schulberg's Marine Corps commission, Folder 8, WWII: Report for duty documents and information for Seymour W. Schulberg, 1943–45, SCD.

38. James T. Fisher, *On the Irish Waterfront: The Crusader, the Movie, and the Soul of the Port of New York* (Ithaca, NY: Cornell University Press, 2009).

39. "Roosevelt Juden drehen Sexfilme," *Innsbrucker Nachrichten*, June 8, 1942, 6; "Hetzfilme aus aller Welt," *Wiener neueste Nachrichten*, September 11, 1938, 26.

40. Yogerst, *Hollywood Hates Hitler!*, 89, 110.

41. Reprint of a handbill, Folder 1, WWII: "The Hollywood Tribune," newspaper, 1939, SCD. Emphasis in the original.

42. *Don't Be a Sucker*, anti-fascist and anti-racist educational film made by US Army Signal Corps, 1945, 1994.119.1, RG-60.2213, Film ID: 857, USHMM.

43. Reprint of a handbill, Folder 1, WWII: "The Hollywood Tribune," newspaper, 1939, SCD.

44. The most exaggerated version of this perspective is Urwand, *The Collaboration*.

45. Thomson, *Warner Bros*.

46. See Steven J. Ross, *Hitler in Los Angeles*.

47. "Was rennt der Sammy so? Ein Roman unter Juden in Hollywood," *Berliner Illustrierte Zeitung* [clipping, only year noted, Nr. 6, 1942], in Folder 4, WWII: *Berliner Illustrierte Zeitung*, German Newspaper, Nr. 6, SCD.

48. Budd Schulberg, *What Makes Sammy Run?* (1941; repr. London: Transworld, 1958), 102.

49. Bennett A. Cerf, President, Random House, Inc., January 22, 1943, Folder 7, WWII, SCD.

50. "ENSIGN BUDD WILSON SCHULBERG, USNR," [one-page resume], SCD.

51. Max Aub, "I Saw It Happen," Joint Anti-Fascist Refugee Committee, 1942, Folder 3, WWII: "I Saw It Happen" by Max Aub, Joint Anti-Fascist Refugee Committee, 1942, SCD; see also Max Aub, *Diario de Djelfa* (México: J. Moritz, 1970), which mainly comprises poems written in the concentration camp.

52. "ENSIGN BUDD WILSON SCHULBERG, USNR," SCD.

53. "A Look Back . . . Budd Schulberg: Documenting the Horrors of the Holocaust," accessed April 12, 2020, https://www.cia.gov/news-information/featured-story-archive/budd-schulberg.html. The CIA account of Schulberg is, for the most part, a helpful and accurate summary of his life and work for the OSS.

54. "ENSIGN BUDD WILSON SCHULBERG, USNR," [one-page CV], SCD.

55. Lowell Mellett to Major Franklin Andreon, United States Marine Corps, January 13, 1943, Folder 7, WWII, SCD.

56. Phillips D. Carleton, Captain, US Marine Corps, to [Budd] Schulberg, September 3, 1943, Folder 8, WWII: Report for duty documents and information for Seymour W. Schulberg, 1943–45, SCD.

57. Budd Schulberg to Ellen Harrington, Academy of Motion Picture Arts & Sciences, July 1, 1994, Folder 43, WWII, Correspondence, 1980–94, SCD.

58. Budd Schulberg to Ellen Harrington, Academy of Motion Picture Arts & Sciences, July 1, 1994, Folder 43, WWII, Correspondence, 1980–94, SCD.

59. Budd Schulberg is now given credit as the screenwriter for *December 7* on the IMDb database, but this most likely did not appear before 2014.

60. *December 7* has an unusually convoluted history, but the credit does not belong to Frank Wead, James Kevin McGuinness, John Ford, and Robert Parrish, as argued by Harris in *Five Came Back*, 208–9.

61. Charles Kaufman to Robert R. Presnell, August 4, 1944, Folder 3: Attack!, Robert Presnell Sr. Coll., Herrick.

62. "WORLD WAR II WOMEN'S RESERVE WAVES U.S. NAVY MOVIE 80984," accessed April 14, 2020, youtube.com/watch?v=PazHV_shhFU.

63. Frances L. Rich, Lieutenant (jg), USNR, Special Assistant to the Director, to Ensign Bud Schulberg, USNR, Office of Strategic Services, Field Photographic Branch, South Agricultural Branch, Washington, DC [undated], Folder 42, World War II: Correspondence, 1943–45, SCD.

64. Buck, *The Price of Illusion*, 15.

65. Frances Rich's papers are held at her alma mater, Smith College, Identifier SSC-MS-00129.

66. The archival staff at Dartmouth cautions that Schulberg may simply have "collected things" that comprise his files. But I suspect that there was some method, and that he tended to save material that he either contributed to or that reflected some kind of stake for himself. It seems plausible that some of the captions on the "Newsmaps" in the collection were written by him. See "Newsmap, 23," US War Department, 1943, Folder 5, WWII: Map, "Newsmap, Number 34," US War Department, 1943, SCD; "NEWSMAP Prepared and distributed by ARMY ORIENTATION COURSE, Morale Services Division, Army Service Forces, WAR DEPT., 2E581 Pentagon Building, Washington DC, Army Air Force distribution by Publications Division, SCD.

67. "Gordon Dean, 52, Was Truman Aide. Victim in Nantucket Crash. Headed A.E.C. for 3 Years—Became an Executive," *New York Times*, August 17, 1958, 78.

68. "Gordon Dean, 52, Was Truman Aide. Victim in Nantucket Crash. Headed A.E.C. for 3 Years—Became an Executive," *New York Times*, August 17, 1958, 78.

69. James Gladstone, *The Man Who Seduced Hollywood: The Life and Loves of Greg Bautzer, Tinseltown's Most Powerful Lawyer* (Chicago: Chicago Review Press, 2013), 65.

70. Schulberg, "The Celluloid Noose" (1946), 1, Folder 39, WWII: "The Celluloid Noose," SCD, 2.

71. Gordon Dean, Lieut, USNR, Office, Chief Counsel, to Lt. (JG) Budd Schulberg, June 2, 1945, Folder 11, WWII: Letter from Gordon Dean to Budd Schulberg regarding film on the subject of war crimes, 1945, SCD.

72. Schulberg, "The Celluloid Noose" (1946), 1, Folder 39, WWII: "The Celluloid Noose," SCD, 1.

73. Schulberg, "The Celluloid Noose" (1946), 1, Folder 39, WWII: "The Celluloid Noose," SCD, 2.

74. Rereleased as *Nuremberg: Its Lesson for Today*, the Schulberg/Waletzky Restoration, 2015.

75. Schulberg, "The Celluloid Noose" (1946), 1, Folder 39, WWII: "The Celluloid Noose," SCD, 2–3.

76. Robert Koehl, *The Black Corps: The Structure and Power Struggles of the SS* (Madison: University of Wisconsin Press, 1983).

77. Schulberg, "The Celluloid Noose" (1946), 1, Folder 39, WWII: "The Celluloid Noose," SCD, 3.

78. Schulberg, "The Celluloid Noose" (1946), 1, Folder 39, WWII: "The Celluloid Noose," SCD, 4.

79. Progress Report, 19, Folder 11, WWII: Memorandum: Progress Report regarding film and recording procurement, OSS, War Crimes Photographic Report with German list of films, 1945, SCD, 1.

80. Progress Report, 19, Folder 11, WWII: Memorandum: Progress Report regarding film and recording procurement, OSS, War Crimes Photographic Report with German list of films, 1945, SCD, 3.

81. Schulberg, "The Celluloid Noose" (1946), 1, Folder 39, WWII: "The Celluloid Noose," SCD, 4.

82. Progress Report, 19, Folder 11, WWII: Memorandum: Progress Report regarding film and recording procurement, OSS, War Crimes Photographic Report with German list of films, 1945, SCD, 4–5.

83. Progress Report, 19, Folder 11, WWII: Memorandum: Progress Report regarding film and recording procurement, OSS, War Crimes Photographic Report with German list of films, 1945, SCD, 10.

84. His interview with Riefenstahl, focused on the attempt to acquire the missing films and her information about other film locations, was included in his report on his "field trip." Lt. Schulberg, USNR, to Cmdr. Donovan, Cmdr. Kellogg, Major Finke, Report on field trip Nov. 4–8, 9, 1945, 1–2, Folder 15, WWII: Memorandum to Cmdrs. Donovan, Kellogg and Major Finke from Budd Schulberg regarding Leni Riefenstahl interview, 1945, SCD.

85. Beck, *Budd Schulberg*, 39, n. 2.

86. Schulberg, "Nazi Pin-Up Girl," Folder 41, WWII: "Nazi Pin-Up Girl," SCD, 16.

87. Progress Report, 19, Folder 11, WWII: Memorandum: Progress Report regarding film and recording procurement, OSS, War Crimes Photographic Report with German list of films, 1945, SCD, 2.

88. Beck, *Budd Schulberg*, 39, n. 2.

89. Schulberg, "Nazi Pin-Up Girl," Folder 41, WWII: "Nazi Pin-Up Girl," SCD, 2.

90. Beck, *Budd Schulberg*, 39, n. 2. The text says that "he found her in Bavaria," which is incorrect. It was Austria, but just over the border.

91. Schulberg, "Nazi Pin-Up Girl," Folder 41, WWII: "Nazi Pin-Up Girl," SCD, 16.

92. Schulberg, "Nazi Pin-Up Girl," Folder 41, WWII: "Nazi Pin-Up Girl," SCD, 12.

93. Schulberg, "Nazi Pin-Up Girl," Folder 41, WWII: "Nazi Pin-Up Girl," SCD, 11.

94. The report, officially unattributed, was either written by Schulberg or taken largely from his account. "American Intelligence Report on Leni Riefenstahl, May 30th, 1945," Source unidentified, 35–38, LENI RIEFENSTAHL, film star and producer, Hitler's alleged mistress, Folder 52, WWII: "American Intelligence Report on Leni Riefenstahl—May 30, 1945," printed publication, undated, SCD; Schulberg, "Nazi Pin-Up Girl," Folder 41, WWII: "Nazi Pin-Up Girl," SCD, 18–24.

95. See Steven Bach, *Leni: The Life and Work of Leni Riefenstahl* (New York: Knopf, 2007), 221–24.

96. "Milton Herman Medenbach, December 31, 1907–January 17, 2007," accessed April 18, 2020, kirkandnicesuburban.com/obituary/medenbah-milton.

97. See Bach, *Leni*, 223; Leni Riefenstahl to Lt. Col. Medenbach, 1945, apparently sent to him at his home in the United States, Folder 14, World War II: Letter from Leni Riefenstahl to Lt. Col. Medenbach, 1945, SCD.

98. "American Intelligence Report on Leni Riefenstahl, May 30th, 1945," Source unidentified, 35–38, LENI RIEFENSTAHL, film star and producer, Hitler's alleged mistress, Folder 52, WWII: "American Intelligence Report on Leni Riefenstahl—May 30, 1945," printed publication, undated, 35, SCD.

99. [Riefenstahl interrogation]/CONFIDENTIAL/German Intelligence Section/Special Interrogation Series No. 3, Donovan Nuremberg Trials Collection, Cornell University, accessed May 30, 2020, lawcollections.library.cornell.edu/Nuremberg/catalog/nur:01264.

100. Bach, *Leni*, 225.

101. "American Intelligence Report on Leni Riefenstahl, May 30th, 1945," Source unidentified, 35–38, LENI RIEFENSTAHL, film star and producer, Hitler's alleged mistress, Folder 52, WWII: "American Intelligence Report on Leni Riefenstahl—May 30, 1945," printed publication, undated, 35, SCD. The chronology here does not make sense and skips over her being "cleared."

102. Lt. Schulberg, USNR, MEMORANDUM to Comdr. Donovan, Cmdr. Kellogg, Major Finke, November 9, 1945, 1, Folder 15, WWII: Memorandum to Cmdrs. Donovan, Kellogg, and Major Finke from Budd Schulberg regarding Leni Riefenstahl interview, 1945, SCD; Schulberg, "Nazi Pin-Up Girl," Folder 41, WWII: "Nazi Pin-Up Girl," SCD, 3.

103. Lt. Schulberg, USNR, MEMORANDUM to Comdr. Donovan, Cmdr. Kellogg, Major Finke, November 9, 1945, 1, Folder 15, WWII: Memorandum to Cmdrs. Donovan, Kellogg, and Major Finke from Budd Schulberg regarding Leni Riefenstahl interview, 1945, SCD.

104. Schulberg, "Nazi Pin-Up Girl," Folder 41, WWII: "Nazi Pin-Up Girl," SCD, 12.

105. Lt. Schulberg, USNR, MEMORANDUM to Comdr. Donovan, Cmdr. Kellogg, Major Finke, November 9, 1945, 1, Folder 15, WWII: Memorandum to Cmdrs. Donovan, Kellogg, and Major Finke from Budd Schulberg regarding Leni Riefenstahl interview, 1945, SCD.

106. Schulberg, "Nazi Pin-Up Girl," Folder 41, WWII: "Nazi Pin-Up Girl," SCD, 12.
107. Schulberg, "Nazi Pin-Up Girl," Folder 41, WWII: "Nazi Pin-Up Girl," SCD, 12–13.
108. Schulberg, "Nazi Pin-Up Girl," Folder 41, WWII: "Nazi Pin-Up Girl," SCD, 13.
109. Schulberg, "Nazi Pin-Up Girl," Folder 41, WWII: "Nazi Pin-Up Girl," SCD, 13.
110. Schulberg, "Nazi Pin-Up Girl," Folder 41, WWII: "Nazi Pin-Up Girl," SCD, 12–14.
111. Schulberg, "Nazi Pin-Up Girl," Folder 41, WWII: "Nazi Pin-Up Girl," SCD, 12–14.
112. Schulberg, "Nazi Pin-Up Girl," Folder 41, WWII: "Nazi Pin-Up Girl," SCD, 15.
113. *Der Sieg des Glaubens*, imdb, accessed April 19, 2020, http://imdb.com/title/tt0516078/plotsummary?ref_=tt_ov_pl#summaries.
114. "Hitler Youth at the 1933 Reich Party Day, Administrative History, Sieg des Glaubens [Victory of Faith], USHMM, accessed April 19, 2020, http://collections.ushmm.org/search/catalog/irn1004350.
115. Schulberg, "Nazi Pin-Up Girl," Folder 41, WWII: "Nazi Pin-Up Girl," SCD, 15.
116. "Leni Riefenstahl-UCLA Retrospective" (2004), accessed April 19, 2020, http://www.germanhollywood.com/rief_retro04.html.
117. Schulberg incorrectly calls him "Hans," not Carl (1897–1984); see Uli Jung, "Carl Junghans," *Encyclopedia of the Documentary Film*, ed. Ian Aitkin (London: Routledge, 2013), 700–701.
118. Progress Report, 19, Folder 11, WWII: Memorandum: Progress Report regarding film and recording procurement, OSS, War Crimes Photographic Report with German list of films, 1945, SCD, 8.
119. Progress Report, 19, Folder 11, WWII: Memorandum: Progress Report regarding film and recording procurement, OSS, War Crimes Photographic Report with German list of films, 1945, SCD, 8.
120. Junghans used unpaid Czech actors; see Hilmar Hoffmann, *The Triumph of Propaganda: Film and National Socialism, 1933–1945* (London: Berghahn Books, 1997), 126.
121. Progress Report, 19, Folder 11, WWII: Memorandum: Progress Report regarding film and recording procurement, OSS, War Crimes Photographic Report with German list of films, 1945, SCD, 8.
122. *Opfer der Vergangenheit* (1937), IMDb database, accessed April 22, 2020, http://imdb.com/title/tt0247595/; "Sterilization; marriage health law, Opfer der Vergangenheit, " see http://collections.ushmm.org/search/catalog/irn1002456.
123. Progress Report, 19, Folder 11, WWII: Memorandum: Progress Report regarding film and recording procurement, OSS, War Crimes Photographic Report with German list of films, 1945, SCD, 16–17; see http://collections.ushmm.org/search/catalog/irn1001940 (accessed April 22, 2020).
124. Henry Friedlander, *The Origins of the Nazi Genocide: From Euthanasia to the Final Solution* (Chapel Hill: University of North Carolina Press, 1995); Christopher Browning, *The Origins of the Final Solution: The Evolution of Nazi Jewish Policy, September 1939–March 1942* (Lincoln: University of Nebraska Press, 2007).
125. Progress Report, 19, Folder 11, WWII: Memorandum: Progress Report regarding film and recording procurement, OSS, War Crimes Photographic Report with German list of films, 1945, SCD, 15.

126. Schulberg, "Nazi Pin-Up Girl," Folder 41, WWII: "Nazi Pin-Up Girl," SCD, 15.

127. *Tiefland*, an opera/drama produced, directed, and cowritten by Riefenstahl, was released in 1954. "French authorities" have been credited with confiscating the film. Most likely Schulberg had something to do with this; see Bach, *Leni*, 229; 197–201. 228–29.

128. Schulberg, "Nazi Pin-Up Girl," Folder 41, WWII: "Nazi Pin-Up Girl," SCD, 13–15.

129. Schulberg, "Nazi Pin-Up Girl," Folder 41, WWII: "Nazi Pin-Up Girl," SCD, 16.

130. Bach, *Leni*, 139. This was not simply a retrospective view. When Riefenstahl's *Olympia* was awarded the first prize at the International Moving Picture Festival in Venice, September 1938, the American and British delegates protested that the decision was a result of interference by "high German officials in Berlin." See "2 Delegates Decry Venice Film Awards. Choice of German Picture Irks U.S. and British Envoys," *New York Times*, September 2, 1938, 21. Leni Riefenstahl is not named in this article.

131. Schulberg, "Nazi Pin-Up Girl," Folder 41, WWII: "Nazi Pin-Up Girl," SCD, 16.

132. See John M. Hoberman, *Sport and Political Ideology* (Austin: University of Texas Press, 1984).

133. See Paul Knepper, *The Invention of International Crime: A Global Issue in the Making, 1881–1914* (Basingstoke, UK: Palgrave Macmillan, 2010); Paul Knepper, *International Crime in the 20th Century: The League of Nations Era, 1919–1939* (New York: Palgrave Macmillan, 2011).

134. Schulberg, "Nazi Pin-Up Girl," Folder 41, WWII: "Nazi Pin-Up Girl," SCD, 16.

135. Schulberg, "Nazi Pin-Up Girl," Folder 41, WWII: "Nazi Pin-Up Girl," SCD, 16–17.

136. Ingar Sletter Kolloen, *Knut Hamsun: Dreamer and Dissenter* (New Haven, CT: Yale University Press, 2009).

137. "Here with Reich Film. Leni Riefenstahl. Here on Visit Only. Leni Riefenstahl Denies She Had Romance with Hitler," *New York Times*, November 5, 1938, 14.

138. Schulberg, "Nazi Pin-Up Girl," Folder 41, WWII: "Nazi Pin-Up Girl," SCD, 17–18.

139. Schulberg, "Nazi Pin-Up Girl," Folder 41, WWII: "Nazi Pin-Up Girl," SCD, 17–18.

140. Schulberg, "Nazi Pin-Up Girl," Folder 41, WWII: "Nazi Pin-Up Girl," SCD, 18.

141. Schulberg, "Nazi Pin-Up Girl," Folder 41, WWII: "Nazi Pin-Up Girl," SCD, 19.

142. Schulberg, "Nazi Pin-Up Girl," Folder 41, WWII: "Nazi Pin-Up Girl," SCD, 19.

143. Schulberg, "Nazi Pin-Up Girl," Folder 41, WWII: "Nazi Pin-Up Girl," SCD, 19.

144. Schulberg, "Nazi Pin-Up Girl," Folder 41, WWII: "Nazi Pin-Up Girl," SCD, 19.

145. Schulberg, "Nazi Pin-Up Girl," Folder 41, WWII: "Nazi Pin-Up Girl," SCD, 19–20.

146. Dolly Haas (1910–94) was born in Hamburg and grew up mainly in England. Her second husband was the cartoonist Al Hirschfeld, and they are the parents of "Nina," whose name is hidden in all of Hirschfeld's portraits. Schulberg, "Nazi Pin-Up Girl," Folder 41, WWII: "Nazi Pin-Up Girl," SCD, 20.

147. Mel Gussow, "Dolly Haas, 84, an Actress and the Wife of Hirschfeld," *New York Times*, September 17, 1994, Section 1, 12.

148. Schulberg, "Nazi Pin-Up Girl," Folder 41, WWII: "Nazi Pin-Up Girl," SCD, 20.

149. Schulberg, "Nazi Pin-Up Girl," Folder 41, WWII: "Nazi Pin-Up Girl," SCD, 22.
150. Schulberg, "Nazi Pin-Up Girl," Folder 41, WWII: "Nazi Pin-Up Girl," SCD, 21.
151. "Leni Riefinstahl Angry. Complains She Was Followed by Detectives in Hollywood," *New York Times*, January 28, 1938, 10.
152. Schulberg, "Nazi Pin-Up Girl," Folder 41, WWII: "Nazi Pin-Up Girl," SCD, 22.
153. Schulberg, "Nazi Pin-Up Girl," Folder 41, WWII: "Nazi Pin-Up Girl," SCD, 22.
154. Winfield R. Sheehan, accessed April 20, 2020, http://theoscarsite.com/whos who/sheehan_w.htm.
155. "Knut Haukelid, 82, Fighter in Resistance to Nazis in Norway," *New York Times*, March 11, 1994, Section B, 9.
156. "Leni Riefenstahl in Paris. Die deutsche Filmschöpferin erzählt unserem Pariser A. L. Vertreter über ihre Amerikareise," in *Mein Film in Wien. Illustrierte Film-und Kinorundscahu*, 3.II.1939 [February 3, 1939], 3.
157. Moorehead, *Sidney Bernstein*, 99–100.
158. Schulberg, "Nazi Pin-Up Girl," Folder 41, WWII: "Nazi Pin-Up Girl," SCD, 22–23.
159. Schulberg, "Nazi Pin-Up Girl," Folder 41, WWII: "Nazi Pin-Up Girl," SCD, 23.
160. Schulberg, "Nazi Pin-Up Girl," Folder 41, WWII: "Nazi Pin-Up Girl," SCD, 23–24.
161. Schulberg, "Nazi Pin-Up Girl," Folder 41, WWII: "Nazi Pin-Up Girl," SCD, 24.
162. Bach, *Leni*, 243, 245.
163. Schulberg, "Nazi Pin-Up Girl," Folder 41, WWII: "Nazi Pin-Up Girl," SCD, 24.
164. Siegbert Salomon Prawer, *Between Two Worlds: The Jewish Presence in German and Austrian Film, 1910–1933* (New York: Berghahn Books, 2005); *Unerwünschtes Kino: der deutschsprachige Emigrantenfilm 1934–1937* (Wien: Filmarchiv Austria, 2000).
165. Schulberg spelled his name two different ways, including "Urinarius" along with "Arinarius" used here. He most likely is referring to Gregory Avenarius, "film expert on the Committee for Cinematographic Affairs." My thanks to David Shneer for this information.
166. Schulberg, "The Celluloid Noose" (1946), 1, Folder 39, WWII: "The Celluloid Noose," SCD, 10.
167. Schulberg, "The Celluloid Noose" (1946), 1, Folder 39, WWII: "The Celluloid Noose," SCD, 11.
168. For a different version of the tale told here, focusing on the importance of John Ford's reputation, see Frank S. Nugent, "Hollywood's Favorite Rebel," *Saturday Evening Post*, July 23, 1949, reprinted in *John Ford Made Westerns*, ed. Gaylyn Studlar and Matthew Bernstein (Bloomington: Indiana University Press, 2001), 262–70, also 1, 34, 12, 64.
169. Schulberg, "The Celluloid Noose" (1946), 1, Folder 39, WWII: "The Celluloid Noose," SCD, 11.
170. Schulberg, "The Celluloid Noose" (1946), 1, Folder 39, WWII: "The Celluloid Noose," SCD, 11.
171. Schulberg, "The Celluloid Noose" (1946), 1, Folder 39, WWII: "The Celluloid Noose," SCD, 11.
172. Schulberg, "The Celluloid Noose" (1946), 1, Folder 39, WWII: "The Celluloid Noose," SCD, 12.

173. Isenberg, *We'll Always Have Casablanca*, 1, 25, 37.
174. Schulberg, "The Celluloid Noose" (1946), 1, Folder 39, WWII: "The Celluloid Noose," SCD, 12.
175. Schulberg, "The Celluloid Noose" (1946), 1, Folder 39, WWII: "The Celluloid Noose," SCD, 12.
176. Schulberg, "The Celluloid Noose" (1946), 1, Folder 39, WWII: "The Celluloid Noose," SCD, 12.
177. Schulberg, "The Celluloid Noose" (1946), 1, Folder 39, WWII: "The Celluloid Noose," SCD, 12–13.
178. Schulberg, "The Celluloid Noose" (1946), 1, Folder 39, WWII: "The Celluloid Noose," SCD, 12–13.
179. Schulberg, "The Celluloid Noose" (1946), 1, Folder 39, WWII: "The Celluloid Noose," SCD, 13.
180. Most likely Aleksandrovitch Kolyshkin. Thanks due to David Shneer for assistance.
181. Schulberg, "The Celluloid Noose" (1946), 1, Folder 39, WWII: "The Celluloid Noose," SCD, 13.
182. Schulberg, "The Celluloid Noose" (1946), 1, Folder 39, WWII: "The Celluloid Noose," SCD, 14.
183. Schulberg, "The Celluloid Noose" (1946), 1, Folder 39, WWII: "The Celluloid Noose," SCD, 15.
184. Schulberg, "The Celluloid Noose" (1946), 1, Folder 39, WWII: "The Celluloid Noose," SCD, 15–16.
185. Beck, *Budd Schulberg*, appendix D, 141.
186. See Doherty, *Hollywood and Hitler*, 121; on the Hollywood response to Mussolini's son, 121–36.
187. Beck, *Budd Schulberg*, appendix D, 141.
188. Schulberg, "Nazi Pin-Up Girl," Folder 41, WWII: "Nazi Pin-Up Girl," SCD, 15–17.
189. Schulberg, "Nazi Pin-Up Girl," Folder 41, WWII: "Nazi Pin-Up Girl," SCD, 3.
190. Bach, *Leni*, 228.
191. Alan Riding, "Leni Riefenstahl, 101, Dies; Film Innovator Tied to Hitler," *New York Times*, September 10, 2003, Section C, 4. See also "An Exchange on Leni Riefenstahl, David B. Hinton, reply by Susan Sontag, in response to 'Fascinating Fascism' from the February 6, 1975, issue," *New York Review of Books*, September 18, 1975, https://www.nybooks.com/articles/1975/09/18/an-exchange-on-leni-riefenstahl/.
192. Bach, *Leni*, 228.
193. Alan Riding, "Leni Riefenstahl, 101, Dies; Film Innovator Tied to Hitler," *New York Times*, September 10, 2003, Section C, 4.
194. About her trip to the United States overall, see Bach, *Leni*, 169–79; Doherty, *Hollywood and Hitler*, 293–310.
195. Leni Riefenstahl, *A Memoir* (New York: Picador, 1995), 239.
196. The song, *L'Apprenti sorcier*, was composed in 1896 by Paul Dukas (1865–1935) and was suggested to Walt Disney by conductor Leopold Stokowski; see "Paul Dukas: The Sorcerer's Apprentice," Our Classic Century, accessed May 19, 2020, http://bbc.co.uk/programmes/p06z3991.

197. Bach, *Leni*, 11.

198. Leo Rosten to Walt Disney, May 21, 1942, RG 208, Office of War Information, NC-148, Entry 295, Box No. 155, File "D"; Robert Spencer Carr to Edgar Dale, February 9, 1942, stressing the role of Kay Kamen, RG 208, Office of War Information, NC-148, Entry 295, Box No. 1555, File "B," NARA.

199. *Movies at War*, vol. 2 (publication of The War Activities Committee—Motion Picture Industry and the Hollywood Victory Committee, 1943), 19.

200. See, for example, *The Ductators* (1942, story by Melvin Millar, produced by Leon Schlesinger), accessed June 4, 2020, http://youtube.com/watch?v+rVtB6afVg9a. Max Fleischer of Paramount produced what has been described as the "answer to Disney's Snow White and the Seven Dwarfs," which "made allusions to contemporary world problems" (Shull and Wilt, *Doing Their Bit*, 71). Schlesinger produced cartoons for Warner Bros. from 1930 to 1944 and then sold his company outright to them upon his retirement, in 1944 (Shull and Wilt, *Doing Their Bit*, 3).

201. Shull and Wilt, *Doing Their Bit*, 75; *Any Bonds Today?* The fast-talking, irreverent Bugs dons Blackface, imitating Al Jolson, accessed June 4, 2020, http://youtube.com/watch?=Ow430mmY6OA.

202. Bach, *Leni*, 223.

203. Ross, *Hitler in Los Angeles*, 194; Bach, *Leni*, 174. It was widely believed, however, that Vittorio Mussolini (1916–97) was opposed "to the race laws promulgated by his father in 1938." See Lee Marshall, "Obituary: Vittorio Mussolini," *Independent* [London], June 14, 1997, http://independent.co.uk/news/people/obituary-vittorio-mussolini-1255848.html; see Doherty, *Hitler and Hollywood*, 121–36.

204. Kwame Anthony Appiah, "The Defender of Differences," *New York Review of Books*, May 28, 2020, 18. This statement appears in the context of a review of three recent books about Franz Boas and the development of anthropology as an academic discipline.

Chapter 6. Reckonings—or Not

1. Most likely the material sent included Siegfried Kracauer's pamphlet, *Propaganda and the Nazi War Film* (New York: Museum of Modern Art Film Library, 1942), which appeared as a "supplement" to his book, *From Caligari to Hitler: A Psychological History of the German Film*, new ed. (Princeton, NJ: Princeton University Press, 1966), 273–307.

2. Leo Rosten to Tristam Coffin, November 2, 1943; Rosten to Alan Cranston, May 26, 1943, File C; Leo Rosten to David Bowes-Lyon, November 4, 1942, File B; RG 298, Office of War Information, NC-1458 Entry E-75, Box No. 232, Leo Rosten, NARA.

3. Rosten, *Passions & Prejudice*, 70.

4. Progress Report, 19, Folder 11, WWII: Memorandum: Progress Report regarding film and recording procurement, OSS, War Crimes Photographic Report with German list of films, 1945, SCD, 17.

5. Progress Report, 19, Folder 11, WWII: Memorandum: Progress Report regarding film and recording procurement, OSS, War Crimes Photographic Report with German list of films, 1945, SCD, 17 (emphasis added).

6. Progress Report, 19, Folder 11, WWII: Memorandum: Progress Report regarding film and recording procurement, OSS, War Crimes Photographic Report with German list of films, 1945, SCD, 18.

7. Lion Feuchtwanger, *The Devil in France: My Encounter with Him in the Summer of 1940*, new ed. (Los Angeles: USC Libraries, Figueroa Press, 2010).

8. "Veit Harlan, 64, a Film Director; Creator of Anti-Semitic 'Jud Suss' for Nazis Is Dead," *New York Times*, April 14, 1964, 37.

9. "Veit Harlan, 64, a Film Director; Creator of Anti-Semitic 'Jud Suss' for Nazis Is Dead," *New York Times*, April 14, 1964, 37.

10. T. S. Kord's discussion of *Jud Süss* and *Der ewige Jude* includes the films *Robert und Bertram* (1939), *Leinen aus Irland* (1939), and *Die Rothschilds* (1940). See T. S. Kord, *Lovable Crooks and Loathsome Jews: Antisemitism in German and Austrian Crime Writing Before the World Wars* (Jefferson, NC: McFarland, 2018), 224–26.

11. "Goebbels in 1945, discussing the film Kolberg," epigraph to Saul Friedländer, *Reflections of Nazism: An Essay on Kitsch and Death*, trans. Thomas Weyr (New York: Harper & Row, 1984).

12. Comment of germant-1, for *Kolberg* (1945), Plot, Summaries, accessed May 6, 2020, http://imdb.com/title/tt0036989/plotsummary?ref_=tt+ov_pl.

13. Peter Paret, "*Kolberg* (Germany, 1945): As Historical Film and Historical Document," in *World War II: Film and History*, ed. John Whiteclay Chambers II and David Culbert (Oxford: Oxford University Press, 1997), 47.

14. Fritz Hippler (1909–2002), the director, and Eberhard Taubert (1907–76), the writer, were never prosecuted. Hippler was "by no means a minor figure in the history of National Socialist filmmaking" (see Roel Vande Winkel, "Nazi Germany's Fritz Hippler, 1909–2002," in *Historical Journal of Film, Radio and Television* 23, no. 2 (2003): 91–99). Taubert, revealed as a leading Nazi in the mid-1950s, had a distinguished career as a fervent 'anti-Communist,' but his role in *Der Ewige Jude* was even then unknown (see "German Propagandist Resigns Following Exposure as Nazi," *Jewish Telegraphic Agency*, September 1, 1955, http://www.jta.org/1955/09/01/archive/german-propagandist-resigns-following.)

15. Progress Report, 19, Folder 11, WWII: Memorandum: Progress Report regarding film and recording procurement, OSS, War Crimes Photographic Report with German list of films, 1945, SCD, 6.

16. Riefenstahl, *A Memoir*, 330–31.

17. Riefenstahl, *A Memoir*, 140.

18. See Harris, *Five Came Back*, 107–9, 206–16, 271, 288, 306, 324–25. Budd Schulberg was not determined to be the screenwriter until after the publication of *Five Came Back*.

19. These were (1) *Ohm Kruger* (1941), anti-British; (2) *Kameraden* (1941), anti-French; (3) *Ich Klage An* (1941), against the handicapped, in favor of so-called euthanasia killing; (4) *Heimkehr* (1941), anti-Polish; (5) *Feind* (1941), anti-Polish; (6) *Dorf im Roten Sturm* (1935), anti-Soviet; (7) *Bismarck* (1940), pro aggressive militarism and conquest; (8) *Kameraden Auf See* (1938), anti-loyalist Spain; (9) *Pour Le Merite* (1938), anti-democracy and anti-republicanism; (10) *Rittmeister Brenken Reited Fuer Deutschland* (1941), anti-World War I adversaries; (11) *Jud Süss* (1940), antisemitic; (12) *Kadetten* (1941), anti-Russian; (13) *Ueber Alles in der Welt* (1941), anti-British, anti-French, and anti-Polish; (14) *Kampfgeschwader Luetzow* (1941), anti-Polish.

20. Johannes von Moltke, "Projektionen der Gewalt: Heimkehr (Gustav Ucicky, 1941)," in *Werkstatt Geschichte* 46 (2007): 84, n. 3. Thanks to Katie Trumpener for informing me of von Moltke's informative article.

21. Progress Report, 19, Folder 11, WWII: Memorandum: Progress Report regarding film and recording procurement, OSS, War Crimes Photographic Report with German list of films, 1945, SCD, 17.

22. "Emil Jannings," accessed May 1, 2020, http://imdb.com/name/nm0417837/?ref_=nmbio_bio_nm.

23. Schulberg, *What Makes Sammy Run?*, 217.

24. Schulberg, *Moving Pictures*, 271–75.

25. Schulberg, *Moving Pictures*, 273.

26. Herman G. Weinberg, *Josef von Sternberg: A Critical Study* (New York: Dutton, 1967), 17.

27. Schulberg, *Moving Pictures*, 279.

28. Schulberg, *Moving Pictures*, 279.

29. Schulberg, *Moving Pictures*, 279. There are a number of similar stories. The best-selling novel of Upton Sinclair, *Dragon's Teeth* (New York: Viking, 1945), described "persons who had an Aryan mother and a Jewish father, or an Aryan grandmother and a Jewish father. . . . who instituted researches as to the morals of their female ancestors, and established themselves as Aryans by proving themselves to be bastards!" 314. Sinclair's "Lanny Budd" novels are occasionally disparaged as antisemitic, which is the opposite of his intention.

30. Steve Shelokhonov, "Viktor Tourjansky. Biography," accessed May 2, 2020, http://www.imdb.com/name/nm069645/bio?ref_=nm_ov_bio_sm.

31. Progress Report, 19, Folder 11, WWII: Memorandum: Progress Report regarding film and recording procurement, OSS, War Crimes Photographic Report with German list of films, 1945, SCD, 18.

32. See Katie Trumpener, "A Eulogy of Failed Remembrance," review of *Air Raid* by Alexander Kluge, translated by Martin Chalmers, afterword by W. G. Sebald, *New York Review of Books*, January 18, 2024, 40–42; von Moltke, "Projektionen der Gewalt, 74–86.

33. Katie Trumpener, "A Eulogy of Failed Remembrance," review of *Air Raid* by Alexander Kluge, translated by Martin Chalmers, afterword by W. G. Sebald, *New York Review of Books*, January 18, 2024, 40–42.

34. William L. Shirer, *This Is Berlin: Reporting from Nazi Germany, 1938–40* (London: Hutchinson, 1999), 183.

35. Schulberg, "The Celluloid Noose" (1946), 1, Folder 39, WWII: "The Celluloid Noose," SCD, 3 (emphasis added).

36. *Heimkehr* is in two parts (no translation or subtitles), at "Nazi propaganda: anti-Polish," Film/Accession Number: 1995.147.1 [RG Number: RG-600902/Film ID: 32 and 33, http://collections.ushmm.org/search/catalog/im1001668 and http://collections.ushmm.org/search/catalog/im1001669, USHMM.

37. Among those he misses completely is Lil Dagover (1897–1980). See Robert Wistrich, *Who's Who In Nazi Germany* (London: Weidenfeld and Nicolson, 1982), 42.

38. The town is not specified in the film, but scenes were said to be shot in Ortelburg (Szcztno) and Chorzele.

39. Progress Report, 19, Folder 11, WWII: Memorandum: Progress Report regarding film and recording procurement, OSS, War Crimes Photographic Report with German list of films, 1945, SCD, 17.

40. Herf, *The Jewish Enemy*, 57.

41. Progress Report, 19, Folder 11, WWII: Memorandum: Progress Report regarding film and recording procurement, OSS, War Crimes Photographic Report with German list of films, 1945, SCD, 17.

42. Progress Report, 19, Folder 11, WWII: Memorandum: Progress Report regarding film and recording procurement, OSS, War Crimes Photographic Report with German list of films, 1945, SCD, 17.

43. "Gustav Ucicky," accessed May 3, 2020, https://www.imdb.com/name/nm0879802/bio?ref_=nm_ov_bio_sm#mini_bio.

44. Anne Marie O'Connor, *The Lady in Gold: The Extraordinary Tale of Gustav Klimt's Masterpiece, Portrait of Adele Bloch-Bauer* (New York: Knopf, 2012).

45. Roslyn Sulcas, "A Klimt for Sale, After a Century," *New York Times*, June 2, 2015, Section C, 3. In defense of Sulcas, the information about Ucicky's career has only appeared online in the last few years.

46. Fulbrook, *Reckonings*, 354.

47. Progress Report, 19, Folder 11, WWII: Memorandum: Progress Report regarding film and recording procurement, OSS, War Crimes Photographic Report with German list of films, 1945, SCD, 18.

48. Progress Report, 19, Folder 11, WWII: Memorandum: Progress Report regarding film and recording procurement, OSS, War Crimes Photographic Report with German list of films, 1945, SCD, 18–19.

49. "Karl Ritter," in *The Concise CineGraph: Encyclopaedia of German Cinema*, by Hans-Michael Bock and Tim Bergfelder (New York: Berghahn Books, 2009), 399; "Karl Ritter, Biography," accessed May 3, 2020, http://imdb.com/name/nm0728774/bio.

50. Fulbrook, *Reckonings*, 214 (emphasis added).

51. Herf, *The Jewish enemy*.

52. Michael Goldmeier had embarked on a study of post-1945 British fascism and then was struck down by COVID-19.

53. Leo Rosten to David Bowes-Lyon, November 4, 1942, File B; Leo Rosten to James Allen, January 2, 1943, File A, RG 298, Office of War Information, NC-1458, Entry E-75, Box No. 232, Leo Rosten, NARA.

54. Leo Rosten to Nelson Poynter, [memos] on June 6, 12 [two separate memos on June 12], 10, (especially) 17, 18, 1942, RG 208, Office of War Information, Entry 264, NC-148, Box No. 1444, File Copies Rosten Memos to Poynter, NARA.

55. Leo Rosen to Dorothy Ducas, May 29, 1943, File D; Leonard V. Finder to Leo Rosten, July 19, 1943, File F, File B; RG 298, Office of War Information, NC-1458 Entry E-75, Box No. 232, Leo Rosten, NARA.

56. Richard Breitman and Norman J. W. Goda, *Hitler's Shadow: Nazi War Criminals, U.S. Intelligence, and the Cold War* (Washington, DC: National Archives and Records Administration, 2010); Richard Breitman, *Official Secrets: What the Nazis Planned, What the British and Americans Knew* (New York: Hill and Wang, 1998).

57. K. R. M. Short, "Hollywood Fights Anti-Semitism, 1940–1945," in *Film & Radio Propaganda in World War II*, ed. K. R. M. Short (London: Croon Helm, 1983), 158–60.

58. PRESS RELEASE, OFF 69, OFFICE OF FACT AND FIGURES, and accompanying note, Leo Rosten to Nelson Poynter, Saturday, June 6, 1942, especially 2; PRESS RELEASE IN MORNING PAPERS OF SUNDAY, JUNE 14, 1942, RG 208,

Office of War Information, Entry 264, NC-148, Box No. 1444, File Copies Rosten Memos to Poynter, NARA.

59. OFF 80, PRESS RELEASE, FOR IMMEDIATE RELEASE, June 13, 1942, RG 208, Office of War Information, Entry 264, NC-148, Box No. 1444, File Copies Rosten Memos to Poynter, NARA.

60. David Kimberley produced a highly original (unpublished) paper on Alexander Korda's engagement with Jewish issues, Department of Hebrew and Jewish Studies, University College London, 2016.

61. Leo Rosten to Nelson Poynter, June 10, 1942, RG 208, Office of War Information, Entry 264, NC-148, Box No. 1444, File Copies Rosten Memos to Poynter, NARA.

62. Leo Rosten to Gardner Cowles Jr., April 14, 1943, File C; Leo Rosten to David Bowes-Lyon, November 4, 1942, File B, RG 298, Office of War Information, NC-1458 Entry E-75, Box No. 232, Leo Rosten, NARA.

63. Navasky, *Naming Names*, 287–302.

64. The first edition was given to US troops, under the imprint of Book Find Club, 1944; later editions included Albert Maltz, *The Cross and the Arrow* (London: George Harrap, 1946).

65. Maltz, *The Cross and the Arrow*, 30.

66. Jerry Belcher, "Writer Albert Maltz, One of the 'Hollywood 10,' Dies," *Los Angeles Times*, April 28, 1985.

67. Navasky, *Naming Names*, 185, 327, 334, 419–20, 287–302.

68. Silver-Lasky, *Hollywood Royalty*, 290.

69. Navasky, *Naming Names*, 229–30, 239–46, 310–12; McGilligan and Buhle, *Tender Comrades*, 44–52, 496–500, 530–35.

70. Doherty, *Show Trial*, 24–27, 31–42.

71. Jesse L. Lasky to Jesse L. Lasky Jr., April 23, 1943, in *Silver-Lasky, Hollywood Royalty*, 276.

72. Andrei Cojoc, "The Message of American Pro-Soviet Movies during World War II—*The North Star, Song of Russia, Mission to Moscow*," in *Journal of Global Politics and Cultural Diplomacy* 1 (2013): 91–104; Doherty, *Show Trial*, 111, 289.

73. Buck, *The Price of Illusion*, 26.

74. Navasky, *Naming Names*, x, 326–27, 343.

75. "Jules Dassin, Biography," accessed May 6, 2020, http://imdb.com/name/nm0202088/bio?ref_=nm_ov_bio_sm.

76. Mel Gussow, "Jules Buck, 83, Film Producer and Battlefield Cameraman," *New York Times*, July 26, 2001, Section B, 9.

77. Buck, *The Price of Illusion*, 28.

78. Sheila Rule, "Philip Dunne, 84, Screenwriter and an Opponent of Blacklisting," *New York Times*, June 4, 1992, Section B, 12; Doherty, *Show Trial*, 92–95.

79. "American propaganda film to educate US soldiers going to France, Film/Accession Number: 1994.119.1/RG Number: RG-60.0969/Film ID: 914, USHMM, accessed May 9, 2020, http://collections.ushmm.org/search/catalog/irn1000826.

80. [Leo Rosten], *112 Gripes About the French*, no publisher or date, printed by Bellenand Fontenay-aux-Roses (Seine), 63.592, LOC.

81. Buck, *The Price of Illusion*, 11–12.

82. Mel Gussow, "Jules Buck, 83, Film Producer and Battlefield Cameraman," *New York Times*, July 26, 2001, Section B, 9.

83. Buck, *The Price of Illusion*, 43.

84. Mel Gussow, "Howard Koch, a Screenwriter for 'Casablanca,' Dies at 93," *New York Times*, Section D, 17.

85. Andrei Cojoc, "The Message of American Pro-Soviet Movies during World War I—*The North Star, Song of Russia, Mission to Moscow*." *Journal of Global Politics and Cultural Diplomacy* 1 (2013): 91–104; see also Robert Fyne, *The Hollywood Propaganda of World War II* (Metuchen, NJ: Scarecrow Press, 1994), 168.

86. Rosten, "Movies and Propaganda"; Rosten, "Oral History."

87. Leo Rosten to Nelson Poynter, June 1, 1942, RG 208, Office of War Information, Entry 264, NC-148, Box No. 1444, File Copies Rosten Memos to Poynter, NARA.

88. Leo Rosten to Nelson Poynter, June 2, 1942, RG 208, Office of War Information, Entry 264, NC-148, Box No. 1444, File Copies Rosten Memos to Poynter, NARA.

89. Leo Rosten to Nelson Poynter, June 2, 1942, RG 208, Office of War Information, Entry 264, NC-148, Box No. 1444, File Copies Rosten Memos to Poynter, NARA.

90. Irwin Shaw was among those who sought to bring attention to Black soldiers entering into combat roles; see Irwin Shaw, "Negro Fighters' First Battle. It was just a routine engagement between P-40s and German planes before the invasion of Sicily but it was a historic event—the first time Americans of their race met the enemy in aerial warfare," *YANK*, August 6, 1943, 8–9.

91. Leo Rosten to Nelson Poynter, June 2, 1942, RG 208, Office of War Information, Entry 264, NC-148, Box No. 1444, File Copies Rosten Memos to Poynter, NARA.

92. *The Negro Soldier* (1944), accessed May 8, 2020 http://youtube.com/watch?v=din2dQyLNVU. Joe Louis also appeared in *This Is the Army* (1943). Matthew Frye Jacobson has analyzed the central musical number, "What the Well Dressed Man in Harlem Will Wear," which includes disparaging racial stereotypes.

93. Leo Rosten to Nelson Poynter, May 14, 1942, RG 208 Office of War Information, Entry 264, NC-148, Box No. 1444, File Copies Rosten Memos to Poynter, NARA.

94. Arch Mercey to Mr. Mellett, 12/2/42 [December 2], RG 208, Office of War Information, Entry 264, NC-148, Box No. 1436, NARA.

95. Arnaud d'Usseau himself was hounded by Senator Joseph McCarthy's Senate Permanent Subcommittee on Investigations and "declined to answer the Senator's questions, citing his constitutional privilege." He was shunned by Hollywood, and moved to France and Spain, where he managed to continue scripting using pseudonyms. See C. Gerald Fraser, "Arnaud d'Usseau, 73, Playwright, Screenplay Writer and Instructor," in *New York Times*, February 1, 1990, Section D, 21.

96. Leo Rosten to Nelson Poynter, memo accompanying material related to American soldiers including Jews, Irish, Italians, and Poles, June 12, 1942, RG 208, Office of War Information, Entry 264, NC-148, Box No. 1444, File Copies Rosten Memos to Poynter, NARA.

97. Among the few references to Leo Rosten in this context suggests that he made some attempt to address the issue and was rebuffed. See Laurie, *The Propaganda Warriors*, 180–81.

98. Memo from Leo Rosten to Lt. Commander Price Gilbert, June 5, 1943, RG 208, Office of War Information, NC-1458, Entry E-75, A-H, Box No. 232 Leo Rosten, NARA.

99. Isenberg, *Casablanca*, 9, 72–74.

100. Isenberg, *Casablanca*, 74.

101. Canada Lee, Biography, IMDB database, accessed June 29, 2020, http://imdb.com/name/nm0496938/bio?ref_=nm_ov_bio_sm.

102. David A. Gerber, "In Search of Al Schmid: War Hero, Blinded Veteran, Everyman," in *Journal of American Studies* 29, no. 1 (April 1995): 10, 1–32.

103. Bosley Crowther, "The Screen; 'Pride of the Marines,' Based on War Career of Al Schmid, in Which John Garfield Stars, at Strand—'Sumarai' at World," in *New York Times*, August 25, 1945. David Gerber brilliantly addresses the human costs of the dissonance between the creation of the myth, and the making of the film, in the lives of those concerned. See David A. Gerber, "In Search of Al Schmid: War Hero, Blinded Veteran, Everyman," in *Journal of American Studies* 29, no. 1 (April 1995): 1–32.

104. Leo Rosten to Jerry Wald, February 25, 1942, RG 208, Office of War Information, NC-148, Entry 294, Box No. 1554, File "W," NARA.

105. "Screen News Here and In Hollywood. Garfield to Star in Film of the Blind Sgt. Schmid—'Snow White' Will Be Revived," *New York Times*, March 22, 1944, 17.

106. Historian David Shneer made this argument with regard to Soviet Jewish photographers and filmmakers during World War II. See Shneer, *Through Soviet Jewish Eyes*.

107. Schulberg, *What Makes Sammy Run?* 240.

108. Doherty, *Show Trial*, 26–41.

Epilogue

1. Rosten, "Movies and Propaganda," 124.

2. "The Council of National Defense: Now a Little Known or Appreciated World War I Federal Agency," National Archives: The Text Message, August 15, 2017, https://text-message.blogs.archives.gov/2017/08/15/the-council-of-national-defense-now-a-little-known-or-appreciated-world-war-i-federal-agency/.

3. Carr, *Hollywood and Anti-Semitism*, 108–31.

4. *Rosten, "Oral History,"* 51–52 and 2192–93.

5. Yogerst, *Hollywood Hates Hitler!*, xvi-ii.

6. Undated, private collection (emphases added).

7. Leo C. Rosten, "President Roosevelt and the Washington Correspondents," *Public Opinion Quarterly* 1, no. 1 (July 1937): 36, 44–47, 52.

8. Budd Schulberg, *The Disenchanted* (1951, repr. London: Allison & Busby, 1983), 124.

9. Schulberg, *Disenchanted*, 21.

10. Schulberg, *Disenchanted*, 79.

11. Ross, *Hitler in Los Angeles*, 71; Eleanor Roosevelt, "My Day" newspaper columns, March 19, 1938, the Eleanor Roosevelt Papers, digital edition, https://www2.gwu.edu/~erpapers/myday/displaydoc.cfm?_y=1938&_f=md054905.

12. Sabine Eckmann and Lutz Koepnick, eds., *Caught by Politics: Hitler Exiles and American Visual Culture* (New York: Palgrave Macmillan, 2007).

13. William E. Leuchtenburg, *Franklin D. Roosevelt and the New Deal, 1932–1940* (New York: Harper & Row, 1963), 277; the Hollywood dimensions are richly illuminated in Carr, *Hollywood and Anti-Semitism*.

14. Axis propaganda, undated document. RG 208, Office of War Information, NC-148, Entry 295, Box No. 1555, File AXIS PROPAGANDA Techniques, NARA.

15. Buck, *The Price of Illusion*, 301.

16. Leo Rosten, "The Myths We Live By," *Journal of General Education* 17, no. 3 (October 1965): 170.

17. *Battle of Peace* [1945], US Army Signal Corps, Film, Accession Number: 2002.549.1, RG-60.3510, Film ID: 2570; *The Pale Horseman* (1946), directed by Irving Jacoby, US Army Signal Corps, Film, Accession Number, 1994.119.1, RG-60.0924, Film ID: 902, USHMM.

18. *Battle of Peace*.

19. Spigelgass, *Bonnet*, 166–67.

20. Shull and Wilt, *Doing Their Bit*, makes a similar argument about the work of animators.

21. Bernard F. Dick, *The Star-Spangled Screen: The American World War II Film* (Lexington: University Press of Kentucky, 1996), 255.

22. Welky, *The Moguls*, 1–10.

23. *Movies at War*, vol. 2, 47.

24. Hart, *Empire of Ideas*.

25. Rosten, *"Oral History,"* 57 and 2198.

26. Rosten, *"Oral History,"* 57 and 2198.

27. Schulberg, *What Makes Sammy Run?*, 217.

28. Rosten, "Movies and Propaganda," 117–18.

29. Rosten, "The Myths We Live By," 174.

30. Rosten, *"Oral History,"* 42–43 and 2183–84.

31. Harpo Marx to FDR, June 30, 1944, and FDR to Harpo Marx, July 7, 1944, "Marx, Harpo" file, PPF 8821, FDR Presidential Library and Museum, Hyde Park, New York. My sincere thanks to Kevin R. Thomas for sharing a copy of this correspondence.

Bibliography

Archives, Libraries, Museums

Academy of Motion Picture Arts and Sciences, Margaret Herrick Library, Los Angeles (Herrick)
Beinecke Library, Yale University, New Haven, Connecticut
British Library, London
Center for Creative Photography, University of Arizona, Tuscon, Arizona
Columbia University Library, New York
Dartmouth College Library, Special Collections, Hanover, New Hampshire (SCD)
Deutsche Kinematek—Museum of Film and Television, Berlin
Franklin D. Roosevelt Presidential Library and Museum, Hyde Park, New York
Firestone Library, Princeton University, Princeton, New Jersey
George Eastman Museum, Rochester, New York
George Washington University Library, Washington, DC
Library of Congress, Washington, DC (LOC)
National Archives, Kew, United Kingdom
National Archives and Records Administration, College Park, Maryland (NARA)
New York Public Library
Ohio State University Library, Columbus, Ohio
United States Holocaust Memorial Museum, Washington, DC (USHMM)
UCLA Library
Wiener Holocaust Library, London
Wisconsin Historical Society, Madison, Wisconsin (WHS)
Yad Vashem, Jerusalem
YIVO Archives, Center for Jewish History, New York

Selected Reference Works

Aitkin, Ian, ed. *Encyclopedia of Documentary Film*. London: Routledge, 2013.
The American Film Institute Catalog of Motion Pictures Produced in the United States, F4 1. Feature Films, 1941–1950. Vol. 4. Berkeley: University of California Press, 1999.
Bock, Hans-Michael, and Tim Bergfelder. *The Concise CineGraph: Encyclopaedia of German Cinema*. New York: Berghahn Books, 2009.

The Encyclopedia of Stanley Kubrick. New York: Checkmark Books, 2002.
Katz, Ephraim. *The International Film Encyclopedia.* New York: Macmillan, 1980.
Mitchell, Glenn. *The Marx Brothers Encyclopedia.* London: B. T. Batsford, 1996.
Movies at War. Vol. 2 (publication of The War Activities Committee—Motion Picture Industry and the Hollywood Victory Committee, 1943).

Books and Articles

Appiah, Kwame Anthony. "The Defender of Differences." *New York Review of Books*, May 28, 2020.
Aub, Max. *Diario de Djelfa.* México: J. Mortiz, 1970.
Bach, Steven. *Leni: The Life and Work of Leni Riefenstahl.* New York: Knopf, 2007.
Baron, Lawrence. *Projecting the Holocaust into the Present: The Changing Focus of Contemporary Holocaust Cinema.* Lanham, MD: Rowman & Littlefield, 2005.
Beck, Nicholas. *Budd Schulberg: A Bio-Bibliography.* Lanham, MD: Scarecrow, 2001.
[Bennett, Charles]. "Charles Bennett: First-Class Constructionist, Interview by Pat McGilligan," in *Backstory 1: Interviews with Screenwriters of Hollywood's Golden Age*, 17–48. Berkeley: University of California Press, 1986.
Berkowitz, Michael. *The Crime of My Very Existence: Nazism and the Myth of Jewish Criminality.* Berkeley: University of California Press, 2007.
Bernstein, Matthew. *Walter Wanger: Hollywood Independent.* Berkeley: University of California Press, 1994.
Birdwell, Michael E. *Celluloid Soldiers: The Warner Bros. Campaign against Nazism.* New York: New York University Press, 1999.
Black, Gregory. *Hollywood Censored: Morality Codes, Catholics, and the Movies.* Cambridge: Cambridge University Press, 1994.
Bohn, Thomas William. *An Historical and Descriptive Analysis of the Why We Fight Series.* New York: Arno Press, 1995.
Breitman, Richard. *Official Secrets: What the Nazis Planned, What the British and Americans Knew.* New York: Hill and Wang, 1998.
Breitman, Richard, and Norman J. W. Goda. *Hitler's Shadow: Nazi War Criminals, U.S. Intelligence, and the Cold War.* Washington, DC: National Archives and Records Administration, 2010.
Breitman, Richard, and Allan J. Lichtman. *FDR and the Jews.* Cambridge, MA: Harvard University Press, 2013.
Brody, Richard. "The Hollywood Movie Made for F.D.R.'s Inauguration." *The New Yorker*, January 20, 2013.
Brook, Vincent. *Driven to Darkness: Jewish Émigré Directors and the Rise of Film Noir.* Piscataway, NJ: Rutgers University Press, 2009.
[Brooks, Richard]. "Richard Brooks: The Professional," interview by Pat McGilligan. In *Backstory 2: Interviews with Screenwriters of the 1940s and 1950s.* Edited by Pat McGilligan, 27–72. Berkeley: University of California Press, 1991.
Brownell, Kathryn Cramer. *Showbiz Politics: Hollywood in American Political Life.* Chapel Hill: University of North Carolina Press, 2014.
Browning, Christopher. *The Origins of the Final Solution: The Evolution of Nazi Jewish Policy, September 1939–March 1942.* Lincoln: University of Nebraska Press, 2007.
Buck, Joan Juliet. *The Price of Illusion: A Memoir.* New York: Atria, 2017.

Buhle, Paul. *From the Lower East Side to Hollywood: Jews in American Popular Culture*. London: Verso, 2004.

Campbell, Tracy. *The Year of Peril: America in 1942*. New Haven, CT: Yale University Press, 2020.

Capua, Michelangelo. *Anatole Litvak: The Life and Films*. Jefferson, NC: McFarland, 2015.

Carr, Steven Alan. *Hollywood and Anti-Semitism: A Cultural History up to World War II*. New York: Cambridge University Press, 2001.

Carruthers, Lee. "Modulations of the Shot: The Quiet Film Style of George Cukor in: *What Price Hollywood?*, *Born Yesterday*, *Sylvia Scarlett*, and *My Fair Lady*." In *George Cukor: Hollywood Master*, edited by Murray Pomerance and R. Burton Palmer, 77–91. Edinburgh: Edinburgh University Press, 2015.

Ceplair, Larry. "Julian Blaustein: An Unusual Movie Producer in Cold War Hollywood." *Film History* 21, no. 3 (2009): 257–75.

Ceplair, Larry, and Steven Englund. *The Inquisition in Hollywood: Politics and the Film Community, 1930–1960*. Urbana: University of Illinois Press, 2003.

Chambers, John Whiteclay II, and David Culbert, eds. *World War II, Film, and History*. New York: Oxford University Press, 1996.

Cohen, Harvey. "The Warner Brothers and Franklin Delano Roosevelt: Connections and Collaborations," [working paper, undated], Kings College London.

Cojoc, Andrei. "The Message of American Pro-Soviet Movies during World War I— *The North Star*, *Song of Russia*, *Mission to Moscow*." *Journal of Global Politics and Cultural Diplomacy* 1 (2013): 91–104.

Cripps, Thomas. *Making Movies Black: The Hollywood Message Movie from World War II to the Civil Rights Era*. New York: Oxford University Press, 1993.

Decker, Christof. "Imaging Axis Terror: War Propaganda and the 1943 'The Nature of the Enemy' Exhibition at Rockefeller Center." In *Imaging the Scenes of War: Aesthetic Crossovers in American Visual Culture*, 85–101. Bielefeld: Transcript Verlag, 2022, 35–60.

deCordova, Richard. *Picture Personalities: The Emergence of the Star System in America*. Urbana: University of Illinois Press, 2001.

Delage, Christian. *Caught on Camera: Film in the Courtroom from the Nuremberg Trials to the Trials of the Khmer Rouge*. Edited and translated by Ralph Schoolcraft and Mary Byrd Kelly. Philadelphia: University of Pennsylvania Press, 2013.

Delage, Christian. "The Judicial Construction of the Genocide of the Jews at Nuremberg: Witnesses on Stand and Screen." In *Holocaust and Justice: Representation and Historiography of the Holocaust in Post-War Trials*, edited by David Bankier and Dan Michman, 101–16. Jerusalem: Yad Vashem; New York: Berghahn Books, 2010.

Dick, Bernard F. *The Star-Spangled Screen: The American World War II Film*. Lexington: University Press of Kentucky, 1996.

Dixon, Wheeler Winston, ed., *American Cinema of the 1940s: Themes and Variations*. New Brunswick, NJ: Rutgers University Press, 2006.

Doherty, Thomas Patrick. *Hollywood and Hitler, 1933–1939*. New York: Columbia University Press, 2013.

Doherty, Thomas Patrick. *Hollywood's Censor: Joseph I. Breen and the Production Code Administration*. New York: Columbia University Press, 2007.

Doherty, Thomas Patrick. *Projections of War: Hollywood, American Culture, and World War II*. New York: Columbia University Press, 1993.
Doherty, Thomas Patrick. *Show Trial: Hollywood, HUAC, and the Birth of the Blacklist*. New York: Columbia University Press, 2018.
Doneson, Judith E. *The Holocaust in American Film*. Philadelphia: The Jewish Publication Society, 1987.
Eckmann, Sabine, and Lutz Koepnick, eds. *Caught by Politics: Hitler Exiles and American Visual Culture*. New York: Palgrave Macmillan, 2007.
Feuchtwanger, Lion. *The Devil in France: My Encounter with Him in the Summer of 1940*. New ed. Los Angeles: USC Libraries, Figueroa Press, 2010.
Fisher, James T. *On the Irish Waterfront: The Crusader, the Movie, and the Soul of the Port of New York*. Ithaca, NY: Cornell University Press, 2009.
Fleischer, Richard. *Out of the Inkwell: Max Fleischer and the Animation Revolution*. Lexington: University Press of Kentucky, 2005.
Frank, Armin Paul. *Off-Canon Pleasures: A Case Study and a Perspective*. Göttingen: University of Göttingen, 2011.
Franks, Jill. *Islands and the Modernists: The Allure of Isolation in Art, Literature, and Science*. Jefferson, NC: McFarland, 2006.
Friedlander, Henry. *The Origins of the Nazi Genocide: From Euthanasia to the Final Solution*. Chapel Hill: University of North Carolina Press, 1995.
Friedlander, Saul. *Reflections on Nazism: An Essay on Kitsch and Death*. Translated by Thomas Wyer. New York: Harper & Row, 1984.
Fulbrook, Mary. *Reckonings: Legacies of Nazi Persecution and the Quest for Justice*. Oxford: Oxford University Press, 2018.
Fyne, Robert. *The Hollywood Propaganda of World War II*. Metuchen, NJ: Scarecrow, 1994.
Gabler, Neal. *An Empire of Their Own: How the Jews Invented Hollywood*. New York: Crown, 1988.
Gallagher, Charles R. *Nazis of Copley Square: The Forgotten Story of the Christian Front*. Cambridge, MA: Harvard University Press, 2021.
Gerber, David A. "In Search of Al Schmid: War Hero, Blinded Veteran, Everyman." *Journal of American Studies* 29, no. 1 (April 1995): 1–32.
German, Kathleen M. *Promises of Citizenship: Film Recruitment of African Americans in World War II*. Oxford: University Press of Mississippi, 2017.
Gladstone, James. *The Man Who Seduced Hollywood: The Life and Loves of Greg Bautzer, Tinseltown's Most Powerful Lawyer*. Chicago: Chicago Review Press, 2013.
Hake, Sabine. *Popular Cinema of the Third Reich*. Austin: University of Texas Press, 2001.
Hansen, Miriam. *Babel and Babylon: Spectatorship in American Silent Film*. Cambridge, MA: Harvard University Press, 1991.
Harris, Mark. *Five Came Back: A Story of Hollywood and the Second World War*. New York: Penguin, 2015.
Harris. Mark. *Pictures at a Revolution: Five Movies and the Birth of the New Hollywood*. New York: Penguin, 1989.
Hart, Bradley W. *Hitler's American Friends: The Third Reich's Supporters in the United States*. New York: Thomas Dunne Books, 2018.

Hart, Justin. *Empire of Ideas: The Origins of Public Diplomacy and the Transformation of U.S. Foreign Policy*. Oxford: Oxford University Press, 2013.
Hayes, Peter. *Why? Explaining the Holocaust*. New York: W. W. Norton, 2017.
Helford, Elyce Rae. *What Price Hollywood? Gender and Sex in the Films of George Cukor*. Lexington: University Press of Kentucky, 2020.
Herf, Jeffrey. *The Jewish Enemy: Nazi Propaganda during World War II and the Holocaust*. Cambridge, MA: The Belknap Press of Harvard University Press, 2006.
Herman, Jan. *A Talent for Trouble: The Life of Hollywood's Most Acclaimed Director, William Wyler*. New York: G. P. Putnam's Sons, 1995.
Hirsch, Francine. *Soviet Judgment at Nuremberg: A New History of the International Military Tribunal after World War II*. Oxford: Oxford University Press, 2020.
Hoberman, John M. *Sport and Political Ideology*. Austin: University of Texas Press, 1984.
Hoffmann, Hilmar. *The Triumph of Propaganda: Film and National Socialism, 1933–1945*. London: Berghahn Books, 1997.
Horowitz, Joseph. *"On My Way": The Untold Story of Rouben Mamoulian, George Gershwin, and "Porgy and Bess."* New York: W. W. Norton, 2013.
Huener, Jonathan, and Francis R. Nicosia, eds. *The Arts in Nazi German: Continuity, Conformity, Change*. Oxford: Berghahn Books, 2009.
Isenberg, Noah. *We'll Always Have Casablanca: The Life, Legend, and Afterlife of Hollywood's Most Beloved Movie*. New York: W. W. Norton, 2017.
Josephson, Matthew. "Profiles: Production Man-I." *New Yorker*, March 8, 1941, 23.
Karnow, Stanley. *Vietnam: A History*. 2nd. rev. and updated ed. New York: Penguin, 1997.
Knepper, Paul. *International Crime in the 20th Century: The League of Nations Era, 1919–1939*. New York: Palgrave Macmillan, 2011.
Knepper, Paul. *The Invention of International Crime: A Global Issue in the Making, 1881–1914*. Basingstoke: Palgrave Macmillan, 2010.
Koehl, Robert. *The Black Corps: The Structure and Power Struggles of the SS*. Madison, WI: University of Wisconsin Press, 1983.
Kolloen, Ingar Sletter. *Knut Hamsun: Dreamer and Dissenter*. New Haven, CT: Yale University Press, 2009.
Kord, T. S. *Lovable Crooks and Loathsome Jews: Antisemitism in German and Austrian Crime Writing before the World Wars*. Jefferson, NC: McFarland, 2018.
Koszarski, Richard. *The Astoria Studio and Its Fabulous Films: A Picture History with 227 Stills and Photographs*. New York: Published in association with the Astoria Motion Picture and Television Foundation by Dover Publications, 1983.
Koszarski, Richard. *Hollywood on the Hudson: Film and Television in New York from Griffith to Sarnoff*. New Brunswick, NJ: Rutgers University Press, 2008.
Koszarski, Richard. "Subway Commandos: Hollywood Filmmakers at the Signal Corps Photographic Center." *Film History* 14 (2002): 296–315.
Kracauer, Siegfried. *From Caligari to Hitler: A Psychological History of the German Film*. New ed. Princeton, NJ: Princeton University Press, 1966.
Kracauer, Siegfried. *Propaganda and the Nazi War Film*. New York: Museum of Modern Art Film Library, 1942.
Laqueur, Walter. *The Terrible Secret: An Investigation into the Suppression of Information about Hitler's "Final Solution."* London: Weidenfeld and Nicolson, 1980.

Lasky, Jesse, with Don Weldon. *I Blow My Own Horn*. London: Victor Gollancz, 1957.
Lasky, Jesse L. Jr. *Whatever Happened to Hollywood?* London: W. H. Allen, 1973.
Laurie, Clayton D. *The Propaganda Warriors: America's Crusade Against Nazi Germany*. Lawrence: University Press of Kansas, 1996.
Lee, Mordecai. "Working for Goodwill: Journalist Lowell Mellett," an extended version of "Working for Goodwill: Journalist Lowell Mellett." In *Traces of Indiana and Midwestern History* (quarterly of the Indiana Historical Society) 27, no. 4 (Fall 2015): 46–55.
Leuchtenburg, William E. *Franklin D. Roosevelt and the New Deal, 1932–1940*. New York: Harper & Row, 1963.
Levant, Oscar. *A Smattering of Ignorance*. Garden City, NY: Garden City Publishing, 1940.
Loacker, Armin, and Martin Prucha, eds. *Unerwünschtes Kino: Der deutschsprachige Emigrantenfilm 1934–1937*. Vienna: Filmarchiv Austria, 2000.
Louvish, Simon. *Monkey Business: The Lives and Legends of the Marx Brothers*. London: Faber & Faber, 1999.
MacLeish, Archibald. *Land of the Free*. New York: Harcourt, Brace, 1938.
MacLeish, Archibald, et al. *Jews in America, by the Editors of Fortune*. New York: Random House, 1936.
Maddow, Rachel. *Prequel: An American Fight Against Fascism*. New York: Random House [Large Print], 2023.
[Maibaum, Richard] "Richard Maibaum: A Pretense of Seriousness," interview by Pat McGilligan. In *Backstory 1: Interviews with Screenwriters of Hollywood's Golden Age*, 266–89. Berkeley: University of California Press, 1986.
Maltz, Albert. *The Cross and the Arrow*. London: George Harrap, 1946.
Marx, Harpo, with Rowland Barber. *Harpo Speaks!* 1962. Reprint, Lanham, MD: Limelight, 2017.
Mascaro, Tom. *Into the Fray: How NBC's Washington Documentary Unit Reinvented the News*. Washington, DC: Potomac Books, 2012.
May, Lary. *The Big Tomorrow: Hollywood and the Politics of the American Way*. Chicago: University of Chicago Press, 2000.
McBride, Joseph. *Frankly: Unmasking Frank Capra*. Springville, UT: Vervanté, 2019.
McGarr, Kathryn J. *City of Newsmen: Public Lies and Professional Secrets in Cold War Washington*. Chicago: University of Chicago Press, 2022.
McGilligan, Patrick. *George Cukor: A Double Life*. Minneapolis: University of Minnesota Press, 2013.
McGilligan, Patrick, ed. *Backstory: Interviews with Screenwriters of Hollywood's Golden Age*. Berkeley: University of California Press, 1986.
McGilligan, Patrick, ed. *Backstory 2: Interviews with Screenwriters of the 1940s and 1950s*. Berkeley: University of California Press, 1991.
McGilligan, Patrick, and Paul Buhle, eds. *Tender Comrades: A Backstory of the Hollywood Blacklist*. New York: St. Martin's Griffin, 1997.
Michalczyk, John J. *Filming the End of the Holocaust: Allied Documentaries, Nuremberg, and the Liberation of the Concentration Camps*. London: Bloomsbury Academic, 2014.
Miller, David. "Leonard Spigelgass: 26 November 1908–15 February 1985." In *WGAw* [Writer's Guild America West] *News*, April 1985: 18–19.

Moltke, Johannes von. "Projektionen der Gewalt: Heimkehr (Gustav Ucicky, 1941)." *Werkstatt Geschichte* 46 (2007): 74–86.

Moorehead, Caroline. *Sidney Bernstein: A Biography*. London: Jonathan Cape, 1984.

Mosse, George L. *The Crisis of German Ideology*. New York: Grosset & Dunlap, 1964.

Muscio, Guiliana. *Hollywood's New Deal*. Philadelphia: Temple University Press, 1996.

Myers, James M. *The Bureau of Motion Pictures: Its Influence on Film Content during World War II: The Reasons for Its Failure*. Lewiston, NY: Edwin Mellen Press, 1998.

Navasky, Victor S. *Naming Names: Historical Perspectives*. London: John Calder, 1982.

O'Connor, Anne Marie. *The Lady in Gold: The Extraordinary Tale of Gustav Klimt's Masterpiece, Portrait of Adele Bloch-Bauer*. New York: Knopf, 2012.

OWI [Office of War Information]. *American Handbook*. Washington, DC: Public Affairs Press, 1945.

Palmer, R. Barton. "The Furthest Side of Paradise: *Two-Faced Woman, A Woman's Face, Hot Spell, Wild Is the Wind,* and *Winged Victory*." In *George Cukor: Hollywood Master*, edited by Murray Pomerance and R. Barton Palmer, 156–72. Edinburgh: Edinburgh University Press, 2015.

Paret, Peter. "*Kolberg* (Germany, 1945): As Historical Film and Historical Document." In *World War II: Film and History*, edited by John Whiteclay Chambers II and David Culbert, 47–66. Oxford: Oxford University Press, 1997.

Peiss, Kathy Lee. *Information Hunters: When Librarians, Soldiers, and Spies Banded Together in World War II Europe*. New York: Oxford University Press, 2020.

Pierce, Todd James. "In Defense of Walt: Walt Disney and Anti-Semitism." Disney History Institute, 2014.

Pogue, Leland. *Frank Capra: Interviews*. Oxford: University of Mississippi Press, 2004.

Prawer, Siegbert Salomon. *Between Two Worlds: The Jewish Presence in German and Austrian Film, 1910–1933*. New York: Berghahn Books, 2005.

Rappak, Wojciech. *Karski's Reports: The Story and the History*. PhD dissertation, University College London, 2021.

Renov, Michael, and Vincent Brook, "Editorial Introduction." In *From Shtetl to Stardom: Jews and Hollywood*, edited by Steven J. Ross, Michael Renov, Vincent Brook, and Lisa Ansell, ix–xiv. West Lafayette, IN: Purdue University Press, 2017.

Rentschler, Eric. "The Legacy of Nazi Cinema: *Triumph of the Will* and *Jew Süss* Revisited." In *The Arts in Nazi Germany: Continuity, Conformity, Change*, edited by Jonathan Huener and Francis R. Nicosia, 63–78. New York: Berghahn Books, 2009.

Reynolds, Kevin Patrick. *That Justice Be Seen: The American Prosecution's Use of Film at the Nuremberg International Military Tribunal*. DPhil thesis, University of Sussex, September 2011.

Riefenstahl, Leni. *A Memoir*. New York: Picador, 1995.

Robinson, David. *Chaplin: His Life and Art*. New York: McGraw-Hill, 1985.

Roeder, George H. Jr. *The Censored War: American Visual Experience during World War Two*. New Haven, CT: Yale University Press, 1993.

Rosenzweig, Laura B. *Hollywood's Spies: The Undercover Surveillance of Nazis in Los Angeles*. New York: New York University Press, 2017.

Ross, Leonard Q. [pseudonym of Leo Rosten] *Adventure in Washington*. New York: Harcourt, Brace and Company, 1940.

Ross, Leonard Q. [pseudonym of Leo Rosten] *Dateline: Europe*. New York: Harcourt, Brace and Company, 1939.

Ross, Leonard Q. [pseudonym of Leo Rosten] *Dors, mon amour* (Sleep, my love). Translated by Elisabeth Granet. Paris: Hatchette, 1948.

Ross, Leonard Q. [pseudonym of Leo Rosten] *Education of Hyman Kaplan*. New York: Editions for the Armed Services, 1943.

Ross, Leonard Q. [pseudonym of Leo Rosten] *Strangest Places*. New York: Harcourt, Brace and Company, 1939.

Ross, Steven J. *Hitler in Los Angeles: How Jews Foiled Nazi Plots against Hollywood and America*. New York: Bloomsbury, 2017.

Ross, Steven J. *Hollywood Left and Right: How Movie Stars Shaped American Politics*. New York: Oxford University Press, 2011.

Ross, Steven J., Michael Renov, Vincent Brook, and Lisa Ansell, eds., *From Shtetl to Stardom: Jews and Hollywood*. West Lafayette, IN: Purdue University Press, 2017.

Rosten, Leo. *The 3:10 to Anywhere*. New York: McGraw-Hill, 1976.

Rosten, Leo. *Captain Newman, M.D.* New York: Harper, 1961.

Rosten, Leo. *Dear "Herm": With a Cast of Dozens*. New York: McGraw-Hill, 1974.

Rosten, Leo. *Education of H*Y*M*A*N K*A*P*L*A*N*. New York: Harcourt, Brace & World, 1965.

Rosten, Leo. *Hollywood: The Movie Colony, the Movie Makers*. New York: Arno Press, 1970.

Rosten, Leo. *Hooray for Yiddish! A Book about English*. New York: Simon and Schuster, 1982.

Rosten, Leo. *The Joys of Yiddish: A Relaxed Lexicon of Yiddish, Hebrew and Yinglish Words Often Encountered in English . . . from the Days of the Bible to Those of the Beatnik*. New York: McGraw-Hill, 1968.

Rosten, Leo. *King Silky!* New York: Harper & Row, 1980.

Rosten, Leo. *The Leo Rosten Bedside Book. Stories, Humour, Social Commentary, Travelogues, Satire, Memoirs, Profiles—& Sundry Entertainments Never Before Published, with a Special Introduction, Background Notes, Revelations and Confessions, Hand-Written and Themselves Worth the Price of Admission*. London: Gollancz, 1965.

Rosten, Leo. *Leo Rosten's Carnival of Wit: And Wisdom, Plus Wisecracks, Ad-Libs, Malapropos, Puns, One-Liners, Quips, Epigrams, Boo-Boos, Dazzling Ironies, and Wizardries of Wording, Plus Surprising Tidbits from Politics, Philosophy, Biography and (Yes!) Gossip*. New York: Dutton, 1994.

Rosten, Leo. *Leo Rosten's Giant Book of Laughter*. New York: Bonanza, 1989.

Rosten, Leo. *Leo Rosten's Treasury of Jewish Quotations*. New York: McGraw-Hill, 1972.

Rosten, Leo. "Leonard Spigelgass: 26 November 1908–15 February 1985." In *WGAw* [Writer's Guild America West] *News* (April 1985): 19–20.

Rosten, Leo. *Many Worlds of L*E*O R*O*S*T*E*N; Stories, Humor, Social Commentary, Travelogues, Satire, Memoirs, Profiles, and Sundry Entertainments Never Before Published; with a Special Intod., Background Notes, Revelations and Confessions, All Hand-Written and Themselves Worth the Price of Admission*. New York: Harper & Row, 1964.

Rosten, Leo. *Most Private Intrigue*. New York: Atheneum, 1957.

Rosten, Leo C. "Movies and Propaganda." *Annals of the American Academy of Political and Social Science* 254 (November 1947): 116–24.
Rosten, Leo. "The Myths We Live By." *Journal of General Education* 17, no. 3 (October 1965): 169–78.
Rosten, Leo. *O K*A*P*L*A*N! My K*A*P*L*A*N!* New York: Harper & Row, 1976.
Rosten, Leo: "Oral History Interview[s] with Leo Calvin Rosten, [June and July] 1959." Interviewed by Joan and Robert Franklin, Popular Arts Project, transcript, Columbia University Libraries.
Rosten, Leo. *Passions & Prejudices: Or, Some of My Best Friends Are People*. New York: McGraw-Hill, 1978.
Rosten, Leo. *People I Have Loved, Known, or Admired*. New York: McGraw-Hill, 1970.
Rosten, Leo. *Power of Positive Nonsense*. New York: McGraw-Hill, 1977.
Rosten, Leo C. "President Roosevelt and the Washington Correspondents." *Public Opinion Quarterly* 1, no. 1 (January 1937): 36–52.
Rosten, Leo. *Return of H*Y*M*A*N K*A*P*L*A*N*. New York: Harper, 1959.
Rosten, Leo. *Rome Wasn't Burned in a Day: The Mischief of Language*. Garden City, NY: Doubleday, 1972.
Rosten, Leo C. "The Social Composition of Washington Correspondents." *Journalism Quarterly* 14, no. 2 (June 1937): 125–32.
Rosten, Leo. *Trumpet for Reason*. Garden City, NY: Doubleday, 1970.
Rosten, Leo. *Washington Correspondents*. New York: Harcourt Brace, 1937.
Rosten, Leo, ed. *Guide to the Religions of America*. New York: Simon and Schuster, 1955.
Rosten, Leo, ed. *Infinite Riches: Gems from a Lifetime of Reading*. New York: McGraw-Hill, 1979.
Rosten, Leo, ed. *Look Book*. New York: H. Abrams, 1975.
Rosten, Leo, ed. *Religions of America: Ferment and Faith in an Age of Crisis: A New Guide and Almanac*. New York: Simon and Schuster, 1975.
Samuelson, Mary Gelsey. "The Patriotic Play: Roosevelt, Antitrust, and the War Activities Committee of the Motion Picture Industry." PhD dissertation, University of California, Los Angeles, 2014.
Sarris, Andrew. *The American Cinema: Directors and Directions, 1929–1968*. New York: Da Capo Press, 1996.
Sarris, Andrew. "The Rise and Fall of the Film Director." In *Hollywood Voices: Interviews with Film Directors*, edited by Andrew Sarris, 7–18. London: Secker & Warburg, 1971.
Sayre, J. *The House without a Roof*. New York: Farrar, 1948.
Schatz, Thomas. *The Genius of the System: Hollywood Filmmaking in the Studio Era*. New York: Pantheon Books, 1988.
Schatz, Thomas. *Hollywood Genres*. Boston: McGraw-Hill, 1981.
Schulberg, Budd. "The Celluloid Noose." in *The Screen Writer: A Publication of the Screen Writers Guild, Inc.*, August 1946, 1–15.
Schulberg, Budd. *The Disenchanted*. 1951. Reprint, London: Allison & Busby, 1983.
Schulberg, Budd. *Moving Pictures: Memories of a Hollywood Prince*. New York: Stein and Day, 1981.
Schulberg, Budd. *What Makes Sammy Run?* 1941. Reprint, London: Transworld, 1958.

Shirer, William L. *This Is Berlin: Reporting from Nazi Germany, 1938–40.* London: Hutchinson, 1999.

Shnayerson, Michael. *Irwin Shaw: A Biography.* New York: G. Putnam's Sons, 1989.

Shneer, David. *Through Soviet Jewish Eyes: Photography, War, and the Holocaust.* New Brunswick, NJ: Rutgers University Press, 2011.

Short, K. R. M., ed. *Film & Radio Propaganda in World War II.* London: Croon Helm, 1983.

Shull, Michael S., and David E. Wilt, *Doing Their Bit: Wartime American Animated Short Films, 1939–1945.* Jefferson, NC: McFarland, 2004.

Silver-Lasky, Pat. *Hollywood Royalty: A Family in Films.* Albany, GA: BearManor Media, undated [2017].

Simms, Brendan. *Hitler: A Global Biography.* New York: Basic Books, 2019.

Sinclair, Upton. *Dragon's Teeth.* New York: Viking, 1945.

Snow, Nancy. "Confessions of a Hollywood Propagandist: Harry Warner, FDR, and Celluloid Persuasion." https://www.researchgate.net/publication/275833924_Confessions_of_a_Hollywood_Propagandist_Harry_Warner_FDR_and_Celluloid_Persuasion.

Spector, Scott. "Was the Third Reich Movie-Made? Interdisciplinarity and the Reframing of 'Ideology.'" *American Historical Review* 106, no. 2 (April 2001): 460–84.

Spicer, Andrew. *Sydney Box.* Manchester: Manchester University Press, 2006.

Spigelgass, Leonard. *The Scuttle under the Bonnet.* Garden City, NY: Doubleday, 1962.

Stevens, George Jr., *Conversations with the Great Moviemakers of Hollywood's Golden Age at the American Film Institute.* New York: Vintage, 2007.

Studlar, Gaylyn, and Matthew Bernstein, eds. *John Ford Made Westerns.* Bloomington: Indiana Univeristy Press, 2001.

[Taradash, Daniel] "Daniel Taradash: Triumph and Chaos," interview by David Thompson. In *Backstory 2: Interviews with Screenwriters of the 1940s and 1950s*, edited by Patrick McGilligan, 309–30. Berkeley: University of California Press, 2006.

Terkel, Studs. *"The Good War": An Oral History of World War II.* New York: New Press, 1984.

Thompson, George Raynor, and Dixie L. Harris. "Army Photography at Home and Overseas." In *United States Army in World War II: The Technical Services*, 540–79. Washington, DC: Office of the Chief of Military History, 1970.

Thompson, George Raynor, and Dixie L. Harris. *The Signal Corps: The Outcome (Mid-1943 through 1945).* Washington, DC: Office of the Chief of Military History, 1966.

Thomson, David. *Warner Bros.: The Making of an American Movie Studio.* New Haven, CT: Yale University Press, 2017.

Trumpener, Katie. "A Eulogy of Failed Remembrance." *New York Review of Books*, January 18, 2004, 40–42.

Urwand, Ben. *The Collaboration: Hollywood's Pact with Hitler.* Cambridge, MA: Belknap Press of Harvard University Press, 2013.

Wagnleitner, Reinhold. *Coca-Colonization and the Cold War: The Cultural Mission in the United States after the Second World War.* Translated by Diana Wolf. Chapel Hill: University of North Carolina Press, 1994.

Walsh, Frank. *Sin and Censorship: The Catholic Church and the Motion Picture Industry.* New Haven, CT: Yale University Press, 1996.

[Wanger, Walter] "Walter Wanger" (oral history interview). In *The Real Tinsel*, edited by Bernard Rosenberg and Harry Silverstein, 80–99. London: Collier-Macmillan, 1970.
Weinberg, Herman G. *Josef von Sternberg: A Critical Study*. New York: Dutton, 1967.
Welky, David. *The Moguls and the Dictators: Hollywood and the Coming of World War II*. Baltimore: Johns Hopkins University Press, 2008.
Willmetts, Simon. *In Secrecy's Shadow: The OSS and CIA in Hollywood Cinema, 1941–1979*. Edinburgh: Edinburgh University Press, 2016.
Winkel, Roel Vande. "Nazi Germany's Fritz Hippler, 1909–2002." *Historical Journal of Film, Radio and Television* 23, no. 2 (2003): 91–99.
Winkler, Allan M. *The Politics of Propaganda: The Office of War Information, 1942–1945*. New Haven, CT: Yale University Press, 1978.
Wistrich, Robert. *Who's Who in Nazi Germany*. London: Weidenfeld and Nicolson, 1982.
Yellin, Emily. *Our Mothers' War: American Women at Home and at the Front during World War II*. New York: Free Press, 2004.
Yogerst, Chris. *Hollywood Hates Hitler! Jew-Baiting, Anti-Nazism, and the Senate Investigation into Warmongering in Motion Pictures*. Jackson: University Press of Mississippi, 2020.
Young, Nancy Beck. *Why We Fight: Congress and the Politics of World War II*. Lawrence: University Press of Kansas, 2013.
Zimmerman, Joshua, ed. *Jews in Italy under Fascist and Nazi Rule*. New York: Cambridge University Press, 2005.

Films

All Through the Night (dir. Vincent Sherman, 1942)
Any Bonds Today? (dir. Robert Clampett, 1942)
Appointment in Tokyo (dir. Jack Hively, 1945)
Attack! The Battle of New Britain (1944)
The Autobiography of a "Jeep" (dirs. Irving Lerner and Joseph Krumgold, 1943)
Battle of Peace [1945]
The Best Years of Our Lives (dir. William Wyler, 1946)
Bismarck (dir. Wolfgang Liebeneiner, 1940) [Nazi]
Body and Soul (dir. Robert Rossen, 1947)
Broken Arrow (dir. Delmer Daves, 1950)
Brought to Action (1945)
Captain Newman, M.D. (dir. David Miller, 1967)
Captains of the Clouds (dir. Michael Curtiz, 1942)
Champion (dir. Stanley Kramer, 1949)
Conspiracy of Hearts (dir. Ralph Thomas, 1960)
The Conspirators (dir. John Neulesco, 1944)
The Cruel Sea (dir. Charles Frend, 1953)
December 7th (dirs. John Ford and Gregg Toland)
Dexterity (1943)
Diary of a Sergeant (dir. Joseph M. Newman, 1945)
Dr. Strangelove (dir. Stanley Kubrick, 1963)

Donne senza nome [Women without names] (dir. Geza von Radvanyi, 1949)
Don't Be a Sucker (1943)
Dorf im Roten Sturm (1935) [Nazi]
The Ductators (dir. Norm McCabe,1942)
A Face in the Crowd (dir. Elia Kazan, 1957)
Feind (1941) [Nazi]
Fellow Americans (dir. Garson Kanin, 1942)
The First Motion Picture Unit of the Army Air Forces (1943)
The 49th Parallel (dir. Michael Powell, 1941), released in the US as *The Invaders*
The Four Feathers (dir. Zoltan Korda, 1949)
Gabriel Over the White House (dir. Gregory La Cava, 1933)
Gentleman's Agreement (dir. Elia Kazan, 1947)
German Concentration Camps Factual Survey (dir. Sidney Bernstein, 1945)
Gypsy (dir. Mervyn LeRoy, 1962)
Heimkehr (dir. Gustav Uckicky, 1941) [Nazi]
The House I Live In (dir. Mervyn LeRoy, 1945)
Ich Klage An (dir. Wolfgang Liebeneiner, 1941) [Nazi]
The Informer (dir. John Ford, 1935)
Jud Süß (dir. Veit Harlan, 1940) [Nazi]
Kadetten (dir. Karl Ritter, 1939) [Nazi]
Kameraden (dir. Ederhard Löseser, 1941 or 1943) [Nazi]
Kampfgeschwader Luetzow (dir. Hans Bertram, 1941) [Nazi]
The Liberation of Rome (1944)
Life Line (aka LIFELINE*)* (1943)
Make Way for Tomorrow (dir. Leo McCarey, 1937)
Man Hunt (dir. Fritz Lang, 1941)
Man with a Movie Camera (dir. Dziga Vertov, 1929)
Manhattan Melodrama (dirs. W. S. Van Dyke, Jack Conway, George Cukor, 1934)
The Memphis Belle: The Story of a Flying Fortress (dir. William Wyler, 1944)
The Men (dir. Stanley Kramer, 1950)
Mister Cory (1957, dir. Blake Edwards)
Mr. Deeds Goes to Town (dir. Frank Capra, 1936)
Mr. Smith Goes to Washington (dir. Frank Capra, 1939)
Mrs. Miniver (dir. William Wyler, 1942)
Mystery Street (dir. John Sturgess, 1950)
The Negro Soldier (dir. Stuart Heisler, 1944)
Nuremberg (dir. Stuart Schulberg, 1948)
Nuremberg: Its Lesson for Today (2010, 2015)
Ohm Krüger (dirs. Hans Steinhoff, Karl Anton, Herbert Maisch, 1941) [Nazi]
On the Beach (dir. Stanley Kramer, 1959)
On the Waterfront (dir. Elia Kazan, 1954)
Opfer der Vergangenheit (dir. Gernot Bock-Stieber and Kurt Botner,1937) [Nazi]
The Pale Horseman (dir. Irving Jacoby,1946)
Pour Le Merite (dir. Karl Ritter, 1938) [Nazi]
Prelude to War: Why We Fight (dir. Frank Capra, Anatole Litvak et al., 1942)
Pride of the Marines (dir. Delmer Daves, 1945)

Private Snafu vs. Malaria Mike (dir. Chuck Jones, 1944)
Resistance and Ohms Law (dir. George Cukor, 1943)
Rhapsody in Blue (dir. Irving Rapper, 1945)
Ring of Steel (dir. Garson Kanin, 1942)
Rittmeister Brenken Reited Fuer Deutschland (1941) [Nazi]
Sahara (dir. Zoltan Korda, 1943)
San Pietro (dir. John Huston, 1945)
Seeds of Destiny (dir. David Miller, 1946)
Sergeant York (dir. Howard Hawks, 1941)
The Seven Year Itch (dir. Billy Wilder, 1955)
Der Sieg des Glaubens (dir. Leni Riefenstahl, 1933) [Nazi]
The Silver Fleet (dirs. Vernon Sewell and Gordon Wellesley, 1943)
Spies (dir. Chuck Jones, 1943)
The Stilwell Road (1945)
Storm Center (dir. Daniel Taradash, 1956)
Target for Today (dir. William Keighley, 1944)
Target for Tonight (dir. Harry Watt, 1942)
That Justice Be Done (dir. George Stevens, 1945)
That Men May Fight (1943 or 1944)
They Were Not Divided (dir. Terrence Young, 1950)
This Is the Army (dir. Michael Curtiz, 1943)
The Train (dir. John Frankenheimer, 1964)
The True Glory (dirs. Garson Kanin and Carol Reed, 1945)
Twenty-Seven Soldiers (1944)
Ueber Alles in der Welt (dir. Karl Ritter, 1941) [Nazi]
Underworld (dir. Josef von Sternberg, 1927)
Walk on East Beacon (dir. Alfred Werker, 1952)

Index

112 Gripes About the French, 190
20th Century-Fox Movietone News, 17, 59, 152, 153
49th Parallel (aka *Forty-Ninth Parallel* and *The Invaders*), 24, 79, 86–87, 89

Abel, Rudolf (William August Fischer), 143
Academy Award(s) (Oscars), 6, 43, 74, 110, 115, 119, 121–22, 141, 142, 150, 166, 179, 187
Across the Pacific (film), 132
Adak, 101. *See also* Alaska and Aleutians
African Americans, 13, 21, 25, 52, 53, 54, 99, 100, 134, 147, 162, 175, 191, 193–94, 200, 252n90, 252n92, 252n95; D'Usseau, Arnaud, 252n95; CHARACTERS: Ben Chaplin, 194; Deacon (Saratoga), 193; Sam, 193; DOCUMENTARY-STYLE COVERAGE: *Negro Colleges in Wartime*, 191; *The Negro Soldier*, 191 IN FILMS: *All Through the Night*, 192, 193, 195; *Body and Soul*, 194; *Casablanca*, 192, 193
Agee, James, 105
Agfacolor, 178
Air Force (film), 83
Air Ministry (UK), 138
the Alamo, 129
Alaska, 93, 101
Aleutians, 93, 103, 106
Alexander's Ragtime Band (film), 119
Algar, James, 167
Algeria, 104, 149
Algiers, 104
Algonquin, 104
Algonquin Round Table, 5, 6, 39; Alexander Woollcott, 5, 6; Harpo Marx, 5, 6
Alien Property Custodian, 153
All Through the Night (film), 6, 34, 83, 93, 192, 193, 195
American Film Center, 4, 74, 78
American Jewish Committee, 49
American Jewish Congress, 186
American Red Cross, 131
Amnesty International, 136
Anastasia (film), 31
Anders als du und ich (film), 182
Annie Oakley, 103
Anschluss, 118, 165
anti-Black racism, 13, 21, 25, 52, 53, 54, 99, 100, 134, 147, 162, 175, 191, 193–94, 200. *See also* African Americans
anti-Catholicism, 20, 51, 99
anti-Nazi resistance, 48–49, 184, 185–86
antisemitism, 6, 19–20, 27–28, 31, 36–37, 38, 40, 50, 51–52, 57, 75, 99, 100, 115,

Index

antisemitism (*continued*)
119, 122, 132, 137, 138, 146–48, 155, 160, 162, 163, 168, 175, 176, 177, 178, 187, 190, 195, 198, 239n39. *See also* Holocaust
antitrust (activity), 7, 16–17
Any Bonds Today? (film), 38, 174, 216n74, 247n201
Appointment in Tokyo (film), 21
Arabic, 192
Argentina, 184
Argonne, 115
Arinarius, Gregory, 169, 170, 171, 245n165
The Arm Behind the Army (film), 82
Army Committee on Welfare and Recreation, 6
Army-Navy Screen Magazine (film series), 39, 81, 90, 93, 96–97, 107, 130, 135, 189, 199
Arthur (king), 6
Arthur, Art, 135
Aryan ideal, 162, 164, 180
Asia, 13, 27
Association of Motion Picture Producers, 119
Astoria, Queens, 12, 26, 59, 92, 95, 103, 104, 112, 127, 130
Atebrine, 131
atrocities, 35, 151, 160, 166, 186
Attack! (film), 124–25, 126, 128, 131–32
Aub, Max (Max Aub Mohrenwitz), 149, 239n51
Auschwitz, 177, 181. *See also* Holocaust
Australia, 82, 98, 125, 134
Austria, 30, 35, 155
The Autobiography of a Jeep (film), 71
Axis (powers), 10, 26. *See also* Germany; Italy; Japan

Babelsberg, 169, 170
Bacall, Lauren, 136
Bach, Steven, 173
Baker, Herbert, 7, 37, 41, 96, 110, 199
Balzano, 161
Banff National Park, 87
Baptists, 119

Barnes, George, 69
barrage balloons, 28, 29
The Battle of New Britain (film), 126, 128. *See also* Pacific theater
Battle of Peace (film), 199
The Battle of San Pietro (film), 106, 128, 132, 189. *See also* Buck, Jules
Beasts of Berlin (film), 93
Bel Canto (novel), 188
Ben Chaplin (film character), 194
Benchley, Robert, 90
Benedek, Laslo, 108
Benigni, Roberto, 137
Bergan, Ronald, 106
Berlin (Germany), 47, 48, 144, 148, 154, 160, 169
Berliner Illustrierte Zeitung, 148
Berman, Henry, 97
Bernstein, Matthew, 40,
Bernstein, Sidney, 35, 167, 185, 217n88
Bernstein, Walter, 104
Best Documentary Short Subject, 150
The Best Years of Our Lives (film), 39, 108–9
Beverly Hills (Los Angeles), 5
Bewildered Youth (film), 182
Big Street (film), 93
Binyon, Claude, 97, 199
Birdwell, Michael, 28, 116, 119, 120
Birgel, Willie, 184
Bittens, Alfred, 184
blacklisting, 43, 68, 123, 136, 137, 167, 180, 188, 189, 190, 194
black market, 72
Blanc, Mel, 37, 81, 96
Blaustein, Julian, 7, 34, 37, 39, 41, 96, 109, 199; *Diary of a Sergeant*, 39
Blockade (film), 33
Blondie (cartoon and film character), 74
blood banks, 131
Bloom, Harold, 35
Bloomsbury Film Society, 167
The Blue Angel (film), 180
The Blue Light (film), 158, 161
Blumberg, Julian, 148
Bock-Stieber, Gernot, 160

Body and Soul (film), 194
Boettiger, John, 20
Bogart, Humphrey, 10, 34, 93, 132, 136, 163, 192, 193; *All Through the Night* (film), 192, 193; *Casablanca* (film), 192, 193; as Rick Blaine, 132, 193
book burning, 181–82
Borzage, Frank, 90
Botner, Kurt, 160
Bott, John, 143
Bourke-White, Margaret, 58
Bowes-Lyon, David, 47, 48; bombing of January 30, 1943, 47–48
Box, Betty E., 137–38; *Conspiracy of Hearts* (film), 137–38
Box, Muriel, 138
Box, Sydney, 138
boxing, 43, 97–98, 140, 191, 194
The Boys from Syracuse (film), 93
"The Boys Write Home," 65, 97
Brady, Thomas, 56
brain trust, 32–33, 46, 198, 201
Brand, Oscar, 217–18n91
Brando, Marlon, 108
Brant, Henry, 37
Breen, Joseph L., 13–14, 22
Breitman, Richard, 50
Brennan, Walter, 71
Bridge of Spies (film), 143
The Bridge Over the River Kwai (film), 91, 110
British Broadcasting Company (BBC), 35
British empire, 4, 12, 30, 64, 104, 180. *See also* United Kingdom
British Information Service, 68
British Press Service, 79
Broken Arrow (film), 109
Brook, Vincent, 18
Brooklyn, 92, 98, 180
Brooklyn College, 41
Brooks, Richard, 22, 211n134
Brought to Action (film), 130, 131
Brownell, Kathryn Cramer, 28
Brownlow, Louis, 32, 45, 46, 57, 198. *See also* brain trust; University of Chicago

Brown University, 41
Bruce (unspecified first name), 28
Brute Force (film), 189
Buck, Joan Juliet, xi–xii, 189, 190
Buck, Joyce, 190
Buck, Jules, xii, 12, 23, 37, 40, 90, 91, 97, 105–6, 109, 120, 128, 131, 141, 151, 189–90, 198–99, 200; anti-communist witch hunt and migration abroad, 189–90; prewar film-related activity, 120; relationship with John Huston in *The Battle of San Pietro* (film), 189
Buck, Pearl S., 74
Bugs Bunny, 38, 174
Bureau of Motion Pictures, 5, 29
Burma, 132, 134

Cairo, 103–4
California, 39, 101, 120. *See also* Los Angeles
California State Infantry, 120
Calvacade (film), 166
cameraman casualties, 134
Campbell, Tracy, 50
Canada, 4, 79, 81, 82, 86–87, 103
Canadian Film Board, 61
Capa, Robert, 104, 105, 211
Capra, Frank, 3, 6, 9, 12, 20, 31, 33, 37, 38, 39, 61, 75, 77, 90, 91, 94, 95, 96, 110, 141, 170, 188, 191, 200
Captain Newman, M.D. (film), 106, 107
Captains of the Clouds (film), 79
Carr, Robert Spence, 59–61
Carr, Steven, x, 9, 28, 31, 119
Carry On (Constable) (film), 138
cartoons, 3, 38, 39. *See also* Disney
Caruso, Anthony, 187
Casablanca (film), 19, 29, 91, 132, 170, 189, 190, 192, 193, 234–35n129; comparison with *All Through the Night* (film), 192, 193
Casaer, Arthur, 121–22
Casaer, Irving, 121
Catholic World (magazine), 115
Catskills, 98
Caught in the Draft (film), 116

"Celluloid Circus," 4, 79
"The Celluloid Noose," 151–54, 170
censorship, 10, 16, 28, 29, 68–70
Ceplair, Larry, 109, 229
Cerf, Bennett, 148
Chambre des Députés, 105
Champion (film), 108, 110
Chandler, Harry, 120
Chaplin, Charlie, 5, 15, 31, 116
Charley Davis (character), 194
Chase National Bank, 44
Chayefsky, Paddy, 37, 90, 134
Cheever, John, 90, 96, 102, 199
Chicago, 96, 98, 110. See also Northwestern University; University of Chicago
Chimen (character), 194
China, 17, 59, 100, 134, 143–44, 169
China-Burma-India front (C-B-I, theater), 132, 134, 143–44
Chodorov, Jerome, 37
Chorzele, 249n38
Christmas, 107
Churchill, Winston, vi, 115, 116, 205
C.I.C. (US Army Counter Intelligence Corps), 155, 157
Cinematic Institute (Moscow), 170
cinematography, 91, 107, 108, 109, 114–15, 127, 198. See also Buck, Cortez; Drell, Wyler
Civilian Committee on Selective Service, 6
Civil War, 197
Clark, Bennett Champ, 119
Clark, Dane, 187
Clark Field, 98
Cleveland (Ohio), 11
Clothier, William, 109
Cohen, Emmanuel, 37, 95, 96
Colliers (magazine), 42, 149
Collins, Claude, 67
Cologne (Germany), 199
Colonel Calhoun (made-up credit), 132–33
Columbia Broadcasting Service (CBS), 64

Columbia Pictures, 15, 87–88, 109, 134, 172
Columbia University, 41, 45, 187
Columbus (Ohio), 103
Comité National Français, 94
Commandments for Health: Use Your Head (film), 68
Committee for the First Amendment, 136
Communism, 19, 25, 32, 44, 53, 63, 106, 107, 108, 110, 123, 134, 136, 159, 187, 188, 189, 190, 191
concentration camps, 35, 149, 161, 165–66, 168, 185. See also Holocaust
Confessions of a Nazi Spy (film), 18, 31, 33, 34, 40
Congressional Medal of Honor, 115, 122
Connecticut, 7
Conspiracy of Hearts (film), 24, 136–38
Contact Bridge, 88
Continental Congress, 46
Cooper, Gary, 115, 117, 130
Cooper, Merian, 123, 232n85
Corlett, Charles H., 101
Cornell University, 41
Corregidor, 98. See also Pacific theater; Philippines
Cortez, Stanley, 37, 91, 97, 107
Coughlin, Charlies, 6, 148
Council of National Defense, 196
Council on Books in Wartime, 41
Crawford, Joan, 18, 189
Creel, George, 8
crimes against humanity, 141, 151. See also Holocaust
Crosland, Alan, 14, 38
The Cross and the Arrow (novel), 187
Crown film unit, 138
Crowther, Bosley, 136–37
Crucifixion, 9
Cuba, 122
Cukor, George, x, 10, 12, 20, 22, 32, 33, 37, 39, 66, 68, 74, 90, 199
Culver City, 15, 97, 120
Curtis, Tony, 106

Curtiz, Michael, 19, 29, 79, 186; *Casablanca* (film), 19, 29
Czechoslovakia, 51, 149, 186

"Dabrowski's Mazurka" (song), 182
Dachau, 105, 165
Daffy Duck, 174
Danaher, John A., 7
Dartmouth College, x, 40–41, 42, 237n16, 240n66
Dassin, Jules, 189
Dauphin, Claude, 134
Daves, Delmer, 83, 109, 187, 189
David, Frank, 74
David, Tess (née Slesinger), 74
Davis, Bette, 117
Davis, Nancy, 93
daylight bombing, 47–48
Day of Freedom (*Tag der Freiheit*) (film), 156, 158
The Day the Earth Stood Still (film), 109
The Day They Robbed the Bank of England (film), 190
D-Day, 52, 104, 186
Deacon (also Saratoga) (character), 193
Dean, Gordon, 151–52
December 7th (film), 150, 178
deCordova, Richard, 210n92
Deep Are the Roots (play), 191
Deerfield Academy, 42, 140
Defense Bonds, 174
The Defiant Ones (film), 108
Delehany, William J., 98
DeMille, Cecil B., 112, 113, 123, 130, 135, 140, 188, 197
Demme, Jonathan, 85
Democratic party, 18
Department of Justice, 17
Depression, Great, 197
(Der) *Ewige Jude*, 178, 181
(Der) *letzte Mann* (film), 179
De Rochemont, Louis, 63, 111
De Rochemont, Richard, 63
Der Sieg des Glaubens (The Victory of Faith) (film), 154, 155, 156, 158, 159, 161

Der Zauberlehrling, 173
Desert Victory (film), 123
Deutsche Arbeitsfront, 153
Dexterity (film), 123, 126, 128. See also Lasky, Jesse, Jr.; Pacific theater; Presnell, Robert
Diamond, Lee, 187
Diary of a Sergeant (film), 39
Dick Tracy (cartoon and film character), 74
The Dick Van Dyke Show, 230–31n32
Dies, Martin A., 19
Dieterle, William, 33
Dietrich, Marlene, 179, 180
Dietrich, Ralph, 96
The Disenchanted, 43, 140
Disney, Walt, 15, 37–38, 39–40, 166–67, 170, 173–75; Leni Riefenstahl visit, 166–67, 173–75
Disney Productions (studios), 15, 16, 37–38, 39–40, 59–60, 166–67, 173–75
Dive Bomber (film), 116
"divide and conquer" as a Nazi tactic, 70, 71
Djelfa, 149
Doctor in Love (film), 138
documentary-style filmmaking, 68–69, 70, 71, 72, 73, 74, 92, 104, 122, 138, 150, 151. See also Rodakiewicz, Henwar
Doherty, Thomas, 28, 29, 33, 206n13, 209n73
Donald Duck (character), 174
Donne senza nome, 236n158
Donovan, James Britt, 143
Donovan, William, 143, 154
Don't Be a Sucker (film), 99, 147, 194
Douglas, Kirk, 108
Douglas, Melvyn, 10
Downs, Lt. Col., 161
Drell, Philip, 12, 35, 91, 97, 104, 105
Dr. Kildare (TV show), 126
Dr. Strangelove (film), 108
The Ductators (film), 247n200
Dukas, Paul, 246n196
Duke, Doris, 143

Dunkirk, 193
Dunne, Philip, 189–90
D'Usseau, Arnaud, 97, 191, 252n95
Dutch East Indes, 64

Early, Stephen T., 20, 45
Eddy, Nelson, 182
Edge of Darkness (film), 190
Eisenhower, Dwight D., 40, 104, 134, 176
Elizabeth (British wartime queen, later queen mother), 47
Elizabeth II (princess, later queen), 47
Empty Rooms Means Idle Machines (film), 61
England, 75, 76, 149, 179. See also British empire; United Kingdom
England's Tithe War (film), 76
Epstein, Julius, 37, 170
Esquire (magazine), 42
The Eternal Jew (film), 178
Ettlinger, Don, 41, 91, 97, 102, 199
Europe, 7, 8, 18–19, 26, 33, 49, 69, 93; film market, 4; theater of war, 12, 16, 21, 93
"euthanasia" program, 160
Evans, Walker, 58
Evening Post (Chicago), 122
Examiner (Chicago), 88
Executive Office of the President, 196
Expeditionary Force, 197

Famous Players-Lasky Hollywood Studio, 112, 139
Fanck, Arnold, 158
Fantasia (film), 167, 174
Farm Security Administration, 58
fascism, 18, 19, 42, 115, 121, 198; fascism in Britain, 250n52. See also Germany; Italy; Mussolini, Benito; Nazis; Riefenstahl, Leni
Federal Bureau of Investigation (FBI), 53, 144
Federal Council of Churches, 29
Federal Security Agency, 71, 78
Feinde (film), 180

Feins, Bernie, 23, 28, 41
Fellow Americans (film), 11, 68
Fenberg, L. Bennett, 97
Feuchtwanger, Lion, 177
Fighting Men: Keep It Clean (film), 66, 68
Finchhaven, 129
Finke, 157
Fischer, William August, 143
Fitzgerald, F. Scott, 43
Five Came Back, 20, 37, 92
Fleischer, Max, 62, 247n200
Fleming, Victor, 14, 74, 179
Fliegerkorps, 153
Flynn, John T., 119
Fonda, Henry, 67
Ford, Henry, 148
Ford, John, 9, 12, 20, 31, 33, 37, 77, 90, 91, 92, 141, 143, 150, 151, 156, 169, 200, 245n168
Foreman, Carl, 37, 41, 90, 91–92, 97, 110
Fort Mayer, 95
Fort Ord, 101
Fort Schuyler, 150
Fort Slocum, 98
Fortune (magazine), 57, 70
Foster, Maurice, 124
Fox Movietone, 152, 153
France, 8, 17, 30, 31, 48–49, 51, 59, 63, 100, 104, 105, 149, 158, 162, 168, 173, 177, 180, 188, 189, 190, 198; defeat by Nazism, 198; resistance, 48–49, 188, 189, 190. See also Rosten, Leo Calvin
Franco, Francisco, 146
Frank, Hans, 153
Freeman, Frank, 119
Freleng, Fritz, 37
French zone of occupation, 157–58
Friedländer, Saul, 248n11
The Front (film), 104
Fulbrook, Mary, 184, 185

Gable, Clark, 18
Gabler, Neal, 30, 205–6n3
Gabriel Over the White House (film), 7
Gallup, George, 63

Garbo, Greta, 5, 166
Garfield, John, 83, 187, 194–95
Garland, Judy, 14, 119
Garnett, Tay, 158
Garroway, Dave, 96
Garson, Greer, 193
Gasparcolor, 167
Gaumont-British, 183
Geisel, Theodor (Dr. Seuss), 96
General Motors Corporation, 8, 59
Geneva (Switzerland), 92
Genevieve, 97
Geoffroy (Lt.), 124
Gerber, David, 253n103
German-American Bund, 122, 146–48
German army, 153, 159
German Communist Party, 159
German Concentration Camps Factual Survey (film), 35, 216n65, 229
German newsreel, 153
German [Reich] Film Archive, 144, 145, 169
Germany, 8, 10, 12, 16, 20, 26, 27, 30, 35, 38, 43, 45, 76, 100, 103, 105, 119, 149, 163, 179; West Germany, 181, 184. *See also* fascism; National Socialism; Riefenstahl, Reni
Gershwin, George, 5, 11, 121
Gerson, Dora, 177
Gerzen, Henry, 35
Getz, Don, 190
Gilbert, Edwin, 85
Gleiwitz, 183
Glory for Me, 109
Gloucester Beach, 125
Gloversville (NY), 112
Gloves (character), 193
"God Bless America" (song), 171
Goebbels, Joseph, 6, 27, 35, 48, 55, 144, 152, 154, 159, 165, 166, 170, 177, 180, 200, 219n116
Goering, Hermann, 48, 49, 152, 219n116
Goethe, Johann Wolfgang von, 173
Gold (beach), 104
Goldfish, Sam, 112. *See also* Goldwyn, Samuel

Goldwyn, Blanche, 112
Goldwyn, Samuel (Sam), 10, 14, 15, 20, 33, 117, 119, 149
The Good Earth, 74
Goofer (character), 81
Goofer Trouble (film), 81
Göring, Hermann, 101, 152
Gorrie, Frank, 102
Gow, James, 97, 191
Grand Kino Lucky, 182–83
Grant, Cary, 103
The Grapes of Wrath (film), 169
The Great Dictator (film), 31, 116
Greenstreet, Sidney, 132
Grimm, Brothers, 173
Grossingers, 98
Grover, Allen, 88, 89
Guadalcanal, 98, 187; Battle of Tenaru River, 187; in *Pride of the Marines* (film), 187. *See also* Pacific theater; *Pride of the Marines* (film); Schmid, Al
Guam, 101
Guardian, 106
Guillerman, John, 190
Guitry, Sacha, 162–63
Gunga Din (film), 103
The Guns of Navarone (film), 110
Gurie, Sigrid, 166
Gurkhas, 134
Gutmann, John, ix, 58, 101
Gypsy (film), 6, 103

Haas, Dolly, 164–65, 244n146
Hamilton, Margaret, 74
Hammid, Alexander, 74
Hamsun, Knut, 162
Hand, David, 167
Handicapped, 106, 107, 200, 201
Hanks, Tom, 143
Harding, Warren, 13
Harlan, Veit, 177
Harlow, Jean, 18
Harman, Hugh, 68
Harmon, Francis, 29, 37
Harpo Speaks!, 5

Harris, Mark, 20, 30, 40, 92, 105, 115–16, 150
Hart, Moss, 39
Hartley, Ruth, 187
Hartmann, Paul, 184
Haruna, 98, 99
Harvard (College, University, and Law School), 40–41
Hatch, Norman, 107
hate films (Hetzfilme), 146
"Hate Leni" (Riefenstahl), 172–73, 175
Hauhausen, 145
Haukelid, Knut, 166
"Hava Negilah" (song), 107
Hawaii, 98. *See also* Pearl Harbor
Hawks, Howard, 7, 83, 85, 102–3, 118
Hawn, Goldie, 85
Hayes, Peter, 50
Hays, Will, 13, 22, 29
Hays Office, 22, 215n53
Hearst Metrotone News, 181
Hebrew, 192
Hecht, Ben, 139
Heidelberg (Germany), 103
Heimkehr (film), 180–81, 182, 183, 192
Heisler, Stuart, 191
Helford, Elyce Rae, 211n137
He Plants for Victory (film), 61
Hershey, Lewis B., 89
Hess, Rudolf, 152, 153, 171
Heydrich, Reinhard, 185–86
Hidden Hunger (film), 71
High Noon (film), 107, 110
Hillcrest (Country Club), 6, 39
Hillman, Sidney, 8
Himmler, Heinrich, 152, 171
Hippler, Fritz, 178
Hirohito, 146
Hirsch, Francine, 237n17
Historically Black Colleges and Universities (Negro colleges), 191
History Channel, 141
Hitchcock, Alfred, 90
Hitler, Adolf, 8, 27–28, 32, 35, 47, 48, 75, 120, 146, 148, 152, 153, 154, 155, 159, 160, 162, 163, 164, 170, 171, 173, 174, 187, 192, 194, 197, 200, 201, 219n116. *See also* National Socialism
Hitler Jugend, 153, 160, 171
Hively, George, 123
Hively, George, Jr., 123
Hively, Jack, 115, 123
hoarding, 72. *See also* rubber
Hoffmann, Heinrich, 237–38n26
Hogan, Ben, 5
Hollywood: The Movie Colony, The Movie Makers, 13
Hollywood Hates Hitler!, 19
Hollywood Ten, 136
Holman, Rufus C., 7
Holocaust, 23, 24, 25, 27–28, 35, 49–50, 52, 54, 108, 141, 168, 173, 185–86, 192, 199, 200
Holocaust (television series), 192
Home of the Brave (film), 108, 110
Hoover, J. Edgar, 53, 63, 220n137
Hopkins, Harry, 4, 6, 94, 202
Horizon Pictures, 189
House (of Representatives) Committee on Un-American Activities (Dies Committee), 19, 43, 110, 136, 188, 189
The House I Live In (song and film), 99, 186–87
The House without a Roof, 103, 228n56
Howard, Leslie, 88
How Green Was My Valley (film), 169
Hugenots, 63
Hull, Cordell, 118
human rights, 20–21, 24, 141. *See also* United Nations
Hungary, 112
Hunt, Marsha, 136
Hurwitz, Leo, 68
Huston, John, 10, 12, 20, 31, 37, 39, 40, 77, 90, 91, 97, 105–6, 118, 120, 128, 132, 136, 141, 151, 189, 200
Hutchins, Robert Maynard, 74

I Blow My Own Horn, 113, 117, 119
Ich Klage An ("I Accuse") (film), 160
I Have Just Begun to Fight, 119
Illinois, 131

Ilsa Lund (film character), 193
Imperial War Museum, 35
India, 63, 134
India at War (film), 63
India in Crisis (film), 63
Information, Education, Orientation (I.E.&O.) program, 45
Information and Education Division (US Army), 6
The Informer (film), 9, 169
Ingles, H. C., 126
Inherit the Wind (film), 108
Intelligence Branch, 151
The International Ice Patrol (film), 74
Inter-Services Film Committee, 21
interventionism, 12, 23–24, 33, 35, 43, 113, 116, 119, 120, 196–97
The Invaders (49th Parallel) (film), 24
Iowa, 122
Ireland, 9; stereotypes, 192–93
Irish Revolution, 9
The Iron Horse (film), 169
Isenberg, Noah, 19, 28, 193
"Is It True What They Say About Dixie?" (song), 121
isolationism, 7, 10, 12, 23–24, 33, 35–36, 197
Italy, 10, 131, 136–38, 149
It Happened One Night (film), 38
It's Everybody's War (film), 67
It's Up to You (film), 73, 74
Ivy League, 32–33, 41, 42
I Was a Male War Bride (film), 91, 102–3

Jackson, Robert, 141, 142, 143, 151, 154, 170–71
Jacob, Eugen ("Peter," "Liebling" or "Jacobs"), 157, 168. *See also* Riefenstahl, Leni
Jacobs, Harold, 35, 37, 59
Jacoby, Irving, 37
Jacoby, Karl, 152
Jahre der Entscheidung (film), 159–60
Jam Handy Organization, 62
Jannings, Emil, 178, 179, 180

Japan (Japanese), 9, 10, 12, 20, 21, 30, 35, 44, 64, 98, 99, 100, 124–26, 132, 146, 178. *See also* Axis (powers)
Japanese Imperial Air Force, 129
The Jazz Singer (film), 14, 38
Jesse L. Lasky Feature Play Company, 112
The Jews of America, 57
John Marshall Law School, 110
Johnny Eager (film), 87
Johns Hopkins University, 155
Jolson, Al, 14
Jones, John Paul, 119
Josephson, Julien, 120
Josephy, Robert, 58
Joyce, James, 148
Joyce, Peggy Hopkins, 5
The Joys of Yiddish, ix
Judas, 9
Judgment at Nuremberg (film), 108, 179–80
Jud Süss (film), 177, 182
Junghans, Carl, 159–60
juvenile delinquency, 108

Kadatten (film), 184
Kahn, Otto, 179
Kaleeshkin (colonel), 171
Kaleidoscope (film), 167
Kanin, Garson, x, 6–7, 10, 11, 12, 20, 33, 35, 37, 40, 90, 97, 104, 134, 189, 190, 199, 209n66
Kantor, MacKinlay, 109
Karski, Jan, 52
Kaufmann, Gunther, 160
Kaufman studios, 26, 92. *See also* Astoria, Queens
Kazan, Elia, 43, 141
Keane, Peter, 127
Kellogg, Ray, 143
Kelly, Colin P., Jr., 98, 99
Kimberley, David, 251n60
King, Henry, 119
King, Jack, 174
Kingsley, Sidney, 41, 97
Kiska, 101–2

Kitchener, Herbert, 179
Kitzbuhel, 154, 155
Klimt, Gustav, 184
Kneitel, Seymour, 21
Knight, Eric, 94
Knudson, William S., 8
Koch, Howard, 190, 191
Kolberg (film), 177–78, 182
Konsularakademie, 155
Kord, T. S., 248n10
Koszarski, Richard, 26, 92, 113, 212n152
Kracauer, Siegfried, 247n1
Kramer, Stanley, x, 7, 12, 20, 37, 39, 41, 81, 90, 96, 107, 108, 110, 186, 199, 229n69
Kristallnacht ("Night of the Broken Glass"), 63, 118, 165, 166, 173
Krumgold, Joseph, 71
Kubrick, Stanley, 22, 63, 108
Ku Klux Klan, 19, 35

La Cava, Gregory, 7
Lagendorf, Ernest, 156
The Land of the Free, 58
Lane Tech, 122, 232n77
Lange, Dorothea, 58
Lasky, Billy, 118
Lasky, Jesse, x, 7, 24, 32, 33, 112–20, 122, 188–89, 196, 203
Lasky, Jesse, Jr., x, 12, 23, 24, 28, 29, 32, 37, 41, 113, 114, 119, 122, 123, 127, 128, 129–30, 131, 135, 138, 139, 140, 141, 188–89, 196, 199, 200, 203; military involvement before the US entry into the war, 120–21; role in shaping photography and film in the Pacific theater, 123–27; sensitivity to treatment of Native Americans (Indians), 129–30
The Last Laugh (film), 179
latrines, 66, 68
Laurents, Arthur, 37, 41
Laurie, Clayton D., ix
Lawrence, Jock, 89
Lawrence of Arabia (film), 190

League of Nations, 92
Lebensraum, 180
Leda Hamilton (character), 193
Lee, Canada, 194
Legion of Merit, 114
Lemarr, Heddy, 18
Lend-Lease program, 4, 59
Leonard, Benny, 5
LeRoy, Mervyn, 6, 99, 103, 186–87
Let There Be Light (film), 106
Leuchtenberg, William E., 198
Levant, Oscar, 5, 11
Levin, Meyer (Mike), 97–98, 99, 187
Lewis, Al, 93
Lewis, Arthur, 7, 37, 41, 96, 199
Lewis, Leon, 19
Lewis, William B., 63–64
Lewton, Val, 140, 146
Leyte, 114, 130
The Liberation of Rome (film), 21
Liberty (magazine), 42
The Library (film), 109
Library of Congress, 57
Lichtman, Allan J., 50
Lidice, 185–86
Liebeneiner, Wolfgang, 160
LIFE, 88
Life Is Beautiful (film), 137
Life Line (film), 130–31
Lindbergh, Charles, 197
Lingayen Gulf, 98
Lissauer, Herman, 217n83
The Little Foxes (film), 117
Litvak, Anatole, x, 6–7, 12, 18, 21, 22, 24, 31, 32, 33, 37, 38, 40, 94, 96, 97, 104, 109, 122, 141, 186, 203, 207n34
Lloyd, Frank, 166
Lodz (Poland), 6, 43, 49
Loeb, Max, 145
Loewes, 15
London, 35, 52, 64, 80, 104
The Long Voyage Home (film), 169
Look (magazine), 41, 47, 88
Looney Tunes, 174
Lorentz, Pare, 20, 68, 70

Los Angeles, 14, 42, 55, 57, 94, 112, 120, 146–48, 151, 165, 172, 177, 197–98. *See also* Hollywood; studio system
Los Angeles Armory, 120
Los Angeles High School, 42
Los Angeles Times, 137, 187–88
Louis, Joe, 191, 252n92
Love Nest (film), 189
The Love of Ours (film), 195
Loy, Myrna, 18
Lubitsch, Ernst, 22, 37
Luce, Henry, 57, 88
Lutze, Viktor, 153
Lye, Len, 167

M-10 tank, 28
MacArthur, Douglas, 98, 114, 123, 126, 129, 188
MacDonald, Grant, 101–2
MacDonald, James, 48
MacLeish, Archibald, 37, 45, 57, 58, 60, 214n33
Maddow, Rachel, 18
Maibaum, Richard, 21–22, 37
Main Street on the March! (film), 63, 222n33
Malaria Mike (cartoon character), 100
Malaya, 64
Maltz, Albert, 186, 187–88, 200–201
Mamoulian, Rouben, 90
Mandatory Palestine, 104
Manhattan, 11
Manhattan Melodrama (film), 121
Mannheim, Al, 148
The Man That I Married (film), 33
Man with a Movie Camera (film), 22
March of Time (film series), 62–63, 76
Marian, Ferdinand, 177
Maria Thomas (character), 181–82
Marshall, George C., 3, 6, 94
Marx, Groucho, 5, 72
Marx, Harpo, 4–5, 39, 202
Marx Brothers, 5, 7, 26, 32, 112, 121
Mason General Hospital, 106
Mass, 137

Massey, Raymond, 88
"Mass Observation," 79
Maugham, Somerset, 5
Maxwell, Elsa, 5–6
Mayer, Louis B., 15, 18, 116, 198
Mayerling (film), 31
McCarey, Leo, 170
McCarthy, Joseph, 23, 25, 28, 107, 123, 188
McClinton, H. L., 62, 63
McDonald, Jeanette, 182
McGarr, Kathryn, 208n58, 209n65
McGowan, Kenneth, 71
Mead, Priscilla, 218n106
Medenbach, Milton H., 155–56, 157
medicine, 131
Meet John Doe (film), 38, 122, 123
Mehls, Martin, 160–61
Mein Kampf, 164–65
Mellett, Lowell, 5, 8, 20, 22, 29, 31–32, 37, 42, 45, 46, 49, 50, 55, 60, 67, 72, 94, 149–50, 186, 188
Memphis Belle, 89, 91, 109
The Men, 110
Mensing (officer), 160
mental illness, 106, 160, 195, 200
Menzel, Gerhard, 178, 183
Mercey, Arch, 67, 70
Merchant Marine, 85
Merchant Seamen Canteen, 66
Merlin, 174
Metro-Goldwyn-Mayer (MGM), 14, 15, 55, 59, 66, 71, 120, 122, 183
Metrotone News (News of the Day), 17
Mexico (and Mexicans), 25, 149, 194, 201
Meyer Levin Day, 98
Mickey Mouse (cartoon character), 173–74
Milestone, Lewis, 190–91
Miller, David, 7, 37, 38, 96, 106, 135, 199
Miller, Herb, 35
Mills, Teddy, 96, 199
Miner, Allen H., 125–26
Ministry of Information (MOI, UK), 75, 76, 77, 80

Ministry of Supply (UK), 77
Mission: Impossible (TV series), 126
Mission to Moscow (film), 188–89, 190–91
Mixson, H. W., 123, 128
Mohrenwitz, Max Aub, 149
Monroe, Marilyn, 143
Monte Carlo, 6
Montgomery, Bernard, 103
Montgomery, Robert, 18
Moore, Mary Tyler, 230–31n32
Morale Branch (US Army), 6
Morgenthau, Henry, 174
morphine, 131
The Mortal Storm (film), 33
Moscow, 170
Mosquito planes, 48
A Mother's Love (film), 183
Motion Picture Bureau, National Defense Advisory Commission, 8, 22, 196
Motion Picture Bureau, OWI, 190
Motion Picture Code, 16
Motion Picture Committee Cooperating for National Defense (later, War Activities Committee), 17, 55
Motion Picture Division, Office of Facts and Figures, 8
Motion Picture Producers and Distributors of America, 13, 29
The Movie Colony, 44
The Movie Makers, 44
Movies at War, 201
Mr. Deeds Goes to Town (film), 9
Mr. Proudfoot, 81–82
Mr. Proudfoot Shows a Light (film), 81–82
Mrs. Miniver (film), vi, 115, 116, 193, 230–31n32, 234–35n129
Mr. Smith Goes to Washington (film), 9, 38
Mueller, 160, 178
Munda, 131
Munich, 53, 145
Munroe, Jack, 143, 171
Munson, Edward L., 95, 96
Murnau, F. W., 179
Murrow, Edward R., 64

Museum of Modern Art (New York), 131, 153
Mussolini, Benito, 146, 175
Mussolini, Vittorio, 175, 247n203
Mutterliebe (film), 183
Myers, James, 28, 206n13, 214n23, 215n45
Mystery Street (film), 6
"The Myths We Live By" (Rosten), 201–2

The Naked City (film), 189
Napoleonic wars, 177
National Association of Broadcasters, 62
National Council of Churches, 29
National Defense Advisory Commission (also Committee), 8, 31, 45, 57, 196
National Emergency Council, 70
National Film Archives, 157
National Socialism (Nazi Germany, Nazism, Hitler, Nazi Party), 23, 27–28, 94, 144
"The Nature of the Enemy," 50–51
Navajo, 129
Navasky, Victor, 23, 213n5
Nazi Agent (film), 189
The Nazi Conspiracy to Seize Power and Wage Aggressive War (film), 171
Nazi film legacy, 145, 176
Nazi party, 163, 171
"The Nazi Pin-Up Girl," 153–55
Nazis, 6, 25–26, 32, 35, 40, 47, 53, 87, 94, 95, 99, 100, 112, 117, 121, 141, 142, 171, 174, 176, 181–82, 184, 187, 193, 200. *See also* Axis (powers); fascism; Germany; National Socialism
Nazi-Soviet Nonaggression Pact, 184, 189
NBC Television News, 143
Negro Colleges in Wartime (film), 191
The Negro Soldier (film), 191
Nelson, Donald, 59
The Netherlands, 51
New Britain, 113, 124–25, 126, 127, 129–30
New Deal, 7, 10, 58, 198; "Jew Deal" charge, 198

Index

New Guinea, 114
New Hampshire, 63
The New Masses (magazine), 187
Newsmaps, 151
newsmen (reporters, press corps), 22, 166, 197, 201
News of the Day, 17
newsreels, 17, 35–36, 58–59, 66, 152, 182
New Testament scripture, 135
The New United States Army (film), 63
New Wave cinema, 20–21
New York (City), 11, 106, 152, 166, 192
New York Harbor, 192
New York Herald Tribune, 44
New York Times, 31, 34, 44, 48, 49, 51, 56, 136–37, 194
New York University, 41, 92
The New Yorker, 4, 8, 41, 42, 47, 103
New Zealand, 134, 167
Nick the Greek, 5
Night Mail (film), 76
Night of the Long Knives, 158
Night Train to Munich (film), 88
N.K.V.D., 169, 171
Noldan, Svend, 184
North American Indians (Native-Indigenous Americans and Canadians), 25, 87, 107, 109, 129–30; *49th Parallel* (film) (aka *Forty-Ninth Parallel* and *The Invaders*), 86–87, 89; view of Jess Lasky Jr., 129–30
The North Star (film), 190
Northwestern University, 41, 110
Norway, 166
Nuremberg (film), 152
Nuremberg: Its Lesson for Today (film), 238n32
Nuremberg (Nazi) Party Day Congress, 153, 158, 161, 171. See also *Triumph of the Will* (film)
Nuremberg trial, x, 92, 140, 141, 142, 143, 144, 145, 151, 152, 153, 154, 156, 160, 169, 176–77, 184–85, 199, 200
Nye, Gerald, 6, 31, 33, 119

Office for Emergency Management, 8, 11, 60, 73, 196
Office of Facts and Figures, 4, 6, 8, 17, 32, 45, 46, 55, 58, 63, 88, 91
Office of Production Management, 8
Office of Strategic Services (OSS), 42, 106, 121, 142, 143, 144, 145, 150, 156, 160, 169, 176, 178, 184
Office of War Information (OWI), ix, 8, 22, 28, 41, 45, 46–47, 68, 69, 149, 190
Office of War Mobilization and Reconversion, 70
Ohm Kruger (film), 179
Olivier, Laurence, 88
Olympia (film), 156, 158, 161, 165, 166
Olympics, 27, 156, 165, 166
Omaha (beach), 104
Once Upon a Time (film), 173
One World or None (film), 62
On the Beach (film), 108
On The Waterfront (film), 43, 141
Operation Justice, 142
Opfer der Vergangenheit: Die Sünde wider Blut und Rasse (film), 160
Oranienberg, 165
Oregon, 7
Ortelburg (Szcztno), 249n38
Osborn, Frederick H., 3, 6, 89, 94, 95, 96
O.S.S. (TV show), 190
O'Toole, Peter, 190
Oxford University, 103

Pabst, G. W., 158
Pacific theater, 32, 59, 115, 123–25, 131, 145, 150, 203
The Pale Horseman (film), 199
Palestine, 104, 136
Palmer, R. Barton, 39
Panavision, 28
Paramount (Pictures), 7, 15, 16, 28, 112, 122, 172, 179
Paramount News, 17
Paret, Peter, 177
Paris, 93, 105, 162, 166, 190, 193
Parker, Dorothy, 188

Parker, Eleanor, 187
Passions and Prejudices: Or, Some of My Best Friends Are People, 47
Pathé News, 17, 58
Patterson, Robert, 66, 126
Patton, George, 104
Paul, Heinz, 184
Paulsen, Harald, 184
Pearl Harbor, 9, 11, 24, 30, 33, 40, 44, 45, 49, 50, 52, 71, 94, 98, 99, 119, 120, 131, 132, 150, 192, 197
Peck, Gregory, 106
Pennsylvania, 131
Perelman, S. J., 32, 41
Perry Mason (TV show), 126
Persian Gulf Command: Some Marvels on the Road to Kazvin, 103
Persilschein, 156–57
Peter Pan, 114
Philippines, 114, 122, 127, 130
Photographic Naval Unit, 169
photography, 58–59, 114–15, 123, 126–27, 131, 145
Pichel, Irving, 143
Pigeon, Walter, 193
Pinchie Winchie, 5
Pitt, Dale, 137
plasma, 131
The Plow That Broke the Plains (film), 68, 70
Plugger (cartoon character), 61
Poland, 6, 17, 27, 30, 43, 51, 52, 54, 153, 180–81, 182
"Poland Is Not Yet Lost" (song), 182
Policek, Magda, 144
Polish film industry, 181
Porky Pig, 38, 174
Postmaster General, 13
post-traumatic stress disorder (PTSD), 106
Powell, Michael, 24, 79, 86, 89
Powell, William, 18
Powers, Francis Gary, 143
Poynter, Nelson, 5, 9, 20, 22, 31–32, 37, 42, 46, 186, 188, 220n1
Prelude to War (film), x, 4, 7, 13, 39

Prequel: An American Fight Against Fascism, 18
Presidents' Day, 99
Presnell, Robert, 24, 41, 90, 115, 122–29, 131–34, 136, 150, 203
Presnell, Robert, Jr., 24, 135–38
Pressburger, Emeric, 86, 89
Pride of the Marines (film), 83, 187, 194–95, 200–201
Prince of Wales, 5
Private Snafu (cartoon character), 3, 81, 96, 100
Production Code Administration, 13–14, 16, 29
Progress Report, 145, 153, 176, 183. *See also* Motion Picture Code
propaganda, ix, 8–9, 11, 31, 33, 120, 161, 191, 201
propaganda ministry, 161
psychiatry, 106, 200
Psychological Warfare Division, SHAEF, 160, 176
Public Broadcasting Service (PBS), 35
public opinion, 45
Purple Heart, 190

quinine sulfate, 131

Rabenalt, Arthur, 184
radio, 64
Ragan, Philip, 61–62
Random House, 42, 148
Rankin, John E., 35
Rank Organization, 137–38
rationing, 72, 73, 76. *See also* rubber
Reader's Digest, 63
Reagan, Ronald, 93
Record Herald (Chicago), 88
Redes (film), 69
Red Scare, 23
Reed, Carol, 88, 134
Reed, George, 194
reenactment(s), 128–29, 189
The Refugee, 63
Rehman, 153
Reinhardt, Gottfried, 37, 97

Reis, Irving, 41, 93, 97, 104
Renault, 49
Rendova Island, 131
Renoir, Jean, 190
Report from the Aleutians (film), 106
Republican National Committee, 13
Republican party, 18, 123, 196–97, 202
Resettlement Administration, 58
Reudersdorf, 144
Reunion in France (film), 189
Rex-Film, 160
"Rhapsody in Blue" (song), 11
Rhodes, Cecil, 179
Rich, Frances, 150–51, 240n65
Rich, Irene, 150
Richardson, Charles S., 31, 46, 55
Rick Blaine, 132, 193
Riefenstahl, Leni, 12, 22, 27, 32, 43, 153, 154–69, 170, 172, 175, 178, 200; interrogation by Budd Schulberg, 153–69
Riegner telegram, 52
Ring of Steel (film), 11
Riskin, Robert, 37
Ritt, Martin, 104
Ritter, Karl, 184
The River, 70
Rivers, Johnny, 187
Riviera, 5
Rivkin, Allen, 60
RKO (Radio-Keith-Orpheum), 7, 15, 99, 122, 149
Roach, Hal, 15, 172
Robson, Mark, 108
Rockefeller Center, 50–51
Rockwell, Francis W., 101
Rodakiewicz, Henwar, 22, 37, 68–74, 89
Rode, Walter, 144
Rogers, James, 46
Röhm, Ernst, 152, 158, 159
Rooney, Mickey, 18
Roosevelt, Eleanor, vi, 33, 198, 217n83, 253n11
Roosevelt, Franklin Delano (FDR, president, administration of), 3, 4, 5, 6, 7, 8, 11, 12–13, 17, 20, 26, 30, 31, 32, 33, 34, 42, 45, 47–48, 50, 53, 55, 58, 60, 84–85, 93, 108, 117, 118–19, 122, 174, 186, 196, 197, 201, 202; as Assistant Secretary to the Navy, 119; FDR Presidential Library and Museum, 254n31; Hollywood aspirations, 118–19
Roosevelt, James, 15, 20, 33
Roosevelt, Kermit, 198
Roosevelt, Teddy, 113
Rosenberg, Alfred, 170
Rosenberg, Ethel, 53, 63
Rosenberg, Ira, 125
Rosenberg, Julius, 53, 63
Rosenheimer, Arthur, Jr., 131–32
Rosenzweig, Laura, 28
Ross, Barney, 97–98
Ross, Frank, 99
Ross, Steven, 28
Rossen, Robert, 186, 190, 191, 194
Rosten, Leo Calvin (Leonard Q. Ross), ix, 6, 8–9, 11–12, 14, 17–19, 21, 23, 24, 29, 31, 32, 34, 35, 38, 41–42, 44, 45, 55, 56, 57, 58, 59–63, 64, 65, 66, 67, 68–75, 76, 77, 78, 79, 80, 81, 82–83, 84–86, 87, 88–89, 90, 91, 92, 93, 106, 110, 115, 117, 132, 150, 174, 176, 185–86, 188, 190, 191, 192, 195, 196, 197, 198, 199, 201, 203, 214n33; *112 Gripes About the French*, 190; *All Through the Night* (film), 6, 34, 83, 85, 192; background and intellectual concerns, 11–12, 43–47; consultation with Henwar Rodakiewicz regarding documentary film, 22, 37, 68–74, 89; *The Education of H*y*m*a*n K*a*p*l*a*n*, 41; evasion of full accounting of his prewar appointment and later service, 45; formulation of critical policy with Donald Shlesinger with British film policy as a model, 72, 73, 74–77, 78, 79, 80; *Hollywood: The Movie Colony, The Movie Makers*, 13, 44, 46; initiation of unprecedented daylight bombing, 47–48; *The Joys of Yiddish*, ix, 41; omission from the official record, 196; *Passions and Prejudices: Or, Some of My Best Friends Are*

Rosten (*continued*)
  People, 47; personal issues, 218n106; PhD dissertation, 45–46. *See also* Office of Facts and Figures
Roth, Beulah, 46, 93
Roth, Sanford, 93
Rothstein, Arthur, 58
Rough Riders, 113, 114
Route 66 (film), 126
Royal Air Force (RAF), 48
rubber, 64–66, 76
Runyon, Damon, 93
Russell, Harold, 109
Russell, Kurt, 85
Russell, Rosalind, 18
Russell, Wallace, 11
Russia, 5, 30, 38, 133. *See also* Soviet Union (USSR)

Salute to France (film), 38, 190
Sam (character, *Casablanca* piano player), 193
Sammy Glick (character), 83
Sam Spade (character), 165
Samuelson, Mary Gelsey, 17–18
San Diego, 150
SANE, 136
San Juan Hill, 114
Saratoga (character), 193
Saroyan, William, 90, 97, 199
Sarris, Andrew, 20, 213n17
Saturday Evening Post, 42, 149, 154, 155, 157, 168, 170, 173
Sayre, Joel, 103, 104
Schatz, Thomas, 14
Schlesinger, Leon, 37, 174, 247n200
Schmid, Al, 187, 194–95
Schoedsack, Ernest, 123
Schoenmetzler, Hans, 160
Schulberg, Ben (B. P.), 139, 140, 179
Schulberg, Budd, 12, 22, 23, 24, 25, 27, 32, 40–41, 42, 43, 47, 50, 83, 92, 108, 139–47, 148–51, 151–74, 176–79, 180, 181–82, 183–86, 188, 196, 200, 201; author of *What Makes Sammy Run?*, 25, 32, 42, 83, 140, 148, 178, 188, 195; *On The Waterfront* (film), 43, 141; personal background, 42–43, 139–41; probing Riefenstahl's relationship with Adolf Hitler, 165–66; role in creating *December 7th* (film), 150, 178; tie to Emil Jannings, 178, 179, 180; tracking down Leni Riefenstahl, 155–57
Schulberg, Sandra, 238n32
Schulberg, Stuart, 41, 144, 152, 185, 196, 237–38n26, 238n32
Schutzstaffel (SS), 153, 165, 171
Schweikart, Hans, 184
Scots, 134
Scott, Adrian, 137
The Screen Writer, 141, 170
Screen Writers Guild, 44, 141, 170, 190
Scuttle under the Bonnet, 94, 95
Seattle, 102, 151
Secretary of War, 8
Seeds of Destiny (film), 135
Selznick, David O., 15, 140, 146
Selznick Pictures (Studios), 15, 140, 146, 149
Sennett, Mack, 170
Sergeant York (film), 7, 24, 33, 84–85, 115–20, 190, 197
The Seven Year Itch (film), 143
Shahn, Ben, 58
Shakespeare, William, 93
Shaw, George Bernard, 5
Shaw, Irwin, 20, 35, 37, 41, 90, 97, 102, 103–4, 105, 199–200, 252n90
Shearer, Norma, 18
Sheehan, Winfield, 166
Sheen, Fulton J., 59
Sheridan, Anne, 103
Sherman, Vincent, 6, 34, 83, 93, 132
Shestopel, Susan, 144
Shirer, William L., 181
Shnayerson, Michael, 103, 104
Shneer, David, 49
Short, K. R. M., 50
Showcross, Hartley, 141
Sidlinger, Albert E., 63
Silver, David, 125
Silver-Lasky, Pat, 7
Silvers, Phil, 192, 209n66

Index

Silver Shirts, 19
Simmons, Chris, 14
Sinatra, Frank, 99, 194. See also *The House I Live In*
Singapore, 64
Skall, William, 109
Skladkowski, Felicjan Slawoj, 182
slavery and Nazism, 23, 162, 191
Slesinger, Donald, 4, 11, 24, 37, 72, 73, 74–77, 78, 79, 80, 91, 199
Slesinger, Stephen, 74
Small, Bernard, 123–24
Small, Edward, 15, 123
Smith, Al, 5
The Snake Pit (film), 31
Snead, Sam, 5
Snow White (film), 167, 173, 247n200
Soil Conservation Service, 69
So ist das Leben/Takovy je zivot (film), 160
Solomon Islands, 131
Song of the Plains, 171
Sorry, Wrong Number (film), 31
SOS Iceberg (film), 158
South America, 79
Soviet-American friendship, 171
Soviet Union (USSR), 5, 10, 30, 49, 59, 100, 108, 133, 145, 169–71, 180, 185
Spain, 10, 33, 146, 149
Spanish Civil War, 33, 146, 148
Special Coverage Unit (SPECOU), 104
Spewack, Samuel, 41
Spicer, Andrew, 138
Spiegel, Sam, 189
Spielberg, Steven, 143
Spigelgass, Leonard, x, 6, 12, 18, 22, 25, 31, 32, 34, 35, 37, 41, 46, 58, 59, 63, 76, 77, 81, 91, 92, 93–94, 95–96, 97, 100, 101–3, 107, 122, 135, 182, 185–86, 188, 191, 192, 195, 199, 200, 203; role in *Army-Navy Screen Magazine*, 39, 81, 90, 93, 96–97, 107, 130, 135, 189, 199
Spingold, Nate, 87–88
Sports Illustrated, 140
The Squaw Man (film), 112
Staff Film Report, 39

Stagecoach (film), 169
Stalder, Fred, 160
Stalin, 159, 171
Stalingrad, 133
Stanford University, 41
Stars and Stripes, 104
"Star System," 16, 112
Steichen, Edward, 107
Steiner, Ralph, 37, 68
Steinhoff, Hans, 179
Stettinius, Ed, 59
Stevens, George, 10, 12, 20, 31, 37, 77, 90, 91, 97, 103, 104, 105, 109, 141, 143, 176–77, 200
Stevenson, Adlai, 93
Stewart, Jimmy, 11, 18
Stieglitz, Alfred, 68
The Stilwell Road (film), 128, 132–34
Stimson, Henry L., 101
Storm Center (film), 109
Story (magazine), 42
Strand, Paul, 68–69
studio system (motion picture industry), 13–18
Sturgess, John, 6
Sturmabteilung (SA) (Brown Shirts), 152, 153, 171, 180
Substitution and Conversion (film), 38
suicide of the Hollywood Motion Picture Industry, 147. See also antisemitism; German-American Bund
sulfa guanidine, 131
sulfanilamide, 131
Supreme Headquarters, Allied Expeditionary Forces (SHAEF), 104, 160, 176
Sutherland, A. Edward, 93
"Swanee" (song), 121
Swerling, Joseph, 90
Swing Shift (film), 85–86, 91, 92
Switzerland, 92, 180
Swope, Herbert Bayard, 5, 202
Sword (beach), 104
Sydney (Australia), 125
Sylvester, 38
Szcztno (Ortelburg), 249n38

Tag der Freiheit (film), 156, 158, 161. See also *Tag der Freiheit-Unsere Wehrmacht*
Tag der Freiheit-Unsere Wehrmacht (film), 158
Tannanbaum, Harold, 37, 97, 109
Taplinger, Robert, 87–88, 89
Taradash, Daniel, 7, 23, 28, 37, 39, 41, 96, 109, 130, 131, 186, 199, 200,
Tarawa, 107
Target for Today (film), 76, 89
Target for Tonight (film), 76, 78, 109
Tarzan, 74
Tati, Jacques, 190
Taylor, Robert, 87
"Tea for Two" (song), 121
Technicolor, 174
Tehran, 103
television, 111, 123, 126, 137, 141, 144, 152, 190, 192
The Ten Commandments (film), 135, 137
Tennessee, 113, 116, 117, 120
Terkel, Studs, 13, 199
Thalberg, Irving, 197–98
That Justice Be Done (film), 143, 176–77
That Men May Fight (film), 150
Then Came Bronson (film), 126
This Is Your Enemy (film), 58, 85
Thomas, Lowell, 181–82
Thomas, Ralph, 24
Three Faces of Eve (film), 107
Tiefland (film), 161, 244n127
Tight Shoes (film), 93
Time (magazine), 59, 88
Time-Life lab, 104
Tin Pan Alley, 121
Tiomkin, Dmitri, 37
Tokyo, 21, 126
Tourjansky, V., 180
Tourou, Leon, 19
Tracy, Spencer, 11, 179
Traube, Shepard, 37, 93, 97
Treasure of the Golden Condor (film), 189
A Tree Grows in Brooklyn (film), 74
Tribune (Chicago), 88, 122

Triumph of the Will (*Triumph des Willens*) (film), 27, 153–54, 155, 156, 158, 161, 162, 174. *See also* Riefenstahl, Leni; Schulberg, Budd
The True Glory (film), 10, 40, 134
Truman, Harry, 54, 57, 171
Trumbo, Dalton, 137
Trumpener, Katie, 181
Tunisia, 103
Turkish, 192
Turner, Lana, 87
Tusalava (film), 167
Twelfth Army (US), 104
Twentieth Century-Fox Film Corporation (Fox; 20th), 15, 67, 93, 116, 122, 166, 189
Twenty-Seven Soldiers (film), 21, 194
The Twilight Zone (TV show), 126
Typke, 160
Tyrolian Alps, 154, 161

Über alles in der Welt (film), 184
Ucicky, Gustav, 180–81, 183
UFA-Film, 180
Ulysses, 148
Unconquered (film), 130
Underworld (film), 139
United Artists, 15, 20
United Kingdom (Great Britain, Britain), 4, 8, 17, 18, 30, 35, 40, 47–49, 59, 75, 78–79, 80–81, 103–4, 106, 134, 137–38, 167, 188
United Nations, 24, 53, 54, 65, 91–92, 123, 134, 135, 136
United Nations Relief and Rehabilitation Administration (UNRRA), 135
United States Army Air Forces Presents the First Motion Picture Unit (film), 91
Universal News, 17, 59
Universal Pictures, 15, 16, 122
University of Chicago, 32, 41, 43, 45, 46, 74, 122, 144
University of Chicago Law School, 74
University of Illinois, 41, 110
University of Iowa, 41
University of Marburg, 155

Index

University of Southern California, 151
University of the Redlands, 151
The Untouchables (TV show), 126
Urwand, Ben, 214n32, 239n44
US Air Force, 83–84, 85, 110
US Alien Property Custodian, 153
US Army, 6, 28, 89
US Army Air Corps, 84, 86, 98
US Army Air Force, 76, 83–84, 130
US Army Counterintelligence Corps (C.I.C.), 155, 157
US Army Moral Services Division, 96
US Army Orientation Films, 6, 94
US Army Public Relations Department, 89
US Army Reserve, 127
US Army Signal Corps Photographic Center (S.C.P.C.), 95–96
US Army Signal Corps (Signal Corps), ix, 25, 34, 35, 59, 66, 94, 96, 114, 121–22, 123, 125, 126, 130, 190, 199
US Bureau of Motion Pictures, 3
US Coast Guard, 130
US Congress, 26, 30, 196–97
US Constitution, 3
US Department of Agriculture, 69, 73, 78
US Executive Office of the President, 196
US Expeditionary Force, 197
US Film Service, 20, 70
US House Military Affairs Committee, 126
US Marine Corps anthem, 171
US Marines (also Marine Corps), 42, 130, 144, 148, 149, 200–201
US Military Government (MG) (Occupation forces), 199
US Naval Reserve, 42, 142, 152
US Navy, 28, 42, 130, 150, 161
US Navy Women's Reserve Corps (WAVES), 150
US Secretary of the Treasury, 174
US Senate, 7, 28, 31, 119
US Steel, 59
Ustinov, Peter, 134

US Treasury Department, 174
Utah (beach), 104

Valentino, Rudolf, 113
Vandenburg, C. M., 82
Variety, 34, 172
Veiller, Anthony, 23, 90, 199, 212n142
Verity Films, 138
Verne, Karen, 193
Vertov, Dziga, 22
Vichy (France) (Nazi-collaborationist regime), 149, 162–63, 177
"Victims of the Past" (and "Victims of the Past: The Sin against Blood and Race") (film), 160
The Victors (film), 110
"The Victory of Faith" (*Der Sieg des Glaubens*) (film), 153, 158, 159
Victory over Europe (V-E) Day, 48
victory shorts, 29
Vienna, 155, 166
Viergang, Yuri, 171
Vietnam, 27
Vining, Robert E., 114
Vogue (magazine), 190
Von Blomberg, Werner, 159
Von Ribbentrop, Joachim, 156
von Shirach, Baldur, 237–38n26
von Sternberg, Josef, 139, 179, 180

Waffen SS, 172
Wagon Train (television show), 126
Wald, Jerry, 83–84, 86, 195
Waletzsky, Josh, 238n32
Walk East on Beacon (film), 53, 63, 111
Walker, G. S. G., 79
A Walk in the Sun (film), 190
Wallenberg, Hans, 156
Wanger, Walter, 7, 15, 37, 40, 41, 84–85, 112, 196
The War, 96–97
War Activities Committee (WAC), 17, 22, 29, 55, 67, 72, 77, 171
war bonds, 38, 174
"War Comes to America" (Orientation Film No. 7), 11, 40

Warner, Harry, 7, 18, 116, 119
Warner, Jack, 18, 40, 117, 208n63
Warner Bros., 7, 15, 33, 55, 58, 76, 83, 84–85, 117, 119, 122, 148, 174, 208n63, 217n83
War Production Board (WPB), 59, 78
Warren, Earl, 202
Warsaw, 52, 172, 184
Washington (DC) press corps, 45–46, 151
Washington, George, 99
Watt, Harry, 76, 109
The Wave (film), 69
The Way of All Flesh (film), 179
Wayne, John, 189
Weaver, John, 97
Wedemeyer, Albert Coady, 169
Wehrmacht, 153, 159, 161
Weidmann, 160
Weill, Kurt, 37, 38
Welcome Home (film), 39
Welles, Orson, 10
Welsh, 134
Werker, Alfred L., 63
Wessely, Paula, 181–82
West End, 190
We Were Strangers (film), 189
What Makes Sammy Run?, 25, 32, 42, 83, 140, 148, 178, 188, 195
Wheeler Field, 98
"When G.I. Johnny Comes Home Again," 21
The White Heat of Pitz Palü (film), 158
White House, 7, 18. *See also* Roosevelt, Franklin Delano
Who's Who, 94
Why We Fight (film series), x, 5, 7, 11, 12, 13, 31, 38, 39, 40, 61, 62, 64, 90, 94, 126, 128, 191
Wien-Film, 183
The Wild One (film), 108
William Morris Agency, 88
Wilson, Arthur ("Dooley"), 193
Winged Victory (film), 39

Winkler, Allan, 28
Winnie the Pooh, 74
Wise, Robert, 109
The Wizard of Oz (film), 14, 74
Wochenschau (film series), 153, 238n33
Women Accepted for Volunteer Emergency Services (WAVES), 150–51
Women's Army Auxiliary Corps (WAACS), 67
Woollcott, Alexander, 4, 6, 202
World Health Organization, 70
World War I (First World War, Great War), 8–9, 122, 196, 197. *See also Sergeant York*
Wright, Mason, 89
Wuertemberg, 177
Wyler, William, 10, 31, 37, 39, 77, 90, 91, 109, 115, 229, 136, 216n72; *The Best Years of Our Lives* (film), 39
Yale University, 41, 74, 126, 187; School of Drama, 187
Yank (newspaper), 104
A Yank in the R.A.F. (film), 116
Yiddish, 41, 135, 182, 193
Yogerst, Chris, 19, 23, 28, 31, 120
Yom Kippur, 137
York, Alvin C., 115, 116–18, 197. *See also Sergeant York*
Yorkville, 153
Young, Collier, 85
The Young and the Brave (film), 83, 85
Young Men's Christian Association (YMCA), 29
Young Mr. Lincoln (film), 169
Young Winston (film), 110

Zanuck, Darryl, 37, 189
Zigman, Joe, 144, 152
Zinnemann, Fred, 107, 110
Zoder (character), 187
Zogbaum, Wilfrid, 128
Zukor, Adolf, 112, 179, 229n3
Zygielbojm, Shmuel, 52

Wisconsin Film Studies

The Film Music of John Williams: Reviving Hollywood's Classical Style,
second edition
EMILIO AUDISSINO

The Foreign Film Renaissance on American Screens, 1946–1973
TINO BALIO

*Hollywood's Unofficial Film Corps:
American Jewish Moviemakers and the War Effort*
MICHAEL BERKOWITZ

Somerset Maugham and the Cinema
ROBERT CALDER

Marked Women: Prostitutes and Prostitution in the Cinema
RUSSELL CAMPBELL

Depth of Field: Stanley Kubrick, Film, and the Uses of History
EDITED BY GEOFFREY COCKS, JAMES DIEDRICK, AND GLENN PERUSEK

Tough as Nails: The Life and Films of Richard Brooks
DOUGLASS K. DANIEL

Making Hollywood Happen: The Story of Film Finances
CHARLES DRAZIN

Dark Laughter: Spanish Film, Comedy, and the Nation
JUAN F. EGEA

Glenn Ford: A Life
PETER FORD

Luis Buñuel: The Red Years, 1929–1939
ROMÁN GUBERN AND PAUL HAMMOND

Screen Nazis: Cinema, History, and Democracy
SABINE HAKE

Peerless: Rouben Mamoulian, Hollywood, and Broadway
KURT JENSEN

A Cinema of Obsession: The Life and Work of Mai Zetterling
MARIAH LARSSON

Continental Films: French Cinema under German Control
CHRISTINE LETEUX

Escape Artist: The Life and Films of John Sturges
GLENN LOVELL

Colonial Tactics and Everyday Life: Workers of the Manchuria Film Association
YUXIN MA

I Thought We Were Making Movies, Not History
WALTER MIRISCH

Giant: George Stevens, a Life on Film
MARILYN ANN MOSS

French Film History, 1895–1946
RICHARD NEUPERT

The Many Lives of Cy Endfield: Film Noir, the Blacklist, and "Zulu"
BRIAN NEVE

Six Turkish Filmmakers
LAURENCE RAW

Jean-Luc Godard: The Permanent Revolutionary
BERT REBHANDL, TRANSLATED BY EDWARD MALTBY

The Cinema of Sergei Parajanov
JAMES STEFFEN